The Brothers Shubert

The Brothers Shubert

by Jerry Stagg

 Random House, New York

FIRST PRINTING

Copyright © 1968 by Jerry Stagg

All rights reserved under International and Pan-American Copyright Conventions. Published in the United States by Random House, Inc., New York, and simultaneously in Canada by Random House of Canada, Limited, Toronto.

Library of Congress Catalog Card Number: 68-28528

MANUFACTURED IN THE UNITED STATES OF AMERICA

For Maxine

who waited a long, long time

Acknowledgments

Thanks go to the thousands of anonymous newsmen who, through the years, chronicled the Shubert story for me. And to the papers which kept the records.

The *New York Times*, without whose index and files this story would have taken even longer to write.

The New York *Daily News*, which generously opened its morgue to me, thus providing an invaluable shortcut.

The defunct New York *Sun*, and its companions in the journalistic cemetery: the New York *World*, the New York *Herald Tribune*, The New York *Journal*, the New York *American*, the New York *Daily Mirror*, *Zit's*, the *Morning Telegraph*, the New York *Dramatic Mirror*, and the Shubert's own New York *Review*.

Thanks, too, to *Variety*, to the Philadelphia *Inquirer*, to the Boston *Globe* and the Boston *Herald*, the San Francisco *Chronicle*, the Los Angeles *Times*, the Los Angeles *Examiner* and the Chicago *Tribune*.

Thanks also to Eliot Norton, of the Boston *Globe*, and formerly of the Boston *Post*, a distinguished critic and a warm host.

To Claudia Cassidy of the Chicago *Tribune*; Sam Zolotow, Bosley Crowther, Brooks Atkinson and Howard Taubman of the *New York Times*, Bob Sylvester of the *Daily News*, Abel Green and Hobie Morrison of *Variety*.

My gratitude to the late Pat Carroll, Librarian of The Players club, and to his cooperative successor, Louis A. Rachow.

To Sylvia Hilton of the New York Society Library, who allowed me to smoke cigars while I read.

To George Freedley and the Fifth Avenue Library Theater collection, who didn't but wanted to.

And my gratitude to the hundreds of people who took time out to talk with me. To Abe Lastfogel, Harry and Nat Kalcheim, Nat Lefkowitz and Joe Schoenfeld of the William Morris Agency; to the late (and that word will reappear all too often in this acknowledgment) Harold Freedman, a fine dramatic agent and a good friend; to the late Jimmy Stroock of Brooks Costume; to Lew Alter; to the late Arthur Klein; the late Sid Piermont; Bill Doll, the peripatetic publicist; to Gerry Collins; to George Abbott; Charles Abramson; the late Ben Sokolow, the Shubert stock broker; Sherman Krellberg; Abe Berman; Spyros Skouras; Arnold Weissberger; Howard Reinheimer; Leonard Sillman; William Zeckendorf; Gilbert Miller; Mrs. Lillian Greneker; Al Lewis;

Max Gordon; Leopold Friedman, formerly president of Loew's; Harry Bestry; Michael Meyerberg; Howard Dietz, and his wife, Lucinda Ballard; the late George Price; Samuel Nagler, of the J. J. Seligman Co.; Warren Caro; Bob Christenberry; Howard Reilly; Richard Rodgers; Morris Jacobs; Vincent Sardi, Sr.; Emma Jean Reissman, secretary to the late William Phillips; William Morris, Jr., for invaluable papers; Bobby North; Harris Clayton, now with MGM, for a time a Shubert attorney; Ed Small; Asher Levy; Sam Kahl; Ken Murray; the late Louis Shurr; George White; Justine Johnstone; Dave Chasen; Mae West; Charles Le Maire; Gypsy Rose Lee, and her equally charming sister, June Havoc; Fred de Cordova, and his lovely mother, the late Margaret de Cordova; Mort Lewis; Ray and Gwen Bolger; Norman Pincus; Viola Carlson; Louis Lurie; George Jessel; Irving Starr; Nora White; John Kenley; Carl Abraham; Ed Scanlon; Sylvia Hahlo; Jack Pearl; Herman Shumlin; Walter Wanger; Jack Warner; Odette Myrtil; Marjorie Gateson; Max Meth; James Proctor; Milton Berle; the late Ed Wynn; the late Eddie Cantor; George Burns; the late Harpo Marx; the late Sophie Tucker; the late Jack Morris; Mr. and Mrs. Milton Weir; William Klein, II, nephew of Willie; Mrs. John Shubert; Abe Cohen and the late Eddie D. Dowling; Julia Sanderson; Sam S. Schwartz; Alfred Strelsin; Irving Maidman; Robert Sinclair; Rudolf Friml; Adolf Zukor, Dick Irving Hyland; John Byram; Vincent Minelli; Arthur Kober; Violet Fisch; Mrs. Maxwell Anderson; Mrs. "Jimmy" Porter; Mr. and Mrs. Howard Cullman; Roger Stevens; the late William Klein, and his late wife, Peggy; Harlan Thompson and his charming wife, Marian Spitzer; Justice Samuel di Falco, and his able staff; Paul Streger; Sol Novin, of Culver Pictures; Lee Sabinson.

There are four special references. The first is to the love of my life, Billie Burke, who really started this book for me almost twenty years ago. Her stories, her memories, her excitement cannot be forgotten.

Ray Whittaker spent untold hours with me, aiding me, not only with his own memories, but in going through my accumulated material to sift out the legends and leave the facts.

Emanuel Seff gave me assistance and interest that I cannot repay. And he gave me free access to his splendid library.

Helen Strauss, formerly of William Morris, now with Seven Arts Warner Brothers, was my agent, my encourager and my friend.

I also want to thank the many people who assisted me in this book, and who specifically asked that their names not be used. Some were Shubert employees; some had been; some had merely known them. They will know who they are and I want them to know I am grateful.

Specific thanks to William Fitelson, my attorney, who has endeavored to keep me out of legal problems, and also for his forty years' worth of theatrical lore.

If I have omitted anyone, I apologize. There must be some.

I would like to thank my son, Christopher, Irwin Denis and Shellie Ritchkoff for assistance in specific research. If there are mistakes, they are mine, not theirs.

The manuscript was typed at various times by Miss Ritchkoff and my wife.

A special thank you to Albert Erskine, my editor. He is a Tennessee gentleman, with Georgian manners, a poor Elizabethan sense of punning, and a Victorian sense of syntax. I cannot say enough.

Finally, to Lee and Sam S. and J.J. Shubert, without whom none of this would have been possible.

Illustrations

The Brothers Shubert

Chapter One

There were three brothers: Samuel S. (S for euphony) Shubert, Jacob J. (J for nothing) Shubert, and Lee (really Levi) Shubert. They invaded New York City in 1900, armed with tireless energy, boundless confidence, a lust for money, power and fame, and $15,000, most of it borrowed.

A quarter of a century later, their worth was estimated at almost half a billion dollars. They revolutionized that most glamorous of all businesses—the theater. They wooed it, and they seduced it, and they took charge of it. They bled it to anemia, and when it lay dying, they pumped back its lifeblood.

They created their own mythology about themselves and became legends in their own times. One part of the myth was the disguise they wore as the great Trust Busters. They fought the trust—the Theatrical Trust—and they compromised with it, and fought it again, and joined it, and fought it again and broke it. Then the Shuberts were the Trust —and more powerful and more ruthless than their predecessor. They fought the Trust and everyone else. Their competitors, their stars, their writers, their directors, their associates, their employees, their partners, their government; singly, and in combination, they took on the press, the Tax Department, Equity, ASCAP, the Dramatists' Guild, local politicians, censors, each other. Sometimes they lost. More often they won. And they had the patience and the pragmatism that converted defeat into victory. They were extraordinary men, these brothers Shubert.

They took control of theater in America. If America bought tickets to see a play, two-thirds of the tickets were Shubert tickets. And one-fourth of the plays America was privileged to see were produced by the Messrs. Shubert.

What a fascinating group of subjects for a biography! Sam and Lee and J. J.—Horatio Algers with a Jewish accent; the immigrant dream; the carving of an empire; the power play in a world of high finance, of make-believe, talent, temperament, and the most beautiful women in the world!

All you need are the facts and the reminiscences of their contemporaries. The newspapers are living records of sixty years of Shuberts; Who's Who has a short biography; there are a hundred sources, a thousand anecdotes, several hundred lawsuits, open scandals and secret ones, Shubert Alley, Shubert theaters; there are wives and wills,

3

relatives alive, and hundreds of people, men and women, who knew them. This is the raw material of biography—this collection of fact and fable, dusty records, grimy newsprint, faded pictures, last wills, tax suits. But who were the men who made the legend? Who, really, were they? For each fact there is a half-truth. And by definition, for every half-truth there is a half-lie. How do you sift through the jigsawed relics of other men's lives to find out what they were like?

The Shuberts were very unusual characters. Early in their lives they began to create a mythology—the Shubert saga. Did they know the myth would outlive them? They must have, you say, because why else did they go to the trouble of carefully concocting lies about the simplest things?

They were born in Syracuse, according to *Who's Who*, and the statement is echoed by men who worked with them for fifty-five years. It is not so. "My older brother, Sam," Lee Shubert used to say lovingly and reflectively. Sam wasn't his older brother.

So, you start from the beginning, and you try to find what appears to be the truth. This is the account of that search through sixty years of the history of the theater as personified by three improbable heroes —the brothers Shubert.

They made an odd procession. They were bone-weary, still dazed by the journeys of the last month which had climaxed a harrowing, dazed year. David Szemanski Shubert paused dramatically at the door of the small house. It was one of four clustered in the backyard—all identical square little boxes huddled together around the two-holer which was the only adornment of the "garden."

He shifted the sleeping baby to his other shoulder and fished for the key. The five older children rushed toward the small stoop (one step) and tried to peer through the windows at the dark interior. The mother, Catherine, stood stolidly beside her husband as he opened the door.

The boxed house was divided into three rooms. A kitchen stretched all across the back of the house; it had a cast-iron stove that heated the house, cooked the food, baked the bread, boiled the water, and consumed incredible amounts of coal, and it also had a sink with running water. There was a bedroom, with no bed, and a parlor with rude pallets slung on the floor.

The father gestured them in. The children's eyes widened in wonderment; they had never seen anything to compare with this in their lives. It was a palace. (There would be much exploring to do. They would have to be reminded about the sink—they had only recently seen running water in a house, and they would have to be taught about the communal two-holer—this they had never seen before.)

The mother smiled gratefully, her face etched with strain and fatigue, looking more like forty-five than the thirty-three years she had lived. "It's very nice, David," she said in a faint voice, and added with concern, "Can we afford such a house?"

The place was Syracuse, New York, and the year was 1882; the arrival was the climax of a year of horror and tragedy, a year of privation and flight, a year of new experiences.

One short year before, in the border town of Shervient in Czarist Lithuania the wave of anti-Semitism had crested. An anarchist assassination of the Czar had loosed a series of pogroms which sent hundreds of thousands of Jews into panic-stricken flight, and exile.

David Szemanski, a pack peddler, had fled to England and then to the United States, leaving behind his wife and six children. He made his bewildered way to Syracuse, discovered that there were similarities between the United States and Vilna province—if you bought something for a nickel and sold it for more, you could afford to buy whiskey, not slivowitz, but whiskey, and David Szemanski Shubert needed whiskey. He was that rara avis—a Jewish lush.

If whiskey was a comfort, what had happened to his name was not. When he arrived at Castle Garden, America's reception center in New York, he had painfully pronounced, "Duvvid Szemanski fun Shervient," and the Tammany beneficiary in the Immigration Department, unwilling or unable to understand, had scrawled "David Shurbent." The "Shurbent" looked like "Shurbart," was mysteriously altered to "Shobart," and finally, in its last mutation to "Shubert."

Somehow he managed to save, beg, borrow enough money to send for his family one year later. He met them at the boat—his bone-weary wife, and his six children, Levi, Sam, little Jacob, Fanny, Sarah, and little Dora, an infant. He took them to the apartment of his wife's relatives the Heilwitz family on the lower East Side. There was so much to do, so much to teach them (including their new name), so much to tell them. And there were things he didn't want to tell them.

These had been hard weeks for David. He was trapped, and he saw no way out. He just did not have the money to get them to Syracuse, and he couldn't tell them he didn't have it, and he could not borrow it from Carrie's relatives, from whom he had already borrowed the money to bring the family here. He ached physically when he thought of the house in Syracuse, *his* house, for which he had paid the rent in cash, sitting there idle and empty.

He ignored Carrie's prodding, and he tried not to drink, even when Samuel was ill, but on Friday night when they all were huddled in the room and he saw Carrie's shame when her cousin suggested that he would lend them *more* money to help them get to Syracuse, it was too much. Did the stingy bastard have to say "more"? He stomped out. When he staggered back, he found his family dressed and waiting for him, their featherbeds and clothes and cooking ware all stacked; they were going to Syracuse. He tried to bluster, but there was nothing left to bluster with. Levi and Samuel never forgave him for the shame of that night. It is doubtful if Catherine ever did.

Nearly half a million immigrants—refugees from Czarist Russia— came into the United States in that year of 1882, almost all of them through Germany and England. What did they find? America was a growing, lusty country. Its towns were becoming cities, and its cities were already beginning to climb into the skies as land values and Sullivan made the skyscraper a historic necessity. The railroads were pushing out in all directions, and mills and factories, from the Mississippi to the Hudson, were belching smoke into the skies. A great steel complex was building in Pittsburgh, Andrew Carnegie was getting richer, John D. Rockefeller had just put together the Standard Oil Trust and was facing the fattest ten years of his life.

Mark Twain was working on *Huckleberry Finn*, and Mark Hanna was building the machine which would control Ohio and elect Presidents. Cyrus Field had lost the fortune he had made by laying the first transatlantic cable, and was building a new millionaire's fund with the first elevated railways in New York. F. W. Woolworth had opened a successful five-cent store in Utica and was expanding rapidly; mass merchandising was being born. William R. Hearst was a practical joker at Harvard, and Thomas Edison was trying to sell his newly invented light bulb, while his restless mind was playing with the idea of moving pictures. The manager of his company in Detroit was a chap called Henry Ford. Harrigan and Hart were the foremost comedy duo in show business, and P. T. Barnum was running the world's largest circus. Except perhaps for the New York State Legislature, where a hot-headed young New York aristocrat was delivering toothy speeches. His name was Theodore Roosevelt.

So, this was the America that greeted them and the first problem they faced was to become American. And despite his good intentions, David was no great help. America may have been bursting its seams as the expansion boom and the trust building continued; the landlords may have been getting rich as they crowded the enormous hordes of

6

immigrants into the already bulging tenements; land values might be soaring as the dispossessed of Europe swept into the countryside; but in Syracuse, in the home of the Shuberts, there was only poverty for these first years—painful, abject, spirit-draining poverty.

There was never enough money, there was never enough food. A tightly knit Jewish community in the city helped out as they could. A Jewish doctor treated Sam through his recurrent illnesses; the rabbi and some influential neighbors tried to "talk sense" to David about his drinking. They gave the Shuberts coal and food and cast-off clothing. There was the problem of learning the language and the customs. School could not be started until a few words of English were mastered. And by the time that the learning process had come that far, Levi faced a harsh fact: he would have to go to work. Someone in the family had to help earn the money to keep them—it would not be David.

What kind of job? What does a boy who is barely ten years old, who speaks the language haltingly, who is just learning to read, what does such a boy do? He shines shoes in the streets, and sells newspapers on corners, and he runs errands and learns to look up appealingly for a tip. And he tries to pick the best "location" to peddle his skills, one which promises business and "rich people" who will pay lavishly.

He opened up shop in downtown Syracuse, fascinating to him, with its horse cars, its three theaters, its shops, its bustle, its buzz. He set up his business "headquarters" in front of the Wieting Theater, where a smart boy could shame the handsome men into lavish tips as they drove up with their lovely ladies. A boy could hold a carriage door open and then, if his expression was just right, keep it from shutting until the proper impressive bribe was paid. That was only one of the many tricks Levi Shubert learned on the streets of Syracuse. He studied the life that went on at night and he filed it in his neat catalogued mind, and he watched the parade of (to him) unbelievable opulence with unblinking, calculating dark eyes.

He became a familiar figure there in front of the Wieting Theater every day from about two o'clock to past midnight, darting like an eel through the horse-drawn traffic, always getting to that carriage door first; he carried parcels for the ladies who were shopping; he sold his newspapers in a high-pitched sing-song, and he sold more papers than any newsboy in town. It was pretty soon recognized that Levi Shubert had the best paper "location" in Syracuse.

Once, they tried to take it away from him, but they only tried once. The challenger was older, and bigger and tougher, and he told the sheeny kid *he* was going to be in front of the Wieting from then on.

7

Levi almost killed him. He did not fight fair and he fought by no rules —skinny, underfed, wiry little stripling that he was, he fought to kill. He was never disturbed again.

The seasons flew by. Winter and summer raced past the front of the Wieting Theater. Winter was money-making time, the season the Shuberts waited for. The knife edge of the wind cut viciously off the lake, driving the numbing snow in swoops and swirls, tearing the breath from chapped lips. But with a charcoal fire in a pail and a throng of customers to serve, winter was a rich time. The summers were slow and drowsy, and the Shuberts reversed the procedures of the squirrels; they stored up their hoard of goodies all winter long, saving for the slow summer months.

Sam had joined Levi in the "business." Undersized, painfully frail, he was like quicksilver, always in motion, always in a hurry, his dark, fawn's eyes fixed on the miracles he watched daily. The boys were twelve and nine, and they were the chief breadwinners in the family. Levi had already taken on the decision making. His mother deferred to him, his father skulked in the background. The bond between the brothers was even closer now, as they spent the long hours together, as coordinated as a drill team in their "business."

There were the rare times when David made a killing—when he arrived home from one of his mysterious nonrewarding trips with the stride of a conquering hero and the attitude of a man who was going to take charge of things. The girls twittered around him, Catherine listened to his exploits, Jacob huddled close to the almost-stranger. The cheerful time never lasted. Soon he was gone again, or off on a bender, to return when he was broke or sunk in self-pity.

Levi and Sam hated the charity, the gifts, the hand-me-downs; they hated the doctor who condescendingly donated his care to the family and the pharmacist who condescendingly filled their prescriptions. More than anything else, the youngsters, so peacock-proud, so quietly arrogant, hated the father who had brought this humiliation upon them.

The manager of the Wieting Theater was a sandy-haired young Scot, John Kerr. He had watched the progress of the Shubert brothers with wry interest. Levi had become his personal errand boy, who brought his paper to him in the box-office, who carried a pot of soup daily from the Kerr house to the theater. One cold slushy night in the winter of 1885, the small figure of Sam Shubert stood by the bucket in which a charcoal fire bloomed, slapping his hands in their mittens, standing guard over the papers piled under the canvas, his breath blowing feathers of steam each time he exhaled. Repeatedly he coughed

—long, racking spasms that shook him from the oversize boots to the woolen cap on his head.

Impulsively Kerr opened the theater door and called to the boy. "When Levi comes back, you come inside and get warm. We got a lot of empty seats tonight." The boy waved to him, and a few minutes later Sam Shubert walked into the theater. For the first time he was ushered inside, and reverently he lowered his small body into the hard seat. His eyes drank in the lighted stage, and his world exploded.

There were beautiful girls in tights and in ballet costumes. There was a castle and there were trees stretching back toward a magic lake. The scene was bathed in light, and never had he seen such beauty, never had he heard such music as the seven men in the pit orchestra were playing. Suddenly, a limelight hissed and then caught; it bathed the scene with such brilliance, he thought he could not live another day unless he too shared in the making of these wonders.

The play was *The Black Crook*, the first girl revue in America; the company was a third-rate, cut-down version, playing a tired performance. But to Sam Shubert, it was the loveliest sight he had ever seen, and the creatures on the stage were kings and queens blessed by the gods. He knew instantly what he would do with his life.

From that day on, his little jockey's body spent the hours in front of the Wieting Theater, but his heart and soul were inside. He tried to tell Levi about the exaltation he had felt, but the words were insufficient. Levi had seen shows; he had not paid to see them, but he had seen them. He was interested in the fact that people *did* pay money to see them.

David Belasco was more theatrical than the plays he wrote and produced. He had roared into New York from San Francisco, a long-haired, fiery, temperamental young genius, had taken over the Madison Square Theater, was trying to muster the courage to reverse his collar so that he would resemble a cleric (he wanted to be the High Priest of the Theater, and he became just exactly that). He would shock and thrill America with plays that Puccini would fall in love with, and make immortal. But in that winter of 1885 *Madame Butterfly* and *The Girl of the Golden West* were off in Belasco's future.

He had opened a piece of treacle called *May Blossom* at the Madison Square Theater, and late that winter he was playing the Wieting Opera House in Syracuse. He needed four little children for his first-act finale, and he was planning to hire them out of school, as he did in every other town he hit on the tour. John Kerr, the Wieting manager, persuaded Belasco to use three children from school and one who didn't bother with school and who therefore could learn any "special business"

9

The Legendary David Belasco, whose attitudes, attire and attainments were the model Sam Shubert took for his own.

Sam S. Shubert, officially posing à la Belasco.

Belasco wanted. Sam Shubert was hired. Salary—one dollar cash a week, for one week. Plus free passes for the family. Although he was ten, he played a six-year-old.

Sam Shubert did not become a star. He worked the week, and he found an idol—for the rest of his life, he would try to emulate Belasco. He began at once. He let his hair grow. And he built a small stage out of scrap wood and cardboard, and in the early morning he would stage imaginary dramas, and his eye would see such beauty, such loveliness in the empty little box, lit by a candle. He was a precociously imaginative dreamer. And a very practical young man.

He secured his first steady job in the theater by persuading the manager of the Bastable Theater in Syracuse to hire him as program boy, at a weekly salary of $1.50. This represented a cut in Shubert income, since the boys had been averaging better than six dollars a week, but as Shuberts they took up the slack at once. Jacob substituted for Sam, and Fanny, the eldest child, became the first Shubert girl to go to work. She started as a seamstress.

In one year, Sam was promoted; he was moved to the Grand Opera House with the title assistant treasurer. The theater, even in its business areas, knows about billing. Assistant treasurer is a much fatter title than ticket seller. Sam had to stand on a wooden crate to reach the window; his pleasant, shyly eager personality made him a favorite with touring companies and customers. From this new "position of power," he was able to throw business to his brothers, as errand boys.

After a year, he was treasurer, keeping the cash drawer and balancing the nightly statement. The Shuberts were all born mathematically able. Levi was doing his arithmetic in a series of jobs: cigar-roller (he never would smoke even in later life because he loathed tobacco forever after), shirt-cutter, haberdashery clerk, and finally, with the son of the Mirvachs, a well-to-do Syracuse family, partner in a haberdashery. Jacob became his clerk at the store, and Sarah and Dora worked there too.

This would be the pattern for the next five years: the entire family working long hours in an unremitting struggle to rise above what had greeted them when they arrived in Syracuse. They pulled themselves up from incredible squalor, from unbelievable poverty, to the point where they were now respectable. They moved to a larger house, a square ugly house, still in the ghetto, and Catherine took in boarders, a parade of Jewish immigrants. David remained David the pack peddler, the irresponsible, and—scandal of scandals in a Jewish community —an alcoholic.

12

But respectability was not enough. There was a lust for power and importance in the young Shubert men. In 1893 God, who had been gently smiling on the Shuberts, decided to grin. Through the persuasive charm of Samuel, Joseph W. Jacobs, a Jewish clothier, entered the lists in behalf of the boy. The Grand Opera House was only the second-best theater in Syracuse, and second-best was not good enough for this young man. He was hired as treasurer of the Wieting, Syracuse's best. He was eighteen years old, five feet tall, a hundred pounds dripping wet—a pint-sized jockey of a man, with king-sized dreams.

It was at this time that the peculiar Shubert predilection for age changing, name changing, history altering, youth-ifying first began to manifest itself. In the census of 1892, David was forty-six, and Carrie forty-three, Fannie was twenty-three, Sarah twenty, Levi (the last time we would see the *vi*) nineteen, Sam sixteen, Jacob fourteen, and Dora twelve. By 1893 Lee had become Sam's younger brother, and Sam had gained a year, while Lee had mysteriously lost two (he would "lose" more in the course of his life). Catherine had gotten younger, and they had all decided they were born in Syracuse. At this point in the Shubert career, Jacob maintained his age. In later years Jacob would add J. to his name, and subtract four years from his age. Seemingly, their mathematical aptitudes did not extend to chronology.

It would become still more bewildering thirteen years later. By 1905, in the thirteen-year span, David would be thirteen years older, but Carrie only eight years older. Sarah would have managed to gain eleven years, as would Jacob (we now have the J.), and Dora would stay with the majority. She too would be eleven years older in thirteen years. Sam would become two *more* years younger and be at the same age as Lee, who had lost another two years. They would decide at this time that they had not been born in Syracuse, although that would not be for publication, but for money.

But even while they were so mysteriously playing the game of "Guess My Age," they were taking their first tentative steps on the road that led to empire. It began with a stroke of luck concealed in a casual remark; it developed when an opportunity presented itself, and the Shuberts leaped at it.

Charles Hale Hoyt, one of America's most successful playwrights of his time, specialized in instant satire, burlesquing the headlines of his day. Just one in a series of hits, *A Stranger in New York*, was on tour, and Hoyt, who had settled in upstate New York, came into Syracuse to catch one of the road companies. And there, at the Wieting, he met young, eager, ingratiating, terribly bright Sam Shubert. He was attracted by the shy charm of the boy, and he suggested to Sam, "If

13

you ever get to New York, look me up. I may be able to throw something your way." He had no idea of the Shubert mentality, to which a suggestion was a promise, and a promise a formal contract. Sam filed the invitation away, and one year later, he "looked up" Mr. Hoyt.

It was a funny meeting. Tiny, dapper Sam Shubert, all five feet of him, went down to New York City and presented himself at Mr. Hoyt's office. He had heard that the road rights to *A Texas Steer* had not been sold. The play was a stunning success in New York, and as owner of the road rights, Sam Shubert hoped to launch his managerial career. What he hadn't heard was that Hoyt was already beginning to show the signs of a mental breakdown, which would lead to hospitalization and a tragic death. Hoyt had no recollection of young Shubert.

It was an awkward situation. There was the fledgling impresario, already in his Belasco makeup, eager to consummate his first "big deal," and there was Hoyt, vague, impatient, brusque—"Who the hell is Sam S. Shubert?" Hoyt's associate and partner finally persuaded Hoyt that in fact he did know Shubert, that Shubert was not a "kid," that he did know theater business, and that Hoyt had promised. Now all that remained was to get the money to secure the rights.

It was the first of the Shubert partnership deals, the first in a parade of partners that would include Tammany Hall, a key figure in a subway scandal, a Kentucky congressman, a respected attorney, the boss of Cincinnati, old-line millionaires, amusement park operators, and Wall Street. This time it was dapper J. W. Jacobs, the Syracuse clothier, who had limped into the Shubert destiny, and who now loaned them a small sum of money to tie up the Hoyt play. The other contributor was stage-struck Jesse Oberdorfer, heir to a small foundry. The Shuberts were in business.

What business? What was the theatrical business, back there in 1894? There was no radio, there was no television, and there was no motion picture industry. Every city and town had one or more theaters, and companies of actors toured from place to place, playing one-week stands, one-night stands, split-week engagements, whatever the traffic could bear. And there were vaudeville theaters, which featured performers in their own acts—jugglers, acrobats, buffoons, clowns, comedians, animal acts, singers, dancers, actors in melodramatic sketches. With the exception of a few scattered burlesque houses, this was the total entertainment of America.

The hallmark for theater was the phrase "direct from New York." And so, every late summer and fall, the owners of theaters from all over the country would stream into New York to attempt to book their attractions for the upcoming season. Each of them wanted the biggest stars, they wanted the tried and true organizations behind the shows, they wanted the marquee values they thought would fill their theaters. They protected themselves in many cases by booking two and three attractions for the same week.

What happened to the two shows that had been contracted for and did not play? They were stranded—a not unusual occurrence. Many times, they went on to another town, many times the cast and company were abandoned by its owner, and actors would find themselves two thousand miles from home with no way of getting back to another job which offered the same gamble. It was an unscrupulous, dirty, back-biting business.

For the producer, it was a matter of scheduling. He would try to route his show logically—from New York to New Haven, from New Haven to Springfield, from Springfield to Boston, and so on. He could lose his shirt by a bad route. If he went to Cincinnati and then to Philadelphia and then doubled back to Columbus, the train fares and the shipping costs could absorb his profit. Since this producer-manager trusted the theater owner with the same kind of faith that the theater owner showed him, he often double-booked his show—scheduling it at two cities for the same night. This guaranteed him one box office collection anyhow. What happened to the poor, miserable theater operator with no attraction to show? Well, he made sure to double-book for next season.

Only a handful of performers could insure themselves of a good route, steady employment, and minimum theft at the box office. To take care of the last, they usually posted a trusted soul at the ticket window with the theater treasurer and thus kept track of every sale. Even this wasn't always a guarantee. There are legends of the theater owner and/or treasurer who religiously presented each company manager with a floor plan of the seats so that the total could be checked against the optimum figure of a sellout. The floor plan was complete except for one thing: three rows of the orchestra were omitted, giving the theater owner three rows of seats which he used to call lovingly "Daddy's hedge against old age."

With a touring show and absentee management, the operation was under the stewardship of the company manager, who usually doubled as the transportation manager and the publicity man. Not content with the kickbacks from the railroads, plus the padding of the account marked "press entertainment," he would make side deals with a venal theater owner and they would cut the melon they withheld from the box-office report to the owner of the show (we call it "ice" now, but

15

it has been with us for a very long time—even the Greeks had a word for it).

Another characteristic of the theater of the era was the dominance of the manager-star. Men like Sothern, or Mansfield, or Booth, or John Drew, or women like Minnie Maddern Fiske operated their own businesses. They were guaranteed their bookings by eager owners; they could plan their routes a year or more in advance; they could put a trusted relative or friend in the manager's job; and they could make a lot of money, most of which was turned over to them.

In this endless playing of "Cheating Cheaters," there were terrible losses, defalcations, embezzlements, bankruptcies, brouhahas, and suicides. It was a situation that cried for the imposition of some logic, and the first attempts were the organization of various regional bookings. Two or three of the "larger" theater owners in an area would try to work out bookings for themselves. This would usually run smoothly until one of two things happened. First, there was the question of who got what attraction for the "slow weeks" at Easter and Christmas. Second, what happened when Partner A cast an avaricious look at a theater in Partner B's town?

But in 1895 a group of men sat down in New York and applied logic to the theater. It was the age of organization, efficiency was creeping up on America and was going to give birth to a whole new world, not so brave and not so perfect, and not so terribly efficient. But it was going to bring order to the theater. It would be called the Trust or the Syndicate, or just plain Klaw and Erlanger. They had a mission —to put some fiscal rationality into the theater—and they charged a fee for their services: millions. They set out to organize the chaos of the booking situation and the road; and they did, and made more millions. They took control, absolute despotic control, of the American theater. And one by-product of the Syndicate was the unique eminence of Abe Erlanger—he became, without a challenger, the most hated man in show business.

The syndicate was born at a luncheon at the old Holland House attended by seven potentates of the theater—the Frohman Brothers, Marc Klaw, Abe Erlanger, Sam Nixon (né Nirdlinger), Alf Hayman, and J. F. Zimmerman, Nixon's partner. Among them, they represented control of theaters in most of the key cities in the country, plus authoritative production control of top plays and leading actors. There is general disagreement about whose idea it was to form a syndicate. It doesn't really matter; in a matter of months, Abe Erlanger was king, booking the theaters. With the club of the theaters they personally controlled, the redoubtable Erlanger could knock heads together over the rest of

16

the country; he put together a nationwide chain, which he booked, controlled, levied on, until he had created a total monopoly. It is doubtful that Abe Erlanger ever heard of Lord Acton, but he was a keen student of Jay Gould and John D. Rockefeller, and he knew the sweet uses of power for profit. In a very short time, in addition to charging the privately owned theaters fees for booking, fees for the attraction, and fees for advertising, the Syndicate was cutting itself in for a percentage of the gross in each theater. This was a sliding-scale arrangement designed by Erlanger to first seduce the theaters into agreement, and then to blackjack them into submission. It worked very well. There are Erlanger detractors who claim he was just the bully boy, and the real evil genii behind the monopoly were Klaw, Frohman, and Hayman, but the end result saw blocky, skinny-legged, bulldog-faced Abe Erlanger crowned the Napoleon of Show Biz.

He took the Napoleon title seriously. A bust of the Corsican graced his office. Uncut Napoleona filled the bookshelves, and Erlanger took to putting his hand into his vest when being interviewed. (Oddly enough, Jake Shubert succumbed to the same curious fixation in later years. He wore his overcoat thrown like a cape over his shoulders, his pudgy left hand clutching it closed at his breastbone.)

The announcement of the formation of the Syndicate was hailed in the press. It promised system and order in a haphazard industry that, as the *New York Times* piously pointed out, "invests $5,000,000 a year in new productions." The *Times* was shorting itself out of a headline. The nationwide gate receipts were many, many times five million. The real-estate taxes, and the real-estate investment that the theater represented aggregated an astronomical sum. It was a major American industry, and Abe Erlanger ruled it.

He had never heard of the Shuberts.

The Syracuse troika was devoting its time to exploiting the opportunity Hoyt had presented. They milked the territory—New York State and New England—with a deft hand; they made a lot of friends, and a little money. Oberdorfer made money, Jacobs made money and had the additional satisfaction of seeing his judgment of Sam Shubert vindicated; and the Shuberts made a little money.

While Sam was using his recipe for success—a soupçon of charm here, a dollop of shyness there, one pinch of greed everywhere—Lee was consolidating the gains. He retained his interest in the haberdashery, just as Sam held on to the job at the Wieting. But they introduced the work pattern the Shuberts would maintain for sixty years—they backed each other up in jobs. Jacob was moved into the Wieting as an assistant; Lee supervised Jacob, and followed Sam into Utica, Rochester, Boston, Portland. Sam made friends, and Lee figured out ways to use them.

The next season saw the Shuberts with the road rights to a second play of Hoyt's, a second investment by Jacobs and Oberdorfer, a tighter booking schedule for the two shows, the family (including Fanny) moved into a larger and better house. Fanny's first child was four, and she had remarried—this time Isaac Isaacs, a pack peddler. They brought forth a son, the second "blood Shubert" born in the United States, named him Milton, and presented him with the dubious favor of calling J. J. Shubert "Uncle."

Lee and Sam had been watching Jacob with puzzled tolerance. He was bigger than either one of them, at five feet six inches. He was stockier. He was fair-complexioned and blue-eyed, and he had the mannerisms of a corner bully, the temper of a tantrum-ridden child, and from some indefinable source, money in his pocket—money that baffled Lee and Sam. The two older brothers were black-eyed, black-haired, short and slender, mild in manner; Sam was outgoing, inventive, could sparkle; Lee was grave in demeanor, reserved, quiet. Both men were shy by nature, but Sam would get excited and the personality wall would come down. Lee lived behind the wall. But Jacob? His sudden violences, his uncontrolled and often unmotivated rages startled his brothers. Lee could usually control him, but not always.

They had come to physical violence only once. It was the winter of Sam's first season at the Bastable. He had laboriously built a miniature stage and was on the floor of the room they shared, admiring his handiwork. He had his usual cough and cold. Jacob was lying on his bed, watching his older brother, and baiting him. Suddenly he rose to his feet, stepped across the small room, and deliberately trampled the model stage. When Sam tried to stop him, he fended off the smaller boy easily, taunting.

Attracted by the noise of the scuffle, Lee, who had been in the kitchen having his meal, catapulted himself into the room. His sisters and his mother followed on his heels. He grabbed Jacob by the shoulder, spun him around, knocking him back on the bed. Lee had gone completely wild.

"You—leave—him—alone!" he said quietly. "You never touch him again!" Jacob began to struggle, and Lee clamped his hands on his throat, forcing him back against the pillows. "You—hear—what—I—say?" He tightened his small, slender fingers, and Jacob's pale skin began to flame red. Frightened by the scene, Catherine began to pound

18

at Lee's back. Lee regained control, and almost contemptuously tossed Jacob back on the bed. "Remember," he said almost conversationally, his high-pitched, sing-song voice hoarse. "You just remember."

Lee and Jake never fought again physically. But Jacob was the third brother from that day on—the outside brother, the "other" Shubert. He was used and worked in the company, but he had no title and very little authority, except as granted by Sam and Lee. He never gave up trying. He served ultimatums and backed off; he worked, as did all the Shuberts, a fifteen- to twenty-hour day. He gloated at his successes and jeered when Sam and Lee had setbacks. He tried desperately for the rest of his life to become a true member of the firm. In the course of years he attained the status of a legal partner, but always he remained "the other Shubert."

In 1897 the Shuberts held a council of war with their advisers— Graff, Oberdorfer, and Jacobs. Sam Shubert was reaching out for bigger things. He and Lee had explored an idea, torn it apart, examined it again, and had come to a conclusion. They were not seeking their advisers' approval; they wanted their endorsement. Sam Shubert was to become a manager—a manager of his own theater. He had selected the Bastable, the very house he had first worked in.

The money was raised, and for the first time in the theatrical pages of America, the title Samuel Shubert, Mgr., appeared. The title as such lasted only one week. The second week's billing referred to him as Sam S. Shubert—and so it would remain for the rest of his career. The decision to take the theater caused a reshuffling of the Shubert brothers. With Sam at the Bastable, Jake moved into the Wieting, and Lee kept the books for both, and became busy in an allied field—he wrote a play.

It was called *A Trip to the Bowery*, a farce-comedy by Lee Shubert, and a company was formed to produce it, headed by Sam S. Shubert and Joe W. Jacobs. They took office space in the block of buildings that housed the Bastable Theater, and long were the hours of creation, and merciful was the final decision on the fate of the play—it was never produced. To those who knew Mr. Lee in the later and glorious years, the Mr. Lee who, it was sworn, could not read a play or recognize one if he fell on it, the enormity of his writing one is incredible. It is symptomatic of the collective Shubert ego. It is a literary loss; there is no script available..

The year that Lee Shubert wrote his epic marks the date of the first Shubert-Erlanger association. Through the efforts of friends of Joe W. Jacobs, a group of businessmen in Rochester agreed to build a theater to be managed by the Shuberts. To insure a flow of attractions for the theater—to be called the Baker—Sam determined to seek out the Syndicate.

He and Lee had agreed privately that their future lay in the theater. With money coming in at a regular rate, and in a business which, Lee pointed out, "was all cash, with no inventory," they had decided on expansion. They had "floated" the Baker; they were in the Bastable, and were making overtures for the Grand Opera House in Syracuse, and they had feelers out for a Utica theater. Lee was going to take over the Grand as soon as conditions warranted it; meanwhile, he managed the business, organized it, lubricated the squeaks, paved Sam's way, and wondered where Jake was getting all that money.

Before Sam and Lee could approach Erlanger, Erlanger called in the Shuberts. Abe Lincoln Erlanger was beginning to crack the whip for the Syndicate. With the nucleus of the theaters and stars they controlled, the Klaw-Erlanger group was rapidly compelling *all* the theaters in America to work with them, and on terms dictated by Abe Erlanger.

If you wanted a show, you cut the Syndicate into the profits, or you just didn't get the show. If there was another theater in town, *it* got the show. If there wasn't another theater, then Klaw and Erlanger might just arrange to build one. Erlanger was shrewd in applying his muscle. The percentage of profit he asked initially was always small; it was only when he had secured his monopoly position that the percentage went up, and up, and up. Mr. Erlanger had learned much from John D. Rockefeller, and Standard Oil. He was applying sound business practice, circa 1897, to the theater. He raised his profit share to 50 percent eventually, and was taking 50 percent of the producer's profit as well—a very nice business and, as Lee Shubert had pointed out, "All cash."

In Rochester, the only first-class house was the Lyceum, and its owner was not in a mood to give Mr. Erlanger any great share of his take. So, Abe Erlanger, on hearing of the Shubert theater being built in Rochester, approached Sam and Lee with a proposition. He would book their new theater with the best attractions; he would take only 5 percent of the profits. He would squeeze the Lyceum out of existence, giving the Shuberts control of theater in the town.

This offer was most appealing to the Shubert sense of morality and bookkeeping; they accepted instantly and laid their plans accordingly. In their conversations they very carefully held out Syracuse from booking agreements, and made no mention of their plans in Utica. To Erlanger, the Shuberts were very small potatoes in a very large stew, and to the Shuberts the great Abe Erlanger was someone they could use in Rochester. It seemed like a healthy arrangement for everyone except the man who owned the Lyceum.

When he saw Abe Erlanger's handwriting on his wall, the owner of the theater had a change of heart. He welcomed little Napoleon as his partner, signed an agreement for what must have been more than 5 percent of the profits, and Mr. Erlanger informed the Shuberts he had reconsidered and was withdrawing his offer. The brothers Shubert tucked the information away for future reference, and if anybody was bothering to keep score, it was one-nothing, Erlanger. It was still, however, very early in the game.

The Rochester operation solved one of the more perplexing Shubert problems. Early in the year, John Kerr, the manager of the Wieting, had walked into the lobby, to find a line at the window and seemingly no one in the box office, where Jacob should have been. Kerr dashed to the box office door, had difficulty opening it, and found Jacob Shubert, wild-eyed, sitting astride his brother Sam, trying to pound his head through the floor. Kerr dragged Jacob off, and Sam fired his brother on the spot. He was banished from all the theaters in Syracuse. Had it not been for his mother's tearful interference, it is quite possible that Lee would have killed him.

For four months, Catherine Shubert worked on Lee and Sam. For four months, she used every persuasion she could think of to convince them that "brothers are brothers" and "brothers must forget and forgive." Finally a compromise was found. Jacob was exiled to Rochester as manager of the Baker Theater. Sam had as little as possible to do with him. Lee supervised the theater, and kept a wary eye on Jacob (known forever after as Jacob J.) and on the till.

And here in Rochester something unsuspected and quite wonderful happened. Jacob J. Shubert was a few days more than nineteen years old. And in this violent, moody, introverted, pugnacious man, there stirred wild visions, wilder dreams, aspirations, and hopes that no one had ever imagined existed. In the main the manager's job was the orderly running of the theater for the attractions booked to play there. But there was also a stock company that could be installed, and Jacob installed it. It was the second such Shubert company, the first, of course, playing the Bastable.

The Baker company became a ringing success. J.J. Shubert proved to be a tempestuous, exacting, tasteless, but always dynamic producer. He surrounded himself with talent; he had a nose for undiscovered abilities in other people. He hired a young man named Owen Davis to work in the box office, write sketches for the stock company, and direct the players. J.J. had discovered himself.

21

All three of the brothers Shubert had also discovered girls. Not *a* girl—girls. Lee's initiation cannot be dated, but Sam's occurred his first year at the Wieting. There were certain privileges to being in the theater, particularly when a girl show was playing. And small Sam, who had begun to feel those first faint stirrings, was drawn backstage time and again. His shy smile, his tiny frame, the eager brown eyes all made him both a favorite of the girls and a natural butt for their teasing. They called him "Sonny" and "Kiddo," and they mothered him and flirted with him, and finally one of them fell in love with the little fellow—at least for one week. Sam had the usual Shubert luck; he won his first major skirmish with only minor disturbance. He felt he understood Belasco better.

He told Lee of his adventure, and Lee smiled enigmatically, then Sam told Jacob, who determined to experiment himself as soon as the opportunity presented itself—and remember, the Shuberts were opportunists. At long last, the Shuberts had found a hobby, and they never gave it up.

The next two years were spent in organization and in solidifying. The Shuberts acquired the Grand Opera House, as per schedule, and young Marcus Heiman was installed as its treasurer. The Heimans were a middle-class Jewish family, who had befriended the Shuberts in the early needy days. Heiman hired as his assistant Sam Kahl, another Syracuse boy. Graff and Jacobs were actively involved in Shubert affairs. They picked up a theater in Utica and leased the Wieting, which gave them total control of Syracuse. Lee still owned his haberdashery, but Jacobs had left the clothing business, and Oberdorfer had removed himself from the family foundry. They were part of the Shubert cadre, and they were planning the next move.

Chapter Two

Sam was no longer content to run stock companies and five theaters; he wanted to produce his own shows, and showcase them in New York City, American headquarters for the stage. It was a new century, and he wanted to help launch it. In March of 1900 Sam and Lee, accompanied by Joe Jacobs, trained to New York City. They were determined not to return to Syracuse before they had consummated a deal for a Manhattan theater to be run by the Shuberts.

The twentieth century was the most saluted century in all of history. In regal disdain of all its predecessors it emerged as the hope of mankind, the day of millennium, and the advent of universal brotherhood—at least, so they said. But never had communications been so full of a universal birthday, and the flood of printed words inundated mankind. It was all the New Year's Eves in history rolled into one.

The theater saluted the new century with pageants. Every producer worth his varsity "p" put together at least one pageant, with girls draped in flags of all nations; every musical director utilized his full orchestra—from four to sixty-four—to arrange medleys of the national anthems; on too many stages the new age was symbolized by an undraped little boy entering the world in pursuit of Father Time.

The Shuberts staged three such salutes to the twentieth century: one in Syracuse, one in Utica, one at J.J.'s in Rochester. No innovators they.

They had become very American. Of the three brothers, only Lee retained the faintest trace of Yiddish accent. They had found models to emulate, and they had imitated well. Sam wore dark suits, jacket buttoned high; he let his hair grow long, wavy, and flowing. His deep brown eyes—poet's eyes—were eager and vulnerable. His hundred-pound body was vulnerable too to an endless series of colds and coughs. He was twenty-three years old, he looked seventeen. Incredibly, he had already had thirteen years of professional experience in the theater. He wanted to be a great impresario, and now he was challenging Broadway. Who was he really? What real talent or genius existed behind the Belasco façade? There is no way to know. He was an outgoing lovely man; he made friends easily, and he liked people, and he liked people to like him. But no one knew him.

Lee was withdrawn. He too had a model—really only half a model. He had met J. W. Jacobs, an elegant, dapper clothier, and Lee dressed like Jacobs, modulated his high-pitched voice to Jacobs' deeper tones, carefully copied Jacobs' quiet and authoritative manner. He stood just under five and a half feet, almost half a foot taller than Sam. He was twenty-five, slender as a reed, courteous, ugly-attractive, with obsidian eyes brooding in his Egyptian face—an inscrutable, poker player's face. He would spend all of his life trying to be courteous, polite, deferential, and always he would be shy and uncertain.

Lee's job in 1900 was simple—he backed the moves that Sam made, backed them with fanatical devotion and love. No matter how wild the scheme, no matter how impossible it might seem to anyone not a Shubert, if Sam wanted it, somehow Lee found a way to make it operational.

A cynic once said, "No greater love hath a man for his brother than to lend him money." Lee found money for Sam. He found backers and partners, and he brought them into the Shubert orbit. He was a precocious spider spinning little webs for the entrapment of the wiser and older insects.

And what about J.J., all nineteen years of him? Somehow, he was the Shubert "original." They had him buried at the Baker in Rochester, a hundred and fifty pounds of concentrated truculence. He had found no model, and he was emulating no one. In the years ahead he would find rivals he hated, men whose work he envied, but J.J. would not copy their mannerisms—only their hits.

So there they were, the peddler's sons, with all the haggling instinct of a peddler, driven by ambitions they never really understood —ambitions that aspired to more than just money, and more than just power. They were reaching outside their skins for substance and satisfactions they never fully comprehended, and they were fortunate men. They were in a country and in a time which smiled on this kind of greed and kindled to this kind of dream. And they were fortunate that there were three of them to wear down the opposition, to outwork the opposition, and to out-think the opposition. They had the telepathic gift of family intuition; they were acquisitive and necessarily greedy; they were tough and ruthless from the shoeshine and newspaper days, tough and ruthless from cold nights in unheated rooms, from pogroms and a failure of a father, from an uncontrollable lust to lunge out of poverty. They were young, but they had been tempered; and they descended on New York City.

The New York sharpies put welcome lamps in their windows for the invaders from Syracuse. The lambs are coming! Sharpen the shears! And when the youthful Shubert brothers zeroed in on the Herald Square Theater (which was located across 35th Street from where Macy's now stands), there were anticipatory snickers from those who "knew the score." The Herald Square was a jinx theater and, except for one or two successes, had housed a dismal parade of flops. Charles Evans, who leased the barn from Hyde and Behman, for "musical attractions," rubbed his hands together and began a protracted negotiation with Lee Shubert, who was acting as the Judas ram for the Syracuse sheep.

Evans kept introducing stiffer and stiffer terms, and Lee Shubert patiently made counteroffers. It took two weeks to bring the negotiation to an end. At the same time Lee ended the lamb legend.

Evans had been hinting at "other producers who were interested"; Lee had countered by suggesting the Shuberts might consider a partnership with these anonymous other producers so that the risk could be shared. Finally after days of this, Lee served an ultimatum. He pointed out to Evans that everyone else *except* Evans was assuring the Shuberts that the Herald Square was a guaranteed disaster. He told Evans curtly that he had made his final offer and demanded a decision by the following day.

Evans was the first New Yorker to negotiate with Lee Shubert. He would not be the last. But he had learned a great deal. Well, perhaps not a great deal—just enough to sign the lease the next day.

How did the brothers celebrate? Did they go to Pastor's? Or Bustanoboy's? Here was little Sam, with the first step up on a flight of stairs that led to all his dreams. Could he sleep that night?

Or did his small silhouette dart up the semi-deserted streets to *his* theater?

(He always walked fast—a small figure at a half-run through life, hurrying toward some destination. It was as if he was throwing his slight torso forward in a dive, while his incredibly small feet—he used to buy his shoes in the children's shoe department at De Pinna's!—on the short, pumping legs were trying to catch up with the body to keep it from tumbling.)

But on this night of nights for him did he visit his theater? Did he climb the work steps from *his* stage to the auditorium? Did he look around him at the naked walls, *his* walls? Did he reach out to caress the worn plush of the seats, to rub the smooth wood of *his* seats? Did he drop into a chair, half-close his eyes, and watch the creations he envisioned? Was there music in his ears, and did he hear salvos of applause? Did he imagine the parade of *his* opening nights, with the great ones of the world he so wanted at his side all coming to pay respect, to see *his* creations in *his* theater? No one knows.

When the terms of the Shubert lease on the Herald Square "leaked out," the wise men of Broadway chortled again—the lads from Syracuse had been had. Not only was the theater too far uptown, but Evans had out-negotiated Lee Shubert in the deal. He had insisted that Shubert respect all prior booking arrangements for the house, which meant, in effect, that although the Shuberts were the lessees, they would have to stand in line to put in their own attractions.

Now, the wise men of the Rialto had no idea of the groundwork the Shuberts had laid; they really had no way of understanding the deviousness of Shubert thinking. And so, when the events of the next ten months unfolded on the theatrical scene, the legend of "the Shubert luck" was born. At first, the Shuberts were resentful of seeing skillful planning attributed to luck, but a little later on they began to encourage the myth—it lent an aura of mysticism to Dalai Lama Lee; it made the spelling out of a deal a little easier when the man across the desk was facing not only Lee, but unknown ghosts who somehow were swinging the luck of the gods to the Shubert side.

(So strongly rooted was this belief in Shubert luck that one angry oldtimer recently stated, "I'll tell you how lucky the Shuberts were. If Lee Shubert were taking his God-damned sunbath on the roof of the Empire State Building and fell, a parachute would open out of his fanny, the wind would be from the South, J.J. would hear about it and start selling tickets, and Lee would float down in Shubert Alley to an S.R.O. house!" Another legend has it that when Lee produced *The Road to Yesterday*, one of his biggest financial successes in straight drama, he had confused it with another play. Shubert luck!)

The facts behind the "luck" in the Herald Square lease had nothing to do with the smiles of the gods. Just before beginning the formal negotiation with Evans, the Shubert boys had sent off a series of telegrams to Richard Mansfield, then one of the leading stars of the American stage. Born in Berlin, Mansfield had served his apprenticeship in Europe. He came to the United States, and after a series of more or less adequate performances, he exploded into prominence with *Dr. Jekyll and Mr. Hyde*. Hit followed hit, and Mansfield became the man who introduced George Bernard Shaw to the American theatergoer, and what was more important in Shubert terms, a man who could guarantee an audience. He was an authentic "star," even by Lee Shubert's definition—he sold tickets.

Mansfield and his wife were on their overlarge houseboat at Old Lyme when the telegrams began to arrive.

WE WOULD LIKE TO MANAGE YOUR PRODUCTIONS   WE
WOULD DEEM IT AN HONOR TO BE ASSOCIATED WITH YOU
IN THE PRESENTATION OF YOUR GREAT INTERPRETATIONS
SAM S AND LEE SHUBERT
THEATRICAL MANAGERS

Mansfield ignored the first wire.

The second was a bit more flowery.

A GREAT ACTOR LIKE RICHARD MANSFIELD WOULD BE THE
MOST IMPORTANT PRESENTATION A THEATRICAL MAN-
AGER COULD MAKE   WE EAGERLY DESIRE TO BRING YOUR
TALENTS IN PLAYS OF YOUR OWN CHOICE TO THE PUBLIC
SAM S AND LEE SHUBERT

Mansfield was intrigued. He showed the wire to his wife.

The third wire was a masterpiece in flattery.

TO PRESENT A MANSFIELD PROGRAM [note the careful
omission of the first name] WOULD BE THE MOST SATISFY-
ING THEATRICAL EXPERIENCE WE COULD ENJOY   MAY
WE DISCUSS IT WITH YOU
SAM S AND LEE SHUBERT

Mansfield succumbed. Not knowing who the Shuberts were, but
from their freedom with telegrams assuming they were important producers, Mansfield invited them to come up to the boat and "discuss."

The story has it that when they arrived— (Lee, then twenty-seven
and looking twenty, Sam twenty-five and looking seventeen—they were
greeted at the gangplank by Mansfield, pince-nez on his Roman nose,
who was puzzled by the sight of two office boys. He asked, "Where
are the Shuberts—the producers?" Sam carefully replied that Mansfield was looking at them. The star studied them through the pince-nez,
shook his head in disbelief, and murmured, " 'Pon my soul," and invited
them aboard. By the time they left, they had a contract with one of
America's leading actors.

That was only the first step in the saga. Even while bombarding
Mansfield, they had made contact with Alf Hayman, Erlanger's partner
in the Trust. They had a chain of theaters in New York State, and a
house (soon) in the city proper, and they knew they had to have
bookings. They were prepared to make a deal with Klaw-Erlanger on
the Herald Square and on their other theaters. They did *not* tell Mr.
Hayman of the Mansfield negotiation.

The sequence of announcements was a study in Shubert planning.
On April 7, 1900, the first story of the leasing of the Herald Square
broke in the *New York Times*. On May 5 the house physically passed
into the hands of the Shuberts, although their lease was to commence
on September 1. On May 18 Richard Mansfield announced his plans for
the forthcoming season, including a "long-run engagement" at the

Herald Square. On May 24 Abe Erlanger announced to his favorite newspaper, the *Morning Telegraph*, that the Shubert brothers had signed a Syndicate agreement and that the Herald Square Theater was a Syndicate house.

The "smart money" in the New York theater sat back and tried to figure out the meaning of all that had happened. And then they cheered up. They *knew* the answer. Abe Erlanger had taken out insurance— it was as simple as that. Everyone knew the Herald Square was a bad house, but Erlanger was smart enough to get his piece of the action from even a bad house. (As a matter of fact, Klaw and Erlanger were in for 25 per cent of the Shubert take on the Herald Square.)

So, the Shuberts, the little boys from Syracuse, had gone to bed for the second time with Erlanger. The first intercourse, in Rochester, had been notably unsuccessful, but the Shuberts were prepared to bet on the second honeymoon. They were not trust-busting, they were no White Knights—they were the peddlers from Syracuse, and they were going to have something in the pack that would sell. At the same time, they were making still another deal for themselves, again without informing their "benefactor," Erlanger.

Among the more colorful characters in a colorful business was a producer named Charles Lederer. Lederer suffered from a congenital inability to balance income and expenses. He was a very successful producer, and he had more than his share of hits, but somehow his bills remained unpaid, his assets were constantly being attached, and in between shrieks of indignation at some legal assault being launched against him, or the sudden discovery that he had been locked out of his apartment for nonpayment, he did manage to produce, in 1897, a smash hit—*The Belle of New York*. It starred a girl called Edna May, and she became the belle of New York, and one year later the belle of London, when Lederer, incensed by some new indignity, transported *The Belle* there. And here another little tile fell into place in the mosaic of Shubert luck. Edna May was a Syracuse girl and a close friend of Jesse Oberdorfer. And as usual, Charles Lederer needed money. The Shuberts needed an attraction. For a very small sum (in cash, $8,000) the Shuberts secured the road rights to *The Belle*.

This was, of course, very much in the pattern of their deals with Hoyt, but instead of getting a corner of New York State and New England, they now had rights for all of the United States except New York City. They toured *The Belle*, and they made a lot of money. They also made a lot of friends in theaters throughout the country—friends who would be most valuable in future wars.

In closing the arrangement with Lederer, Sam Shubert became the first of the brothers to return to Europe. He sailed first class, with Oberdorfer as his traveling companion. Of whatever memories of his first ocean voyage that may have plagued little Sam we have no record. It can be assumed he looked into the steerage compartment and then took a bracing walk around the first-class deck. He enjoyed London. Because of Lederer and because of Edna May, he and Oberdorfer were thrown into the company of the cream of London stage society. He met English impresarios; he looked at English theaters, and he lined up two English musicals to bring to "his" theater—if he ever got it.

The month of May in 1900 saw one other interesting development in the New York theater. A man named Keith—B. F. Keith—who ran a vaudeville chain, had been studying the Klaw-Erlanger operation. And he liked what he saw. He thought it could be translated into vaudeville. So, in May he announced the opening steps in his campaign to organize vaudeville "intelligently and logically." The beginning of the Keith Booking Office, which became the United Booking Office, was theatrical history. It happened in May 1900.

Sam returned from Europe and compared notes with Lee; he wistfully inquired whether the Herald Square was prebooked and sadly learned that it was. Kirk LaShelle was going to bring in his production of a new play, *Arizona*. Leaving Lee in charge of the New York front, Sam went north to see his family and his theaters. He and Lee laughed a little over the war going on between Minnie Maddern Fiske and Abe Erlanger, a matter which was getting more than a little attention from the press.

Mrs. Fiske, one of the truly great actresses of her era, had flatly refused to join the Syndicate, book through the Syndicate, have anything to do with the Syndicate. Her productions were supervised by her husband, who incidentally published that most authoritative theatrical weekly the *New York Dramatic Mirror*. Harrison Fiske was the great fighter of lost causes. For eight long years he bucked Abe Erlanger and never won a battle. He raged and he fulminated, in and out of his paper, and he really had just one strong weapon—his wife. Minnie Maddern could sell out in New York or Dubuque with equal ease, and she didn't need Abe Erlanger's theaters. She could rent her own, and in her second-rate barn she could outdraw the Syndicate's best show. She was an independent, by marriage and by inclination, and her husband rallied the forces of Right behind him, and gallantly he went to war with Erlanger, time after time—and time after time, poor Harrison Fiske watched his allies defect, his bookings vanish. He was accused of anti-Semitism (which was probably true), and he was sued for it by Frohman, and he sued Frohman to prove the claim was libelous.

Some Day There'll Be A City Here. Climax in the last act of *Arizona*, Herald Square Theater, New York, 1900. This was the play that spawned the unique American art form—the Western.

They settled out of court, which meant that he wasn't legally anti-Semitic. He welcomed new allies, and he formed new coalitions; and every time he found himself on the loser's side, with pudgy Abe Erlanger the winner. (Since the entire Syndicate was Jewish, it would be a living wonder if Fiske wasn't an anti-Semite by the time he died.)

But to the Shuberts it was a wry joke. And to the Shuberts Fiske was stupid. Why fight them when you could do business with them? So Sam took the train to Syracuse, wondering to himself what kind of silly show would call itself *Arizona*; he saw his father and his mother, his nephews and his oldest sister and her husband. He visited Jacob J. in Rochester, where the theater was doing excellent business, and what is more, getting fantastically good reviews.

In Syracuse, Sam went to the Bastable and displayed a typical Sam Shubert characteristic. Sam Kahl was the coat room attendant, Marc Heiman the treasurer, and they had a pleasant reunion, comparing notes, catching up on what had happened, marveling at the good fortune that had blessed them all. Back at the theater (it was opening week, in September) Sam Shubert stood nervously in the back of the lobby, watching the people file into *his* theater. He would never cease to be nervous about his audiences, and he would never lose the charming eagerness which made him wonder if all the good things that were happening to him could really be true.

His restless glance watched young Kahl as he checked the coats. He walked up to the youngster and studied his "job." As Sam Kahl grew more and more nervous under the steady scrutiny, Shubert broke the silence. "Sammy, is there any charge for checking coats?"

"No, sir," replied Kahl.

"Do me a favor, please—a *personal* favor."

"Of course, Mr. Shubert."

"I don't mind if you make a dollar. But," and here Sam Shubert paused for emphasis, "Sammy, if people ask if there's a charge for checking, you tell them that in a Shubert theater there is never a charge for checking. But if they don't ask?" He paused again meaningfully. "You put out a saucer with some change in it—mostly dimes and quarters, so they get the idea." He shrugged. "You don't have to *tell* them anything, Sammy. Only if they ask."

Sam Shubert returned to New York City for the opening of *his* theater with someone else's play, *Arizona*, a melodrama of the West by Augustus Thomas, produced by Kirk LaShelle. It was a smash hit. It starred Arthur Byron as a dashing young officer, and a young actor in a minor role attracted attention—his name was Lionel Barrymore.

The success of *Arizona* contributed to the legend of the Shubert luck. The play sold out for a hundred and forty consecutive performances, a smashing run for those days. The "jinx" was lifted from the Herald Square Theater. From a bad house it had become one of the most successful theaters in the United States. The Shuberts were still falling uphill.

But the effect of *Arizona* transcended the fortunes of the Shuberts. It started a vogue called "the Western." It generated an enormous interest in Western art, Western stories, Western folklore. A whole series of imitations appeared: *New Mexico, California, Wyoming*. Owen Wister pounded out *The Virginian*, and a generation adopted the phrase "When you say that, pardner, smile." The Western had happened to America, and American audiences would see an endless parade of shootouts, wagon trains, forts, cowboys, Indians, dancehall girls with hearts of gold, rustlers, nesters, cavalry charges, mesquite, chapparal, mustangs, you name it. We had entered the era of the "fast draw," and God save us, we have not left it. But it began with *Arizona*.

The Shuberts were enjoying schizophrenic emotions. On the one hand, the money was rolling in. Their theater was a financial success, their upstate circuit was doing well, and *The Belle* was adding to the bank account. Financially, it was heaven. But they were still not producing their own shows. The Shuberts were not "presenting." It was frustrating for Sam—Jacob J. was having all the fun. Finally, Sam and Lee came to a decision.

They would introduce a program for the development of new playwrights. On those matinee days when the Herald Square was dark, they would present new plays by new authors with professional casts. The plays would be chosen by Sam S. Shubert, and would be produced under his "personal supervision."

Sam instantly began to personally supervise the reading of a flood of manuscripts, and in a month he had decided on his first presentation, *Sold and Paid For*, by John C. Dixon. It opened on the afternoon of December 7, 1900. Among the kinder reviews was one in the *New York Times*, which stated, "Nothing nearly as awful has been seen in twenty years." Undaunted, Sam presented his second—a dramatization of a novel, *Cashel Byron*, by George Bernard Shaw. The spirit of Christmas, 1900, did not help the cause. The second Sam S. Shubert production was brutally received by the critics. Always the pragmatist, Sam decided that possibly new dramatists would be better encouraged by other producers. It was the end of the "experiments." The Shuberts would present, during Sam's lifetime, only one more New Dramatist— Sam Shubert.

The Shuberts still couldn't "produce"; Sam sat in their Herald Square office and chewed his nails. No sooner was *Arizona* sent out on on the road to milk the provinces than Frohman put *The Girl from Up There* into the theater, and it too was a minor hit. The Shuberts had bought an English play, *The Brixton Burglary*, and they had to sit on it while Frohman ran out his string on *The Girl from Up There* and finally moved it to London. Just as the first faint stirrings of hope were exciting Sam Shubert, the Syndicate moved in a play called *The Prima Donna*. It was panned by the critics. Finally, at long last, Sam S. Shubert went into Broadway production.

Chapter Three

The first Shubert show in Manhattan opened in May of 1901. Lionel Barrymore played another of his small supporting roles, and the play received lukewarm notices, with some praise for the "care with which the production was mounted." It ran for forty-eight performances, and no one in New York realized that some kind of theatrical history was being made. There would be nearly a thousand Shubert productions of some six hundred-odd plays and musicals—an absolutely astounding feat—but the British import was the first ever to be "presented by" the Shuberts.

When it closed and was sent out on tour, Sam found his own theater fully booked for all of the next year! He couldn't squeeze in, he couldn't be a producer. Salt was poured into his wounds when Jacob J. tried out an Owen Davis play, *Under Two Flags*, in Rochester, and it was a smash.

Sam went to Rochester to see the play, and discovered that Davis had made his own plans for its New York presentation. The Shuberts couldn't even have their own "find." To make sure the entire trip wasn't wasted, Sam and Lee rented the Griswold Opera House in Troy, extending their upstate circuit. At the same time, they were acquiring rights to foreign plays—melodramas, farces—the bread-and-butter plays of the theater of the time.

Sam took off for London. The Shuberts were beginning to establish a traveling pattern which would continue for half a century. One or another Shubert was sailing to or from Europe almost every month. The shipping news of the first quarter of the twentieth century indicates that Sam or Lee, and later J.J., was perpetually in motion.

In England, Sam bought the American rights to a posthumous piece by Sir Arthur Sullivan and cabled Lee about the purchase. He wanted a theater.

Lee wanted one too. There were disquieting rumors on the Rialto: now that the Herald Square was a success, the Shuberts weren't going to have it long. Lee focused his sights on the Casino Theater on 39th Street. It was a very complicated affair.

The theater was a real-estate investment for the Bixby family of Brooklyn. They had leased it to a very impetuous, high-strung pair of theatrical speculators, the Sire brothers, as renowned for their temper as for their toughness. The Sires, in turn, had leased their lease to our old friend Charles Lederer.

35

The theater was a sort of Moorish nightmare—a series of arches, garish plaster ornamentation, and resplendent vulgarity, which would not be imitated until Marcus Loew and his fellow movie-moguls determined to bring culture to America. The Casino had housed the original *Florodora*, and each girl in the original sextet had married a millionaire. Lee liked the sound of it.

Lederer was experiencing another of his periods of acute penury and was glad to sell his lease to Lee Shubert for a comparatively small sum—just as long as it was in cash. He did not tell Shubert that he was delinquent on his rent and was about to be evicted. Lee didn't tell Lederer that he had examined the Bixby lease, discovered that Lederer's lease and the Sire brothers' sublease expired at the same time, and had side-stepped all negotiation with the Sires, and had concentrated on the Bixbys.

In later years, Lee Shubert once confided to someone, "To me, a negotiation is like a love affair. All the excitement is in the preliminaries; closing the deal isn't half so much fun." The Brooklyn Bixbys, predictably, succumbed. Lee cabled Sam that he had the Casino. He added that there were some problems in Syracuse.

Lee Shubert in his later years was a sentimental man. His eyes would grow liquid, he was known to cry, he helped friends in need, he donated to charity, sometimes even generously. But in 1901, he had small room for generosity. He had determined to convert the Bastable Theater in Syracuse, the very theater where Sam had had his first theatrical job, into a vaudeville house, and the owners of the theater were not pleased. They served notice of their intention to sue. It was the first of hundreds of lawsuits which the brothers would enjoy. One Broadway historian has stated that "where to most people a litigation was a breakdown in human relations, to the Shuberts, as to Clausewitz, it was an arm of diplomacy." Their attorney in Syracuse was Robert Rubin, who would go on to Metro-Goldwyn-Mayer and fortune, and their New York representative was William Klein, a well-known theatrical attorney.

A series of petty annoyances kept the Shuberts on their toes while they argued about Syracuse. An unknown gentleman with a love for typography had printed vast quantities of seats for the Herald Square Theater—without a contract to do so. He didn't have a contract to sell seats either, but this did not deter him, and as a result many was the night there were two and three people wanting the same seat in the theater, each claiming to have paid for it. The Shubert solution was to fire a whole lot of people, including ushers, and to replace the ushers with Columbia College students. This precipitated a backstage strike

36

and loud screams from the fired employees, who felt this was less a dedication to higher education than a love for lower wages.

Lee Shubert's response was quick and typical. He fired the strikers and replaced *them* with Columbia students. Finally, when a boycott was threatened, Lee fired the students and rehired the employees. It kept life interesting. What kept Sam's life interesting was the knowledge that before the end of the year, Richard Mansfield was finally going to appear in a Shubert theater—the Herald Square—in *Monsieur Beaucaire.*

At the same time, Mr. Lederer was engaged in legal fisticuffs with the Shuberts. He had returned from England, made his usual announcements of future plans, and then gotten into a disagreement with the Shuberts over the planned use of the Casino Theater, which he had leased to them, and which they still did not have! The theater was booked under an existing contract. The Shuberts remained sensible in this comedy of errors and won all their points.

The first week in December of 1901 saw two important Shubert firsts. They announced the leasing of American rights to a London hit, *A Chinese Honeymoon*, and they saw Mansfield open in *Beaucaire* at the Herald Square. Financially, it had been a great year. From Sam's viewpoint, it had been dull.

The Theatrical Trust was in high gear. Since the story of the Shuberts is the theatrical world, it seems proper that their relationship with the Trust be stated in dramatic terms. It is an old Hollywood truism that a hero is just about as good as the villain he conquers. Abe Erlanger was the best available villain—the very best. He had sharpened his claws and his contracts to the point where he controlled almost 95 percent of what America saw on its stages, except for Mr. Keith's private world of vaudeville. (And Mr. Erlanger had some ideas about *that* too.) He was getting a percentage of every show that booked a Syndicate theater—percentages that ran as high as half the profits. In addition, producers who were planning shows in New York, with the bonanza of the road to come, were eagerly offering Erlanger part of the ownership of the show to encourage his road bookings on the show's behalf. The nicest thing about Mr. Erlanger's position was the fact that there was no competition. If a producer became recalcitrant, and a few rash souls did, little Napoleon could play rough—very rough. One such intrepid fellow, Frank Perley, found himself routed from Philadelphia to Liverpool, Ohio, to Dowagiac, Michigan, to Charlotte, North Carolina, to Saginaw, Michigan! The show made money in every

37

place, and so did the railroads that carried the scenery, costumes, and company. The Syndicate made money. The theaters made money. Everybody made money—except Perley.

When Henrietta Crossman, a star of her day, "bucked" little Honest Abe, they finally gave her a complete road booking in her production of *Mistress Nell*. It was only after the contracts were signed and the tour started that Miss Crossman discovered that her show religiously followed by one week into every town a Syndicate production cunningly titled *Sweet Nell of Old Drury*.

When Belasco felt that 50 percent of his brain, sweat, and tears was too much to pay Erlanger, and then needed the Syndicate Routing to tour his Japanese play, *Darling of the Gods*, it somehow was preceded, week by week, by a specially designed Klaw-Erlanger production, *The Japanese Nightingale*. Dramatic sukiyaki just wasn't that popular.

So Mr. Erlanger, together with his associates, wielded the big stick and spoke loudly, and this during the very time that Theodore Roosevelt, the trust buster, had succeeded to the presidency and inaugurated his vigorous attacks on business monopoly! How? Well, there was an ingenuous legal theory held by the members of the Syndicate: since the theatrical business was in no sense a *necessity*, it could not be held in restraint of trade—therefore, the Syndicate could break all rules, starve actors and producers, extort vast sums of money, make or break theater owners, and then claim that since it really had nothing to do with commerce or money and was not essential to public welfare, it was exempt from rulings which applied to business. Naïve? The Supreme Court of the United States, in the 1900s, equally naïve, considered the theory valid and so ruled. Mr. Erlanger was given a free hand. If Franz Kafka, not yet twenty years old, was writing, this had to be his first script.

An old friend of Erlanger's, a producer named Ziegler, was walking up Broadway with him during this period, and Erlanger was basking in the reflection of his own glory. He had brought order, intelligence, and business organization to the theater, and he resented the lack of gratitude being displayed by the various "beneficiaries" of his wisdom. Ziegler, who had his own pomposity, pointed out that half the newspapers in the country were already attacking Klaw and Erlanger as pirates, that actors and producers were up in arms, that others would soon be challenging the Syndicate strangle hold.

"Who?" demanded Erlanger belligerently.

"Well," said Ziegler apologetically, "the Shuberts, for one."

"The Shuberts?" sneered Honest Abe. "If I squeezed my hand—

like this," and he suited action to words, crumpling his cigar, "I would put them out of business in two weeks."

"Why don't you?"

"Why should I bother? It's always good to have one independent for the people to throw rocks at. Ziegler, do me a favor. Leave me alone with the Shuberts. Nixon and Zimmerman are their partners, and I own Nixon and Zimmerman. The Shuberts are mosquitoes and I'm too busy to swat them."

In the first part of 1902, Erlanger was healthy as well as prosperous; but Sam Shubert was not so lucky—he fell seriously ill. He and Lee and their old friend Evans, of Herald Square negotiation, had been dickering on taking over the old upstairs Theatre Comique on 29th Street and running it as the third Shubert house in Manhattan. In the midst of the wheeling and dealing, Sam came down with a cold, which quickly turned into pneumonia. He was ill for three months. His invalidism brought his mother down from Syracuse—her first semipermanent separation from David—to nurse him, to cook for him, and to make a home for the two unmarried sisters who accompanied her. So, for three months, Lee ran all the Shubert business affairs.

He regretfully rejected Jacob J.'s offer to come down to help out. He closed the deal with Evans to rent the Comique, to redo the interior, and to rename it the Princess. He renegotiated the lease on the Casino for an additional five years, at an annual rental of $22,500 per annum. He sent Jacob J. to Boston and then to Chicago to investigate the possibilities of securing theaters in those cities.

During Sam's convalescence, J.J. gave some indication of his resourcefulness as a theater man. In the midst of an exceptionally bad storm in northern New York, a touring company of *For Her Sake* was booked into J.J.'s Rochester house. The theater was sold out; the company arrived on time, but in the confusion caused by the near-blizzard, the scenery and costumes were lost. J.J. made a curtain speech and then put the show on without scenery or costumes to tumultuous applause from the audience. J.J. was all Shubert when it came to avoiding the refunding of money.

It was in this same period that the Shuberts made their first really important financial alliance. They were quickly outgrowing the financial resources of their Syracuse associates. They needed larger money and more important money to open up Chicago and Boston, to lease the Hyperion Theater in New Haven, to take on a fourth house in New York, to explore St. Louis, to make arrangements in London, to poke an inquisitive nose into Philadelphia. Again it was Lee who found the "partners."

Samuel Untermyer was an important New York attorney. He was then in his early forties, and his clients included the rich and famous in New York—old-line Jewish banking and investing families, and some of the new-rich who with Tammany backing were carving fortunes out of the New York City expansion. Among this latter group was a mysterious man—Andrew Freedman. A bachelor, an intimate of the powers in the city, a man with real, if hard-to-nail-down, associations with the House of Morgan, his interests were varied and lucrative. He owned the New York Giants baseball team; he had invested heavily in New York real estate; and most important, he was one of the privileged, small group that was building New York's first subway, the IRT, under a generous contract. He and Untermyer took a long, hard look at the burgeoning theater and decided it was a good business for realistic investment. And they zeroed in on the Shuberts as "comers"—young men who seemed to know what they were doing. It was Lee they dealt with, and Lee who piloted their arrangement. They were very quiet partners, invisible and anonymous at the beginning. They were influential and rich; more important, they made available to the young Shuberts the world of political influence and the world of established money—respectable money, big money.

By the time Sam was able to return to work, the deal had been set. Lee and Sam hotly denied rumors that they were leasing a Chicago theater, or a Boston theater, or the New Haven theater; and then, a month or so later, the Hyperion in New Haven came under Shubert control, and the New Haven acquisition would be followed by the Chicago house; Boston would take a little longer. When Boston happened, Erlanger would move. The war for control of the theater would begin, and the Shuberts were getting strong allies in the wings.

These weird "we deny—we affirm" shenanigans were another strange pattern of Shubert behavior: the heated denial of a thing about to happen; the event; then, a look of injured innocence as the Shuberts explained what had occurred. They *did* have an excellent sense of publicity, which might explain this particular idiosyncrasy—it gave them *three* public announcements instead of one.

The brothers were humorless men. They occasionally enjoyed a joke, and in his later years Lee even got a small reputation as a raconteur, a mimic, even as a minor-league mot-coiner. But essentially they were sober, serious men. Their approach to a dollar was reverent, and it colored their approach to everything else. They just plain lacked humor. But like Sam Goldwyn, things they said and things they did were funny. In the long years of Shubert participation in the theater, anecdote after anecdote—some true, some false—was told about the brothers.

40

Stories were attributed to them—some of them the same stories that had been attributed to Erlanger a few years before and probably to every theatrical figure since the first play was produced. The Shuberts were guilty of occasional malapropisms, and when he got excited, Lee's high-pitched stuttering words were occasionally amusing. J. J. was never amusing. At his best, he was genial; and at his worst, terrifying. Occasionally he was unintentionally comic, but J. J. was never amusing. If one sign of fame is having jokes made *about* you, the Shuberts first began to become famous in the completely adolescent high jinks that led up to their taking physical control of the Casino Theater.

Sam had just returned to work after his convalescence. An agreement had been reached with the owners of the theater; the two lessees —the Sire brothers and George Lederer—had presumably accepted the Shubert take-over. Lederer had received money. Sam put his English import *A Chinese Honeymoon* into rehearsal. And on the 1st of May in 1902 the Shuberts were given the keys to the theater by the owners. The Sire brothers paid no attention to anything that had taken place. *They* were the lessees; *they* intended to remain there. They insisted Lee Shubert pay them too if he wanted them to leave.

Lee ignored the request. Their lease was to begin May 1st, so on May 1st Sam went to the theater, and was refused admission. The newspapers duly chronicled it. On the 2nd of May, Sam led a task force to the Casino. It consisted of himself, all five feet of him; Willie Klein, their attorney, a five-foot-three-inch giant; and short, roly-poly Abe Thalheimer, who was part of the Shubert organization. They found the doors to the theater locked, and the keys they had been given no longer fit. What to do? General Sam Shubert relied on strategy. He called a hasty council of war in the street outside the theater and determined on a flanking action.

Off the stairway to the upstairs lobby of the Casino was a door to a tavern-restaurant which shared the premises. Stealthily the Shubert invaders made their way to the tavern through its door into the theater entrance. There, they were met in force by the outraged Sire brothers. There was nothing to be said in the face of the superior defense team, and the Shuberts repaired to their office to summon reinforcements.

Two private policemen (one of them a real, honest-to-God federal marshal) flanked the next Shubert attack. Back to the tavern they stormed—three short generals and two tall soldiers. They threw open the door to the theater, and found facing them a solid wooden wall, hastily erected by the defending Sires. Sam surveyed the situation for as long as ten seconds and then ordered the wall broken down.

With a borrowed set of tools the Shubert legions began to tear down the board barrier. They splintered two of the planks, making an opening wide enough for little Sam to squeeze through and to take over control of *his* theater. He was met by an imposing gentleman in a watchman's uniform, armed with a very large revolver, which he waved genially at the attackers. The Shuberts beat a hasty retreat again, to reorganize.

The newspapers blazoned the story: "Shuberts Driven Off at Gunpoint." The battle of the Casino was left with the Sires in the theater, the street doors sealed, the tavern open, and the splintered barrier now guarded on both sides.

The third day of the "incident Casino" was spent in watchful waiting and legal preparation. The Sires moved first, with a legal step to prevent the Shuberts from getting the theater. On May 7th the court ruled; the Sires were awarded the theater, and the Shuberts promised an immediate appeal. On the 15th they filed their appeal. Willie Klein saw Untermyer; he saw Lee; he saw Sam; he met with the Sire lawyers. Lee meanwhile had grown tired of the whole thing. A cast was in rehearsal for "A Sam Shubert Presents," and there was something logical about the Sires' claiming that if Lee Shubert could give money to Lederer he ought to give them some too.

Like many another Shubert cause célèbre, the case was settled out of court. Lee paid the Sires $20,000 for the lease, and on the last day of May, Sam Shubert moved his cast into the Casino. Sire had insisted on one additional clause in the agreement. Three nights a week he was to have a private box, in his name, at the Casino Theater. That plus the $20,000 was what it cost to end the silliness, and it wasn't really ended.

Three days later, Sam opened *Chinese Honeymoon* at the theater, and the Shuberts had their first New York smash hit. To read the story line is a waste of time. It was a typically incredible plot line—Samuel Pineapple (*sic*), an English stockbroker, marries his typist and takes her for a honeymoon to a mythical part of China. Not only is Yiang Yiang a myth, but it has local mythical customs and harbors a long-lost nephew of Mr. Pineapple. Into this "tight" libretto were woven songs and dances and several topical tunes on the news of the day. The audience loved it; Sam delivered a charming curtain speech. The show ran and ran and ran.

It spawned road companies, and it rained dollars. But more than anything else, it established the brothers Shubert as more than theater operators and scavengers of rights. It gave them a Broadway (and eventually a national) reputation as creative producers of stage entertainment. They had made a hit. It made Untermyer and Freedman certain they had moved into a good thing. True, Erlanger had his hand in the pie, and Nixon and Zimmerman, original partners in the Syndicate and Erlanger's partners still, were co-presenters with Sam Shubert. But the word was out that it was a Shubert operation.

Lee lost little time consolidating the Shubert position. Positive now that he would lose the Herald Square, he announced the first Shubert real estate *purchase* in New York. They bought the area from 107 to 113 on West 39th Street opposite the Casino, and on it they proposed to erect a new theater, to be owned by Lee and Sam and to be managed by Sam. Then Lee, newly born world traveler, set out for Europe "to acquire properties and seek new talent."

The New York papers noted his departure and commented on the rapid growth of Shubert holdings. Could this be a split in the Syndicate? Were Nixon and Zimmerman leaving Erlanger to cast their future fortune with the Shuberts? Read tomorrow's rumors to confirm.

No sooner had Lee and Oberdorfer sailed than Joe W. Jacobs, newly named Shubert general manager, announced the lease of the Hyperion Theater in New Haven, the theater to be managed and booked by the Shuberts for ten years, beginning in 1904. This meant ten Shubert houses. Sam celebrated by taking the Casino chorus girls on an outing for the Sunday; hansom cabs, food, entertainment. (This was one way of showing gratitude which did not cost too much.)

Either the excitement of *Honeymoon* or the terrible heat of that summer was the cause of it—Sam Shubert was soon gravely ill again. Lee rushed back from Europe to hold bedside conferences with his brother; to hotly deny that J. J. was in Chicago locking up the Dearborn Theater deal; and to announce that Lionel Grossmith, one of London's bigger stars, was going to open the Shubert Princess Theater in *Night of the Party.*

A few weeks later Sam, thin and drawn from his illness, announced that the Shuberts had secured the Dearborn in Chicago. Now it was time to "hotly deny" the pending acquisition of the Colonial in Boston.

It had been a great season and a busy summer, and as their first fall presentation on September 1, 1902, Sam S. presented that posthumous Sir Arthur Sullivan piece *The Emerald Isle* at the Herald Square. It received rave notices from the critics, it did good business, and it enhanced the growing Shubert reputation still more. Abe Erlanger decided that it was time to kill some mosquitoes.

Erlanger began with milk and honey carefully prepared for the Shuberts. Nixon arranged a meeting between Lee and Erlanger in little Napoleon's office. What Erlanger proposed interested the Shuberts.

Erlanger told Lee how much he and his partners admired the Shubert skills; how they saw in Sam and Lee valuable manpower for the good of the theater; how they wanted to cement their ties with the Shuberts in an overall agreement on bookings, new productions, etc. What he proposed was a marriage of their organizations, with the Shuberts getting the bargain basement Syndicate rate of twenty-five percent paid to the Trust. It was a very attractive offer. The meeting ended on a friendly, optimistic note, with Lee and the ubiquitous Willie Klein promising to get back to Honest Abe in a few days.

Shubert decisions had become a bit more complicated now than they had been in the earlier days. Untermyer and Freedman had to be consulted; Sam, who was euphoric with success, relied on Lee for judgment; Joe W. Jacobs, as general manager, was an important source of counsel. So, the Shuberts huddled, talked out the deal, felt that it was something they could not afford to pass up, and Lee called Nixon to tell him to set a second meeting with Erlanger. It was still milk and honey.

At the second meeting, an area of general agreement was found. Papers were to be drawn by the Trust lawyers, and the Shuberts and the Syndicate would be almost one. None of this, however, deterred Lee from proceeding with his own plans. Jacob J. "commuted" from Boston to Chicago to Syracuse to New York. Sam S. was supervising the preparation of new productions. The Princess Theater was refurbished in gold and red and was prepared for opening. Lee personally bought a site for an additional theater in New York City—this one on 42d Street. None of this escaped the covetous eye of pugnacious Abe Erlanger, a man whose acquisitive instincts were insatiable. He had control of almost all the theaters in the United States—he was up to his von Stroheim neck in theaters, more damned theaters than he really needed—but he didn't want anyone else having any. He pushed the attornies; he wanted that Shubert deal closed. He barked at Willie Klein, "What's the matter with Lee Shubert? Is he going into the real estate business?" Klein reported back to Lee, and Lee, smiling enigmatically, softly mentioned that "Theodore Roosevelt says investment in land is a very good thing."

Finally the papers were ready, the deal ironed out, and in a small ceremony Sam and Lee Shubert and Abe Erlanger solemnly affixed their signatures to the contracts. The Syndicate had gotten control of the brothers Shubert. Now, Erlanger lowered the boom.

Only a few days after the contract was signed, Erlanger sent a note to Lee Shubert requesting an amendment to the contract. Erlanger was "requesting" that the Shuberts agree, in writing, that they would not extend their circuit, by the purchase, lease, or erection of any new theater. It took the Shuberts just about five seconds to refuse. What Erlanger was saying in effect was that as the lease on each property expired, the Shuberts would lose that property and be unable to replace it. Eventually, they would be without playhouses. The Shuberts worded a careful reply, indicating their joy with the existing contract and their reluctance to change it.

The Erlanger reply was predictable: because of the Shubert breach of contract they were hereby notified that Klaw and Erlanger could no longer continue to book Shubert attractions in Syndicate houses. When the Shuberts politely asked just what breach of contract had occurred, Erlanger's reply was classic: "You know God-damned well what breach!"

Lee then attempted to see Erlanger, and no appointment could be arranged. Willie Klein had similar luck with the Syndicate attorney. At a dinner party, Erlanger announced to one and all that the Shuberts would be out of business in sixty days. He, Abe Erlanger, had spoken. The next attack came from an expected source; Hyde and Behman publicly issued the statement that they were not renewing the lease on the Herald Square with the Shuberts. (This, of course, the Shuberts had foreseen, and had protected against. They had the Casino and the Princess and would soon have the Madison Square, plus "real estate.")

In a private meeting with Lee Shubert, Hyde told Lee that he had been forced to this decision by Erlanger, who had sworn to "destroy Hyde and Behman, if necessary, to get rid of the Shuberts." Nixon, the Shubert partner in production, was embarrassed but unable to do anything. Finally, after much huddling, Jacob J. was called into town to meet with Alf Hayman, Erlanger's partner.

The meeting was a farce. Hayman, portly, mustached, in his late fifties, sat behind the desk listening to young Jacob J., already tenacious as a bulldog and twice as aggressive. Where was the breach, Jacob J. wanted to know. How had the Shuberts breached their contract? Hayman's answer was beautiful. The Shuberts had refused an attraction in Troy, New York. Jacob J. pointed out that the contract called for Shubert approval of shows booked into their theaters. He, Jacob J., had not approved. "Tell Erlanger," stormed J. J., "that we are living up to *our* contract. We expect him to do likewise." Hyman nodded. J. J. jammed his hat over his curly hair and said, "And tell Erlanger that in sixty days we'll still be in business, and sixty days after that, too!" And that is how it was left.

Erlanger's next move was to pour all the power of the Syndicate, as businessmen and as individuals, into a systematic attack on the Shu-

45

berts. The leading theatrical daily of the time was the *Morning Telegraph*, now better known for its racing information. The sheet was pro-syndicate, a mouthpiece for Erlanger, and in the opinion of many experts, bought and paid for by Honest Abe. It began loosing tirades on Shubert greed, nefarious practices, collusion with scalpers, etc. The Shuberts made no reply. The next step was a whispering campaign; little Sam S. Shubert, he of the mild manner, ready shy smile and the deep brown eyes, was labeled a homosexual. (Strangely enough, in later years the same odd charge would be made against Lee and against J. J. Since the Shuberts gained a rather impressive reputation as bedroom athletes, the charge was laughable.) No one in his right mind ever accused Lee or J. J. of being a romantic; for them, women were more or less isometric exercises—they were healthful, they gave a man a sense of physical well-being, and they could be taken during business hours. Almost five thousand beautiful girls graced Shubert productions. Although they did not invent the casting couch, it is believed that the Shuberts developed its functions. Lee would trot into the back of his theater, call an usher, and say in a high whisper, "The third girl from the left—what's her name—tell her I would like to see her in my office after the show." The girls came, they saw, and they never talked about it. J. J., who specialized in musicals, was saluted for his harem (the chorus and the show girls), about which he was most possessive. They were very active males, these Shuberts, and if they didn't love with a deathless devotion, they certainly worked at love with admirable industry.

There was no defense against the whispering campaign except controlled amusement. But in the case of the *Telegraph*, Lee had a weapon—he cut the Shubert advertising from the paper. It was not a great sum of money they were spending each week, but in Shubert thinking it was a telling blow—it hit the pocketbook which, the Shuberts always felt, was a most sensitive area. It signaled the first Shubert engagement in a war with the press, a war they extended to all papers, a war which never really ended until there were no more Shuberts.

The Shubert philosophy about newspapers was a simple statement of pragmatic clarity. The Shuberts were businessmen, went their argument, and they manufactured a product. They spent hard-earned money to advertise the product they manufactured, and this money went to already rich newspapers. Why then should a newspaper attack them or their product? Why should the very paper that ran an ad for a Shubert Presents run adjacent to that ad a column in which the critic tore the product apart? To Lee Shubert and to J. J. it made no sense. Their reaction was simple and elemental: remove the critic or we remove the ad.

In the case of the *Telegraph*, the ads were in and out, depending on the virulence of the attack on the Shuberts. In other cases, the Shuberts tried to control the critic by the threat of the advertising budget. The Shubert press department walked a tightrope between outraged Shuberts and even more outraged editors. Freedom of the press, to Lee and Jacob J., was the right of the Shuberts to read favorable notices.

In defending this Shubert right, the brothers fought some epic battles—even up to the United States Supreme Court! They barred critics from their theaters and, in later years, gossip columnists. They published two theatrical sheets of their own, making a profit on one of them. They threatened and cajoled, and they served ultimatums and subpoenas.

J. J. came to Chicago and decided to run a contest in the press awarding two tickets to opening night, plus a cash bonus, to the person who picked the best name for their brand-new theater. Percy Hammond, later dean of critics in New York on the *Herald Tribune*, was then the drama editor for the *Chicago Evening Post*. In his column he drily suggested that having seen several Shubert productions, he wanted to enter the contest. In memory of the redolence of past Shubert shows, why didn't they call the new theater The Onion? J. J. blew.

When the screaming and the profanity had died down, Hammond was barred from the Shubert houses in Chicago. It took several weeks for the Shubert management in Chicago to calm down J. J.'s choler and to restore seating privileges to Hammond, an important outlet for theatrical news.

Some time later, the new theater opened with great fanfare, presenting Eddie Foy in *The Orchid*, another Shubert English musical import. The anonymous critic for a now-defunct newspaper, *The Chicago Interocean*, in reviewing the Shubert opus, wryly remarked that "since the Shuberts did not see fit to adopt Percy Hammond's suggestion for the name of the theater, perhaps they would take a close look at the "entertainment" they brought to Chicago last night, *The Orchid*, and change *its* title to *The Onion*. The effect of this on J. J. was instantaneous. He erupted into a temper tantrum, and when the dust had settled, he barred *Hammond* again! Not the other critic. Hammond. It makes one wonder.

The attacks by the critics were a problem, but only a minor problem. The Shuberts were engaged in a much more vital fight—a fight for survival in the face of promised destruction by Erlanger.

47

As could be predicted, the Shuberts went about their war in the most unpredictable way. Young Gandhi had returned to India, but hardly anyone in the United States had ever heard of him—certainly the Shuberts hadn't. But they adopted a policy of passive resistance, and with it they drove Abe Erlanger to distraction.

The worthy brothers simply refused to acknowledge a state of hostility; they recognized no breach of their contract with the Syndicate. They scrupulously rendered their accountings, piously made their payments on time, and smiled enigmatically when anyone suggested that their relationship with Erlanger was less than perfect. And all the time, they were consolidating their real estate, extending their circuit, adding allies, digging their trenches. And Abe Erlanger knew what they were doing and couldn't find a damned thing to do about it.

The Shuberts had fallen into a job-division pattern that worked to everyone's satisfaction. Sam was the titular head of the company and its driving creative force. Lee sat in Sam's shadow, discreetly planning the logistics; and J. J. was in charge of "out-of-town," supervising theater redecoration and construction, watching the box offices, hiring and firing, and always having more money in his pockets than Lee or Sam could understand.

The three brothers were indefatigable; they worked an eighteen-hour day, they were on so many trains and boats in such rapid succession that often it must have seemed to Erlanger that there were at least six brothers.

There was only one problem. Sam could not come up with another *Chinese Honeymoon*. Whether he produced plays alone or in association with Nixon and Zimmerman of the Syndicate, they didn't work. And because he could not keep a flow of attractions for the Shubert theaters, the brothers were forced to outside booking to keep the lights on in their houses. Although the practice was profitable, it was bad for Sam's ego. His series of no hits and near flops need not be listed. Only one play of the period is important in Shubert history. They brought the English version of *Heidelberg*, originally a German romance, to New York, where it opened and closed with embarrassing reviews. It died on the road; they couldn't even book it into their own chain. They were stubborn men—twice they would revive *Heidelberg*. First revival: a bomb. The second? The biggest moneymaker in theatrical history.

For Sam, there were very few gratifications in this endless parade of nondescript attractions. He met a girl called Harriet Sawyer, and he saw a lot of her, and he met a star, Lulu Glaser, and he saw a lot of her. He told his best friends that he had fallen in love with Julia Sanderson, a sixteen-year-old singer in the chorus of an epic called *Win-*

Julia Sanderson. Sam never told her he loved her.

some Winnie that Sam and his Syndicate partners had produced in a moment of weakness. Sam neglected to tell Miss Sanderson of his undying love. However, it is rumored that he *did* tell Miss Sawyer, and she promptly took an overdose of pills. Sam went to London.

Lee was buying and selling real estate, starting the first Shubert theater in Boston, encouraging J. J. to find a second house in Chicago and to explore St. Louis, an Erlanger monopoly. He had arranged to sell his 42nd Street property to Reginald de Koven, a composer who was still very, very rich from his *Robin Hood*, and de Koven was building America's "most beautiful" theater on the site; called the Lyric, it was leased back to the Shuberts for twenty-one years, and they promptly made plans to move their offices to the new building. They hired A. Toxen Worm, a portly, imperious Dane, as the head of their press department. But A. Toxen, an impressive fellow, quickly outgrew that position and played a key role in Shubert affairs for the rest of his life.

Meanwhile, Erlanger was becoming incredibly rich. His concept of the Syndicate was proving itself over and over again. A thousand theaters from coast to coast were pouring in profits. Since almost every production in those theaters was kicking back a percentage to the Syndicate, Abe and his partners were slicing larger and larger melons. They published no financial reports, their books were a well-kept secret. But money makes its own news. And in every city in the country, men who had money, who liked it and wanted more were sniffing the heady atmosphere of the theater and finding the aroma irresistible. They wanted in. But the Syndicate was a tightly held corporation. Erlanger's recipe for success was providing potential allies for the Shuberts.

There followed a series of seemingly unconnected events. Each of them might have been changed by Erlanger, but he did nothing; together they brought the cold war to open battle, and together, Erlanger's small mistakes, plus one catastrophe beyond his control, established the Shubert Empire.

Belasco, the high priest of melodrama, and Sam's god, grew increasingly enraged at the fifty percent of his play that the Syndicate was taking. Finally, he sued for an accounting, and he filed a suit under the comparatively new antitrust laws. His attorney was Samuel Untermyer, the Shubert "silent" partner.

The Syndicate went through all the legal motions, and rather than relax its strangle hold on the business Erlanger felt that, if anything, he must now be even more rigid in his disciplining of the "independent" producers. He had watched the Nixon-Zimmerman-Shubert partnership with schizoid reactions. On the one hand, he approved of it, since

50

it gave him a pipeline into Shubert affairs. On the other hand, he resented the idea that *his* partners were subsidizing the young upstarts. He sneered knowingly when *The Runaways*, done by the coalition, turned out to be the most expensive bomb of the season—seventy-five thousand dollars' worth of not-so-good. With the Belasco suit a reality, Erlanger started to clamp down on the Shubert-Nixon-Zimmerman production of *The Girl from Dixie*. He was going to teach the Shuberts a lesson, and in doing so, he was going to prove to the theatrical industry that Abe Erlanger was going to continue to write the rules.

On December 30, 1903, 1,600 people packed the Iroquois Theater in Chicago, the Klaw and Erlanger flagship theater in the Middle West. It was a matinée in the heart of the holiday season, and the audience was mostly women and children. The show was a musical extravaganza, *Mr. Bluebeard*, starring Eddie Foy.

The audience was enchanted as one exotic setting followed another, and the broad comedy of Foy had them happy and relaxed while they listened to the lilting music. Suddenly, high on the proscenium arch, a tiny puff of smoke billowed out toward the audience. Hardly anyone noticed. But in seconds, tongues of flame were licking at the flimsy scenery and the gauze draperies.

Foy stepped to the footlights as the audience began to panic. Incongruous in his outlandish costume he told the audience there was nothing to worry about. "The theater is fireproof. We will have it under control in a few minutes." He waved to the orchestra leader, and the musicians began to play the overture.

Backstage, members of the company were beginning to edge toward the exit door; a stagehand opened it, and a gust of cold air swept into the stage area, and the flames soared. A skylight above the stage shattered and now the entire stage area of the nearly new theater was a giant chimney. The curtain man began lowering the asbestos curtain, and halfway down, it jammed on its rollers. Two more skylights exploded in a shower of tinkling glass, and a wall of hot gas and flame exploded into the theater, chuting under the half-lowered curtain.

The panic hit—screams, stampede, a mad crush of people surging toward the exit doors. Some in the orchestra section did not move from their seats. That first gust of flame and gas had incinerated them in their places.

Despite the presence of standees and congestion in every door, the orchestra ticket holders suffered relatively few casualties. In the balcony the story was tragic.

51

The aisles were badly planned; the exit doors, in most cases, were sealed shut. The architects of the "fireproof theater" had planned iron fire escapes all along the solid-brick alley wall, and here, through those doors that opened the mob hurtled out onto the iron platforms and the steep staircases. Maddened by fear, they charged into the hordes trampling out of adjoining doors and clogged the staircase at one point until the bodies were piled twenty feet high.

Inside, people were trapped against the unyielding doors, crushed by those behind them, choking in the thick smoke, clawing at each other for escape.

The fire lasted less than fifteen minutes. More than six hundred people perished. The scandal rocked Chicago, and the shock wave roared across the United States.

There were many theories about how the fire had started. One said that a corner of the rich red curtain had brushed against one of the "revolutionary" new electric floodlights, caught fire and sent it on to the canvas and wood of the scenery. A second hypothesis was that the overloaded electric wiring had shorted, caught fire, and set off the chain holocaust which brought the terrible tragedy.

But the theories didn't really matter; the facts were grisly enough. Horror and indignation flared in every city. Theaters were closed down. City administrations put their inspectors on overtime, and laboriously they went through every house, checking fire doors, exits, seating arrangements, and making strong recommendations. Thousands of actors were out of work. Thousands of theaters were closed. Some would never reopen. Amazingly, no convictions ever came out of the Iroquois fire. Although indictments were handed down, no penalty was assessed, no theater owner or manager paid a fine or went to jail, although the violations were flagrant.

In New York, almost all of what is today's fire code for theaters and other places of public assembly was written in the weeks that followed the Chicago catastrophe. All the Shubert theaters were closed; one, the Madison Square, permanently. But new theaters would have to be built, not only in New York but all over the United States, and someone was going to build them, operate them, and plan attractions for them. The lines were being drawn.

James Metcalfe, an artist-critic for the old *Life* magazine, drew a vicious cartoon, caricaturing Erlanger with the blazing theater in the background, and Erlanger promptly sued *Life* for $100,000, charging libel. But *Life* was only one publication; all over the United States, editorials harangued against the "callous Theatrical Trust," and against

Erlanger, and publishers searched for someone to play the hero in their columns, which had already cast Erlanger as the villain.

A few days after the Iroquois fire, little Sam Shubert impulsively paid a call on Abe Erlanger. He was weary of the endless strain of bickering, conflict, pressure; in his own mind, there was room for all in the theater. He was determined to find a way to coexist with the Syndicate. All of this he told Honest Abe, and ended the meeting by offering the Syndicate the use of the Shubert house in Chicago until the Iroquois could be rebuilt. It was a generous, almost unbelievable offer, and it seemed to guarantee peace between the factions. Erlanger was touched, he gratefully accepted Sam's gesture, and Sam returned to Shubert headquarters to report that everything was in order, that the war was over.

Two weeks later Erlanger, for reasons that can't be explained, changed his mind. Perhaps it was the press campaign against him; perhaps it was a series of Belasco diatribes; but Erlanger called in Nixon and ordered him to drop his association with Shubert. Nixon tried to calm Erlanger, but nothing he said would make Abe alter his decision. Nixon pointed out that *The Girl from Dixie*, a joint production, had been brought to Chicago for polishing before New York. He and Sam Shubert had been working on it for four months. Erlanger was adamant. He served his ultimatum to Nixon: End the Shubert relationship or leave the Syndicate! Nixon, a normally cocky man, flushed, bit his tongue, and walked out of the office. By the time he reported the news to Shubert, their route had been canceled, their stars had resigned, and their company was out of business. *The Girl from Dixie* was dead.

Furious at Erlanger's betrayal, and especially so because it followed so closely the expressions of undying gratitude Erlanger had made to Sam, the Shuberts moved quickly. Sam sailed for London and began negotiations on the New Waldorf Theater. The Shuberts would lease it for sixteen years. He met with George Bernard Shaw to discuss some of Mr. Shaw's productions in the United States. Lee was holding interminable meetings with Untermyer, Freedman, Fiske, Belasco, and all other disgruntled independents. When Sam came home, Lee sailed for London to nail down the details on the New Waldorf deal, and to have his visit with Mr. Shaw. Shaw remarked to Granville Barker, "I am being Shubert-ized. In small packages."

All the "little" Erlanger moves, the trivia of his anti-Shubert campaign, were coming together. Belasco was now an Erlanger-manufactured Shubert ally; so was Fiske. The Iroquois Theater disaster would compel the building of a thousand new theaters. And Honest Abe's insistence on a closely held monopoly left large investors on the outside looking for a rival investment. The Shuberts were waiting. Finally, his feud with the press left a "hero"-vacuum in the theater. Erlanger had helped create the Shuberts.

During the Shuberts' short truce with Erlanger, the Syndicate invited Sam into the organization of a theatrical managers association; two months later it was formed, with no Shubert as a member. Willie Klein and Untermyer, realizing that the Shubert fortunes were being seriously menaced by Erlanger's implacable enmity, began to incorporate the various branches of the little empire. Significantly, Sam and Lee were officers of each of the eight corporations that were organized; J. J. was an incorporator only in those that were the owners of theaters outside New York.

On April 18, 1904, the brothers sat in their new offices in the Lyric Theater with an eager insurance salesman. They were each handed insurance applications to be filled out. They were applying for policies of $50,000 to cover each of them, plus a joint policy on all three brothers of $100,000. They were a long way from Sam's first policy for $2,500, taken out when he had become treasurer of the Wieting.

Each of them went to his desk and filled out the form. Sam gave his age as twenty-six, and his place of birth as Syracuse. (He was twenty-nine, and born, as mentioned, in Poland.) Lee, who was thirty-one, listed himself as twenty-eight, born in Syracuse; but Jacob J., in a rare moment of chronological honesty, said he was twenty-five, which he was.

Sam, in giving the requested information on the structure of the family, wrote that he had had three brothers, one of whom died in infancy, and that the two survivors were aged thirty (for Lee, he took an average) and twenty-five. There were three sisters, he wrote, thirty-five, twenty-nine, and twenty-two.

Lee, seated in the same room, at the same time, had only two brothers, both living, aged twenty-seven and twenty-six respectively. He grudgingly agreed with Sam that there were three living sisters, but his estimate of their ages was thirty-three, twenty-seven, and twenty-one. Since Lee had decided that Sam also was twenty-seven, it would seem that their mother had enjoyed a busy year.

Jacob J. was filling in his application at the same time, and as far as brothers were concerned, he joined with Sam in putting the number at three, one of whom had died in infancy. But he asserted his independence when it came to the respective ages of the living and disagreed with both Sam and Lee. Lee was thirty-one, according to J. J., and Sam was thirty. He left the ages of the three sisters blank.

One looks at the three forms and marvels; one knows that the eager agent must have looked at the three forms; one is just positive that someone in the main office of the insurance company examined the forms, and yet, despite all the discrepancies the policies were issued. (Before making their first payment, the brothers Shubert canceled the joint policy but held on to the individual coverage.)

When the doctor for the insurance company examined the men, he was annoyed at the fact that each of them had made himself taller than he actually was in his stockinged feet. Now, why had they made themselves younger? Were taller and younger both mere indications of vanity? Was it just plain I-don't-give-a-damn irritation at the red tape of the questionnaire? Motivation is in the eye of the beholder.

Actually, by diminishing their ages the Shuberts were diminishing their premiums—it was just that simple.

One terrifying fact came out of the medical examination. In his first report the doctor recommended against the policy covering Sam's life. Preliminary diagnosis: tubercular. It took two additional physicals before Sam's application was approved. Sam laughed it off, but whenever Sam coughed, Lee winced.

Chapter Four

The brothers went their separate ways in their careers. J. J. was now based in Chicago, building in St. Louis, and trying to keep his finger in the pie in upstate New York. Lee was back in London, closing the lease on the New Waldorf. Sam was "producing," co-producing, and finally, collaborating. He and Robert Smith were working on a musical extravaganza called *Fantana*. Like his brother Lee, Sam was going to be a writer.

To backstop J. J.'s operation, A. Toxen Worm was now in Chicago, and Channing Pollock was brought in to head the press department in New York. And to pick up manpower in the Syracuse-Rochester-Utica operation, the Shuberts "amalgamated" their interests with those of Hurtig and Seamon. They were stripping down for battle.

If the Shuberts and their employees were all very busy, none was busier than Willie Klein, their indefatigable attorney.

In producing *their Heidelberg*, the Shuberts had entered into a co-production deal with William Brady, a very successful entrepreneur of the theater, better known perhaps as the husband of Grace George and as the father of Alice Brady, and best known as the manager of Jim Corbett, the world's heavyweight champion. (One of Mr. Brady's hits was *Gentleman Jack*, starring Corbett.)

The Shuberts claimed to have the American rights to *Heidelberg*, and even though the show did not do well, Aubrey Boucicault, a writer who claimed *he* had the rights, sued the good brothers and Brady for $50,000. The Shuberts indignantly filed a countersuit for $60,000. No one could out-sue a Shubert. In the free and easy days of theatrical rights, it is quite possible that (a) neither of them had the rights, or (b) both of them had firm contracts. It did not matter much.

During this same period, the building on West 39th Street, where the Shuberts stored sets and costumes, suffered a fire. Channing Pollock announced the estimated damage as being $50,000. (This figure was one the Shuberts employed again and again in estimating losses, damages, injuries. It was the roundness of the number, or perhaps all those zeroes, that pleased them, but it appears and reappears in Shubert litigations.) The police chief of the city of New York, a Mr. Duane, estimated the damage at $2,000. Sam and Lee wanted to sue *him*, but the cautious Mr. Klein suggested they settle out of court with the insurance company. They collected just over $3,000.

Mr. Sire was keeping Klein busy with demands for accountings on

LYRIC THEATRE

REGINALD DeKOVEN, - - - - - - - - Proprietor.
SAM S. AND LEE SHUBERT, - - - - - - - Managers.

WEEK COMMENCING MONDAY EVENING, JANUARY 16, 1905
Matinees Wednesdays and Saturdays.

SAM S. SHUBERT
—OFFERS—

The Jefferson De Angelis Company

In the Japanese-American Musical Comedy,

FANTANA

Book by SAM S. SHUBERT and ROBERT B. SMITH.
Lyrics by Robert B. Smith.
Music by RAYMOND HUBBELL.   Staged by R. H. BURNSIDE.

CHARACTERS.

COMMODORE EVERETT, a retired naval officer, at present a California wine
  merchant, and owner of the vineyard "Fantana"..............HUBERT WILKE
HAWKINS, valet to the Commodore................**JEFFERSON DE ANGELIS**
LIEUT. SINCLAIR WARREN, of H. M. S. "Pontiac," anchored off 'Frisco.
                         FRANK RUSHWORTH
FRED EVERETT, a recent graduate of Annapolis, nephew of Commodore
  Everett.......................   ..   .. DOUGLAS FAIRANKS
HENRI PASDOIT, a waiter in the Café Odion, Paris, traveling as a count, and
  seeking his fortune in the wine business ....GEORGE BEBAN
HON. KOGORA HIRATAKA, Japanese Minister to America ...   PHILIP LEIGH
THE MARQUIS KIQTO, Governor of Kinshin Province, Japan..ROBT. BRODERICK
FANNY EVERETT, daughter of Commodore Everett, nicknamed "Fantana"
  by her father after his vineyard......................**ADELE RITCHIE**
JESSIE, her maid...... .... **KATIE BARRY**
ELSIE STURTEVANT, a New York belle, schoolmate of Fanny's...JULIA SANDERSON
MLLE. ANITA, a Parisian vaudeville artist and secretly married to Pasdoit,
                         ELEANOR BROWNING
THE KID....... ....ADELAIDE SHARP
MABEL..............⎫ Leaders' ⎧......................ROMA SNYDER
LILLIAN ....⎪ of the ⎪.........................AMY DALE
FLORENCE ....⎬ younger set at ⎨...............JEAN CALDUCCI
JEANETTE..... ...⎭ the hotel. ⎩...... ....CATHERINE COOPER
LOLA SAN....⎫ Geisha Girls, ⎧.............. ....LYNN D'ARCY
HELA KORA..⎭   ⎩.............. ....VICTORIA STUART

VASSAR GIRLS VISITING THEIR COLLEAGUE, FANNY EVERETT—Misses Sybil Anderson,
    Carlotta Doty, Aurora Piatt, Mabel Courtney and Louise Barthel.
MAIDS—Misses Grace Wilson, Lotta Ettinger, Neva West, Carol Oty, Dorothy
    Knight and Amy Dale.
VALETS—Misses Lyun D'Arcy, Nina Clemens, Olive Quimby, Kathryne Hyland,
    Gertrude Mandell and Victoria Stuart.
OFFICERS OF H. M. S "PONTIAC"—Messrs. Harvey A. Kelly, Edward Hallaran,
    Frank Greene, George Picard, Henry Davis.
CADETS OF THE ANNAPOLIS NAVAL ACADEMY—Messrs. R. T. Kirkwood, Chas.
    Wright, Jack Carlyle, Henry Dyer and Frances Cameron.
Hotel Guests, Attendants, Japanese Men, Giesha Voyagers, Maids and Valets.

Fantana. "Written" by Sam S. Shubert—but not in Chicago. Playing the role of
Fred Everett, a young juvenile—Douglas Fairbanks (Senior, that is).

his reserved seats at the Casino, and the courts were endlessly awarding $25,000 to Lee Shubert, and then reversing themselves and giving the same amount to Mr. Sire. (Together, the sums add up to that magical $50,000.)

When the Casino had *its* fire—fortunately not during a performance —and the theater was gutted, the Shuberts determined to rebuild it as a street-level theater, instead of the original one-flight-up. In the course of the alterations, Mr. Wolf, the café owner who had been caught in the middle of the Sires-Shubert war, now found himself in a fracas with Sam Shubert, who angrily walled the lobby off from the café. Mr. Wolf sued, and Mr. Klein countersued.

When the Shuberts secured an injunction against a hapless performer, claiming a contract breach, the young lady, Annie d'Angeles, found herself not working. Marie Dressler, who periodically suffered her own financial embarrassments—this was long, long before *Min and Bill* or *Anna Christie*—announced a benefit for herself one night, and Miss d'Angeles volunteered to perform. She did, and was promptly haled into court by the omnipresent Mr. Klein, and the court fined her $50 for contempt of the injunction.

Della Fox, a leading comedienne of the time, was married to a Broadway gentleman in the jewelry business and known affectionately as "Diamond Jack" Levy. He "helped" the Shuberts star his wife in an epic at the Princess Theater, *West Point Cadet*, the forerunner of many Ruby Keeler–Dick Powell service academy pictures, and it opened and closed in the wink of a diamond. Mr. Levy lost his jewelry store, and the Shuberts lost the costumes. The chorus kept them, since they had not been paid for their seven weeks of rehearsal. Mr. Klein sued the chorines for the costumes, and the unlucky "Diamond Jack" was also named. Mr. Levy, officially the producer of the piece—it was public knowledge, however, that the Shuberts were doing the work—wished to spare his wife any embarrassment and had announced that the closing of the hopeless show was occasioned by Della Fox's "laryngitis." The Shuberts now asked Mr. Levy for the theater rental, with Mr. Klein doing the requesting.

While Mr. Klein kept himself happy in litigations, he did not neglect his corporate work for the brothers. A tiny item appeared in the *New York Press*, announcing the forming of the F. Ray Comstock Company, a theatrical organization which would specialize in attractions for summer resorts. Mr. Comstock, a fairly well-known Broadway producer was president, Sam was vice president, Lee the secretary, and Willie Klein the attorney. It was Mr. Comstock's honor to become the first wholly owned Shubert subsidiary. And Sam Shubert announced that he would book the theater at Manhattan Beach, a New York summer resort near Coney Island, and do the same for the Shubert Garrick Theater in Chicago during the summer season—this last in open conflict with the Syndicate.

The results were immediate. Erlanger, who had been silently enjoying Sam's series of bad shows, now advised that the Syndicate contract with the Shuberts would not be extended to include the new theater in St. Louis. Sam was in St. Louis with Joe W. Jacobs, visiting J.J. when Erlanger made the announcement.

J.J. exploded. Not only had Sam failed to come up with shows for the Shubert circuit, but he had also succeeded in fouling up their still-unopened theater. Sam was calm. He told Jacob that the Garrick in St. Louis (they had given up all contests for naming theaters) would be a first-run Shubert house. "What do we open with," demanded J.J., "*Taps?*" (A recent Sam flop.) "Or do we bring back *Heidelberg?*" Sam began to get angry. But J.J. was not to be stopped. "I don't want you here for the opening. And I don't want Lee. You're both jinxes. Fourteen-carat hoodoos. Everything you touch turns to shit. Stay out of my theater for the opening so you don't rub off on me." White-faced, Sam left the Garrick.

Sam went directly to Chicago to see the final rehearsals of *Fantana* and to placate Robert B. Smith. Mr. Smith, later to do the lyrics on *Sweethearts* for Victor Herbert, was more than a little incensed with the state of affairs. He had been approached by Sam Shubert, who suggested a skimpy plot line to him, and he had proceeded to write *Fantana*, conferring from time to time with his producer, Mr. Shubert. Smith felt that he had done all the work, while Sam had gotten all the publicity. This, plus the normal tension of preparing a new show, made Mr. Smith an angry collaborator. To placate him Sam called a press conference and hotly denied any "rumor that he was the coauthor of the book of *Fantana.*"

Two days later the play opened in Chicago to great praise, with particular attention paid to "the lavish Shubert production." *Fantana* was a hit, and Sam immediately started preparations for the New York opening. He approved the programs for the opening at the Lyric; the program read, "Sam S. Shubert presents *Fantana*, with book by Sam S. Shubert and Robert B. Smith. . . ." He may have been the nicest of the Shuberts, but he was a Shubert and knew a good credit when he saw it.

Lee, who had only recently returned to New York, after another meeting with Shaw and with a number of properties and the locked-up lease on the Waldorf, found nothing but grief waiting for him. Nothing had been booked for the opening in St. Louis; the Lyric and Princess were leased out to non-Shubert productions; the Casino was dark; J. J.

was sending letters and wires from St. Louis; Erlanger's press department was spreading the rumor that the Shuberts were going to sell the Garrick in St. Louis because they didn't have an attraction to put in. Lee asked Sam to get back to New York. There was work to do.

They informed J. J. that his opening attraction would be Ada Rehan, a most important actress, in *The Taming of the Shrew*. J.J. raised hell. This was the best they could do? Why couldn't he have an important attraction? For *his* theater? Lee corrected him icily, and finally, grudgingly J.J. agreed, but reiterated his stipulation: No Lee and no Sam at the opening—he was not going to have the "Jonahs" there to kill him. Lee hung up, and he made the announcement of the opening attraction at the newest Shubert theater, the twelfth theater in the United States under the "personal management of Sam S. and Lee Shubert." The failure to mention J.J. was deliberate.

As reported in the *Sun*, Lee went on solemnly, "We are pleased to bring an artist of Mme. Rehan's caliber to St. Louis. We were also considering a story called *Romeo and Juliet*. And I wish to announce that we have asked a very prominent playwright to prepare a script on this story for the approval of Mme. Rehan and my brother." He took the stunned silence of the press as a tribute.

In St. Louis, J.J. was going through the last frantic days of opening a new theater with a new production staff, and a new backstage crew. He was a restless dynamo of energy, and despite the presence of J. W. Jacobs, who was there as Sam's watchman, he controlled his violent temper very well. J.J. was very much an Erlanger type. To him, war was war. The Syndicate had two successful houses operating in St. Louis, and their affairs in the city were in the capable hands of Pat Short, a pleasant, smiling advance man, who enjoyed excellent relations with the press.

Sam Kahl, who had started with the brothers in Syracuse in the cloakroom of the Bastable, was the treasurer of the new house. He had listened to J.J.'s belligerent pronouncements for more than two weeks. "Two Syndicate houses bucking us! Not one, but two. And my idiot brothers send me Rehan! We got to fight, Sam. We got to fight!"

Kahl, a mild and gentle man, saw no reason for guerilla tactics, some of which Jake had suggested. On opening night, the genial Mr. Short sent a huge basket of flowers to the Garrick, with a card enclosed, wishing the Shuberts luck. It was a civilized and gentlemanly act; and after all, with two well-booked houses against the Shubert's one, Short could afford the gesture. When J.J. came tearing through the theater to the box office to check with Kahl on how the sales were going, he spotted Short's bouquet.

"Who sent the flowers?" J.J. demanded, "Who sent the flowers?" (Even at this early time, his speech pattern was set. Almost always he repeated every question, and almost always in a challenging tone. J.J. had the happy faculty of sounding angry when he was in his most euphoric mood. "He never asked you how you were," said one old employee. "He demanded to know.")

So, "Who sent the flowers?"

Kahl replied tactfully that they had come from Pat Short.

"That momser," muttered Jake. Kahl held his peace. Jake looked at the flowers in their elaborate basket and then wheeled on Kahl. "You got a card?"

Kahl stalled. "Card? What kind of card?"

"A card!" exploded Jake. "A God-damned card! What kind of a lousy box office is this, you ain't got a card?"

Kahl shrugged helplessly. "What kind of card?"

"A gift card that goes with flowers," barked Jake.

Kahl bridled. "Now, Jake," he said. "What in God's name would I be doing with a gift card in the box office?"

J.J. grudgingly agreed that Kahl was right. "So, don't stand there," J.J. ordered. "Go to a store and get me a card. I'll cover for you."

Kahl went across the street to a stationery store and bought a simple white card, with accompanying envelope. Silently, afraid to ask, he handed it to J.J.

Laboriously J.J. inscribed on the card: "To Mme. Ada Rehan, With all my admiration, J.J. Shubert." Carefully he tore Pat Short's card from the basket and, just as carefully, attached his own. "Here," he ordered Kahl, "take these back to Rehan and present them to her." J.J. rushed out of the ticket office and made his way backstage to see if there was any other outlet for his nervous truculence. He was very pleased later that night when Mme. Rehan thanked him for "his lovely flowers."

The Shuberts saw the year out in a blaze of glory. The St. Louis Garrick opened and was hailed as an immediate Shubert triumph. It was new, it had started with Shakespeare, it was a little independent fighting the Trust, and it was a success. Neither Lee nor Sam was there for the opening, and J.J. took the bows and the praise with surprising humility.

In New York, one week later, Sam presented *Lady Teazle*, starring Lillian Russell. *Teazle* was a musical adaptation of *The School for Scandal*, which the brothers had imported from London, and if it was a little odd to see the king-sized hourglass which was Miss Russell in the Sheridan comedy, it didn't matter to the audience. They loved it, and they bought tickets.

61

Lillian Russell as Lady Teazle in the musical version of Sheridan's *The School for Scandal*.

Sam was once again riding high. In another week he was "present-ing" *Fantana*, and he thought he had a hit. He was right. He delivered a charming curtain speech on opening night, and he and Lee had a little party for the cast, which, by coincidence, included Miss Julia Sanderson in a small role. Sam had still not gotten around to telling her of his un-dying love. He just confided it to a few friends.

Right after the success of *Fantana* was assured, Sam took the train to St. Louis. He wanted to see the new theater in use, and he was pleased with what he found. J.J. had done a good job. Business was brisk, the theater immaculate, and J.J. extraordinarily pleasant, as he gave his report. On his way out of the theater, Sam Shubert stopped by the box office to chat with Sam Kahl. After an exchange of amenities, Shubert asked Kahl if he had any plans for after the show, and when Kahl indicated that he was free, Shubert said, "Good. We can have a bite at the hotel and catch up on things."

As soon as Kahl had completed his bookkeeping for the night's performance, he and Sam Shubert, joined by J. J., went to the hotel for a late supper. Friendly, curious Sam Shubert wanted to know all about their old friends from Syracuse. For some reason, Kahl heard regularly from the upstate city and was a fund of information.

"Kaufman?" he said delightedly. "In the glove business. Doing very well. Started about three years ago, in business for himself, and right now, he's thinking of expanding."

Sam smiled warmly. "Little Freddie Kaufman! His own business! Isn't that wonderful?"

J.J. just glowered.

"What about Gilder?" asked Sam.

Kahl beamed. "Gilder is married—expecting his second child. He is working for a lingerie company, and they have given him the whole upstate New York territory."

"Married!" echoed Sam Shubert. "A second child—isn't that won-derful?"

J.J. grunted.

Kahl was waxing enthusiastic. "Yes, most of the old Syracuse gang is really doing well. Remember Grady?"

"Grady?" asked Sam Shubert. He shook his head. "Grady? What Grady?"

"The one who used to bum around with Lee."

Sam's face lit up. "*Grady!*" he said excitedly. "Why didn't you say so? What's he doing?"

"He just opened his own small cigar factory."

Sam was pleased, and J.J. muttered into his coffee.

"And do you know what happened to Lennie Friedman?" Kahl went on. "He is engaged. He went to law school. He could have been appointed to the district attorney's office, but he decided he wanted his own office. Well, let me tell you what happened. An insurance company asked him if he would be their attorney in Syracuse. Well, from that . . ."

Sam shook his head admiringly. "Little Lennie!" he said. "Imagine it—little Lennie already a lawyer!"

Kahl continued. "He represents several corporations in addition. I think he has a great future."

Jake interrupted in his tactful way. "I think you are a God-damned liar."

The two Sams looked at him in dismay.

"Everybody from that lousy Syracuse is a success except us, hey?" bellowed Jake. "We stink, I suppose. I think you made up the whole crock."

As Kahl shrugged in resignation, Sam Shubert, ignoring his brother, turned to Kahl. "Don't pay any attention to him. I tell you, you could put ten thousand people in a desert, and never find one who would envy me for being J.J.'s brother."

They separated, as Kahl went back to his apartment, and Sam turned to J.J. "Was that necessary?"

"What?" asked J.J. "Was what necessary?" He squared his shoulders. "Joe Schmuck is worth a million. Abe Nothing is governor. Morris What's-his-name owns City Hall. Kahl was just trying to make me feel bad. We ain't doing so bad, are we?"

When Sam returned to New York, the newspapers were carrying the story of the court decision on the Erlanger vs. Metcalfe and *Life* case. The court had thrown out Erlanger's complaint, despite the unnecessary Frohman statement that the *Life* cartoon was anti-Semitic in intent. Erlanger, furious at the decision, instantly barred Metcalfe from all Syndicate theaters, and the Shuberts went along with Erlanger's fiat. It was a costly move that Erlanger had made. Nationwide, the press began to attack him as a dictator.

Buried in the maze of newspaper stories was a pathetic little item. Harrison Fiske's announcement that his transcontinental booking office, which he and Belasco had tried to establish in competition with the Trust, was closing. Fiske blamed it on Richard Mansfield, who had left the Shuberts and was back with Honest Abe.

Lee took the opportunity to announce their thirteenth theater, to be built in Utica and to be called, of all things, the Garrick. They already had the Majestic in Utica, but "renewal difficulties" made the change necessary. Translate "renewal difficulties" into Syndicate pressure. Sam came back from London to announce the Waldorf opening—Eleanora Duse, the legendary Italian star, would open the theater, and then alternate with Emma Calve, the great soprano. The brothers were getting terribly high-brow.

The Belasco suit was in the courts, waiting its turn on the calendar, and everywhere the press was assailing the Trust for depriving cities of attractions, gouging its associates, interfering with the freedom of the press. The Shuberts were still suffering Erlanger attacks in New York papers, and despite all Trust efforts, were trying to "live with" their contract. In an effort to counter the anti-Shubert barrage they determined to publish their own magazine, *The Show*, edited by Channing Pollock, to sell for ten cents for a yearly supscription or one cent per copy at newsstands and theaters. The first issue appeared in April 1905, with a picture of Miss Sanderson included.

Sam's latest production, *The Earl and the Girl*, starring Eddie Foy, was in St. Louis, and J. J. was sending frantic wires. What would follow it? They had planned on a show moving in from the Shubert Garrick in Chicago, but Erlanger refused to allow the St. Louis booking. Lee had taken a steamer for London—Duse had changed her mind; Calve was ill. What would open the new theater?

For Sam, it suddenly was all too much. He had been meeting with Belasco and with Fiske. He and Lee had laid very careful plans. Untermyer and Freedman were in complete accord. The newspapers of the country, and a lot of moneyed people, wanted to see the Theatrical Trust broken. Now was the time. A huge barn of a theater, the Duquesne, was available in Pittsburgh. There had been conversations, and now impatiently Sam determined to act. He had exhausted every route of conciliation with Erlanger. If it had to be war, then war it would be. He and Lee had tried to plan for every eventuality, and now he was coming to the end of choices.

The decision to take the night train to Pittsburgh was made at the last possible minute. The continuing skirmish with the Sire brothers was due for trial on May 11, and when it was unexpectedly postponed, Sam saw that he could save a day by getting to Pittsburgh, closing the deal on the Duquesne Theater, and rushing right back to New York. Despite the fact that the Shuberts were pretty well known at the Pennsylvania Railroad ticket office, it was extremely difficult to get space.

They tried to get two drawing rooms—Willie Klein had to be there, Abe Thalheimer was along to help Sam on the physical appraisal of the theater, and Belasco was coming for the ride. The last was fast becoming an integral part of the Shubert forces, invaluable to them for the prestige of his name and his offerings and as a source of supply for

65

their theaters. Belasco's plans changed, and he couldn't make the trip. It was just as well. The best space they could secure on the crack train was two lower berths in one car, and a third lower in an adjoining car for Thalheimer.

They joked about what Belasco might have said if he had been stuck in an upper, and Sam was exultant about the whole twenty-four hours he was saving. He was a very busy man. He had a copy of the second issue of *The Show*, and they chuckled over parts of it.

Pulitzer's *New York World* had conducted a survey of the eighty-six chorus girls in *Lady Teazle*—eighty-six in the chorus was typical of the lavish productions called "musical extravaganzas"—and the results were thought-provoking. Of the eighty-six, twenty were married, twenty-one had been married and were now divorced, six had divorces in process, and thirty-nine were single. The youngest girl in the chorus was sixteen. No one claimed to be the oldest girl in the chorus, so that little tidbit is forever missing. The survey went on to reveal that the average girl in the *Teazle* chorus worked twenty weeks out of the year and was rewarded with $18 per week, for each week of employment. Nonetheless, on this $360 a year, seven of them had automobiles (a terribly new and expensive luxury, since the "average" car cost about $5,000), seventy-eight of the young ladies listed "jewelry and furs" as assets, and seven boasted of coming to rehearsal in their own carriages. Forty-eight listed "independent means." Obviously, the girls had stumbled on a brand-new theory of economics.

At about 10:30, the men retired to their berths, and as May 11, 1905, was drawing to a close, the speeding train was hurtling down the track toward Harrisburg.

From that point on, all press reports are contradictory and garbled. Earlier in the day, a work train, repairing track, had hitched onto a freight car moving toward Pittsburgh. It had been shunted to a siding outside Harrisburg for the night, a siding that arched around a lazy curve. Were two cars derailed in that process? One paper says so. Other reports indicate that the work train was not derailed but that it was parked on a curve and that therefore the angle forced two of the cars out from the track. Then, say these reports, the passenger express, speeding at well beyond a margin of safety and swaying from side to side on the iron rails, brushed into the jutting side of the work train.

All reports agree on one thing. In complete disregard of elementary rules of safety, the work train contained a dynamite car, and it was attached to the regular freight. And this was the car that the passenger train sideswiped. There were three tremendous explosions, followed by the menacing crackle of flames. The passenger train careened off its track and stretched on its side along the uprooted roadbed. There were screams of agony from the injured, the hiss of escaping steam, and then, frantic attempts to escape from the holocaust.

From this point on, the stories again disagree. The New York *Evening World* printed an interview it alleged it obtained from Sam Shubert via telephone at 5:00 A.M. on the morning of the 12th. "The first I knew of the accident was when there was a sudden stop as our engine butted into the overturned wreck of the freight train. There was an explosion which shook the very earth. The glass from the wreck was heaped about our heads. I seemed to be pinned to my berth in some way. I tried to get out, but I must have been practically stunned. I heard cries all about me. The lamp crashed down, and instantly the coach seemed blazing from end to end. The second explosion seemed to bring me to my senses. Then too, I could feel the flame curling up into the side of my berth and it was eating into my legs."

Thalheimer, in the next car, had smashed through the window with his hand, cutting himself badly in the process. He located Shubert, who was pinned in his berth. He was helpless for a moment, and then ran back to his own berth, and using the hammock from it as a ladder, managed to clamber up to the broken window beside Shubert. He freed the injured man, whose legs by this time were horribly charred, and helped him out onto the side of the car. Sam Shubert's account continued:

"On the adjoining track and on the side of the car out of which we climbed was the freight train, turned over and burning. Every car on the freight was on fire, and every car in the express was blazing. . . .

"Thalheimer lowered himself down the hammock after I had reached the ground, and walked over the blazing cars with me on his back. He wore no shoes, and flames caught our pajamas and burned them off of us."

Thalheimer then went back and yanked a semiconscious Willie Klein out of the wreckage of the train, making his way through the burning Pullman and carrying Klein to safety. This was presumably Sam Shubert's own story. The *New York Times* carried a different account, but one thing is certain—Thalheimer was heroic.

While Thalheimer was on his second errand of mercy, a mill boy, Charles Garner, noticed the badly burned Shubert by the side of the burning wreckage and covered him with his coat. Half-delirious with pain (which makes the *World* interview slightly suspect) he asked the boy to stay by him and to call him by his first name. The boy stayed with him to the extent of going to the Commonwealth Hotel in Harrisburg, where Sam was taken as quickly as help could be summoned.

Thalheimer, despite his injuries, kept his head in the panic that surrounded him. Bleeding from the gashes in his hand and forearm and badly burned, he managed to call Sam Nixon in Philadelphia and Jacobs in New York. Nixon rushed his own physician to Sam's bedside, and it was Jacobs who had the torment of notifying the Shubert family.

Jacob J. took charge. He made the first possible connection to Harrisburg; he was accompanied by Joe W. Jacobs. His mother and Dora and Sarah were on the next train. Dr. Leiser, Sam's personal physician, went with Jacobs and J. J. By the time they arrived at the Commonwealth, Sam Shubert was in a coma, and at nine thirty on the morning of May 12th, he was dead.

Old David, exiled in Syracuse, collapsed when the news came to him. He relapsed into his native Yiddish, and sat in a chair, helplessly holding a picture of his son, while tears streamed down his cheeks and into his beard and as, from some deep well of memory, he repeated the Kaddish, the Hebrew prayer for the dead.

The women of the family were prostrate. In London, Lee, up to his neck in the opening of the new theater, was given the news at his hotel. He collapsed completely. Disbelieving, half-hysterical, he so alarmed his associates that they called a doctor, who poured sedation into Lee until he finally fell into a fitful sleep.

Sam's body was brought back to New York in a special baggage car furnished by the railroad and was taken to the family home on West 79th Street, where on Sunday, May 14, 1905, the funeral was held. His body was then placed in a vault at Salem Fields Cemetery, in Westchester, to await the return of Lee before interment.

He was thirty years old. He had just begun to attain true importance in the theater. It was a tragic waste, a sharp, inane end to what had only begun. He and Lee had made such plans! They had dreamed such dreams! They had foreseen everything—everything except a dynamite car and an aborted trip to Pittsburgh.

An ocean away, Lee Shubert lay in a darkened hotel room, his mind refusing to accept what the cable had so coldly stated. To love, to truly love one person—one person in the world, and to know that insanely that one human being was dead! He cried silently, the tears making little streams down his Indian-head face. He was an emotional man, but all his life he would find it hard to be emotionally involved with people—except with Sam. Sam he loved, Sam he had nursed, Sam he had watched over, protected and guarded. There were wild angers in him and wild sorrows, and he lay there helpless, half-drugged, the tears flowing, and he wanted to pray, but to him there had never been a

God, and now, when he needed Him most, he didn't know how to address Him.

But in the madness that lasted three days, and most of all, on the Sunday of the funeral he could not attend, Lee Shubert made vows to himself and contracts with life. Somehow, through him, Sam would have life. That much, he swore, I can do. But how?

Shubert activities halted completely, awaiting Lee's return from London. He was a very disturbed man when he arrived in New York, and he went directly to the family home on West 79th Street, where he remained under a physician's care for another week. He used the time. First, it was essential that he get a grip on himself, to control his grief, his sense of desolation, his feeling that it was *his* life that had ended. Second, there were important decisions to make. He held a few business conferences with J. J. and with trusted advisers like Jacobs and Willie Klein, who was slowly recuperating from his brush with death. Lee's gratitude to Thalheimer and Klein could not be expressed. Garner, the young mill boy who had been with Sam those last harrowing hours, was brought to New York and given a job in the Shubert organization.

The newspapers delivered minor eulogies to the "twenty-seven-year-old theatrical figure," and the smart money along the Rialto predicted that, with Sam gone, the Shuberts would liquidate their business, probably to Erlanger, and find other outlets for their skills. The smart money was very close to being right.

Lee Shubert was a shrewd, calculating mind; he was a more than capable opponent in a skirmish or a negotiation. But he was an illiterate, superstitious man. (In walking down a sidewalk, for example, he would skip in stride to avoid stepping on a crack. Obviously, this caused him to stare downward when walking, and because of this characteristic he gained a reputation as a man who walked buried in profound thought!) And as a man who believed in all sorts of superstitious fancies, he saw in the death of his brother some supernatural sign.

How much of this was deeply psychological cannot be determined. Was he concerned about his own ability to carry on the business, with the assistance of Jake and the staff? Was he frightened by the supernatural omen that the gods were against him? Or was he tired of the fight, wanting to find some peace?

Finally, one day during these black times when Lee was physically incapable of work, he brought up the question of liquidation with Willie Klein, J. W. Jacobs, and, of course, his younger brother, Jake. What was the use, Lee wanted to know. Why go on?

Pugnacious, belligerent Jake hit the ceiling. In righteous anger, he insisted that they had no choice but to go on. "F—k Erlanger, and f—k Frohman!" he bellowed. "The Shuberts can outproduce them!" He was backed by Klein and Jacobs. When Lee persisted in his melancholy, they called in Thalheimer and Untermyer as reinforcements. Lee was out of bed by now and walking around in the darkened apartment. He had been outdoors once—to go to Salem Fields Cemetery and watch a coffin lowered into a grave that was a brown scar on the green grass.

He went out for the second time in early June. He had come to his decision, and he made an appointment to see Abe Erlanger.

Erlanger received him alone. He made the expected perfunctory remarks about how sorry he was about Sam, and Lee came quickly to the purpose of the meeting. Lee did not wish to continue the various Shubert enterprises; he was tired, he had no desire to do it all alone; he was prepared to begin a negotiation with Erlanger on a buy-out! Erlanger was not too surprised. He had been anticipating this from the moment he learned of Sam's death, an event he did not find too depressing.

But now Shubert made his first condition. Before his death, Sam had signed a contract with Belasco, guaranteeing him certain out-of-New York bookings. It was Lee's stipulation that any negotiation for an Erlanger take-over of the Shubert companies was predicated on the assumption that Erlanger would honor the Belasco agreement.

Erlanger, who was in the midst of multiple litigation with Belasco, flatly refused. He chose an unfortunate phrase to express his rejection. Chewing his dead cigar, he growled, "I don't honor contracts with dead men."

Lee Shubert turned pale with rage. He stood up, bobbed his head in his formal bow, and stalked out. He walked across 42nd Street to his own offices, where J. J. and Klein were waiting, and reported the incidents. Jake glowered. "We'll kill the son of a bitch," he said angrily.

Jake did not let up the pressure on Lee. And finally, by sheer force of will, he convinced Lee that they must go on. In the shock of Sam's death and in the tension of the weeks that had followed, Lee and Jake had become closer than they had ever been. Lee seemed to lean on his brother's sturdiness, and draw strength from it. This too was soon shattered.

In the days following Sam's death, Jake had made the usual claim on the insurance companies involved. There were three policies on Sam's life: one for $2,500, one for $25,000, and the large new policy for $50,000. The insurance company, going through its own "scandal" at the time, was most reluctant to part with fifty thousand green bills on a policy which had only two premiums paid to it. And they were disturbed by certain contradictions in the news accounts of Sam's death, and the information he had sworn to on the policy application. They assigned an investigator to the case, and payment was being held up.

When that dreadful May 12 occurred, it was presumed that Sam had died intestate; it was so stated in many papers, and his estate was "estimated" at $500,000. When Willie Klein was sufficiently recovered from his own injuries to resume work, he produced Sam's will. It was a short document—short and to the point. According to it, Sam Shubert left everything "to my loving brother, Lee, with full confidence that he will take care of my mother and my sisters." Not only was there no mention of Jake, it was a patent snub. He was once again "the other brother."

Sam's estate was a lot less than $500,000. It was less than half that amount, including the insurance, plus the claim against the Pennsylvania Railroad. And now, the insurance company was balking at the payment of the $50,000 claim.

In Syracuse they could find no birth certificate and no record of attendance at any school. (In partial explanation, it must be said that record keeping in the eighties and nineties was most incomplete.) Even superficial questioning revealed that Sam was not the twenty-seven-year-old his policy claimed him to be. He was probably at least thirty. His mother executed a curt affidavit that he had been born in Poland; actually, it was Lithuania. Finally, after much hesitation, the claim was paid, without even the subtraction of the monies that the Shuberts had saved in premium payments by Sam's deduction of a few years. The money was paid into the estate and administered by Lee.

Recovered now, and determined, Lee Shubert resumed direction of the Shubert empire. There were thirteen theaters in all, including the London operation. There were properties they had purchased, contracts with actors and composers, and there were routings and tours to be arranged. In the next two years, Lee Shubert was going to astound the theatrical world. The single greatest expansion in the history of the theater was about to take place.

Chapter Five

It began with a stunning announcement made to the press by Lee Shubert. He informed the papers that Fiske, Belasco, and the Shuberts were joining forces, and inviting other "independent producers" to join them. This, in itself, was not startling; in effect, it had been going on for several months. But he went on to say that among the Shubert attractions for the coming season was the farewell tour of Mme. Sarah Bernhardt—the divine Sarah. This was news. Lee was deluged with questions. How had it come about? Was this what had taken him to London? His reply was that the idea had been a "hunch" with his brother Sam, and he had done the negotiating while in London. (The truth of this is unimportant; it was the first step in the myth of Sam Shubert.)

He went on to accuse Erlanger of cold-blooded attempts to force the Shuberts out of business. "He told me that if I broke my contract with Belasco, he would give me anything I wanted. But if I did not, no Shubert attraction would play in any Syndicate house, and no attraction that played a Shubert house would ever play a Syndicate theater." This was an obvious threat to all independents—a ukase by Erlanger demanding a boycott of Shubert houses, on pain of being starved out. Shubert continued. "I refuse to be dictated to. . . ." He concluded by stating that he was severing all connections with K & E.

On that same date, Belasco, in London, accused Frohman of being a party to the Trust and of trying to extend its tentacles to London. It seemed like more than mere coincidence that both statements were made on the same day.

Now the announcements began to come like salvoes. An arrangement with Henry Miller, as a Shubert associate. The confirmations of the acquisition of the Duquesne. The Empire in Newark, and the Empire in Cleveland. The incorporation of the Sam Shubert Booking Agency (in New Jersey) to book attractions throughout the country, organized, in Lee Shubert's statement, "to perpetuate the name of Sam S. Shubert." The Lyceum in Baltimore came under the Shubert banner, and so did the Lyceum in Buffalo. Lee announced that they would build a theater in Cincinnati and one in Kansas City—which would mean twenty-three theaters under Shubert management. Lee purchased 219 West 43rd Street as a prospective theater site, and Eddie Foy, an important Syndicate star, joined the Shuberts as the star of *Earl and the Girl*, which would open the new Lyric Theater in Philadelphia. Frank Perley, the producer who had been "disciplined" by the Syndicate, withdrew from it and placed himself in the Shubert camp.

Now the press had found its hero: its shining knight on the white steed. The Syndicate (Erlanger) was bad; ergo the Shuberts were good. The hangover of sentiment attendant on the untimely death of Sam carried over to Lee. And in most of the major cities in the United States, the name Shubert became familiar. Their every move was hailed as a blow for freedom and for "good theater." Lee Shubert was becoming the Trust Buster.

In London, George Bernard Shaw, the *enfant terrible* of the theater, was interviewed on the subject, and was, as usual, sardonic and far-sighted. He stated flatly that *he* was on the side of the Trust. Consternation! Why?

"Well, there is the choice of three monopolists," said the newly socialist redhead. "A playwright has the unhappy choice of (1) some obscure speculator, seedy, illiterate, shabby and opportunistic, or (2) a municipal theater, politically run for and by Puritans, to whom thought is frightening, or (3) the Trust—organized, financed, competent, and competed with by rival managers like Belasco or the Shuberts, whose anti-Trust is nothing but a new trust." Did that mean he would have his works produced by the Trust? "My plays will be done by those well-financed managers who can give me the most generous terms," said Mr. Shaw.

Lee Shubert replied to Shaw's remarks. "We have not formed an opposition Trust or Syndicate." Then, with his gift for coining clichés, he continued. "Competition is the life of trade. The times when a manager who could not get bookings from the Syndicate had to give up are gone. We expect to give everyone the fair treatment for which we looked in vain."

He announced that, from this day on, the Duquesne Theater in Pittsburgh was to be known as the Belasco, that it would open with Margaret Anglin in *Zira*, and that he had completed the formation of a corporation in Albany, capitalized at one million four hundred thousand American dollars, under the title of Sam S. Shubert and Lee Shubert, Incorporated. Its purpose: to conduct theatrical enterprises. His brother J. J. was a director, as was Willie Klein. He added that the Shubert interests had acquired eighteen theaters in four weeks.

The flood of announcements never slowed—theaters and more theaters, productions, affiliations, real estate purchases. And if people began to wonder what the Shuberts were using for money—after all, Freedman hadn't made *that* much on the building of the first subway in New York—their questions were answered on the morning of October 5, 1905. Five months after the death of Sam Shubert, a press release informed the interested of the existence of a new theatrical partnership. The Shuberts had associated themselves with George B. Cox of Ohio and Joseph L. Rhinock of Kentucky. It was a pregnant alliance.

George Cox, described by *McClure's* as "the massive, coarse saloon-keeper who was Republican boss of Cincinnati, . . . the worst-governed city in the United States," was a ham-handed, ponderous, self-made man. He had climbed the ladder from bartender, through ward heeler, to political boss, patronage dispenser, kingmaker, real estate mogul, millionaire. There were many suspicions as to where the money came from, but no questions as to its presence.

He was a strange man, devoted to his wife, opposed to profanity, and eager to convert some of his money (there were those who called it "boodle" and "slush funds") to high-interest investments. He talked to Rhinock, a "neighbor" across the river, in Covington, Kentucky.

Rhinock had been elected to Congress from Covington, and although not as rich as Cox he was wealthy enough to have extensive race track interests, real estate holdings and other money-making involvements. He and Cox had been looking at the theater situation in the Midwest, and now they came to a decision. They liked the press that the Shuberts were getting; they saw advantage for themselves in allying with a popular cause; they felt that a theatrical boom was imminent; they had no place in the existing colossus, the Klaw and Erlanger group. Logic drove them into Lee Shubert's short, skinny arms.

That opening salvo committed a certain "Anderson" and Rhinock to undertake the immediate construction of eighteen new theaters to be operated by the Shuberts. Anderson was Max C. Anderson, fronting for Cox, and a man with some experience in the "theater"—he had booked animal acts. The wording of the statement was cautious; Willie Klein's hand, and Untermyer's, could be seen in the penmanship. Cox and Rhinock would have no interest in the theatrical presentations; the Shuberts would have no interest in the brick and mortar of the theaters, although "Lee Shubert had been persuaded to take stock in several of the projected theaters." That must have been an interesting arm-twisting session. But it was apparent that the new combine was sedulously avoiding antitrust jeopardies. No one believed a word of the statement. Rhinock was given an office adjoining Lee's, in the Shubert headquarters.

One day later, the Shubert Theatrical Corporation filed papers in Albany—Lee Shubert, president; J. J., vice president.

And the theaters seemed to be reproducing by multiple fission. Two in Iowa, one in Maine; a new house in Ohio, and another in Kansas. It rained Shubert theaters. But the houses they were securing were not the proper nucleus for a successful operation. They were older theaters, in the main—large, out-of-date public halls and opera houses, old barns, off-location theaters. But they needed outlets for the producers they were seducing, and they needed a nationwide route if they were to compete with Erlanger.

But in the now six months since Sam's death, Lee had quadrupled the chain, planned five memorial theaters to honor Sam, tried frantically to find the productions to keep the theaters working, and was facing the Bernhardt tour. He worked a twenty-hour day, seven days a week, as did Jake. All of this business expansion Lee retained in his head—from the seating capacity of the theater in Niagara Falls to the price of Lillian Russell's underdrawers.

Mme. Bernhardt arrived in New York just before Thanksgiving, and Lee Shubert held a reception for her. The divine one was sixty-one years old, looked thirty-five, and was accompanied by a large entourage that included a young man to make her feel thirty-five. She spoke little English; Shubert spoke no French. Their conversation was conducted through Frank Connor, her manager and co-sponsor of the tour with the Shuberts. Lee had never heard of *Camille* and told his associates he was "worried about a play where the heroine dies coughing," but he went forward bravely with his plans. Each time he tried to explain the routing to Sarah Bernhardt, she volleyed in a barrage of French, which always seemed to translate into "How much?"

In later years Lee would imitate Mme. Bernhardt, his clumsy hands aping her expressive gestures, and his ridiculous pipsqueak voice trying to rrroll the dramatic octaves of the Bernhardt vocalization. Since he still didn't speak French, he would say, "Comment allez-vous? Il n'ya pas de quoi," over and over again in varying inflections as he sailed around his office. Then he would stop and, in his own little whisper, say admiringly, "English she couldn't talk; English she couldn't pronounce; but boy, could she count in English!"

What Lee Shubert hadn't told Mme. Bernhardt was that the tour was running into snags. Erlanger, harassed by the Belasco trial, stunned by the Shubert eruption, started to fight back. And stupidly he came to another arrogantly inept decision. He would make his fight on Bernhardt. No Syndicate theaters would be available to her; with this weapon he would break Shubert. The order went out to every Syndicate house; they were not to book Bernhardt, on pain of blacklist.

The first inkling of this came to Lee when he discovered that he could not get a theater in Syracuse, a town which, with Shubert sentimentality, they had abandoned. Lee's reply was instantaneous. He arranged for a theater in Auburn, New York, and announced special trains from the Syracuse area to ferry the customers.

In Portland, Maine, when the Shuberts could find no theater for Bernhardt, they sought permission to use the City Hall for her performance. Erlanger protested violently; no public building should be made available for a paid attraction. But driven by the attack of the newspapers, who declared that the Syndicate "was depriving Portland of a cultural experience," the mayor and city council voted to permit the divine Sarah to use the building.

Across the nation, the press picked up the Syndicate boycott, and universally they attacked it. Bernhardt was exactly the wrong attraction for Erlanger to have used as an example. But Abe Erlanger was a stubborn man, and he persisted in the fight. He sat in his office on 42nd Street, and listened to J. J. crow about the twenty-five theaters he had secured in Illinois and Iowa for the Shubert chain, and heard Lee announce that a new theater would be built next to the Lyric (directly across from Erlanger's own office!) for Shubert management. His cup flowed over when Lee, together with the divine Sarah, called a press conference to tell the world that he was going to build the Sarah Bernhardt Theater on 39th Street in partnership with Madame. Erlanger clamped down harder.

In the South and in the Southwest, where the Shuberts were weakest, he made it impossible for them to tour. There just weren't theaters to be had. Lee's riposte was to rent a tent from the Barnum and Bailey circus and to truck it into every town where he was barred. The tent seated three times as many people as a theater; the Shuberts made three times as much money, and it wasn't long before Lee was using the tent in cities where theaters *were* available. Everywhere they went, the Shubert press department played up the "boycott," inflamed the press, and sold tent tickets at the same prices as comfortable theater seats. The tour was a stunning success, partly because Erlanger had fought it so bitterly.

There was other theatrical news, most of it buried by the Shubert-Syndicate war. In London, where the Waldorf was proving a real headache, George Bernard Shaw fulminated against the closing of his New York production of *Mrs. Warren's Profession*, which the police called immoral. And in New York, the same group of fat cats who had founded the Metropolitan Opera, as a sort of private Culture Club for conspicuous consumption, now announced the formation of the New Theater, which would be America's national theater, repertory in concept, loftily artistic in goals, and of course provided with a ring of private boxes, à la the Met. It would be headed by Heinrich Conried,

76

Counting the House. The Divine Sarah in front of the Shubert tent, Cycle Park, Dallas, Texas.

manager of the Metropolitan Opera, and the names of the founders seemed to indicate that Ward McAllister had organized it out of his four hundred families. John Jacob Astor, J. P. Morgan, August Belmont, Otto Kahn, the Vanderbilts, the Whitneys, the Mackays—all would have boxes.

Erlanger had two small moments of pleasure as 1906 came to an end. The treasurer of the Shubert Hyperion Theater in New Haven had shorted the accounts, and the Shuberts had him arrested. And in New York, the court decided against Belasco and for the Syndicate in the long suit. It was an utterly surprising decision, but Honest Abe had very little time to enjoy it. District Attorney Jerome of New York publicly stated that he was beginning an immediate investigation of the Trust for possible criminal action. Was Freedman behind the D.A.? Or Untermyer? The damned Shuberts, thought Erlanger, the God-damned Shuberts.

The Shubert explosion continued. It seemed that every issue of a newspaper carried the story of another theater, another group joining the Independents, another editorial tearing into the Syndicate and praising Lee Shubert. The Bernhardt tour produced a fountain of newspaper stories, as Erlanger continued his stubborn boycott of the French star. In Jacksonville, Florida, she played *Phaedre* in a skating rink; she covered Texas like a tent in a tent, except for Austin, where the Attorney General insisted that the performance play in the Opera House, which had signed contracts with Erlanger giving him exclusive booking. That made headlines. So did the tent, with its forty-two hundred seats, which was packed in Dallas and in Waco.

Lee Shubert was being three people, and none of them was idle. He was producing; he was financing; and he was publicizing. Everywhere Lee wasn't, Jake was. Lee wrote a letter to a critic in Kansas City who disliked *Camille* but praised Bernhardt. "Making love and dying are her two long suits," said the critic, "but she is better at dying." From Kansas City, the swooning Madame went to Chicago, where the Shuberts had two theaters; she played the tent in a benefit for the victims of the San Francisco earthquake, grossed twenty thousand in one performance, and sent three fourths of it to the stricken city. The West Coast papers blazoned the headline "Madame Bernhardt forced to play quake benefit in tent!" Other papers picked it up, and now, in addition to attacks on Erlanger and applause for Lee Shubert, they added a peculiar third theme—they implored the embattled brothers to "bring Shubert theaters" to their starved towns!

The Syndicate and the Independents were building recklessly, leasing foolishly, coming to face-to-face confrontations in towns that could not possibly support two ordinary attractions, and the cold facts were that there weren't enough star attractions to go around. The value of stars was becoming more and more apparent, and so the two factions began a systematic raid on each other. Sothern and Marlowe left Klaw and Erlanger to book through Shubert; so did Lew Fields, of Weber and Fields.

And B. F. Keith, who was emulating the Syndicate in his organization of vaudeville, sat back and purred contentedly—there would be a lot of theaters available. Keith had just about gotten his monopoly on bookings; only a young impresario, William Morris, still bucked him, with the aid of a few tough independents in the vaudeville business. Now came a sudden rumor that worried Keith. He heard that Shubert was planning vaudeville for some of his theaters—theaters he could not supply with entertainment in any other way. Keith made a hasty appointment with Erlanger.

J. J. went to Europe, with a mission: to get rid of the Waldorf lease. Bad luck had dogged the theater from the beginning. No attractions seemed to work. And trying to run it was a time-consuming task, at a moment when neither brother could spare the time. J. J. was to get the damned place working, or get out of the lease. He settled on the first course, and started a publicity campaign for the debut of Sothern and Marlowe in London. He picked up additional European plays and musicals and returned to New York in time for a farewell dinner for Sarah Bernhardt.

She had closed her tour in Springfield, Massachusetts, playing the tent. Erlanger was obviously the kind of man who, once determined to swim the Atlantic, would rather drown in it than be rescued. Stubborn to the end, he closed his four Springfield theaters to the French star—they were the only theaters in town. The Shuberts proceeded calmly with the tent, peddled their tickets from an ice and coal office, and sold out.

The dinner in honor of Bernhardt was held at the Café des Beaux Arts, and the figures for the tour were announced, in English: two hundred and twenty-six performances, with a dollar gross of just over a million dollars. A million dollars in 1906 dollars. The good lady received $305,000 as her share of the take, while the Shuberts pocketed $210,000. They also were the beneficiaries of millions upon millions of dollars worth of the best kind of publicity, the kind that could not be bought, not at any price. And if the Shuberts knew anything about show business, they knew about publicity.

They had learned that publicity draws large money, important money, and they learned too that important money and large com-

The Boys from Syracuse. The Messrs. Shubert, already feeling success—Lee (left), Jake (right).

"Honest" Abe Erlanger. The theater's iron fist in the iron glove. For a time, his grasp equaled his reach.

mitments generate publicity. They became masters of the art. Lee had also learned that there were several kinds of important money, some clean and pure—money from banks, bankers and civic leaders—some "boodle" money and not so pure—from civic bosses, gamblers, speculators. And he had learned one other thing: *all* money liked the fact that the theater was *cash* business, with a high profit; and the bricks and the mortar, the canvas flats and the costumes, the actors and the chorus girls—all of these never did care which kind of money it was. He never forgot this.

A statistical breakdown of their "announced" theaters would total well over one hundred twenty, and in addition, they had produced through Lee and Sam S. Shubert, Incorporated, some twelve shows— then a fantastic achievement. Sam had been dead only a year. Lee had taken over, and J. J. had moved up. There were more than a hundred employees now; and a payroll that Lee carried in his head; daily grosses to be totaled, which Lee carried in his head; real estate accumulating all over the country, which Lee and J. J. carried in their heads; and intricate financial arrangements with the top negotiators in the country, which again, Lee had memorized. He had found millions of dollars for his companies; he had performed an incredible money-raising job, and miraculously, he had achieved all of it without once surrendering control of *any* of his companies. He and Willie Klein had organized more than thirty corporations for the various Shubert endeavors, and Lee Shubert voted at least 51 percent of each of them. How he managed this with Cox and Rhinock, with Freedman and Untermyer, is something to confound a philosopher.

Their own press conferences were often unintentionally hilarious. On his return from Europe, J. J. called in the papers to tell of his European adventures, and in the course of it he held forth on the differences between European and American dramas. "European drama," he stated with assurance, "is much more Continental than American drama." J. J. was fond of the word "Continental."

Lee Shubert, who lived by an old Willie Hammerstein adage that "the best seats in a theater, for a producer, were seats with asses in them," was studying the situation with the same absorption as Keith. He knew that in the rapid Shubert expansion he had been forced into taking less desirable theaters in town after town, merely to meet the competition of the Syndicate and to provide a route for the attractions he was booking. He knew too that the new houses under construction or on the drawing boards would take time to complete, and that in the interim he had to support the older houses. He started to look at vaudeville, as Keith had guessed, and when the papers started printing predictions that the Shuberts were moving on to vaudeville and were going to start by taking over the largest theater in America, the New York Hippodrome, Lee "hotly denied" the rumor. "The next thing you know," he said graciously, "you newspaper fellows will give me the New Amsterdam." The New Amsterdam was the Syndicate flagship in Manhattan and the home office for Abe Erlanger.

The papers the next week duly reported the departure for Europe of Catherine Shubert (the mother), accompanied by Dora and Sarah, making their first trip abroad—a present from the brothers.

A day later the headlines shrieked that millionaire Harry Thaw had shot and killed Stanford White, the architect, in jealousy over Evelyn Nesbitt Thaw. Evelyn Nesbitt had enjoyed a small role in the ill-fated *Girl from Dixie*, the play that had precipitated the Shubert war.

Discreetly buried in the same papers was the announcement of the incorporation of the Shubert-Anderson Company, to produce theatrical entertainment. And inevitably, in the Shubert pattern, two weeks after the hot denial, Lee told the world he and Anderson had leased the Hippodrome. "We are following two big men," he said pompously, "and it will be a job to equal them. After all, the yearly rent is $250,000." He made this last comment in an awed voice. "This does not mean we are interested in vaudeville," he continued, "despite all the loose talk you may hear. We are in the legitimate theater."

The summer had been enlivened by various additional theater acquisitions, a few bitterly contested. Willie Klein was earning his keep. And the press continued its pro-Shubert campaign. In London the Shuberts announced that Sothern and Marlowe would open the season at the New Waldorf, and George Bernard Shaw refused to come to America. "I am afraid of being naturalized and elected President," he told the *Daily Mail*. "I much prefer the quiet and retirement of London." Since the picture spread which accompanied the story displayed G.B.S. in the altogether, spindly shanked and red-bearded, it would seem that London was not giving him much retirement.

In Albany the Shubert Theatrical Company doubled its capitalization and listed its stockholders, which for the first time mentioned Rhinock and Anderson (Cox). Willie Klein lost his first case for the Shuberts when a song in the show at the Casino was declared by the courts to be a steal, but he won several others. Buried in the real estate section of the *Times* was a tiny item stating that Frank Connor (Bernhardt's manager) and Lee Shubert had sold 536 lots at the east end of the Blackwell's Island bridge for $500,000. There is no record of what they paid for them; but they did not take a loss.

The first of the Sam S. Shubert memorial theaters built by the combine opened in Kansas City, and when there was public protest at the ticket scale, the Kansas City *Journal* dutifully editorialized, "The Shuberts are businessmen with the single idea of making money. They did not come to Kansas City to establish a philanthropic enterprise." In all of America no truer editorial statement had ever been made, as the local financiers of the Sam S. Shubert Memorial Theater could testify. Lee had commissioned oil paintings of his beloved brother to be hung in the lobby of every "memorial theater." He sent the painting to Kansas City, had it hung in the lobby, and then sent a bill for the painting— one thousand dollars—to the gentlemen who had paid for the theater. They refused to honor the bill, not quite understanding Lee's "sentiments." Ever practical, Lee ceased commissioning oil paintings and switched to photographs.

Arnold Daly, actor-producer, introducer of Shaw to the American audience, went bankrupt; he owed an undisclosed amount to Lee Shubert, who had used him as the soft underbelly of G.B.S. Lee had endorsed a note to a bank for over $5,000, and he was stuck for that too. Disgusted, Lee closed down *The Show*, the Shubert house organ, and announced plans for the first Shubert extravaganza at the Hippodrome, which would be "under his general supervision" and which, mysteriously, would have "a tank."

J.J., who had been annoyed not a little by the incessant publicity enjoyed by Lee, started "supervising" productions. One opulent Oriental piece had been in rehearsal for several weeks when J.J. paid his first visit. The action called for an actor to enter, stalk to center stage, and declaim," I am Omar Khayyam." No sooner had the performer made his entrance when J.J. darted from his seat in the orchestra, shouting, "No, no, no!" He hurried to the footlights and stared up condescendingly at the hapless actor. "You're a good-looking fellow," said J.J. pityingly. "You got a nice voice, you want people should think you're a dope?" He paused for dramatic effect. "I am Omar Khayyam," he said contemptuously. "I am Omar *of* Khayyam." There was a delicate hush in the theater as Jake stalked back to his seat. The actor shrugged, walked into the wings, and at Jake's signal, reentered. As he did so, the troubled director slid into a seat beside J.J. and whispered, "Mr. Shubert, it's not Omar of Khayyam. It's the man's name. Omar Khayyam." Jake nodded vigorously and grunted to himself. Then he called, "All right, pick it up." Standing at stage center, the actor declaimed, "I am Omar of Khayyam." "No, no, no, hold it, hold it!" shouted Jake, his blocky figure hurrying down the aisle. He stared at the actor for a moment, rubbing his chin reflectively. "Tell you what," said Jake thoughtfully, "better cut the 'of.' The scene plays too long."

The Hippodrome. The famous tank, New York's greatest spectacular. Finale of *The Golden Garden*, 1910.

Lee opened his first Hippodrome production, *Pioneer Days*. It was a spectacle full of stage magic, involving cowboys, Indians, the U.S. cavalry. Circus acts were staggered through the piece, but it was the production's finale that made the show the talk of the theatrical world. It used that mysterious tank. A hundred chorus girls in their spangled tights marched in unison down a flight of stairs into the tank, which was forty feet deep and filled with water. They disappeared. It was a wonderful illusion, and the Hippodrome tank finales became a trademark. The explanation of the apparent miracle was simple: at the foot of the steps was a small airtight chamber, very much like a diving bell, and the girls would enter this and, after two or three seconds in the water, walk through the "bell" to another flight of steps that led backstage. The Shuberts kept a sentry on the telephone to count the girls at every performance and to report to the stage manager. They never lost one.

The show was an instantaneous smash. Lines formed at all eight ticket windows of the Hippodrome, and in the course of one working day they took in $91,000 in advanced sales. Lee beamed in his stone-faced way, and J. J. glowered. He had not been cut in on the land deal with Connor. He had not been asked to help with the Hippodrome. And his last two productions in Chicago had been roasted. Now Lee was a successful impresario as well as the man in the headlines. Jake chewed a sour cud when Lee announced that the estimated weekly gross at the Hippodrome would be $60,000.

Shortly after, the city of New York opened hearings on the activities of the Theatrical Trust. Lee Shubert was the only witness called, and a few days later, the New York Grand Jury indicted Erlanger, Klaw, Frohman, Hayman, Nixon, and Zimmerman for conspiracy in restraint of trade.

The indictment served to fan the flames of war. Erlanger, furious at Shubert's testimony, clamped down even harder. Theater owners found themselves caught in the middle. The newspapers were solidly behind the Shuberts, and the fighting was getting dirty. Under pressure from the St. Joseph, Missouri, *Star*, the manager of the theater there announced that his was not a Syndicate house. Shubert tried to book an attraction into the theater, and the unhappy manager replied that he was solidly booked for the year. The Shubert press department went to work on the *Star*, and the neutral manager suddenly found himself under vicious attack in his own town.

Lee Shubert announced a series of one-night stands, starring some "of the biggest names in the theater." His list included Sothern, Marlowe, Nazimova, Henry Miller, Lew Fields, Mrs. Fiske, and David

Warfield. He solemnly stated that "only with one-night stands can touring shows make a real profit." The facts were that (a) he had found a one-night-stand impresario to take over this part of Shubert booking, and (b) he couldn't fill his theaters with regular attractions.

Interestingly enough, when the impresario decamped to the Syndicate (he got better houses to play) with his one-night-stand tour, Lee Shubert stated that no one-night stand could make money, and they were bad for the theater. He was a very flexible fellow.

Keith took over the two remaining important holdouts and closed his monopoly on vaudeville. Percy Williams and Willie Hammerstein had succumbed, and Keith announced the United Booking Office, through which all acts for his theaters would be hired. It was more powerful and more efficient than Erlanger's operation, and he didn't have any opposition, except for William Morris, who had no place to run. He ran to Erlanger, who issued loud threats that he was going to invade the vaudeville field.

Lee Shubert said nothing. He had been instrumental in forming the Society of Independent Managers, with Belasco and Fiske, and he was busy appearing in court. Lee's case against Ziegfeld came up during this period, and here the head Shubert was apoplectic. It seems that Florenz Ziegfeld, one of whose greatest talents was spending just a little bit more money than he had, was in Europe with his soon-to-be wife, Anna Held. He needed $1,000 to get him back to the States, and he cabled Lee for a loan. Shubert, who would give money away, but hated to lend it, made an agreement with Ziegfeld to tour Held, and then sent Ziegfeld the thousand "to come back and sign the contracts." Ziegfeld came back and signed the contract for the Held tour, but he signed it with Abe Erlanger. Lee Shubert had been raped, and with small pleasure. He collected his thousand, and he hated Ziegfeld from that day on. Jake hated Ziegfeld as part of the obligation of the partnership, but when in a few years Jake became a musical impresario, he began to hate Ziegfeld personally. Ziegfeld always got the good reviews.

Right after the Ziegfeld case was settled, Willie Klein was called on again. Lee Shubert, at this stage of his career, hated ticket speculators. He had no objection to getting more money for a seat than the price printed on the ticket, but he had a personal aversion to that money's going anywhere except into Shubert pockets. So, annoyed at speculators who were standing outside *his* theater, shouting to *his* prospective customers to avoid the line and get served immediately, Lee hired three gentlemen, equipped them with megaphones, stationed them strategically outside his theater, where they shouted to the passers-by to purchase their seats "only at the box-office." A naïve policeman arrested the three men for disturbing the peace and haled them into court, where they laid the onus on Shubert. Willie Klein straightened that one out just in time to bring Lee into court to testify in the Sire case. Yes, the Sires were back.

It takes a long memory, but way back in 1901, when the Shuberts leased the Casino, the Sires had demanded that they be bought out for $20,000. To get them out, Lee had paid. But he had never liked the idea. With Willie Klein, he decided to sue to regain his money, and now, finally, six years later, the court awarded him his $20,000 plus five years' worth of interest, compounded at 6 percent.

George Cox and Joe Rhinock had been putting their heads together. The Panic of 1907 had gripped the country. Money was tight, businesses were failing, banks were closing. The war between the Shuberts and the Syndicate was ruinous for both sides. There simply were not enough attractions to keep everyone happy. Box-office receipts had dropped, and the continuing expansion was draining resources. (Whether they knew it or not, in their endless competition for important actors, the Syndicate and the Shuberts were aggrandizing the "star system.") What Lee Shubert had told them was true: the theater was a cash business, and the hard-money flow was comforting. But they looked at Keith's operation—Keith who had no competitors—and they did not like the comparison. Cox and Rhinock decided to do something about it.

There was a series of secret meetings, and then, at the very time that Standard Oil was about to be socked for $27,000,000 worth of penalties on their monopolistic railroad rebates, the front pages of every newspaper in the country carried a startling headline. It announced the incorporation in New Jersey of the United States Amusement Company, to be capitalized at $100,000,000. The president of the company was Abe Erlanger; the vice president was Lee Shubert. Among those on the board were Klaw, Erlanger, Hayman, Lee, J. J., Cox, and Rhinock. Their counsel was Willie Klein. The executive committee consisted of Erlanger, Lee Shubert, and Klaw. Fourteen Shubert houses were pooled with Syndicate houses, and the purpose of the United States Amusement Company was to set up a world-wide vaudeville chain.

The first reaction was one of stunned shock. Then came a chorus of outrage, particularly from the press, which felt it had been betrayed by the Shuberts. Harrison Fiske and David Belasco were furious, but remained silent. To them too it looked like a sellout.

Belasco called a meeting of the Society of Independent Managers, which was attended by Lee. And from that meeting, because of the apprehensions among the independents, a statement was issued. Lee stated, "We have not sold out to the Trust. This has nothing to do with the legitimate theater. We have taken houses which were not theatrical successes and are turning them over to vaudeville; they will be vaudeville successes."

William Morris was retained by the company to supervise their bookings, and Erlanger buried himself in his new venture. Not only would he be the Napoleon of the theater, now he could be the Alexander of vaudeville.

The Shuberts went quietly about their business. They had transferred into Shubert Theatrical the theaters "donated" to the combine. In most cases these had been the older theaters or the new ones that hadn't done business. They kept adding to their holdings, and they kept signing important actors. They closed the Hippodrome for the summer, after having grossed nearly one and a half million dollars at the box office. Willie Klein went to Albany and again they increased the stock of Shubert Theatrical Corporation, and for the first time, Cox himself appeared as a listed stockholder. Prior to this date, Anderson had fronted for Cox.

There was great fanfare when ground was broken for the New Theater on Central Park West just north of Columbus Circle, and not very much attention was paid to the item that the antitrust indictment leveled against the Syndicate had been dismissed. As stated before, the reasoning was curious. Trade, said the court, implies that the commodity is vital to life. Ergo, restraint of trade would be wrong. But the theater is not vital to life; therefore, it cannot be in restraint of trade. Erlanger was home free. J.J. was busy in Europe. Lee was buying real estate and planning theaters. Joe W. Jacobs was preparing contracts for twenty-seven companies for the new season. The new Hippodrome spectacle was in rehearsal.

And no one paid any attention to a strange phenomenon that had been occurring. In little stores, in penny arcades, in upstairs lofts, moving shadow pictures were being shown, and people were finding them exciting. They cost a nickel, and quickly they got the name "nickelodeon." It was so insignificant that it attracted no attention. But it had suddenly moved into the entertainment world, and it was going to revolutionize it.

Chapter Six

The armistice in the theatrical war worked for everyone—Erlanger, Lee Shubert, Keith, Cox, Rhinock. Everyone except J.J. who needed hostility as much as a diabetic requires insulin. In 1908 he became the first Shubert to be married. Of course, the marriage did not *start* with a war, but Jake was resourceful.

He had met a young, almost-beautiful girl in one of his choruses. Her name was Catherine Dealy, and the marriage was a surprise to everyone. As a matter of fact, most people didn't know about it at all. Like the source of Jake's money and the legendary bank accounts across the country in various names, the marriage too was private to J.J. He and Miss Dealy took up residence, and *he* left for Europe. It was one hell of a honeymoon.

The Messrs. Shubert, Lee and Jacob J., behaved in a very peculiar manner vis-à-vis the other sex. They started early, and it became a way of life. They took a feudal view of their enterprises, and in their own way they were benevolent despots, who "took care" of their vassals, and exercised the rights and prerogatives of the ruling classes. They liked girls. Both men were particularly attracted to long-legged girls, although J.J. was a bit of a bosom man too. Yet, essentially, both men were insecure. They were ashamed of their illiteracy, they were always afraid of betraying ignorance and they covered it—by bluster in J.J.'s case and by rigid politeness in Lee's. To protect themselves against potential embarrassments, they cultivated the company of those whose "literacy" did not endanger Shubert egos or those who would be impressed by the name Shubert. It was a pattern Lee managed to break; J.J. never did.

This in almost all their "romances" relieved them of the necessity of wooing and pursuing. They summoned girls to their offices: they contracted for them, they ordered them, they negotiated with them. And there were many, many girls. Some went on to stardom; others married into "society" and became social leaders; some vanished into the same obscurity from which a Shubert chorus call had lured them.

Jake was the "cruder" of the two, and legion are the tales of his assignations—in dressing rooms, in telephone booths, in corridors, behind scenery flats and, of course, in hotel rooms and apartments. Lee, with his endless hours of work and his mathematical brain which calculated that time was money, made his office a convenient place. To one side of it (after he moved to the Shubert Theater Building in New

York) he had an apartment, complete with bedroom. To the other side of his office was a small, meagerly furnished room which, to be sure, also contained a bed. A former secretary of Lee Shubert's remarked, "It was a traffic problem. You see, the bedroom was for stars and important people. The room—well, that was just for girls." He paused thoughtfully. "The room got most of the action."

So, Jake's marriage, when the story broke, came as a surprise. Everyone knew that the Shuberts were capable of love. They had evidenced this in their attitude toward money and toward real estate. But to find J.J. guilty of a *human* weakness surprised a good many people. His solo honeymoon did not. That was Jake.

He had much to keep him busy in Europe. The first matter to dispose of was the New Waldorf Theater. Three years ago, Lee had signed a five-year lease on the house. In July, when Jake arrived in London, he handed the keys to the theater over to the owners. They did not want to take them. Jake left for the Continent, and the owners consulted their solicitor. That gentleman was mildly helpless; he finally appealed to the English court to serve the Shuberts with a suit outside the court's jurisdiction. His clients wanted their money for the full term of the lease, and they wanted damages. The theater, they claimed, had been "left insecurely fastened, and without a guard or a fireman."

Jake replied, "We gave up the theater because the owning company attempted to take advantage of us. When we went in there, it was agreed that the house should be furnished . . . but later the owners made improvements costing fifteen thousand dollars . . . They claimed that this was done through a verbal agreement with my brother [Sam], then in charge for the firm in London. It couldn't be. The lease called for a house complete in all its details. When the bill for fifteen thousand dollars was put up to us, we stepped out."

When Lee was asked about it, he merely commented, "I don't want another theater in London, you can be sure of that." The facts were simple: the New Waldorf had been a loser and a headache. More and more, the Shuberts were buying their properties in Europe. More and more they were pushing into musicals and into American productions. They wanted out, and to Shubert thinking, verbal agreements with dead men were not binding.

While J.J. was being Continental, and Lee was setting up the Shubert fall schedule, Erlanger was hard at work getting ready to take over vaudeville. It seems fairly evident that the reason he had acceded to the Cox suggestion to make some sort of truce with the Shuberts was that he didn't want the Shuberts as enemies, not while he was writing more than a million and a half dollars' worth of vaudeville contracts. He also needed certain of the Shubert houses, which, as stated before, were in many cases larger "halls," and thus better for vaudeville purposes than the Syndicate theaters.

Not all the Shubert affiliates were happy with this new turn of events. The spanking new Mary Anderson Theater in Louisville sued the Shuberts, claiming that vaudeville would "kill the status of the Anderson theater." Willie Klein denied that any damage would be done. The Lyric in Buffalo had to be sued, closed, and a receiver appointed by the court before the vaudeville shows could be moved in.

In September the new vaudeville circuit opened, with enormous publicity and enormous payrolls. At the same time, the Shubert season began with *Anna Karenina*, presented by Lee and Sam S. Shubert, which was critically hailed and attended poorly, followed one week later by Nazimova in *The Master Builder*, which got the same reception. In fact, almost everything the brothers tried that season didn't do too well, except for a Lew Fields' production of *The Girl Behind the Counter*.

Vague rumblings had been emanating from the Keith camp, and now Keith issued a press release, implying an imminent invasion of the legitimate theater. Lee Shubert welcomed him to the fold, hailing "all competition that would tend to advance the drama."

The Shuberts were advancing the drama by leaps and bounds. They presented some twenty-odd attractions during the season, and by any standards they were not good. They now controlled about 10 percent of the number of theaters that Erlanger was running. From a tiny skin irritation, they had grown to a major boil on Honest Abe's neck.

Erlanger was completely engrossed in his vaudeville chain, losing money hand over fist, while Lee Shubert kibitzed from the sidelines— a silent partner, relieved of unprofitable houses, free to concentrate on his plans, and reaping critical acclaim for his new smash production at the Hippodrome. (Yes, there was a new routine using the tank.)

Willie Klein was suing with great abandon, enjoining here, appealing there, counterfiling in another place. Klein, who had been anybody's theatrical lawyer a few short years ago, was becoming a Shubert monopoly. There was something about Shubert contracts, and something about J. J.'s sweet-tempered disposition, that led inevitably to litigation.

And all the while, motion pictures were fascinating the public. Vaudeville houses, hit hard by the competition, introduced films to their programs. The theater lobby forced a municipal ordinance in New York which made all motion-picture houses close for a day because they were unsafe, and the motion-picture lobby secured a permanent injunction against the ordinance, and then applied for licenses to put vaudeville acts into *its* theaters. The guardians of public morality were disturbed by the fact that motion pictures required dark, dark rooms in which to project; what vulgarities would men and women perform under the curtain of blackness? One prudent operator separated the men and the women in his audience, seating them on opposite sides of the aisle to protect them against temptation. He was severely beaten by one respectable married lady who resented the protection.

There were already four hundred nickel theaters in New York City, two hundred and fifty in Chicago. A young man named Marcus Loew had opened his first movie house in a penny arcade in Cincinnati, seen it prosper, and taken over an arcade on New York's 14th Street. He had been a successful furrier, and was on his way to becoming a motion picture tycoon. He came to see Lee Shubert.

Loew had vision, and unlike the Belascos and the Fiskes who were positive that the motion picture was a passing fad, a "mechanical trick" which would soon lose its popularity, Loew could see chains of theaters devoted to motion-picture presentation. Theaters meant two people— Erlanger or Lee Shubert. And where had Loew started? In George Cox's backyard in Cincinnati. Naturally, he came to see Lee Shubert about theaters.

He picked a very fine time. Erlanger was losing Klaw's shirt in vaudeville. He was presenting some of the very best vaudeville ever seen; he was certainly raising the level for the audience, but he was going broke in the process. And Keith, compelled to fight back, was raising salaries to protect his stars from Erlanger raids, and booking motion pictures to avert audience loss to the nickelodeons.

There was only one logical conclusion, and Keith and Erlanger were pragmatic men. Keith bought out Erlanger, and Erlanger bought off the Shuberts. Keith's monopoly was intact, and William Morris had been beautifully doublecrossed. The smart money was positive that Erlanger had outfoxed Lee Shubert in the deal, but nothing could have been as wrong as that assumption. Lee did very well.

The smart boys said that Erlanger had been paid a million and a half dollars by Keith. The actual settlement had Keith assuming Erlanger's commitments to actors, contract by contract. In addition, he paid Erlanger a quarter of a million dollars, for which Abe agreed to stay out of vaudeville for ten years. To close that deal, Honest Abe had to guarantee that the Shuberts would respect that agreement, and to close *that* deal, he paid Lee Shubert half of the buy-out.

In effect, Lee Shubert had unloaded fourteen distinctly unprofitable theaters, had seen Erlanger tied up with vaudeville while Lee was free to make theatrical hay, had done absolutely no work in the vaudeville venture, and had been exceedingly well paid for it—$125,000.

Some of the theaters came back to the Shuberts, and it was then that Marcus Loew paid his call. He "leased," at very liberal terms, several Shubert houses in remote Brooklyn and upper Manhattan. It was a good association for both men—it would last for many years. But it was Lee Shubert, as shrewd a businessman as ever invaded Broadway, who foresaw the impending "squeeze" that the motion pictures promised.

It is very hard to find lasting Lee Shubert contributions to the theater, except for brick walls that make up theaters. But certain of his innovations are still alive, and the first of these was the introduction of girl ushers at the Casino Theater in 1908. Since women would work for less than men, it was a logical Shubert move. But these were the first females to direct patrons to their seats.

Some other Shubert contributions might be mentioned here. That little coin machine with its paper cups that hangs beside the drinking-water tap in Shubert theaters is a monument to Lee. Once the cups had been free, but that was before Lee noticed that thirsty people were prepared to pay for them.

Then, there's that bilious orange fluid that comes in waxed containers now, but once came in glass bottles, and is sold at intermissions. This usually was run by one or another indigent Shubert relative. At one time, the mixing room was in a theater basement, from which the concoction was delivered to all New York Shubert houses. One employee swears that Lee himself supervised the mix.

The ticket racks and the "count-up" room—where each night's tally is made on the receipts for each theater—are another Shubert first. In the endless battle between the management and the employees over an honest count, the Shuberts devised as foolproof a system as could be found. It's used by all theaters now.

And no account would be complete that failed to mention the hot-water tap in the "lounges"—the hot-water tap that never yields water. Another Shubert idea. (In the early forties a Shubert descendant was using the men's room facilities in the Empire Theater, a non-Shubert house, and when he washed his hands he used honest-to-goodness hot water which flowed from the tap marked "hot." He turned to his companion and remarked, "Now I know this isn't one of our theaters; the hot water runs.")

In the midst of all this innovating, the Shuberts were going about their business. They acquired more and more property in and around what is now the New York theatrical district. And they looked for plays and fought with playwrights, natural enemies to Lee since they had to be paid money. He never conceded that a playwright was worth anything, and more than once stated that "a playwright ought to get a share of the producer's profit, not of the gross. Different plays cost more money, and before the playwright gets any the producer ought to get back his investment." Or so he told the *New York Dramatic Mirror* on April 25, 1908. This seemed logical enough until certain actors, playwrights, and other "partners" protested that no one ever seemed to make a profit in a Shubert production.

The uneasy truce between the massive Syndicate and the expanding Shuberts was still on. They had all become members of the newly formed Theatre Managers' Association, with an elaborate arbitration system to settle disputes between rival managers and a framework of a code which would control the enemies of all producers—actors, writers, composers, etc., and they dueled for control of the Association.

And while they were jockeying for power within the infant Association, neither the Syndicate nor the Shuberts paid very much attention to the new monster, the motion picture, which already, unbelievably, was housed in seventy-five hundred theaters in the United States!

In New York City, thirteen legitimate or vaudeville houses had been converted to motion picture theaters. Despite the enormous proliferation of producers—glove salesmen, tired actors, furriers, dressmakers, truckdrivers, real estate salesmen, who all became film makers—there was not enough product. The rerun, later to be emulated by TV, made its appearance, and the theater owners made the happy discovery that audiences not only didn't mind seeing the same picture two or three times, they even liked it.

Tucked away in the little columns of the theatrical trade papers was the handwriting on the wall. Week by week, a repertory company, a cheap-seat theater devoted to melodramas, or a grind vaudeville house was going out of business. They could not stand the competition of the motion-picture action, the motion-picture novelty, and the motion-picture price, now rising to a dime.

Equally unnoticed by the trade press, was the birth of the first Shubert born on American soil—J. J.'s son, John.

The big Shubert news did make headlines. In a move that surprised every "artistic" figure in the theater, and made Erlanger a furious man, the New Theater announced that Winthrop Ames was to be artistic director and that Lee Shubert was to be business director. The most prestigious job in the theater in the United States—the control of the first national theater—had been handed to Lee Shubert.

It was an extraordinary tribute to the man. He was comparatively young—thirty-five years old—and his formal education, even charitably stated, was limited. He had been in the business just about ten years, only eight of them at headquarters—New York. There were men of prominence and stature on both sides of the Atlantic who desperately wanted the spotlight of the job, men who seemed better equipped and certainly "less Jewish." But so strong was the impact of his quiet personality, and so impressive the business pragmatism he had displayed, that it was Shubert the New Theater turned to.

If any single thing could be calculated to set Erlanger off, this was it. Heading the New Theater, in association with the most important names in New York society and American finance, was something that Erlanger had hoped for. He had issued many a public statement, filled with piety, humility, and mush, and when his overtures had not even elicited a nibble he took another tack. If Erlanger was not to direct the destiny of the New Theater, obviously no American should. Honest Abe declared that what the New Theater required was a *European* director.

But Shubert! Erlanger issued a long, scathing interview attacking the choice and the New Theater, and he salted it with thinly veiled attacks on Shubert's ability, taste, honesty. Belasco, who had also wanted the job, said nothing for the record, and Fiske, who thought Fiske ought to have the position, also maintained a discreet silence publicly. To his wife, Fiske said, "The choice is incomprehensible. The man can't read; is the New Theater to be the Hippodrome?"

The truce, which had been forced on both parties, patently could not continue much longer. Erlanger's attack was not enough of a pretext for Lee Shubert to make the open break, although he was furious at the insults. He had to find something else.

He found it in the Theater Managers' Association. There was a series of strategy meetings held in the Shubert offices, great comings and goings; Rhinock, Anderson (on behalf of Cox), Fiske, Belasco and, as always, Willie Klein. A terse statement was made that J.J. would be leaving for the West Coast to set up a Shubert-booked circuit there.

J.J.'s marriage was already tempestuous. His wife and infant son were ensconced in a West Side apartment, and after his first glow at having topped Lee by having a child, J. J. was conspicuous by his absence. He was "on the road," supervising "out-of-town," running Chicago and St. Louis, and spending as little time as possible at home. Essentially insecure and shy, he blustered, bumbled, and crackled, his moods changed with Heathcliffe rapidity, and his attitude toward wife and son was ambivalent. They were his, possessions to be paraded, and at the same time they were obligations and annoyances, and the best way to avoid them was to be busy.

As soon as J.J. had attended the wedding of his sister Dora to Milton Wolfe, he took off for the West Coast. On November 10, 1908, Lee called a rambling press conference.

It began with announcements of new theaters to be built in New York, wandered to the subject of "prurient" entertainment, which was being deplored in pulpits and attacked in editorials. Lee stated that "the public is the best censor." He declaimed about "freedom," and finally he came to the point of his meeting. He dropped his bombshell: the Shuberts had withdrawn from the Managers' Association.

"We have fourteen theaters in New York City," he said, "and no other member has more than three. But the vote is not weighted. We vote once, and so does the man with one theater." He went on to assert that the Association consistently voted against the Shubert interests. He cited the Ziegfeld-Nora Bayes incident.

Nora Bayes, the "Shine On, Harvest Moon" star, had left the Shuberts to join Ziegfeld's *Follies*. Ziegfeld asserted that this was not contract jumping; he claimed to have a prior contract. The Shuberts furiously denied any prior contract and submitted their protest to the arbitration machinery set up in the Theater Managers' Association by-laws.

"The arbitration hearing was postponed," said Lee bitterly, "and postponed again, and all the time, Miss Bayes was rehearsing for Mr. Ziegfeld."

Lee went on to other complaints. The *New York Press*, a current newspaper, had attacked Oscar Hammerstein, Sr., an "insider" in the Syndicate clique. Instantly, the Association had voted to withhold all advertising from that paper. The *Telegraph* had never ceased its virulent campaign against the Shuberts.

"We demanded that the Association take similar action against the *Telegraph*," said Lee. "The Association refused. At this meeting," Lee continued, "Max Anderson resigned, and my brother warned that we might form our own Association."

He hinted that Erlanger's ill-timed, badly phrased attacks on the New Theater might just possibly help the Shuberts in their future financing. Men like Vanderbilt and Mackay of Postal Telegraph were incensed.

"For all these reasons," said Lee softly, "we have resigned from the Association."

The interview was news. So was the resignation from the Association of Belasco and then Fiske.

Lee demonstrated his independence of the Association ruling by restoring Shubert advertising to *The Press*. He dramatized his own independence of his own ruling by resuming advertising in the *Telegraph*.

One month later, Erlanger called his conference and announced that Fiske, Belasco, and Klaw-Erlanger would "mutually book." The lines were shifting, and Lee Shubert commented drily, "I am gratified that our efforts have helped the 'open door' policy. We will continue to book. We already have forty attractions and are adding more daily. When my brother returns in a few days, he will have an important announcement."

Jake's announcement was important. It restated the "open door" policy, and in Jake's inimitable fashion. "I can book East to West for forty weeks, with no assistance from anyone. Despite what you may have heard, Mr. Fiske will continue to book with the Shuberts. I have made arrangements in the larger cities to control and operate new theatres. . . . These various theaters will follow the 'open door' policy." He announced a "deal" with the Association of Western Managers making available to the Shuberts two hundred theaters; in addition, new theaters would be erected in key Coast cities.

"Messrs. Shubert will next season present sixty productions, constituting more dramatic and musical offerings under their own direction than have ever before in the history of the world been presented by one management, thus taking upon themselves the lead in supplying offerings to meet the new conditions, even while making alliances with other producers."

Sixty productions! Out of one office! Erlanger bided his time. He still controlled the best routing, and more important, he had the attractions. Klaw went west to arrange for commitments, and the Syndicate put its collective strength into one project—book against the Shuberts. Town by town, city by city, it would be a bigger star, a bigger show against each Shubert attraction. There were intimidation of theater owners, threats of reprisal, threat of bankruptcy. The war was on again.

There were about three thousand theaters in the United States, and of this number about a thousand were lucrative for booking. Most of these Erlanger held. To invade properly, the Shuberts would have to wean the houses away from the Syndicate or build new houses. In Pittsburgh, they were frozen out of the city. In Philadelphia, they had only one house and that not too profitable.

The U.S. Amusement Company, the symbol of the peace, was quietly dissolved, and the New Theater opened on November 6, 1909, with *Antony and Cleopatra*, starring E. H. Sothern and Julia Marlowe. It was an artistic achievement and a box-office failure. Other pretentious fare followed, and the New Theater limped along. Erlanger chortled, J. J. asked embarrassing questions, and the boxholders were disturbed.

The board called a meeting, attended by their theatrical advisers,

Ames, Shubert, and Frank Corbin, literary head of the New Theater. Ames stated that the theater was in the black, a contention which could not be supported. The amateurs of the board asked Lee Shubert to explain the lack of success, and his reply was, "I want to know why we aren't doing better plays, plays that will attract attention."

Corbin, feeling that he was under attack, demanded, "Mr. Shubert, what play on Broadway is better than the productions we are presenting?"

Lee named the reigning hit, *Passing of the Third Floor Back.*

Corbin replied, "But I practically wept on your shoulder, Mr. Shubert, begging you to buy it. But you procrastinated, you couldn't make your mind up, and eventually it was bought for Broadway. By you!"

There was a strained silence, and the next week Corbin was fired.

The next New Theater production was staged by J. C. Huffman, Shubert stage director. It was *A Son of the People* and it met with a tepid reception.

The pressure on Lee Shubert through this period was enormous. There were the sixty productions to mount; there was the New Theater to supervise; there were vast real estate negotiations to conduct; there were the never-ending lawsuits to fight, to appeal, to direct; there was the constant necessity to firm up alliances, to protect existing affiliations against encroachment, and to make systematic raids on the Erlanger star list. And there were theaters to build.

In the midst of all this pressure, the Shuberts lost a lawsuit that infuriated Lee. Laurette Taylor, then a snip of an ingénue, had appeared in a Shubert production. Lee had been much taken with her and signed her to a long contract, with a salary of seventy-five dollars per week. He had liked her so much, he had *voluntarily* raised her to a hundred. When the play closed, George M. Cohan had persuaded Shubert to "lend" Miss Taylor for the ingénue role in *Alias Jimmy Valentine.* Shubert had agreed, and Miss Taylor got the hundred a week for that too. Now, Cohan had a comedy for Miss Taylor, and when she asked Shubert's permission to appear in it, Lee told her that she wasn't funny —"You don't belong in comedy." Miss Taylor took the part. Mr. Shubert sued, asking an injunction against her appearing anywhere except under his contract.

The court came up with a curious verdict. It decided that since Miss Taylor's contract with him called for seventy-five dollars per week, when Lee raised the salary to a hundred, he had in effect broken the contract. Miss Taylor was free to sign with Cohan. Shubert was apoplectic, and he never spoke to Miss Taylor again. Later on, he would say,

"Every time I start being generous, I remember that silly judge. He doesn't even know how many actors he cost money!"

It must not be assumed that Lee Shubert was constantly fighting off this generous impulse. He was not, by nature, a generous man. On Sam's death, he had adopted one of Sam's more endearing characteristics. Sam had a long handout list—tired actors, broken-down writers, the typical hangers-on in the theatrical district. As little Sam would come bouncing down the street, they would wait for him, and with each handshake, there was passed a rolled-up piece of currency. It was done tactfully and nicely.

Lee inherited the handout list, and added to it year by year. He also imitated Sam's walk, bouncing on his small feet across streets and down aisles, his Egyptian-Indian face, with its sallow skin, peering downward (to avoid stepping on a crack), his black hair always combed, his clothes impeccable. He liked the walking. It was exercise, it got him away from the office, and it gave him a chance to appraise real estate.

Shubert would go for walks late at night, his shrewd eyes examining New York's midtown, block by block. He would purchase one piece of property, and then to "protect it" from another theater's being built by competitors, he would buy various frontages along the block, so that no two adjacent pieces were large enough for a theater building.

And all along his routes, there would be the charity list. If anyone else tried to give them money, Lee would grow angry. They were *his*.

On one of these late-night walks, this time accompanied by William Brady, he persuaded Brady that his fortune lay with the Shuberts and the open door, and Brady left the Syndicate. Brady was a top producer, planning twenty attractions, and a million-dollar corporation was formed, with Brady as president, Lee vice president, and J.J. secretary-treasurer.

Erlanger countered with the announcement of an alliance of producing managers, which sounded very much like a Who's Who of theatrical impresarios, all of whom would be booking through the Syndicate; it lacked only the Shuberts, Fiske, Liebler, and the new ally, Brady. Belasco had gone over to his "mortal enemy," Erlanger.

The theater as an institution is not notable for its loyalties. The lack of them can be blamed on bruised egos, sensitive temperaments, or just plain avarice. But the history of the American stage in the twentieth century is a chronicle of double-dealing, contract breaking, changes of affiliation, piracy, theft, and rivalries. If Diogenes's honest man had decided to become an impresario, he would have had a hard time maintaining his character. If it wasn't his "creative talents" who were gouging him, he would discover that his box-office manager was selling tickets at scalpers' prices and pocketing the difference. And if he turned his back, his star, his playwright, and his composer would be dealing with his enemy. Since Lee Shubert was not discovered by Diogenes, he accepted all of the ground rules with commendable philosophic cynicism. Jake would scream, rant, rave, and punch, when these shifts happened. Lee would smile thoughtfully, mark it down in his mental black book and file it. His memory was long (so was Jake's), and he never forgot a betrayal and never forgave one either, except when he needed the betrayer for another production. He then let bygones alone, and reserved his vengeance for a more convenient time.

In this never-ending changing of allegiance, it was Shubert's turn to strike the next blow. J. J.'s trip to the West continued to pay dividends. Whether it was Cox's pressure, J. J.'s charm, or dissatisfaction with the Syndicate is hard to tell, but successively, Moses Reis, who operated seventy-five theaters in New York, Pennsylvania, New Jersey, Maryland, and Ohio, and John Cort, the leading chain operator in the West, subscribed to the open door policy. Cort, who controlled the National Association of Theater Managers, saw to it that Erlanger and his strongest allies were expelled from the Association.

Erlanger started a rival association, and then set up a $5,000,000 corporation in Chicago to buck the Cort interests. That corporation was to be the first of five such ventures nationwide, and its cast of characters was the same: Klaw, Erlanger, Hayman, etc., etc., plus Belasco!

The High Priest of Drama had an unbelievable capacity for feuds. Having thrown his lot in with Erlanger, Belasco now demanded that the name of the Belasco Theater, in Washington, D.C., which he operated with the Shuberts, be changed. He wanted his name off. The Shuberts refused, and Willie Klein, who was fighting some twenty litigations at this time, added another to the list.

Although the Shuberts were massively committed to a nationwide chain of theaters, Lee kept zeroed in on New York. He had several theories, based upon those early days in Syracuse. A show advertised as "direct from New York" sold more tickets than a show that was not so advertised. He felt that New York's geography was changing, and that inevitably the theatrical district was moving north along Broadway. He could feel the impact of motion pictures and of the mixture of vaudeville and motion pictures that Keith was featuring, and shrewdly he felt that the heartland of theater would be Manhattan Island. Finally, midtown New York real estate was worth money and in Lee's opinion would be worth more.

Through his work at the New Theater, he had met Alfred Gwynne Vanderbilt, and that Dutchman owned a horse stable, The American Horse Exchange, on 50th Street between Broadway and Seventh Avenue. The automobile was beginning to clog Manhattan streets, and a stable on Broadway was not a particularly attractive moneymaker. Vanderbilt and Shubert shared a reverence for money. The Shuberts leased the stable, and began a complete overhaul of the building. It would be J. J.'s pride and joy, and it was he who named it the Winter Garden.

The relentless struggle for theaters in key cities continued. It was a dirty, bloody business, as Shubert and Erlanger maneuvered, probed, offered, served ultimatums. There was legal sniping, and there were meetings in smoke-filled rooms. To further illustrate "theatrical loyalty," Erlanger triumphantly announced that Mme. Bernhardt, the divine Sarah, was going to make yet another farewell tour, this time under Syndicate management. Shubert offered to rent Erlanger a tent.

Somehow, in the midst of all this vast theatrical activity, with all the headaches of sixty productions and intricate routing, Lee Shubert found time to organize a syndicate to purchase almost the entire square block fronting on Broadway between 35th and 36th streets. This included the old Herald Square Theater, plus some twenty-five various apartment houses, stores, brownstones, and a hotel. The announced price was $6,000,000. The original plan was to build a theater and office building, but Shubert's instinct that the center was pushing north finally made it a commercial building site. The Herald Square was razed.

Shubert's partners, Cox and Rhinock, were remaining active. Under Cox's tender guidance, Keith took over the Orpheum circuit, headed by Martin Beck, the largest in the Middle West. This completed the strangle hold on all vaudeville in the country. In arranging this deal, Cox sold to Keith various theaters acquired originally for the Shuberts and never suited to legitimate theatrical presentations. Three of the theaters in which the Shuberts had financial stakes went in the trans-action—at a profit to the brothers.

Marcus Loew incorporated Loew's Theatrical Enterprises for $5,000,000, and on the board of directors was Rhinock. Joe Schenck, who with his brother was running an amusement park on the Palisades, plus several theaters, was also present. Loew, now building three new theaters in addition to the fourteen in operation, was leaning heavily on Lee Shubert for advice—and theaters.

Brady, who had been in London, came back to tell the world that he and the Shuberts (who had sworn never to have another theater in

London) had just leased three theaters in London. J. J. left for a tour of the West, accompanied by Joe Rhinock. The main point of the mission was to see Cort; that worthy had just signed contracts with Erlanger, opening up a whole territory to Honest Abe. When Shubert protested, Cort's bland reply was, "An Open Door is an Open Door."

Shubert productions continued to flow, and to remain undistinguished, except for those at the Hippodrome. And on September 28, 1910, Lee, described as "the brains of the New Theater and head of the Shubert empire," received his first feature interview, with Harrison Fiske in the *New York Dramatic Mirror*. It described him as "mild, gentle, precise, almost prim." What the theater needed, Lee said, was good plays. "The theater is first a luxury, then a habit; now it is a necessity. Take the Hippodrome; seven thousand people twice a day!" Was the Hippodrome representative? And how did he reconcile the need for plays with his continuing battle with the people who wrote plays? Lee was up to the task. "Playwrights are important, but actors are more important. It takes more than printer's ink and electric lights to make a star. A star is an actor who has a following." He stared complacently at the press representative.

Then he decided to wax philosophical. "I began my career as a manager in assisting my elder brother who founded the firm and died." (This was the first time that the Shuberts *publicly* reversed their ages. Prior to this epic date, they had reserved their chronological unorthodoxy for insurance companies.) "I took up the work where he left off." Lee's eyes filled, and he was obviously emotionally shaken. "Every theater we own in New York will have a picture of my brother Sam hanging in the lobby," he said, "and shortly, every Shubert house in the world will also have a picture." For all his sentiment, Lee remained Lee. He would learn that somehow naming a theater "The Sam S. Shubert Memorial Theater" left a kind of pall in the air, a depressing, funereal quality. The "memorial" theaters—all five of them—gradually became known as the "Shuberts."

"I love to succeed," he went on candidly. "The greater the difficulties, the greater the joy in succeeding. I take such pleasure in the work I ask nothing better than to stay in my office. Work has become such a habit, I need no recreation to make me happy."

He wound up the interview by stating that all Shubert tickets could be had directly from the box office. They would be delivered by that new-fangled contraption called a motorcycle, and no theater-ticket brokers would have seats available for Shubert-controlled houses.

J.J.'s major interest was the Winter Garden. He spent as much time there as he could, supervising the painters, the carpenters, the

103

electricians, and finding time to visit the Hippodrome (Lee's bailiwick) just often enough to get into a fist fight with Burnside, the stage director, who quit. Nothing Lee could do would persuade Burnside to return.

A few Shubert plays were still rehearsing and opening, and going out on tour. Douglas Fairbanks opened at the Comedy Theater in *The Cub*, a Brady production, and it was a smash. Mary Pickford was already a star, but they were yet to meet. At the Nazimova Theater, the Messrs. Shubert presented *Mr. Preedy and the Countess*, and a bit player called Lynn Fontanne got moderate reviews in the press. And a young juvenile, Sidney Greenstreet, was working in another Shubert opus.

The motion-picture industry had discovered Los Angeles, and the Biograph Company, the eastern kingpin in production, was setting up a unit out there in the boondocks. Hollywood was being born. Two hundred and fifty pictures were being made each month in the United States, but production could not keep up with the demand, and this despite the fact that an additional two hundred were being imported. Carl Laemmle in Chicago kept experimenting with talking pictures. J.J., in an attempt to boost box-office receipts in the newly acquired Great Northern Theater (which J.J. promptly renamed the Lyric), converted it to motion pictures.

It was a jinx house for J.J. The theater had two entrances, both of them, as Jake once said, "carefully hidden from anybody who was looking for them." He had rented the theater at $1,500 a week, and his first week's receipts from motion-picture exhibition came to a fat $375. He was in trouble, and he knew it.

In Minneapolis a bright young showman named Rothafel was doing interesting stage shows and a lot of business. J.J. hired him to "pep up" the Lyric, paying Rothafel a hundred dollars a week. Rothafel introduced an orchestra and, to give tone to the house, placed potted palms on stage, trying to make the Shubert theater a temple of culture. The second week's receipts rose to $700, but Jake was a wee bit more in the hole than he had been, since the additional Rothafel touches had added to his costs. He sent a volley of concerned telegrams to the young man and to the theater manager. J.J. was particularly incensed with the florist's bill for the palms.

Working night and day, Rothafel brought the gross up to $1,300 in another two weeks, and J.J. fired him—by wire. "Why did you snake me out of Minneapolis?" demanded Rothafel. "I was doing all right there. And business is building here."

Jake's reply was, by wire, "You are fired. Go back to Minneapolis and take the God-damned palms with you." J.J. came out to Chicago and personally surveyed the situation, finally coming to the conclusion that he would imitate Woolworth—he would lower the prices slightly and increase the volume. The Lyric lost more money. In disgust, J.J. sublet it to a "grind" vaudeville company, and they made a fortune.

Every time J.J. passed the Lyric, he would carefully spit into the gutter. And much later (1926), when Rothafel became better known as "Roxy" and built the till-then most luxurious theater in the country in New York, J.J. was among the invited guests at the opening. He stalked through the overwhelming marble lobby, and came face to face with a potted palm. "Ahah!" he exclaimed, "the son of a bitch is still crazy about palms! In Florida he should have theaters!"

During that same unhappy Lyric episode in Chicago, J.J. showed his delicate understanding of the drama. Winchell Smith, a well-known theatrical manager, was in Chicago with a company of Shaw's *Candida*. When the Shuberts booked it into Chicago, with Arnold Daly starring, it was mutually understood that the piece was prestige booking. The show did not lose money in Chicago, but it didn't make any, and J.J. wired Smith, "Cut expenses. We are losing our shirts." Smith fired back a wire, "Cut how? Wire suggestions." Jake wired back, "Write out one or two parts!" Smith wired back, "Fire me!"

Someone in New York explained that *Candida* could not be cut in this fashion. And no, Mr. Shubert, girls could not be added to boost business.

If J.J. had absolutely no conception of dramatic productions, he did have box-office brains when it came to musicals. From the beginning, in the queer hierarchy of the Shubert organization, the Winter Garden was Jake's theater. He staffed it carefully, with J. C. Huffman and William J. Wilson as stage directors (both with Hippodrome experience), Arthur Voegtlin, for years with the Hippodrome, and Melville Ellis, who had been with the Shuberts for five years now—starting as chorus boy, writing incidental music, designing sets and costumes, in charge of costumes and everything else he could lay a hand on. All of them reported to Jake, and there was never any doubt about who was running the show. Jake announced the opening for March of 1911, starring a Broadway newcomer, Al Jolson.

The two important names on the list are Jolson, who would make millions for the Shuberts, and Melville Ellis, who for years would add dash and tone to J.J.'s productions.

Chapter Seven

The popular musical theater in America for the first two decades of the twentieth century was a curious collection of derivative art forms frantically searching for its own identity. There were three basic types of musical offering. The operetta, imported from Europe, was occasionally Americanized, but more often was "adapted"—translated, and supplied with new lyrics, some additional music, all pinned on the usual Graustarkian plot. Then, there was the musical comedy, in which a skimpy, usually incredible plot line was employed to hook together girls, songs, and comedians in a kind of theatrical bundling-bed; the ingredients could touch each other but they rarely consummated a relationship. Finally, there was the revue, a fast-paced mélange of song and skit and dance—actually, just smart, high-priced vaudeville.

The audience had changed. Prior to the introduction of the Gilbert and Sullivan operettas, very few women—ladies, that is—and no children attended the theater. But when the English team was introduced to the United States, women began to flock to the theater. It became smart, social, and acceptable.

The Shuberts were concerned with all three varieties of musicals. J. J. had a deep affection for the schmaltzy Viennese sound in music, and through the years, J. J. was the leading importer of three-quarter-time composers from Mittel Europa. He would hear a "genius" in a rathskeller, sign him to contract, bring him to America, and since so few could satisfy the Broadway criterion, it may be presumed that half the trios, pianists, small groups that entertained at "Continental" restaurants in New York had been brought here by the Shuberts.

For his Winter Garden opening, Jake didn't trust any of his new talents. The production was *La Belle Paree*, and the score was by Louis Hirsch, a gifted and successful Broadway composer; there were additional tunes by Jerome Kern. But what really exploded the Winter Garden into instantaneous popularity was the dynamic Broadway debut of Al Jolson. The entertainer had been "threatening" New York for years with ads in the trade papers reading, "Watch me, boys, I'm coming East," signed "Al Jolson." Lee put him under contract at $250, and after March 20, 1911, the date of the Winter Garden opening, Jolson was worth his weight in gold.

The reviews were ecstatic; the critics and the audience liked the show, the theater, the production. It was all Jake's. He was in the clouds. And to make his triumph complete, within a week of the opening of the Winter Garden, the shutters went up on the New Theater. It was a total fiasco.

But the Winter Garden started something else in the Shubert family. It sowed the seeds for a peculiar agreement, never written but one which would slowly evolve. It would become "understood" that the musical end of Shubert productions would lie in Jake's bailiwick; the "legitimate" theater would be Lee's. New York theaters and real estate would be Lee's; out-of-town would be Jake's baby. Booking all theatres, arranging for attractions, signing stars to contracts—Lee. Hiring dancers, composers, etc.—Jake.

Two separate, independent organizations would emerge in the Shubert hierarchy, each responsible to, and loyal to, one of the brothers, and in bitter competition with the other. There was a complete sharing of profits and of losses, but the interchange between the Lees and the Jakes was minimal. Some of the bitterest wrangles between the brothers resulted from Lee's "invasions" of Jake's province. And this occurred with annoying frequency, prompted by Lee's cultural "advisers," his own desire to compete, or an empty theater that needed a show. J.J. would blow like a wounded whale, and then be torn between his natural avarice, which wanted the Shuberts collectively to have a hit, and his elemental ego, which wanted "the other Shubert" to have a flop.

There was more than the fraternal war to bother the Shuberts. The impact of motion pictures on the stage box office was enormous, and there didn't seem to be an end in sight. The motion-picture business was expanding with unbelievable rapidity, and it had long stopped being a "gimmick" and a "curiosity"—the self-comforting words of the stage die-hards. Its effect was most keenly felt in those city theaters that were not in the main theatrical district, and in smaller cities and towns. What the motion picture wasn't stealing from the traditional stage audience, Keith-Albee vaudeville was gouging into. Theaters were dying, and the Shubert-Syndicate war didn't help matters at all.

Films were being attacked for their violence and their subject matter. "They pervert the sensibilities of the young," thundered a Brooklyn minister.

The theater, long under this kind of attack, was now suffering it in more violent form. In its never-ending fight for the dollar, in competing with film, it had become more and more daring in theme and in presentation. Lee had been having his own troubles with various Shubert presentations, which he always contended were "serious, moral plays," but which other people, less sensitive, found "salacious." Lee was essentially a prim man, and he found this kind of criticism painful.

One peaceful night, in April 1911, he was seated at an opening in

King Jolson. Al Jolson, the Shubert's biggest moneymaker, as Gus in *Honey-moon Express*, Winter Garden Theater, New York, 1913.

a Shubert house when word got to him that the paddy wagons were marshaling at *his* Maxine Elliott Theater, which he had rented to the Abbey Players of Dublin.

It was the American debut of Synge's *Playboy of the Western World*. The Irish-American colony was up in arms at the play. They felt that Synge and his Dublin actors were doing a great disservice to Ireland and slandering an ancient and honorable race. To make sure that their displeasure would be known, they had bought tickets, and brought vegetables. They disrupted the performance, a riot started, and the police were called.

Lee, who knew nothing of the play's background—his ignorance here equaled his knowledge of Synge and the Abbey players—did know the word "playboy," and filled with trepidation, he hurried to the Maxine Elliott, sure of the worst. As he came up to the theater, he ran into a reporter for the *New York Times* and shouted at him in his high voice, "If I had known there was one thing off-color about this show, I wouldn't have let them have the house."

Shortly after, on June 28, 1911, for the first time in seven years, Lee left for England and the Continent, this time accompanied by Brady. He was a very busy Shubert. He had another of his epic meetings with George Bernard Shaw, and came away with the rights to a new work, *Fanny's First Play*, which unfortunately would come across the footlights as if it were Shaw's first play. In France, he bought several French farce epics, and signed Gaby de Lys to a Shubert contract. Gaby was the singing sensation of the Continent, and she fitted nicely into Lee's plans. In Berlin, he held protracted meetings with Max Reinhardt, the most exciting stage figure in Europe. He had made the Deutsches Theater world-famous for his productions of *Faust, Salome, Oedipus Rex*, etc. Lee did not know the plays, but he had heard the name Reinhardt, and he persuaded Reinhardt that art and Max would be served by signing with the Shuberts.

The incredible part of all of this remains the undeniable fact that this was the man who had been brought in as an "expert" on America's first real repertory theater. True, it had failed, but the failure was in no way attributed to Lee Shubert. He came off a cultural hero, and Winthrop Ames, the Artistic head of the defunct New Theater, was making plans with Lee to build a theater or two between 44th and 45th Streets, in back of the Astor Hotel. It would create a small, private alley, and on its southwest corner would be erected the Sam S. Shubert Memorial Theater—complete with Sam's picture in the lobby.

The business aspect of the theater had worsened during Lee's short absence. Keith, prodded by his general manager, Albee, was

110

introducing motion pictures into most of the theaters he booked. But the abortive Erlanger-Shubert raid on vaudeville had driven the price of acts higher and higher, and pricing them down again was not simple, not even with a monopoly position.

Albee applied every pressure—threat of blacklisting, bad routing, bad bookings; all of this was possible since nearly all vaudeville was being booked through the Albee-run, Keith-controlled United Booking Office. When the performers tried to fight back, largely through activating a social club, The White Rats, into an active union, Albee countered by organizing his own vaudeville artists' union, and successfully broke the independent group. But the germ of a performers' union was planted. Actors' Equity was being conceived.

Shubert had tried vaudeville; he was flirting with motion pictures (making far more announcements than films), and he had leased some houses to Marcus Loew. Now he expanded the Loew tie-up. Under the Sunday laws in New York, no theatrical performances were allowed by legitimate theaters. They tried to get around it by performing the so-called Sacred Concerts, on Sundays, which the police pretended not to see as entertainment. Their myopia was helped along by generous cash contributions from the various managers. Lee made arrangements with Loew to lease a number of Shubert theaters to Loew for Sunday use—days when the theaters were normally dark.

While J.J. had been producing, and Lee was in Europe, the usual flow of litigations had kept Klein busy. His box score was pretty good; the Shuberts had lost only a small percentage of the twenty-odd cases on the docket, and the bulk of these Klein had settled out of court. Some cases were still pending. A Mrs. Bridget Murphy of 336 East 34th Street wanted two thousand Shubert dollars, claiming that she had been "contused, abraded, frightened into nervousness," when she was run over by a Shubert elephant. She claimed to have been sweeping the stoop of her house when an elephant had tried to enter said house, pushing past her in the process. In so doing, said elephant had inflicted various unspecified injuries. The elephant was on its way to the Hippodrome, and so it was a Shubert responsibility. The court had reserved decision, and Lee smilingly told Klein to give the lady a little money; anybody "who got run over by a Shubert elephant shouldn't go unpaid."

Lee stopped smiling when Willie Klein went into detail on the case of Kitty Gordon, "the girl with the $50,000 back," who had filed suit for $2,700. She had signed for $1,000 a week at the Winter Garden, had received only $300, and was suing for the rest. Lee thought for a moment, and then his face brightened.

No Longer "Memorial." A program for the Sam S. Shubert Theater. It was better for comedy.

The Monument. Laying the cornerstone of the Sam S. Shubert Memorial Theater, 44th Street and the "Alley." Lee at right; beside him, Lew Fields of Weber and Fields.

"Doesn't that contract call for Sunday-night 'concert' performances?" Lee asked.

"Sure," said Klein. "All our contracts on the Winter Garden have that clause."

"Then the contract is illegal," said Lee, beginning to purr again. "That's against the state law!"

"But *I* drew the contract," protested Klein. "And *you* signed it."

Lee's eyes twinkled. "Would we want anyone to hold us to an illegal contract?" he asked. "Didn't we make the same answer in the De Angeles case?"

Klein nodded dazedly. "Lee, we can't just keep on drawing illegal contracts and then use them as an excuse not to pay people."

Lee smiled benignly. "Would I suggest it?"

Not much later, he did suggest it, and this time it came back to bite him. The Winter Garden signed a Shubert contract with a Miss Kathleen Clifford for four Sunday-night performances. After the first appearance, she was offered half the salary the contract stipulated. She refused to accept it, the Shuberts canceled, and Miss Clifford took it to court.

Willie Klein used the standard Shubert gambit—illegal Sunday-night concert equaled illegal contract. The court again agreed with this peculiar logic, and the Shuberts had won again. But Miss Clifford was stubborn. Illegal the concerts might be, but somebody was making an awful lot of money out of them. When Miss Clifford's attorney presented that thought to the court, it decided that possibly this was a police matter.

It was lost in channels—the Shuberts had a free list for the police department—and finally the new Equity Council wrote to the Corporation Counsel in New York and, to everyone's surprise, received a reply stating the case had been settled out of court.

Actually, the Shuberts had been fined $500, but more important, one week later, they canceled the Sunday-night concerts—for the time being. This was one of the painful Shubert retreats, since it cost them money. And since the Winter Garden was J.J.'s very own showplace, J.J. became even more resentful of Lee.

The meeting Lee held with his brother, after his return from Europe was acrimonious. Buoyed by his stunning success with the Winter Garden, Jake felt entitled to greater recognition and more authority within the organization. In his never-humble opinion, Jake was not only the real dollar man of the combination, but its artistic genius too. Hadn't he arranged with Morris Gest to present the Ameri-

113

can premiere of *Les Sylphides* and *Scheherazade?* He gratuitously added, for Lee's benefit, that during Lee's absence the Shuberts had been invited by Chicago's *haut monde* to set up and supervise a New Theater in the Illinois city. Perhaps, J.J. suggested caustically, with Lee's experience in repertory and "class production," he would like to take it on? Further, said Jake, he was tired of "Sam S. and Lee Shubert Present" on the billboards. He wasn't even too fond of "The Messrs. Shubert"; he, Jake, was doing all the work and wanted the credit.

Lee was impassive. He refused the gambit of the Chicago New Theater. He refused to retire "Sam S. and Lee"—they would continue to "present." He would not enter into any discussion that touched on Jake's limiting or circumscribing his activities. And what he *did* want to talk about was the new Shubert Theatrical Corporation, set up in New Jersey, which would assume the assets of the New York corporation of the same name. He thought they would have more flexibility in the new corporation—translated, it meant easier switching back and forth of assets from the proliferating Shubert-controlled corporations.

Jake grumblingly agreed; if it saved money, or made money, J.J. was all for it. He now pressed his own plans for the upcoming season. He hated Ziegfeld, and envied him. He hated the glowing reviews of the *Ziegfeld Follies*, the "new idea" Ziegfeld had begun in 1907. He had paid Ziegfeld the supreme Jake Shubert compliment, when one year later he had produced *The Mimic World*, a very close imitation of Ziegfeld's imitation of a Paris revue. On the music score of *The Mimic World* had appeared the phrase "Follies of 1908," and Ziegfeld, who felt he owned the word, wanted to sue to have the subtitle removed from the music score!

Now J.J. wanted to surpass Ziegfeld. He wanted to do a revue at the Winter Garden and call it *The Passing Show*. He started to describe it, and Lee quietly told him to go ahead. Lee may have thought he owed Jake one.

There was much more ground to cover. Although the editorial pages of the press had made heroes of the Boys from Syracuse, theater critics had been taking a different approach. And the Shubert feuds with critics were juicy news items. From Jake's modest amateur beginning in Chicago, where he barred Percy Hammond twice, the brothers earned their professional standing in the years that followed. They took on critics from coast to coast.

Channing Pollock had been a Shubert press agent and the publisher of *The Show*, the short-lived penny magazine they had published. When he left the employ of the brothers, they threw him a dinner and presented him with a diamond-studded, gold cigarette case, which Pollock used to lovingly refer to as "my whorehouse humidor."

When Pollock was hired by the hated *Telegraph* as drama critic, the Shuberts were gleeful—they had a friend in the enemy camp. But Pollock was an honest critic, and he called them as he saw them, and much of the Shubert output that he saw he just plain didn't like.

The brothers felt betrayed, and by one of their own. They barred him from all Shubert theaters. Pollock didn't give up easily. In various disguises, he managed to attend, and to review. It became a fashion joke.

What would Channing Pollock wear to the next Shubert opening? He wore beards, wigs, dark glasses—on one occasion, even a putty nose! Once, as Gilbert Miller's guest, Pollock came as Pollock. Miller, a formidable physical fellow, bulled him into the theater, past the protesting house manager, Harry Hyams. The critic panned the play *Fanny's First Play*, by George Bernard Shaw—and the Shuberts fired Hyams.

In Chicago, Jake barred Charles Collins, who had replaced Percy Hammond on the *Post*, and kept him barred for four years! The critic felt that he was being barred in memory of Hammond.

In Boston, Jake barred the distinguished critic Philip Hale, and then George Holland. Holland was a resourceful fellow. He had himself appointed an acting fire marshal and, by an odd coincidence, only inspected the Shubert theaters for fire violations on opening nights.

Not to be outdone by his younger brother, Lee barred Heywood Broun of Pulitzer's *World*, Alexander Woollcott of the *Times*, and Gilbert Gabriel of the *Sun*.

J.J. countered by barring Goodman Ace, then a twenty-year-old critic for the Kansas City *Post*.

The odds were all with Lee—there were more critics in New York. He successively barred Leonard Lyons and Walter Winchell from his theaters. Winchell commented, "I do not mind missing Shubert openings. I can always go the second night and see the closing. . . ." (Harpo Marx once loaned Winchell his blond fright wig, and Winchell, disguised as the zany Marx, entered the stage door and reviewed the show from the wings. J. J. never forgave Marx.)

But barring the critics didn't stop the reviews. From the beginning, the *Morning Telegraph*, the leading theatrical paper of the day, had crucified the Shuberts. Pulitzer's *World* was not far behind. The brothers came up with a typically Shubert solution to their problem. With no friend at court, they built their own court. They set up a weekly newspaper, *The New York Review*, the only newspaper which never panned

115

any of Jake's superproductions. One of their publicists, Sam Weller, was named editor and publisher, and he did what he could to fan up pro-Shubert sentiment. He even made money with the paper!

The attacks of the *Review* on the *Telegraph* were spicy, but they somehow lacked the bite of what the *Telegraph* was saying about the Shuberts. "This paper will not libel the Shuberts. It would be as cruel as it is unnecessary," was one sample. Jake and Lee took both pride and interest in their paper. Jake liked to read the reviews of his plays over and over again, particularly when the criticism of the less protective papers was other than laudatory. The brothers also "dug" items for their favorite paper. And it was Jake who turned out to be particularly good at smelling out scandal in the rival camp.

Jake came rushing in to Weller just before press time with the story of a scandalous party at the Erlanger estate in Lawrence, Long Island. There was very little fact in the yarn, as written, but a lot of innuendo and a lot of headline. J.J. named names of the young chorines present and tied Erlanger to the whole scene. J.J. got a big kick out of the story, and all of Broadway was laughing at it.

There were only two things wrong with the story. One, it had not occurred; and two, the Erlanger estate in Lawrence did not belong to Honest Abe but to his brother, a sedate and staid judge. He had never heard of the wild party or of any of the ladies presumed present.

Abe Erlanger bellowed for his legal department, which moved for an indictment against the paper and the Shuberts on the charge of criminal libel. The grand jury held hearings, and the matter dawdled back and forth. Finally, word was leaked that the jury had been reading the *Telegraph* and the *Review* and was of the opinion that no indictment should be filed—as a matter of fact, they felt that Erlanger and the Shuberts should be held for trial on identical charges.

Willie Klein was called in to help write the story, dug by an energetic Shubert employee. Since there had been no formal announcement from the jury, the *story* would have to be written in a most careful fashion. But it was Klein's opinion that they could print any sort of picture they felt appropriate. The cartoon drawn showed Honest Abe being tossed out of the grand-jury room, and landing on an unsavory heap of garbage.

Where the story of the nonexistent party had not been libelous, the grand jury found the cartoon very libelous, and on that ground served up an indictment. Sam Weller was arraigned and let out on bail. Like so many Shubert-involved actions, it was settled out of court. The Shuberts agreed that the *Review* never again would assail the reputation of a certain young lady, and Erlanger dropped the libel charge.

The *Telegraph* never printed a word about the story, and the *Review* shut its mouth on the issue. Both sides had legally been singed and became a little bit more cautious in the future.

One tangible result of the *Review* story appeared discreetly some six months later. In January of 1912, Adelaide Louise Erlanger received a divorce decree ending her marriage to Abraham Lincoln Erlanger. Mrs. Erlanger had not liked the "wild party" that never happened any more than the ones that had.

Erlanger's plight put J.J. in a mellow mood. He was the sort of man who empathized positively with another man's troubles. And J.J. had a lot to be mellow about. His Winter Garden shows were being imitated! He screamed to heaven about "piracy" at the same time he was preparing his *Follies* copy. But imitated he was and recognized he was. He was no longer merely "the younger Shubert." He had become J.J. He liked it.

It even threw him back into a half-hearted attempt at making his marriage work. His son was three, still a little too young to share Jake's time; nonetheless, he brought the boy to the theater, sat him backstage in the care of a wardrobe girl or a chorine, and went on about his business. John Shubert by the age of five had probably seen more naked female epidermis than any child his age outside a nudist camp. When someone remonstrated with J.J. that perhaps this was not the most exemplary way to raise a child, Jake shrugged and said, "Let him get it out of his system now." (The boy was five when that philosophy was voiced.)

For Catherine Dealy Shubert the marriage was a trampoline act. Jake's moods were unpredictable, and one day's pleasantries might just be that night's screaming onslaught. She had moved to an apartment on 72nd Street and Riverside Drive and lived in constant terror that her husband would have her evicted. During one prolonged siege, she barricaded herself into the house with her young son and, with the aid of a cooperative building attendant, hoisted baskets of food up to her window from the street. She was afraid that opening the door meant an invasion by Jake's attorneys.

The brothers Shubert were undoubtedly the two busiest entrepreneurs in New York that year (1911–1912). Productions, theaters, real estate, corporations. Jake's Winter Garden continued to make news, and Lee's productions were adequate, and no more.

Gaby de Lys, the "sexy French chanteuse," made her American debut at the Winter Garden, and ran into difficulties—her smart lyrics were not understood, and her voice was not all that thrilling. A comic, Frank Tinney, stole the notices from everyone except Jolson. And to make sure that nothing happened with their new star, the Shuberts signed Jolson to a long-term contract, which guaranteed him a piece of the profits. They didn't sign another young performer who appeared in the revue. He was also the rehearsal pianist, turned actor, and they didn't think Irving Berlin was going to make it.

Jake came right back with *Vera Violetta*, starring Jolson again and a Mlle. de Lys with slightly improved diction, and she caught on too. The curtain raiser, an "artistic" ballet, *Undine*, starred Annette Kellerman, who exchanged her sensational one-piece suit for a one-piece tutu, and drew audience. The Jolson piece also starred an hour-glass-shaped female, Mae West, who brought her own unique gifts to the Shubert stable.

Lee was having tougher sledding. In association with Winthrop Ames, he brought Reinhardt to the Casino in a magnificent production, with his Deutsches Theater troupe, of a tableau entitled *Sumurun*. Lee took no credit; he left it all to Ames. It was undoubtedly the most exciting theatrical presentation of its time; the sets were spare, "modern," the staging imaginative, ahead of its time. It was an erotic fantasy, which was criticized for its shocking content, applauded for its artistic triumph, and ran a mere sixty-two performances. For the moment, Shubert had had art.

The most interesting part of Reinhardt's stage theory, in addition to its lyric unity, was the attempt to break down the invisible wall between audience and players. He built an apron out beyond the footlights, over several rows of seats, and brought his performers into almost physical contact with the audience. It was the first "thrust" stage. (When Reinhardt started bridging and, of course, sacrificing seats in the Casino, Lee Shubert raised bloody hell. Ames had a hard time convincing him.)

Of all the Reinhardt contributions, this device was the one J. J. seized. He had a runway built at the Winter Garden, and now the audience could almost touch, and really see, see, see the eighty, count them —eighty, chorus girls. J.J. tried it first in *The Whirl of Society*, and when it clicked, he planned its use for the first *Passing Show* in 1912.

Whether it was Jake Shubert or the changing times cannot be determined—but the chorus girl underwent a change. Ziegfeld had been using his "American Beauties," but in the main the style in female beauty leaned toward a hefty beef-trust chorus line. With the "runway," the girls started getting slimmer, younger, and nuder. (But the Shuberts always had a warm spot in their hearts for some of their "older" chorus girls—girls who had been with them in many shows. They kept employing them—some long beyond the time they should have been working in a chorus. This occasionally elicited some cavalier sneers from audience and critic, who did not share the brothers' sense of feudal responsibility.)

The Shubert chorus was divided into three groups of girls: the "show girls," who were tall, statuesque, no-clothes horses, the "mediums," and the "ponies." J.J. liked them all. Lee leaned toward the show girls.

That first *Passing Show* did not use Jolson, but it introduced from vaudeville Willie and Eugene Howard as comedy stars and an eccentric dancer, Charlotte Greenwood, and featured a song by that rehearsal pianist Irving Berlin. Jerome Kern also contributed a number.

The *Passing Shows* came regularly thereafter, always using the Reinhardt runway, always running for a smashing (for those days) twenty weeks, and then going out on tour. They were Jake's bread-and-butter presentations, filled with spectacle, girls, comedy, girls, fantasy, girls, music, and girls. John Charles Thomas made his initial Broadway appearance in the second *Passing Show*, and the chorus kept getting younger and slimmer.

By the time of the 1914 version the transformation was complete. The age of the slender, shapely all-American girl was here. The runway was still there, but the bald-headed tenants of the best seats were getting a run for their money. Younger men, gay blades, the playboys of the era, the Ivy League stage-door Johnnies were now competing for those choice aisle seats. The girls' costumes were just as different. The legs, which had slowly been inching out of the tights and leotards, were bare for the first time. The bare midriff on stage was the result of another of Jake's insights. And with the same uncanny eye for talent the brothers always seemed to have, they introduced a dancing sprite— mercurial, lovely Marilynn Miller. (She had not yet dropped the second *n* in her first name.)

The new chorines not only looked slimmer, they danced on stage instead of parading in mass formations. They tapped, they kicked, they even went through simple pirouettes and arabesques of the ballet. The show, of course, was a stunning success.

Jake did not allow success to go to his head. He remained his unpleasant, irascible self. He fumed at Lee and Lee's flops; he was enraged at what he considered a lack of appreciation for his "artistic productions"; his terrible temper kept getting him into trouble. Miss Helen White, a chorus girl from New York, attached the box-office receipts in the Boston Shubert theater, claiming salary for two and a half weeks, plus her fare to New York.

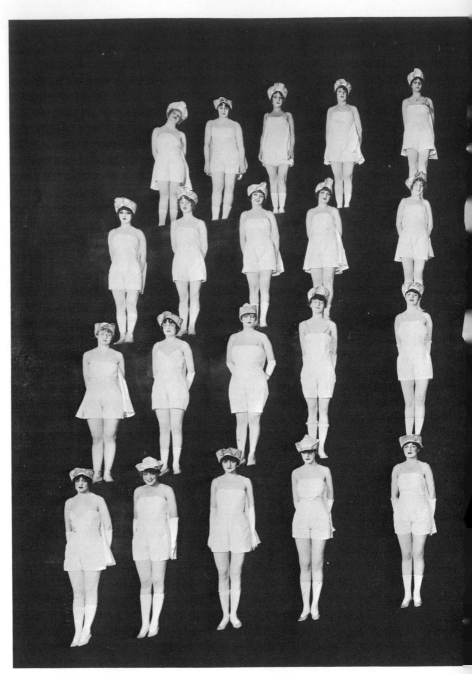

Girls, Girls, Girls. Forty-four of them! A J.J. production number, this from *The Passing Show of 1914.*

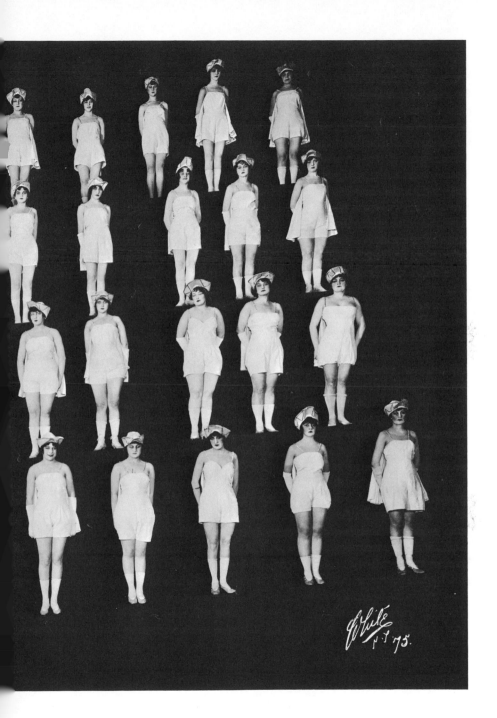

The Shubert manager had given the girls half checks and notice, which the girls refused to accept. When J.J. came to Boston, he refused to see the girls, and Miss White enterprisingly tracked him to the Copley Plaza. She hit him with the summons in the lobby and Jake hit her—with a right cross.

Like most of Jake's violences, the incident was settled out of court by Willie Klein.

Jake's return to New York did not diminish his pugnacity. Almost always, his terrible rages required a physical outlet, and when he got into an altercation with a young show girl, Peggy Forbes, at the Winter Garden, Jake lost his temper in an interchange of pretty dull repartee. He followed Miss Forbes backstage, and he physically assaulted her. She was a badly bruised girl, one eye swollen shut, scratches on one cheek, a cut lip—a pretty sad sight. She was good copy for the papers when she swore out a warrant for J.J.'s arrest; it turned out she was the great-granddaughter of a former President of the United States, Zachary Taylor.

The hearing was acrimonious, and marked by a totally unexpected blindness on the part of the Shubert employees who had witnessed the attack. They could not remember having seen it, and when the smoke cleared, Willie Klein quietly settled the matter—out of court, to be sure.

Klein used two techniques in handling the affairs of the brothers. When Lee was a litigant, as either plaintiff or defendant, he liked to have Lee appear—Lee was a convincing witness. When it was Jake who was the litigant, Klein tried to keep him out of court. J.J. had become the complete producer, and to him all the world was a stage, and he was the boss. He was an intolerant witness and overbearing toward judge and jury.

In 1910, during one of their expansion wars with Klaw and Erlanger, J.J. had rented the Tootle Theater in St. Joseph, Missouri, at a monthly rental of $666. The entire transaction had been handled through intermediaries and agents, and in the winter of that year the Shuberts put a melodrama into the house. The action called for a sweaty, hot summer scene, and so the stage was set. Unfortunately, there were gaping holes in the roof, a blizzard hit St. Jo, and in the midst of the Shubert's short, hot summer, snowflakes were falling, and actors were wrapping themselves in shawls even as they were emoting, "I declare, I never knew it to be so warm!"

Jake refused to pay the rent, the Tootle owners sued, Jake appeared in court and attempted to tell the jury what had been done to him. He was very funny in court, but somehow the jury, after having laughed at Jake's description of the scene, awarded Tootle almost $9,000.

Jake was stunned, but only for a moment. He charged toward the judge's bench, and his voice was a bellowing roar. Klein tried to head him off, and Jake told judge, jury, court, St. Jo, the Tootle staff what he thought of them. Tootle promptly sued for damages, but this time Klein kept Jake out of the picture, and the Shuberts were rid of the Tootles.

Jake's success was financially beneficial to the Shubert fortunes, but Lee's failures were not. By contract, they needed a large number of attractions to keep entertainment streaming into their theaters across the country. The counterbooking of the Erlanger group was a constant threat. The Shuberts needed hits, and Lee kept trying to supply them. And one other item was taking a larger and larger part of Lee's thinking: he wanted recognition not only as a commercial supplier of entertainment but as an artistic producer.

The Shubert attempts at straight plays had not been marked by either success or distinction. But Lee kept trying. A superstitious man, and not exactly a literate one, he was overwhelmed when Augustus Thomas approached him with a play called *The Witching Hour.* Thomas had offered the play to Frohman but Frohman thought that a play about telepathy, mesmerism, and the occult was too far out, and so, in Frohman's opinion, was Mr. Thomas. Frohman dropped it.

Shubert, enthralled with the extrasensory idea and wanting very much to prove that he was far more scientific than Frohman, bought the play. It was a hit, and it ran all season, but it did not get Lee Shubert the kind of reviews he wanted. One thing it did do for him: it showed that a drama could make as much money as a musical, and a drama didn't need a chorus, didn't need a composer, an orchestra (not then, at least) or fancy spectacular scenery. It was a good way to make a *dollar.* He would spend the rest of his life chasing the elusive artistic muse.

If Thomas paid off, others did not. He tried twice with a young actor turned director, Cecil B. De Mille, and he failed twice. When Mr. De Mille decided that film was his medium (by this time, we were seeing three-reel pictures—twenty-seven minutes on one subject), he could not persuade Lee Shubert to back his venture. Lee had beeen burned twice and was therefore twice educated.

To fulfill his booking contracts, Lee kept buying European plays. He preferred plays that had already been translated from one language to another, and preferably from the second into English. A German play, adapted for the French, and then adapted from the French into English was his dearest dream. "That way," he would say, "you get three great writers working on it before you even start, and it doesn't cost a cent."

In 1912, when the European operetta was in the doldrums, the Shuberts presented a little epic by Johann Strauss under the title *The Merry Countess*. It featured the Dolly Sisters, and was stolen from *Die Fledermaus*. It proved to be a hit, and the Shuberts tucked it away for later reference, after cashing in nicely. They had neglected to secure rights from the Strauss estate, and they were roundly sued by the widow. It was fortunate that she had not seen a *Fledermaus* featuring the Dolly Sisters. Instead of suing for mere piracy, she might have had a case in damages.

But despite all the foreign purchases, and despite the endless invitations to writers and stars, the two huge production empires—the Shuberts and the Syndicate—could not supply attractions and make money. In Ohio, Cox was getting restless. His partners the Shuberts, it seemed to him, were spending half their time in Europe, buying shows that weren't making a great deal of money here. Erlanger and Frohman were equally busy keeping Cunard happy. At Cox's invitation, new talks commenced.

Lee interrupted the discussions for a trip to England, where in righteous indignation he stated, "It was like I never left home. Every theater I visited, I heard American ragtime from *my* shows, and nobody asked me for permission or paid me for the use. I intend to put a stop to this kind of action. From now on, every Shubert production will be copyrighted in Europe." (His steal from *Die Fledermaus* was still running on Broadway.)

During Lee's absence, J.J. and Rhinock went to Cincinnati for meetings with Erlanger and Cox. They were working out the terms of a truce, which would bring order and peace (again) to the booking of shows and, it was devoutly hoped, money to the backers.

The disillusioned newspaper fraternity had now caught up with George Bernard Shaw's earlier appraisal—they recognized the Shuberts as a new syndicate, and the heroes were getting a tarnishing treatment. They played up a suit for fraud, $185,000 worth of fraud, launched against J.J. by the widow of an Iowa theater owner. They gave a great deal of attention to various other actions filed by Shubert "associates," demanding "fair accountings," and "proper percentages of profits."

But in Cincinnati the terms of the agreement were being hammered out, and for the second time the Syndicate and the Shuberts were joining forces. This time it was a far stronger Shubert army demanding its concessions.

Lee got back to New York in November of 1913, just in time to help draw the final agreement and to be party to the joint statement. The Shuberts and the Syndicate would exchange stars under contract to each organization. Shubert attractions would appear in Erlanger houses, and Erlanger shows would be presented in Shubert houses. No longer would there be rival bookings—no Shubert musical would provide the competition for a Syndicate musical, and no Syndicate drama would be booked against a Shubert drama. Instead, "The audience would have both varieties of entertainment to select from." And Lee pointed out that now a theater could be "cast" to the play it would house, just as accurately as an actor was cast. A play that worked best in an "intimate" house would be booked there, instead of into a large theater.

This was what was published. The newspapers hinted that another announcement could be expected shortly. With the agreement, there would be unused theaters in both camps. The sages of the press said that the Shuberts and the Syndicate would join in "a giant combine" to make films, films of plays they controlled, and these films would be distributed to the soon-to-be-available theaters. It made all kinds of sense, except that it wasn't true.

What was true was even more interesting. Erlanger and Lee Shubert were making "secret" deals with Keith on theater leases, and in addition, Lee was making deals, "secret" from Keith and Erlanger, with Loew! And he had his own plans about motion pictures. De Mille was making his first full-length feature. The demand for product was increasing daily. The longer form had come in, and the courts had ruled that copyright laws applied to films, and Lee Shubert saw dollars in old plays he controlled. Didn't he have copyrights?

The funniest part of the "binding agreement" between the warring factions was Lee's statement to the papers when he and Erlanger announced that all their houses in New York were now going to a three-dollar top, from the two-and-a-half that had prevailed. "Inter-booking has begun," said Shubert, "and it will discourage the opening of any more new theaters. Some old houses may be converted to other uses. Actors will perhaps get less, but they will work a longer season, so that in the end they will get more. Until now we have not been able to go ahead along the lines we have outlined. We were not quite sure, either of us, I imagine, that the other really meant business. But now we are all satisfied that each has the interest of the whole business at heart."

The actors started Equity immediately. Shubert had warned them.

And Willie Klein started new forms for contracts, carefully designed to circumvent the brand-new agreement so piously entered into.

Lee was a busy man at this time—busier than usual. He was arranging for the dedication of the Samuel S. Shubert Memorial Theater on 44th Street and the Alley. He referred to the new theater as "a temple of dramatic art," "a place of beauty and dedication," and he really meant what he said. An impressive number of notables were invited to a preview reception at the theater, prior to its official opening, and on the day they were received, Lee had a troublesome time reconciling "art," "dedication," and "beauty" with the headlines in the New York papers.

The Shuberts had presented a play, *The Lure*, a white slavery epic, with all the probing depth and sensitivity of a marked-down dime pulp novel. The city claimed the play was "lewd and immoral" and ordered it closed. Lee protested violently and vociferously. The play, he said, was a moral tract, preaching against a life of sin.

The preaching, one columnist remarked drily, was spelled out, lurid step by lurid step. Lee stated that the Police Commissioner himself had attended the play on opening night and enjoyed it. Despite the Shubert protests, the play was closed, but only temporarily. The presiding judge, McAdoo, had said flatly that the play was no moral tract, that it was designed purely to make money, and he was issuing orders to close it. Old faithful, Willie Klein, asked for an extension for twenty-four hours so that Samuel Untermyer, the Shubert "guest attorney," might be able to see it.

Instead, in a precedential ruling, the judge ordered the show closed until the entire grand jury could see it and rule on its suitability for public presentation.

Two days later, the prosecutor, the grand jury (twenty-three strong), Sam Untermyer, and Lee Shubert attended the eeriest performance of a play ever seen on Broadway. Buried in the darkness of the theater, an audience of twenty-six watched a complete presentation of *The Lure*. It was weird. Not a sound came from the audience—not a cough, not a sigh. For that matter, no verdict was forthcoming, either. They reserved judgment, sat the next day, listened to an impassioned Lee deliver a speech defending "freedom of expression," and remained unmoved. Sensing this, Lee, who had stated that "nothing could stop him in his fight for an artist's right to express himself," offered to have the objectionable scenes rewritten. The grand jury dropped the entire mess, and such is the value of notoriety that *The Lure*, recipient of all the scandalous publicity, attracted more customers than it normally would have. It passed the Shubert test of quality—it made money.

126

Meanwhile, on October 28, 1913, the Sam Shubert Theater opened with much fanfare, and with a success. It starred Sir Johnston Forbes-Robertson in *Anthony and Cleopatra*, and Lee basked in the spotlight. He had made Sam immortal on Broadway, in concrete and lights, with his picture in the lobby, and he had found a semipermanent home for the Shubert enterprises. In the floors above the theater, he set up Shubert headquarters—his own office in the turret on the corner, J.J. diagonally across from him. It is significant that the vault adjoined Lee's office.

The board of directors of the Stratford-on-Avon company provided some fireworks for the theatrical world when they announced the cancellation of plans to bring the troupe to the United States for a tour. "The level of the theatre in America," they said, "is far too low." The howls of protest could be heard clear across the Atlantic.

American producers, led by Frohman, whose talent for vituperation was unexcelled, defended their "art." Lee Shubert was more temperate, and came up with a typical Shubert summation. "The important question," he said seriously, "is—could they get a theater?" First things first.

He had his own surprise in store. Andrew Freedman and Untermyer were selling their stock in Shubert Theatrical to George Cox. They had done very well. Their relatively small investment was bought out for more than half a million dollars, and Rhinock's office in the new Shubert building took on added importance. Of all their various associates, partners, and backers, the Shuberts had narrowed it down to Cox and Rhinock. And Lee remarked when questioned about the sale, "No matter who sells any of our stock, I [*sic*] have a majority of it. There will be no change in the business policy of the Shubert firm."

Freedman and Untermyer retained their interest in the real estate end of the Shubert business but were separated from the theatrical ventures. It is interesting to speculate on the reasons behind the sale. Freedman and his associates in the building of the IRT subway in New York were facing a scandalous investigation. Untermyer was looking to a possible political career. Most important—the Shuberts had made so much money in the past few years they were looking forward to control of their own business, and not by owning majorities of stock in a tightly held corporation. They were looking forward to business without consultation. It suited their temperaments, and it would confine the decisions to two men—Lee and J.J.

Chapter Eight

There are and were five ways to make money out of the business called theater—five ways, that is, for a businessman who is an entrepreneur. Actors and playwrights and composers, set designers and directors and choreographers all drink from the financial mainstream that the audience supplies, but they are the raw material of the theater. The *business* of the art is to combine the creative talents and mold them into a machine that makes dollars.

The five ways need to be spelled out. Men make money out of show business by owning real estate—theatrical real estate which is leased at fixed fees, or percentages of the receipts, or combinations of both. Men also make money by finding a play and a cast, renting a theater, and hoping that the public likes the play and will buy a sufficient number of tickets to leave a surplus for the producer for a lot of weeks. A third moneymaking system is to have supplies that producers need to mount their plays—scenery, costumes, lights, the mechanical gadgets that help to create the illusion. (For some strange reason, there has seldom been a bankruptcy in this group. They are paid in cash, the risk is calculable, and they resemble the only perpetually solvent group at the race track, the feed store.) The fourth standard method of manufacturing income out of the theater is to "book a route." The Theater Guild does it today. You "line up" theaters in convenient large cities, and you supply them with attractions. If you are smart, you will collect from the theater *and* the producer. This was the core idea of the Syndicate and, of course, of the Shuberts.

The fifth dollar generator is the secret one—the unspoken evil, the ever-present undercover practice of ticket "scalping." There have been ticket brokers since the first gladiator got billing. There have usually been "understandings" between ticket broker and producer and theater owner, limiting the overcharge for the service rendered. In latter years, these fees have been pinned by law as a fixed charge set by the state or the city.

But when a show is "hot," when it's a sellout, a smash, a "hard ticket," there is no known way to control the price that a box-office man on the make, or a scalper, or even a legitimate broker will demand (and get) for his tickets. "Agreements" have been overlooked, the laws have been flouted. Lee Shubert used to say, "When the Stock Exchange puts a ceiling on AT&T, we will be able to enforce a ceiling on theater tickets."

This gouge, commonly called "ice," has plagued producers as long as there have been hit shows. They did not object to "ice" on moral grounds. Not at all. They resented the fact that *their* show was selling seats for two and three times the printed price, and none—repeat, none—of the extra money was coming to them. They fired box-office men, they tried to cut off the supply to brokers, they took action against "scalpers" hawking their tickets outside the theater. But the "ice" age never ended. It hasn't today. (The term "ice" has an interesting derivation. The unfortunate producer, when being short-changed, was likely to find that certain sums charged against his production were lumped under the heading Incidental Company Expenses—abbreviated for convenience to I.C.E., or ice.)

Now the Shuberts had put their fingers into the first four money-making methods with avaricious precocity. They owned and leased theaters, into which they booked their own productions or the shows of others, and they had a costume inventory, a set inventory (and even a shoe factory which compelled all dancers to buy their dancing shoes from the Shuberts). They made a profit on all except productions, where they took their percentage of flops and averaged out on hits.

But the ice they didn't get their share of! It galled the Shubert soul. They fought the scalpers, they tried to control the box-office personnel by putting Shubert relatives into the cages as soon as they could count, they threatened ticket brokers, and all to no avail. Finally, Lee came to a decision. If you can't lick them, then you join them.

Ray Comstock, an "independent" producer who was backed, booked, and controlled by the Shuberts, bought an interest in the Tyson Ticket Agency which, in addition to a main office, had stalls in the leading hotels in New York. It was a juicy item for the press, and J.J. vigorously denied any Shubert interest in the ticket office, but no one believed him.

Certainly, Erlanger didn't. The uneasy armistice was still in effect, but here was a new Shubert wrinkle. Erlanger announced that no Syndicate show would sell tickets to the Tyson agency "since it was only a front for the Shuberts."

New York's district attorney followed up with an announcement that his office was beginning an investigation of the ticket agencies. It was his intention to restrict the sale of theater tickets to theater box offices. Comstock, the man in the middle, remonstrated that he saw the investment in Tyson's as "a chance to make money." He went on to state that agencies were a convenience to the public and, as such, ought to be treated well instead of persecuted. Shubert shut Comstock up and, eager to keep the district attorney out of the picture, told the public that they, the producers, would "agree on ticket management. We will solve the problem ourselves."

The "ticket scandal" simmered down and vanished from the newspapers, for the time being. It would keep coming up, again and again; it became a kind of teething ring for young district attorneys—they would learn about ice, go into shock, serve subpoenas, conduct investigations, give interviews to the press, enjoy the headlines, make proposals, and become discouraged. A few weeks later, if a lover of the theater wanted two on the aisle, he couldn't find them at the box office, but he could get them at a broker's—or from "someone"—at a price. It made work for the *next* district attorney, and it still does.

Producers never really warm up to investigations of the "ticket situation," although they enthusiastically endorse them, and theater owners are even less eager. There is a reason. In every play contract and in every theater lease there is a cunning little clause touching on what is euphemistically known as the "house seats." These are blocks of seats, reserved for each performance for the producer, the theater owner, and in later years, the director and the star(s).

The "house seat" began as a courtesy. When the Shuberts first rented the Casino, it will be recalled, "a box, three nights a week," was reserved for the use of the Sires. The Sires undoubtedly hoped to sell them if the Shuberts had a hit. But from a courtesy, the "house seat" became a lucrative business. In some contracts, a producer "reserved" for the theater owner as many as seventy and more seats per performance, to be disposed of by the owner. These "house seats" are always in choice locations in the orchestra, and with a smash show, selling seventy tickets can make a profitable day's work. Very profitable if a $6 ticket goes for $25 or $40, with no tax to report.

In addition, the producer himself keeps a number of the house seats for his own use. If the producer is Jake Shubert, he hasn't enough friends to sit in two seats for more than one performance. What did he do with the rest of the tickets? Did they go to the brokers? Back to the box office? It may be presumed that they were not burned.

While Lee was fending off the district attorney in the Tyson case, Willie Klein was defending one of the more embarrassing Shubert lawsuits. Clyde Fitch, the fabulously successful American playwright, had been called in by Lee to adapt a play from the German which Lee had acquired. It was called *The Blue Mouse*, and Fitch's deal called for him to receive 30 percent of the profits as his royalty. Shortly after the deal was made, Lee came back to Fitch and pleaded poverty. His deal with the German authors gave them 50 percent of the profits as a royalty, and here he had given 30 percent to Fitch, leaving him, the

J.J. and Family. During a truce.

producer, with a mere 20 percent as his share. It wasn't fair. Since the play looked pretty good, Fitch quickly agreed to split it with Lee, each taking 50 percent of the net profit. The German team was not paid, and Fitch died in 1909, and he was not paid. The play was a huge money maker.

The Fitch estate brought suit for their share of the profits, and in the course of putting his case together, the Fitch attorney made a startling discovery. Before the show ever opened, and while Fitch was still pledged 30 percent, the Shuberts had bought out the Germans for a small cash payment, plus 3 percent of the gross. Lee had neglected to inform Fitch, and now the estate asked for $50,000, plus interest. It was settled—out of court.

In the spring of 1914 Lee had sailed to Europe to secure properties and, on his return, held a press conference. He announced more than fifty projects in various stages of work, the proudest being the production of *Pygmalion*, starring Mrs. Patrick Campbell.

The press was interested in motion pictures. Were the Shuberts going to enter the burgeoning field? No comment. Was it true that Brady and the Shuberts were taking over World Films? No comment. Did the Shuberts have an interest in World Films? Yes, they had an "interest" in the company. No, there were no plans for changing its name to Shubert Theatrical Films, Incorporated.

Weren't the Shuberts and Cox and Rhinock planning a $2,000,000 film company? "Where would I find two million dollars?" He closed the interview with that one.

With Lee back, Jake could become Continental again. In one last attempt to solidify his marriage, Jake took Catherine and young John, aged seven, to Europe with him. The brothers never were out of the country at the same time, and from the time of Sam's death they never traveled on the same vehicle—train or boat or plane. Theirs was a huge business by this time, and someone was always minding the store.

It wasn't J.J.'s fault, but their trip to Europe was interrupted by the outbreak of World War I. J.J. brought his family home from Europe, together with some European artists for his various new productions. And the war would present new problems for the brothers, and for show business. It wasn't our war yet, but its effect was felt in the box office. Business was down. The new season got off to a limping start, and Lee stated, as he would always state, "A hit show will make money. So-so shows will no longer be able to survive." And he watched Keith and Albee use the excuse of bad business to cut back vaudeville salaries and wondered if he could apply it to the contracts for his "legitimate" shows.

With the business slump, it seemed appropriate for the "arrangement" between the Syndicate and the brothers to be amplified. The road reflected the general national slowdown at the box office, and in a joint statement, the rulers of theater explained that because of the success of the joint effort in Boston, St. Louis, Philadelphia, and Chicago, it had been agreed to extend the agreement to cover the rest of the nation, except for New York. In this new phase, London and Paris would also come under the agreement. Willie Klein trumpeted gleefully that now both sides "could close unprofitable houses," and with the war on, "tying up England will be easy."

It meant that about 99 percent of the legitimate theater in the United States, exclusive of the island of Manhattan, would be "controlled." Would the Shuberts book? Or would the booking be done by Klaw and Erlanger? The rumors flew thick and fast, and the smart money predicted that a new office would be formed, very much like Keith's invention, the United Booking Office, to book the entire country and to be jointly controlled by the brothers and Erlanger. Peace reigned, and George Cox smiled. It was January, in 1915, a very ironic moment. The need for efficiency and economy, which had first given rise to the Syndicate and which had just as logically created its rival, the Shuberts, now was cementing the marriage between them. Mergers make strange bedfellows.

All of this had fallen to Lee to negotiate. J.J. was busy. He had celebrated his return to this country by beginning seven productions. Sigmund Romberg, who turned out music in absolutely unbelievable quantity, had written his first operetta, *The Blue Paradise*, for the Casino, and also had added a few new members for his *Passing Show of 1914*, still running at the Winter Garden. Jake had other fish to fry, and one of them was the Hippodrome, more or less left to the guardianship of Voegtlin, Wilson, and Manny Klein.

The Winter Garden roof extravaganza, under Jake, was to open on the Saturday night that the Hippodrome would present its new attraction, and they both paralleled the final preparations for *Blue Paradise*. Jake was a harried man. He was giving the Winter Garden rehearsal his personal touch when he suddenly decided he needed a larger pit orchestra. It was Thursday afternoon before Saturday night opening, and he sent an emissary over to the Hippodrome, to "borrow four trumpets and four drums."

The Hippodrome, undoubtedly the most complicated theater in

133

Winter Garden Program. Typical of the covers of the time; this one was for Jake's *Artists and Models.*

J.J. Took Two by K.O., One by Default. Manny Klein, at the piano, Arthur Voegtlin and R. H. Burnside, the creative team at the Hippodrome and sometimes J.J.'s sparring partners. Wilson was decked by J.J.; Burnside missed all the fun.

the world in terms of production problems, lighting spectaculars, cast size and backstage-crew complexity, was enjoying its own madhouse when Jake's message arrived. Wilson, the stage director, a calm and courteous man, told the messenger to tell Mr. Shubert "we can't spare the instruments."

On Friday, with the deadline looming ahead and the frenzy mounting at the Hippodrome as well as at the Winter Garden, the same errand was assigned by Jake to his "runner." Four drums and four trumpets. Wilson was a bit more brusque this time, as he watched Voegtlin trying to bring a semblance of order into a chorus of two hundred and a set that was supposed to rotate and become a Siamese temple. "We can't spare the instruments," he said in a strangled voice. "Tell Mr. Shubert that we just can't spare them."

Saturday evening, Voegtlin, Wilson, and Manny Klein, each attired in crisp evening clothes for the opening, were surveying their domain, satisfied that after a sleepless night and a rehearsal-filled day, they had a show. They were surprised to see J.J., a sartorial vision in evening suit, stride forcefully into the Hippodrome, followed by three teamsters. J.J. ignored their greetings, and as the three "creative heads" of the Hippodrome followed him in curiosity, J.J. bounced down the aisle to the orchestra pit. While the three men watched him in bewilderment, he slowly walked across the arc of the pit, counting the instruments. He turned to the three truckers, and pointing at four trumpets and four drums, Jake barked, "Them! Take them to the Winter Garden!" Aghast, Voegtlin rushed to Jake's side. "Mr. Shubert," he said, "you can't do this! The orchestrations! The effects! Everything is ready for tonight."

Jake fixed him with a bloodshot blue eye. "What did you say?" he roared. "Whose theater is this?"

"Yours," said Voegtlin. "But we— You just can't do this!"

Jake wheeled on him. "If it's my theater, I will—well, do what I want—take the God-damned drums and horns."

"But you can't," began Voegtlin, and he got no further, as Jake hit him. Voegtlin fell back, Jake slugged him again, and grabbing the dazed artistic-director-and-general-manager, he dragged him to the door, where he casually tossed him out. "And keep him out!" he ordered the guard.

Wilson, who had followed this incredible scene helplessly, now flared. "You can't do that to Mr. Voegtlin," he said in anger. "And I am not going to have him . . ." And that's where Jake ended Mr. Wilson's declaration. Checked by a short hook, and propelled by Jake, Mr. Wilson joined Voegtlin in the alley.

At this point, Jake was a bellowing bull. He bore down on little Manny Klein. "You got something to say?" Jake demanded. "You maybe got two cents you want to put in?" Klein, a pianist-composer, careful about his hands, placed them behind his back and said mildly, "You can't do it, Mr. Shubert," and before Jake could react, Klein walked quickly to the door, nodded politely to the guard who opened the door, and Klein joined his fellows of the artistic department of the Hippodrome. J.J. shrugged and motioned to the three awed truckers, and supervised them in the loading of *his* instruments. As he started back for the Winter Garden, he called to the dumbstruck guard, "And the bastards stay out! Hear me?"

Both shows opened, both were well received. Ziegfeld welcomed the exiled trio, and they never worked for the Shuberts again. J.J. never understood this.

It was a belligerent month for Jake. Shortly after their return from Europe, he and Catherine had argued again, and he had taken his own quarters, leaving her to barricade herself once more in the Riverside Drive fortress. Not long after the Hippodrome contretemps, Jake decided to come calling on his wife, and she didn't want to see him. He forced his way into the apartment and began his strident vocal abuse. Catherine and young John cowered in the living room, and the superintendent, attracted by the clamor, arrived with the doorman. Jake began to drive them out, and in the course of the argument, they forcibly imprisoned him in a bedroom until he calmed down. When Catherine attempted to plead with him not to frighten the boy, Jake had shrilled, "He ain't my kid! You know it damned well. I ain't the father! Don't use that crap with me!" John was nine years old when he heard the accusation.

It was a time of war in Europe, and a time of war for the brothers Shubert. No sooner had Jake declared his son a bastard, than Erlanger called all the Shuberts bastards. Dramatically, he called off all agreements, proclaimed various and sundry legal actions to be immediately forthcoming, and publicly stated that the Shuberts had broken their word, had stolen money from him, had issued fraudulent statements, and that he and his associates were determined to crush the brothers, once and for all. It was a tired litany, he had said it before, but this time he meant it more than ever before.

What had brought about the crisis was Erlanger's discovery that in making his "peace" with the Shuberts, he had been taken again. Under the terms of the agreement, all Erlanger attractions playing Shubert houses were to receive 60 percent of the gross, and all Shubert attractions playing Erlanger houses were to get the same percentage.

All other managers would get a 50 percent split. This had been the percentage arrangement from the beginning.

But now Erlanger found that whereas the Syndicate enjoyed participation in only a few of their attractions, the Shuberts had an owner-interest in almost every show produced by their allied managers. Thus, the Shuberts were sharing income in many, many shows that were presumably booked by the pool agreement, and they were getting money that they didn't have to share with their "partners" in the pool. This was not a situation which Erlanger proposed to live with, and at the same time he did not want to publicly confess that he had signed so one-sided an agreement—one-sided against him. He chose instead to attack, with accusations of fraud, false returns, and so on.

So, the war was on again, and in higher gear than ever. But things had changed. The underdog Shuberts were no longer the underdogs. Time had been creeping up on the Syndicate owners. Erlanger was fifty-five, Klaw almost sixty. Hayman was dead. And within a few months of the resumption of hostilities, Frohman, the key producer in the Syndicate ranks, would die on the *Lusitania*. It was the Shuberts who were surging ahead, with the momentum of youth and the impetus of endless ambition. The Syndicate was a little tired, a little worn—a weary old champion tossed in with a lusty young challenger. This time, it was almost no contest.

Repercussions in show business were immediate. Actors' Equity already concerned with the show-business slump and its effect on actors' earnings, sought to strengthen its position by affiliation with the A.F.L. The producers, despite the schism in their own ranks, united to fight the threat.

To recapitulate, the Shuberts were now engaged in a great number of battles. Lee was fighting Jake; Jake was fighting Lee, Catherine, and everyone else; Willie Klein had some thirty legal cases on the active file; collectively the brothers were fighting the Syndicate, George M. Cohan *and* the actors; and this was the time they chose to take on the *New York Times* and its drama critic, Alexander Woollcott.

In the hullabaloo of the moves and countermoves of the Woollcott case, of consultant attorneys, important comment, and the usual hoopla which accompanies legal circuses, the fruits of Jake's left hook were reaped. The Hippodrome, which had lost its creative leadership, was given up by the Shuberts and taken over by Dillingham. Lee was philosophic—business had been off, anyway.

The Woollcott affair got almost as much space in the national press as another "incident" taking place at the same time—World War I. It all began with a play called *Taking Chances*—in the light of what happened, a prophetic title. It seems fairly obvious now, with hindsight, that the Shuberts were not at all confident of the success of the play. They took ads in fifteen newspapers, *before the opening*, to advise the public: "Don't pay any attention to the reviewers." *Taking Chances* opened that night.

The reviews broke down to good—one; noncommittal—six; bad—eight.

The "good" came from the Shubert house organ, *The New York Review*. Among the eight roasts was Woollcott's in the *Times*. The Shuberts barred Woollcott from all Shubert theaters. And the *Times* was not about to accept the Shubert suggestion that Woollcott be replaced or else. Woollcott, with the paper's approval, filed for an injunction against the Shuberts to prevent them from barring him. Interestingly, on the day the injunction was served, Woollcott gave a rave review to an all-star revival of *Trilby*, produced by the Shuberts at the Sam S. Shubert Theater. That was the same day that the *Times* informed the Shubert office that their ads would no longer be accepted by the paper, as of April 4, 1915.

It fanned into a national issue. Every newspaper saw a threat to its right to editorial freedom. In court, Max Steuer, for the Shuberts, attacked Woollcott as personally biased and young, alleging that Woollcott was engaged in a vendetta, for his own reasons, against this estimable theatrical house. He cited hostile reviews to prove his point.

The next day, the *Times* attorney cited Woollcott reviews favorable to the Shuberts. While the court was listening to the arguments, the New York State Legislature saw a bill introduced under the heading "Drama Critics Protection Bill." The Shuberts, by this time politically powerful, sent J. J. to Albany, where, flanked by Syracuse and New York City solons, he had the bill killed. The court reserved its decision, but eleven days after it began, the ruling was announced: Woollcott won. On that same day, the *Lusitania* went down; among those lost, Charles Frohman, ace producer of the Syndicate.

The Shuberts had thirty days in which to file an appeal, and it took them only twenty to retain another lawyer, Charles Tuttle, to handle the appeal. The clamor nationally increased; editorials were written about the sanctity of free criticism and free editorial policy. The Shuberts were villains. Lee, ever practical, had begun to regret the entire Woollcott fiasco; but he was committed. Finally, the court of appeals announced its verdict: the lower court was reversed, the Shuberts were declared the victors. The court decided that the Fourteenth Amendment was not involved, since in the opinion of the court no civil right had been abrogated. (If Woollcott had been a Negro, the court might have ruled otherwise!) In effect, the court had ruled that a theater was private property, and the owners of same could seat or not seat according to their wishes. Woollcott announced now that *he* would appeal.

The Harvard Law Review wrote a treatise on the case, indicating that, in their opinion, Woollcott was morally right and might have been legally right, but that he had taken the wrong route by law in making his case.

And Lee Shubert, weary of the whole thing, personally notified the *New York Times* that Alexander Woollcott was completely acceptable to the Shuberts as a critic.

Despite victory, J.J. was unmollified. Seemingly, he liked to time his own assaults with history. World War I had sparked a series of fistic triumphs for Jake, and now that Black Jack Pershing was leading our forces against Villa in Mexico, Jake got himself into another scrape.

He had a new musical production in New Haven, at the new ShuBert Theater there, and had motored up for the opening. After the show, a young Yale undergraduate, Hartley, approached Miss Nancy G. Williams, a member of the Shubert chorus, and tried to engage her in conversation. Perhaps he wanted her to join his fraternity, or perhaps he was a predecessor of the Welcome Wagon. In any event, J.J., crossing the lobby toward Miss Williams, in whom he had more than a passing interest, took umbrage at Mr. Hartley and his intentions. Words led to words, and Jake hit him. Jake's tactics were such that Mr. Hartley's course in self-defense at Yale left him defenseless; Jake pummeled the young man into a convenient sofa and left the hotel, accompanied by Miss Williams.

Hartley's friends followed the pair and had Jake arrested. The house manager and the Shuberts' New Haven lawyer arranged bail, and Jake was released, to rejoin Miss Williams.

For Catherine, this was the final straw. On J.J.'s return to New York, an acrimonious confrontation took place, and Jake, the apotheosis of gentlemanliness, took space in the Public Notice column of the *Times*, telling one and all he would not be responsible for debts in the name of Mrs. Jacob J. Shubert, nor would he be responsible for goods delivered to Mrs. Shubert's address.

This last was really a dirty trick, since Catherine had only recently ordered new furnishings from W. & J. Sloane, and with Jake's notice, Sloane refused delivery. Catherine lost her Irish temper, filed two lawsuits on the same day. The first was against Jake, and the second against Sloane. Her suit against Jake accused him of desertion, and multiple adulteries, with three women named specifically, Miss Williams among them. She assessed Jake's wealth as more than a million and demanded her fair share for herself and their child.

Jake filed a countersuit, Willie Klein doing the filing, and this time against his better judgment. In his countersuit, Jake reiterated the charge that John J. Shubert was not his child. Willie Klein finally prevailed upon Jake to let him arrange an amicable settlement with Catherine.

While Jake was fighting his multi-fronted personal war, Lee carried on for the brothers. Belasco and Daniel Frohman stated that it "was undignified for actors to join 'labor.'" Lee went one step further; he insisted on following Keith's lead and referred to Equity as a social club. "It means nothing to me," said Lee, "how many clubs or organizations the actors have. I will run my business, and they can run theirs and have all the societies they wish. I am violently against a union of actors. If they go through with this foolish plan, I will turn my theaters into movie houses."

To make sure he would have more than enough theaters to convert, he bought the Astor Theater, bringing the New York City total to twelve Shubert houses; it would be fourteen when construction was completed on the two already under way. Lee also whistled loudly in the dark. "I and my brother have confidence in the theater-ticket buyer. Our new season will be bigger than ever. We will have more shows on tour than ever before, and with the fine-quality shows we will bring, the road will be very good."

The Shubert "luck" was still there. The first reactions to the war boom were being felt in America. This was the eve of our own entrance into the hostilities, production was increasing, money was getting freer, the Shuberts were going to cash in on their renewed anti-Erlanger attitude. The watchword for the theater was "war," and the Shuberts interjected "patriotic" and "war" sketches in their numerous revues (at the Winter Garden, Jake did a Salome sketch, with the head of the Kaiser substituted for that of John the Baptist!) and even their musical comedies, part of their "quality" presentations for the year, were based on war plots.

Jake not only produced, he directed *Her Soldier Boy*, a silly operetta about a soldier presumed dead, who had not seen his mother for fifteen years. The "dead man's" best friend comes to bring the sad news to the mother, learns that Mama has a weak heart, and poses as the long-absent son. Naturally, he falls in love with the sister, who has strong emotions about *him* but rejects incest as a love theme. At long, long last, brother is found on the battlefield, un-dead in time for a clinch and a playoff. J.J. milked it for every drop of schmaltz and cried during rehearsals when mother and son were reunited. It was a dreadful play.

Not to be outdone, Lee produced, although he did not direct, an equally silly musical, *Love O' Mike*, with songs by Jerome Kern. Mike is really Sir Michael Kildare, who falls in live with the fair maiden. But she can love only a real, honest-to-goodness hero. After much plodding plot, during which Mike stages a fake fire so that he can perform a fake rescue, it turns out that he is a fourteen-carat war hero, and his Victoria Cross wins the girl.

It was typical of the kind of play the 1916–1917 audience could watch. The chorus girls always had one number, à la 1898, in which one or more was wrapped in the flag, and all sang a rousing patriotic number. The difference was not in the brothers' patriotism but in the size of the flag. Under J.J.'s guidance, the flags were smaller, although the girls were the same size. It was the era of "A Rose That Grows in No-Man's Land," of "Tipperary," of "Long, Long Trail A-Winding."

The most spectacular Shubert production of the year was never seen by the public. It was staged by Willie Klein. In October he persuaded Catherine Shubert to drop her divorce suit against Jake, and Klein told the papers that Mr. and Mrs. Shubert "had agreed on a division of effects." In nonlegal language, this meant that Catherine got the furniture from Sloane's, and Jake paid for it.

In February of 1917 Klein and Catherine showed up in Buffalo, where, on a Saturday morning, the New York State Supreme Court awarded Catherine a divorce. The grounds were adultery, and Catherine named only one girl. Willie Klein had done a good job. Catherine could have named a hundred.

The terms of the divorce settlement were not made public, and the papers were sealed. It is most unusual for supreme court sessions to be held on a Saturday; it is even more unusual for two residents of New York City to receive a New York State divorce in Buffalo; and most divorce cases do not conclude with sealed records. But Klein had arranged it, and the growing Shubert "muscle" in New York had bulled it through.

Under the agreement, Catherine received $100,000, to be paid to her at the rate of $7,500 per year. It was not a generous settlement for a man of J.J.'s wealth, but no one ever accused J.J. of being a generous man.

Soon after, his wife and rejected son moved to a small house in Long Branch, New Jersey, and the boy was enrolled in a private Catholic school. That took more money than the $7,500 allowed, and Catherine asked J.J. to assume the costs. He didn't bother to reply. J.J.

141

For Those under 24. Ed Wynn. The great comedian, aged thirty, and an unidentified show girl in a bit from *The Passing Show of 1916*.

was a good hater, and right at the moment he was hating Catherine. When she found out that one of her son's classes was in ballet (the bulk of the students were girls), she withdrew him at once, stating that no child of hers was going to become a fairy. It was the first in a series of short-term school stays for young John. It would leave its mark.

It had been a trying year again for Willie Klein. As the Shubert empire grew, so did the litigations multiply. His value to the brothers cannot be estimated. Not only did he fight their legal battles, but he also managed their contracts, negotiated them in and out of theater leases, helped smother some of their scandals, used every device of a devious man to further Shubert interests and, as a by-product, created a large part of today's theatrical law. He was small in size, but a titan for the Shuberts, and as tough and ruthless as if he had been born into the line. He was not an originator or an architect for them, but a tremendous administrative and legal force.

While J.J. was getting his personal life in some sort of order, and producing his endless stream of operettas, musicals, and revues, Lee was planning the largest theatrical purchase in history. In October of 1916 George Cox had died in Cincinnati, leaving a large estate and a crippled political machine. His widow was the executrix, and the brothers Shubert found a new problem in the administration of their affairs.

Rhinock, whose office adjoined Lee's, was on hand for consultation and quick decision. But the other major "outside" shareholder in Shubert enterprises was the elderly widow in Cincinnati with almost no knowledge of the affairs that had made her husband one of America's richest men. It was awkward for business and particularly trying for Lee, who in any negotiation would listen and listen and stall and stall until he felt it was time to move—then Lee liked to move quickly and dynamically. (One theory was that by listening so long, he felt he might not have to face a problem, and thus be saved from the need of making a decision. This might have been true in regard to a play, where Lee really never was sure, but not in real estate, where he almost always was.)

Lee determined to buy out the Cox holdings. Cox was the largest single theatrical-property holder in the world. Virtually every major city had one or more theaters owned by Cox, either as an individual or in association with others. In addition, he was a sizable participant in the Shubert holdings.

In July of 1917 the brothers Shubert, with Rhinock picking up part of the obligation, bought out the Cox estate. It was a gigantic financial deal—as stated before, the largest in theatrical history—going as high as an estimated eight figures. It definitely made the theater a Shubert business. In twenty short years they had assembled the dominant theatrical empire in the United States, and in the world. In a short time, forty major American theatrical producers would be booked exclusively by the Shuberts, ending once and for all the "rivalry" with the Syndicate. In addition, the Shubert brothers—these two strange young men from Russia, by way of Syracuse—would personally produce more plays than any office in history. And from Lee's seat, he had achieved the one most important result. The business was controlled by *him*.

The United States had been at war a few short months when the Cox purchase was accomplished, and where others might have taken time to digest the huge purchase, Lee kept adding houses in New York, by purchase and by construction. "People want to be amused," said Lee in the *New York Times* on November 4, 1917. "And the amusement center, I believe, is fixed for many years to come in New York . . . Times Square. But it is expanding northward, and in the next few years, I believe more theaters will be seen from 45th Street to 59th Street. The great theatrical artery will be Broadway."

He was a pretty good prophet, and unlike most such seers Lee Shubert had the money to make sure it happened as predicted. He had just about "cornered" the theater holdings on 44th and 45th streets, and he himself was pushing north when he announced the construction of the Apollo, the twenty-first Shubert theater on Manhattan Island, to be built at the southwest corner of Broadway and 47th Street.

Three weeks later, disturbed by a slump in box-office receipts and intensive Liberty Loan drives from Washington, Shubert betrayed the enormous naïveté he was capable of when it came to matters nontheatrical or nonfinancial. His philosophy on the war was issued in an interview with the *New York Times*, and it sums up Lee's awareness of the world outside Shubert Alley.

> There is a slump in the theatrical business and it is due to false issues that have been raised in Washington and our daily newspapers. While there is a need for conservation of food, coal and other supplies, there is no reason why legitimate industries should be paralyzed. Theatrical enterprise represents capital. Without capital, the nation would be in a sorry plight. [*He actually said it!*] Capital supports labor and gives employment to the nation's workers. If the industries representing capital are crippled, the government will soon feel their loss. Business should be kept at high pressure. The public should be discouraged from hoarding their money. Money hoarded in banks does the government no good . . . it is false economy to cripple industries that are supporting the nation. I am in favor of the conservation of foodstuffs

and other vital resources, but I firmly believe the public should patronize the theaters, for in doing this, not only are they enjoying excellent entertainment, but they are assisting capital in supporting the government. . . .

Translated into the vernacular, it is the honest credo of a dedicated man —dedicated to making money out of the theater. It is the statement of a man who never voted in an election in his life, who never discussed politics except as it affected his business and his dollars. Lee Shubert hated anything which promised inflation, he hated anything which kept people out of *his* theaters, and he hated anything which made his job of theater running more difficult. So, it would soon be easy for him to hate Actors' Equity.

Right now, as 1917 drew near its end, he could luxuriate in not hating Erlanger. Lee couldn't be bothered. The peace that Cox had engineered was being ignored by both parties, but contracts still existed, financial arrangements still were binding.

Early in December, in Philadelphia, Erlanger filed for an injunction restraining the Shuberts from playing first-class attractions at either the Chestnut Street Opera House or the new Shubert at Broad and Locust. Under the Cox truce, first-class attractions could be booked only at the Adelphi or Lyric theaters operated by the Shuberts.

The Shuberts countered by tersely announcing the severing of *all* booking and pooling arrangements in Chicago, Philadelphia, Boston, Baltimore, and St. Louis. J.J. vindictively added that the reason for this action was not the Philadelphia suit. Their contract with the Syndicate called for financial settlements to be made the first day of every February and August. No settlement had been made, no statements had been received. Therefore, the Shuberts were ending the relationship.

Klaw replied that the statements and settlements were all prepared. But they would not be issued. A Shubert accountant in Chicago had brought charges against the Shuberts, claiming fraud. "The Messrs. Shubert," said Klaw, "almost before the ink was dry upon the original contracts began evading and violating their obligations." Klaw went on to suggest that the Shuberts kept two kinds of books, theirs and their partners'. It is a charge that would be leveled again and again at the good brothers.

This time, Klaw announced that they were filing suit for an accounting in Chicago—to begin with, "since he had reason to suspect the accounts were not 'truly' kept." Lee fired back a countersuit, demanding an accounting from Klaw and Erlanger, and added a penalty suit for default on the 1917 settlements, the ones held back by Erlanger.

The World War was going on, but for the brothers Shubert it

145

The Exquisite Miss Peggy Wood. As ingénue lead in the original Shubert production of *Maytime*. Three decades later, she charmed a new generation as the star of TV's *I Remember Mama*.

was merely something that required occasional benefits and donations, made coal hard to get, presented unfair competition with shows like *Yip, Yip, Yaphank* booked into a non-Shubert theater, and made travel more arduous. They grew very fat.

Jake had come up with another smash hit, *Maytime*, from Romberg's pen. Romberg, who seemed to write tunes without effort, had determined to concentrate on operettas after the success of *Blue Paradise*. He had left the Shuberts to make it on his own, and over J. J.'s never-polite protests. He had two flops, and J. J. approached him with a highly improbable German operetta. Romberg, starved for an outlet for the Viennese melodies that had been bubbling in his Hungarian head, really let himself go with *Maytime*, and he turned out a lovely, lovely score. *Maytime* became one of the all-time operetta hits on Broadway—so successful that a second company was opened to play at the 44th Street Theater, in addition to the original company at the Shubert. This is the only time two companies performing the same play ran simultaneously on Broadway.

Less than one year later the indefatigable Romberg wrote *Sinbad* for Jolson and J.J.! This was another Jolson extravaganza at the Winter Garden, and like all of Jake's shows there, works of other composers were interpolated into the show, although Romberg had ten tunes in the production. Four of the interpolated numbers became all-time hits. "Swanee," "Rock-a-Bye Your Baby with a Dixie Melody," "Chloe," and "Mammy" became a lasting part of the Jolson repertoire and earned a permanent place in the American musical scene.

Who picked the songs? Who "found" Romberg? Who was responsible for the success of these various Shubert ventures? If Jake is to be excoriated for his lack of taste, lambasted for his vulgarity, slugged for his deficiencies, then perhaps it is only just to credit him for his triumphs. Perhaps he didn't discover Romberg, or find the tunes, or latch on to the comic. Perhaps it was his kitchen cabinet of talented hetero- and homo-sexuals who sold Jake on the talents of the people he employed. But they did happen in Jake's shows. And if Jake wasn't musical, if he couldn't sing the song—by God, he hummed well.

Lee, on the other hand, was stone tone-deaf. He could not, as one composer said, "carry a tune in a brief case." Many was the time that Lee would inform director and composer, "Right here, we need a good song. Something like . . ." and then he would begin to hum in an awesomely monotonous chant a series of high-pitched grunts. He did this for more than ten years, desperately instructing his associates in the musical art and never achieving communication. In 1930 Herman Hupfeld had a tune in a non-Shubert production. It was "Sing Something

147

Jolie. Al Jolson with show girl Hazel Cox, in the Shuberts' *Sinbad*, 1919. Three popular classics came from this show: "Mammy," "Swanee" and "Rock-A-Bye Your Baby with A Dixie Melody."

Simple," and when the tune became a hit, a group of stunned theatrical talents stared at each other and muttered, "That's Lee's song." It was the tune he had been repeating so long. But Lee never recognized it. For twenty years after "Sing Something Simple," Lee Shubert would beg composers to write a tune that went like this . . . and then would come the muezzin's lament, "Sing Something Simple" without melody. It was Lee's song.

So the brothers Shubert buried themselves in their business and their productions, with various assignations during and after business hours. And together they watched the money grow. There were minor setbacks, like lawsuits. And annoyances like the government, which wanted to raise the admission tax from 10 to 20 percent for the wartime emergency. The theatrical managers rose unanimously to fight this. They threatened to close their theaters; they were just not about to become twice as patriotic as they had been before. Lee Shubert, number-one man in the theatrical world, solemnly served warning on President Wilson. People would be priced out of the theater, said Lee. They would be forced into the motion-picture houses and the vaudeville shows, since they were in dire need of entertainment. These cheaper forms, said Lee, would cost the government needed money. "Twenty percent of a fifty-cent ticket," said Lee, "is a dime. But ten percent of a two-dollar ticket for the theater is twenty cents. Does the government want to lose money and drive us out of business besides?" The government didn't.

As he was threatening to go out of business, Lee expressed his faith in America's future by acquiring the Boston Opera House, plus an interest in the three Selwyn theaters in Manhattan. The Opera House purchase started the rumor that J.J. was about to embark on a grand opera production schedule—a rumor J.J. encouraged. It brought terror to the hearts of opera lovers.

Lee refused to comment. He was very busy, this czar of the American stage. He was running an empire, spinning large dreams, working eighteen hours a day, and worrying about a strange occurrence. Lee Shubert had fallen in love.

Chapter Nine

It would seem that the Shuberts followed a pattern when they fell in love—they might mention what had happened to others, but invariably they neglected to inform the female involved. Sam had never told Julia Sanderson, although he had confided in various intimates; Jake never bothered with the emotion; and when Lee found himself enamored, he, like Sam, shyly confessed his state to associates, but somehow he never got around to telling Justine Johnstone.

Miss Johnstone was one of the most beautiful women in the world. Blonde, shapely, breathtakingly arresting, she had graced a number of Ziegfeld productions, had starred in her own shows, headed the Justine Johnstone Girls, and broken the hearts of any number of New York's most eligible men. Broadway paraded a great many beauties in those palmy days, but if there was a queen, it was Justine.

And Lee had met her, and Lee had tumbled. Broadway's leading holdout bachelor had fallen. It was a brand-new sensation, and Lee had no idea how to cope with it. Feeling protective, tender—wanting to give and to cherish—well, Lee had felt that way about Sam. He assumed that he "ought to" take care of his sisters and their offspring, and the men they married. (God knows he didn't have to take care of Jake.) But why should he suddenly feel *this* way about an absolute stranger? It puzzled him. Another thing that puzzled him was how one went about doing something about it.

It was not that he was inexperienced. There is no official tally, but Lee enjoyed a well-earned reputation as an active bedroom athlete. His relationships with girls had been simple. If there was any complication, the relationship had been negotiable. And, at negotiation, he had no peer.

But acting like a suitor was a startling new experience, and Lee didn't know how to begin. For an opener he decided to produce a play, starring Miss Johnstone.

It was a wartime revue, labeled *Over the Top*, with a built-in salute to the American public which had gone "over the top" in the war effort. It starred Miss Johnstone and the Justine Johnstone Girls, marked the Broadway debut of a brother-sister dancing team called the Astaires, and opened at the 44th Street Roof Theater, which, logically enough, was on the roof of the 44th Street Theater (now the site of the *New York Times*).

From the beginning, it was Lee's production, although it was another in the long and undistinguished line of the "Messrs. Shubert

Justine Johnstone. Lee never told her he loved her.

Present." He had the bandbox theater redecorated for the opening, and much time and money were spent on the star's dressing room.

Lee, approaching forty-five, admitted to forty-one. (He would lop off additional years as the fancy struck him.) Short, sallow-complexioned, with piercing black eyes, coal-black hair, he was a slender, dapper Broadway figure. The King of Broadway had found his toga—a dark suit, the vest with white satin lining and piping, small pointed shoes and a round black derby.

Johnstone was barely twenty, the toast of New York, and to her, Lee Shubert was a Broadway producer who wanted to star her in a show, and someone to be disabused of any other ideas. Like everyone else in the business, she had heard the legends of Shubert niggardliness, Shubert contracts, Shubert chiseling, Shubert arrogance toward actors, Shubert Shubertism. Wary, cautious, she found herself completely disarmed by the most cooperative producer she had ever known. Her dressing room was perfect; her every comment about a costume was translated into instant needlework; her criticism of a musical number called for a new tune or a rewrite; her suggestions on production had the set builders on the ready—it was red-carpet treatment.

Miss Johnstone had little time to ponder the superstar handling because everywhere she turned, there was Lee Shubert. Lee, whose cash-register mentality had made him eager to do small, tight dramas (ah, the money that could be saved on costumes and chorus girls!) and who had never had sufficient time (or talent) to give them the love and attention such presentations required, now enveloped *Over the Top* with his presence. Romberg had done a "jazz" score, somehow finding inspiration and sheer hours in between writing *Maytime* and *Sinbad*, and from the first day of rehearsal Lee danced attendance. He was at readings, he sat through rehearsals, he was a constant visitor in Miss Johnstone's dressing room, took her to dinner after the day's work, drove her home. He discussed the props, tried to conceal his distaste for woman suffrage, which she devoutly espoused, he made plans for the after-the-curtain "Little Club," which was part of the show's gimmick, and spent the bulk of his time feeling frustrated. He just didn't know how to get to the next step.

Here he was, the Sultan of Show Business, the entrepreneur of a thousand assignations, behaving like a tongue-tied, calf-eyed sophomore. One night, over supper, he blurted, "Justine, you ought to get out of the business."

Since the show had opened to only lukewarm notices, she interpreted it as a criticism. "Is my work that bad?"

He hastily reassured her that it wasn't her work he was thinking about. "You ought to get out of the business because you don't belong; you were put together missing things."

She tried to be light. "I thought I was complete. What is it you think I lack, Lee?"

He stared at her out of his coal-black eyes. "Greed," he said in his soft voice.

"Greed?"

"That's what makes the world go 'round," said Shubert, leaning forward in his chair, his high voice purposeful and hard. "Greed. It's what makes some people successful. It's what makes some actors stars, and the rest just actors. Greed is the difference."

Miss Johnstone stared at him, fascinated. His black eyes were almost reptilian, and he himself seemed hypnotized by his own thinking. "You have to want something more than anyone else wants it. You have to want it so much, you can taste it," he went on. "You have to feel greed."

Lee's luckless pursuit continued. Patient and persistent, he wooed; but like *Over the Top*, he didn't please the audience. That show closed, and shortly after, Miss Johnstone rang down the curtain on Lee; she married Walter Wanger.

Lee's grief was perfunctory. There were a lot of other things to worry about, and his sorrow could be eased with any number of fresh conquests. Girls were part of *his* business, and anyway there was work to do.

The Shuberts did manage to salvage the young Astaires to star in their 1918 *Passing Show*—the first starring appearance for the youngsters on Broadway. Although Romberg wrote the score, as usual, the show is best rememberd for two interpolated tunes—"Smiles" and "I'm Forever Blowing Bubbles." It was a busy wartime season for the Messrs., and completely undistinguished save for a monumental disaster called *Freedom*, a patriotic pageant with music, staged personally by Lee, and secondly, by an incident which turned the tide of history for Jake—an actor slugged him.

J.J. had been his usual sunny self, profanely berating the cast, director, composers, conductor—anyone—and during the production of *Little Simplicity*, he made the mistake of physically attacking Walter Catlett. Catlett knocked him over the footlights, and Jake came up with one of the loveliest of his many Shubert lines. As he lay in the pit, stunned, he waved a shaky finger at Catlett and said, "You can't walk out! I'll hold you to your contract if I go broke suing you!" Yes, J.J. was indomitable. Catlett did not leave the cast. He didn't have to.

Within the next few months, everybody left all Shubert casts, and

Girls, Girls, Girls. Ten this time. J. J.'s *Passing Show* of 1918. Nita Naldi, the soon-to-be vamp of the silent screen, is featured, third from the right, front row.

The 1919 Equity Strike—The Committee. Front row, seated left to right: Marie Dressler, Ed Wynn, Doris Raulsen and Ivy Sawyer. Back row, left to right: Lionel Barrymore, Ethel Barrymore, Conway Tearle, John Charles Thomas, Pearl "Perils of Pauline" White, Brandon Tynan, Joseph Santley and Louise MacIntosh.

Broadway went dark. The great Equity strike was called, and since the Shuberts were the leading (in numbers, anyway) production company, Lee was thoroughly embroiled in the strike and its negotiations.

The war was over, bringing a merciful end to the parade of "patriotic" sketches, songs, production numbers, and whole plays. The theater turned to "normal" fare, and in the first months of peace, business was good. But the country was swept by a wave of unrest. Wartime dislocations were echoed by postwar reactions. The labor force, fearing cutbacks, militantly organized unionization drives. The Socialist movement attracted adherents. There was violence and anarchy in the ranks. Paralleling a crippling steel strike, the actors determined that their time was now.

Early in August of 1919 Equity, after months of fruitless negotiation with the managers, after endless about-faces on the part of the management negotiators, called its strike. One by one, theaters closed their doors—and not only in New York. Chicago, Boston, the West Coast joined in the action. The actors, for the first time solidly backed by the A.F.L. stagehands, shut down show business as far as the legitimate theater was concerned. They were almost unanimous in their actions; only a few sided with the producers. Some like George M. Cohan *were* producers. Others felt that an "artist" didn't belong in a union of labor. But the overwhelming majority fought bitterly and well.

Opposed to them was the united force of the men who controlled the theater, either as producers, as house owners, or as brokers. There were threats and attempts at intimidation, but the sentiment of the country was with the actors. It was a time of labor change. Lee Shubert was a pivotal force in the managerial group. He issued his customary threat to close all his theaters permanently. He would convert, he promised, to motion pictures. No one believed him. He enlisted various trusted "stars" to attempt to break Equity. He played a vital role in forming a rival group.

On the "inside"—among his fellow-managers—he was more easygoing and a lot more ready to compromise. He even urged them to compromise. Lee was being hurt in his most sensitive area, his pocketbook. At one meeting he screamed, "This strike is costing me ten thousand dollars a day!" That was real pain.

In the first days of the walkout, the Messrs. struggled manfully to keep at least the Winter Garden open. Lee ran the backstage operation, and pulled the curtain; J. J., who always felt he was a lighting genius, supervised the lights. Other Shubert executives manned the box office, seated the patrons, moved the scenery. It was a side of Shubert character that they never lost—this was *their* theater, *their* show, and by

"The Spirit of Equity." A rare photograph of Miss Ethel Barrymore.

God, no one was going to prevent them from collecting *their* money. Equity did. Even after the wrenching effort of combining the remnants of three productions (*Gaieties, Vogues, Passing Show*) into the Winter Garden presentation, they were forced to shut down.

There were noble attempts to save face; there were long, tense negotiations. It was Willie Klein who carried the bulk of the responsibility for hammering out the final agreement with Equity, and to everyone on Broadway, that indicated one thing. The shots were being called by Klein's boss, Lee Shubert. He had become the dominant voice in the Managers' Association. There were managers who didn't approve of the settlement, and Erlanger remarked, "That son of a bitch, Lee Shubert, he sold us out!"

As in all conflicts, the Equity strike had its own sidelights—some amusing, some revelatory. It taught Lee Shubert one significant thing. There were perils inherent in bigness. When the strike hit high gear, the Managers' Association wanted to collect a war chest, and it proposed that each production be assessed a fixed amount of money, a sort of head tax. Since the Shuberts were the largest single fountain of productions, it meant a walloping sum that they were being taxed. At the same time, as only *one* member of the Association, they were limited to one vote (plus the votes they could control from their satellite producers). Lee screamed like a stuck pig at the unfairness, the undemocratic spirit, the downright injustice of this kind of thinking, echoing his protest when he quit the Theater Managers' Association in 1908. Since one of the few things that will unite producers is a threat to their incomes—like an actors' strike—the Shuberts had to live with injustice for the duration. But long before the Supreme Court came to its epic decision, Lee Shubert had reached his. One dollar, one vote. When the issue arose again, he had his proposal ready. When it came to Shubert money, Lee wanted to be more than equal.

When the strike was called, Ziegfeld went to court to seek an injunction preventing the actors from walking out. The Shuberts took a typically different route. Willie Klein, on behalf of the brothers, sued Equity for half a million dollars—Equity, collectively, and a hundred and eighty-four members of Equity, individually—asserting that this round sum was an approximation of the money the strike was costing the Shuberts. Neither legal maneuver worked. Ziegfeld's cast walked out, the judge refused the injunction, and Shubert's case was thrown out of court. But the brothers had added a postscript to the most famous cliché in show business. Not only must the show go on, but, in Shubert translation, if it doesn't, then the Messrs. want the money they would have made if it had! It was Lee-and-Jake financial logic.

160

Ed Wynn was a pivotal force in Equity. With almost all of Broadway dark, and the city hungry for entertainment, Equity, whose members were just plain hungry, determined to run a giant variety show as a fund raiser for the strike war chest. It was one of the all-time all-star bills in theatrical annals, and everyone who was an Equity member and a star appeared on the stage of the Lexington Avenue Opera House, to a packed house. Ed Wynn, under court injunction not to appear, was seated in the audience. He suddenly rose to his feet and said, "Justice Lydon has forbidden me to appear on stage tonight. I am very sorry that this has occurred, but of course the orders of the court must be obeyed. If I had been able to appear tonight, I had in mind telling you a story . . ." and he told it then, and Wynn went on and on from his place in the audience, explaining step-by-performing-step just what he would have said if he had been allowed on the stage. He brought down the house.

There were many hostilities born during the strike. Lifelong friendships came to an end when certain actors, in complete conscience, could not back the strike. George M. Cohan was a particularly tragic figure.

For years the acknowledged spokesman for actors, Cohan, now a successful producer, tried to ride two horses. He addressed the actors group, begging them to trust him, to rely on him to achieve a fair agreement, and they hooted him off the stage. Crushed and embittered, he announced his retirement from the theater which was his raison d'être, and to which he had given so much.

Among the producers—with their competitive positions, their current animosities, their suspicions—schisms arose that took years to heal.

One point of unanimity for the actors, striking or otherwise, was the Shuberts. And on this villain, a majority of the producers could agree. *Everyone* united against them.

During the strike, Lillian Russell had sent a wire from Chicago. Still smarting from the court decision which had ruled that the Shuberts did not owe her money, she claimed that $100,000 was due her from the brothers. She offered this sum to Equity, "if any miracle worker can be found who can collect it."

And at The Players clubhouse bar one strike evening, three male stars were getting mulled as they discussed the progress of the strike. "It's the Shuberts!" mumbled one, in a rolling stage mumble. "It's the God-damned Shuberts! They're crooks!"

"You're right," offered the second in a mellifluous baritone. "They're crooks, and they're bastards, and they lie, and cheat and steal and welsh on contracts!"

"They're the lowest form of theatrical life," said the first actor judiciously, if slightly thick-tongued. "As a matter of fact, they're the lowest form of any kind of life."

The third actor, who had been listening attentively, now interrupted in his clipped stage British. "Now, now, they can't be all that bad," he protested.

The first gentleman examined him in drunken dignity. "They can't?" he said belligerently. "They can't? Then tell me this," he added, with irrefutable logic, "if they're not so bad, tell me why they're called Shubert."

The brothers from Syracuse had made a position for themselves. Not only did they have a street named for them, but they had become an epithet. There was a certain connotation to being in a "Shubert" production or signed to a "Shubert" contract. It wasn't a good connotation. Shubert shows had their own flavor or lack of it, and Shubert employees were stigmatized by comments like "He only does what Lee Shubert tells him," or "J.J.'s got his brand on him."

With Equity a reality, the Shuberts made their peace with the actors and went back to work. They put their heads together to start laying plans to torpedo the union, but in the meantime there was work to be done. Their control of the business was growing stronger every day. They had a small army of retainers; they were mounting show after show to keep the lights on in their New York houses and to feed to their almost a thousand theaters across the country.

There were two kinds of Shubert presentations now: the Messrs. present, and Lee presents. Jake never presented, but the bulk of the big musicals that came out of the office were "under the personal supervision of Mr. J. J. Shubert"; and, of course, within the sacred precincts of the Shubert offices this became "under the personal stupid vision of etc." Now, Jake wanted to present, just as Lee did, but Lee wouldn't allow it, and the only victory Jake managed was a formal request to all papers to stop referring to "Lee and Jake," and to use the term "the Messrs. Shubert." Jake resented the billing situation, and he even resented "Jake." Anyone addressing him was to use the more refined "Mr. J.J." Since the second "J" was purely arbitrary and had no name that it belonged to, it provided lovely material for certain unimpressed journalists. They would write, "Lee and Jacob J. (formerly Jacob) Shubert are in the midst of . . ." Or "Lee-n-Jake, now known as Lee-n-J, are preparing to . . ." Each time such an item appeared, Jake would haul the Shubert press man across the office coals. "It ain't dignified!" he would bellow. "You tell that son of a bitch, I wanna be treated with dignity!"

He really did. He never did quite forgive Marjorie Gateson's "disloyalty" when she joined the Equity strike. This made Miss Gateson almost unique in the theatrical profession—she was viewed with disfavor by *both* Shuberts.

When Lee planned the production of *Fancy Free*, he had designed it to star Marilyn Miller, the elfin beauty of Broadway, with a starring role in it for Miss Gateson. Miss Miller had started in English vaudeville and had been brought to Broadway by the Shuberts, who had her locked into an ironclad contract, filled with some of the most delicious Willie Klein clauses. With *Fancy Free* ready to go, Miss Miller was offered the lead in a *Ziegfeld Follies*, and like any other musical star of the time, this was the show she wanted.

Miss Miller was in a peculiarly embarrassing position since her father was a company manager with the Shuberts. She asked Miss Gateson to "speak to Mr. Lee, since you're so good with him." Miss Gateson, choosing discretion rather than the alternative, told Marilyn she could not interfere.

Broadway is a broad avenue, but rumor crosses it quickly. Lee had heard that Mr. Ziegfeld, by now one of Lee's arch enemies, had been trying to lure away his star. So *he* called in Gateson and suggested, "You talk to Marilyn, and tell her she is being badly advised." Miss Gateson decided to maintain her neutral position.

Now, the Miller attorney discovered a rather interesting fact. When the Shuberts had imported the act *The Columbian Trio* to play the Winter Garden, Marilyn had been under age. Her mother had signed her contract! It was very simple to have the court decide the contract was not binding because Marilyn was a minor at signature time; so Miss Miller went into the Follies, and Mr. Shubert went into a rage. Included in his royal tantrum as objects of his enmity was Miss Gateson. So she had a place on two lists: Jake's *and* Lee's.

The uniqueness of this position cannot be stressed sufficiently. Usually, if *one* Shubert disliked an actor, that automatically insured that actor the liking of the other Shubert brother. In fact, there are those who believe that the Shuberts really cultivated dislikes on a calculated basis. The theory went like this: if Jake needed performer A, he would arrange with Lee to have a disagreement with A so that he, Jake, could then call in A and assure him that despite Lee's resistance Jake wanted his talents for his production—since Lee presumably was against the hiring, there was a fighting chance to chop the salary of the performer. In a number of cases, the theory worked.

So, Miss Gateson could work for either of the Shubert brothers or for neither! Since the brothers were pragmatic fellows, when they needed her she worked for them.

Despite their endless feuds with actors, or possibly because of them,

163

the Shuberts inadvertently became the single greatest unifying force in the history of performers. Actors who, out of sheer professional jealousy, could have strangled, clawed, assassinated each other found themselves sharing a common, binding emotion. They hated the Shuberts.

They distrusted their contracts, their chiseling, their outright cheating. They disliked Jake's truculence just about as much as they feared Lee's soft-voiced wheedling. Actors found themselves sharing a theatrical dugout with their fellows in the common war. Playwrights joined and strengthened the Dramatists' Guild; and so did musicians, reinforcing ASCAP. The Shuberts didn't plan it that way. It just happened to them.

But in 1920 the Shuberts were not really paying too much attention to what actors were thinking. Four or five more interesting vistas had caught the brothers' attention.

In the Middle West, the Orpheum Circuit, founded by Martin Beck and including Marc Heiman, Asher Levy, et al.—all former Shubert associates from Syracuse—had "gone public." They had issued stock, under the guidance of one William Phillips, a Wall Street investment banker, and they had made a lot of money, personally.

This was a new way to get money as far as theatrical thinking was concerned and as such, predictably, would intrigue Lee Shubert. He had met Mr. Phillips, who was a literate man about town, and now he began to cultivate him. If there was a new way to get money, personally, Lee Shubert wanted to find out about it.

Second, more than ten years had passed since the vaudeville truce had been signed with Keith. And Lee had contracted to stay out of vaudeville for only ten years. For all those years, Lee had reflected unhappily on the flow of dollars into Keith's monopoly. If money went into a box office, Shubert wanted some. He determined to reopen a vaudeville war with Keith, and to start with, he hired a Keith booker who had been friendly with Sam and instrumental in bringing Jolson into the Shubert fold. His name was Arthur Klein, who although not related to the redoubtable Willie was cut from the same short length of cloth.

Klein, Arthur, was a small, dapper man who had booked some of the biggest acts in vaudeville. He had known the Shuberts for years, and he welcomed the assignment of opening a new vaudeville circuit. He also provided Lee with companionship in the late hours of the night, when the calls were coming in from the theaters across the country, giving the dollar take for the night's performance. He went to work on building attractions for vaudeville.

Third, to keep his hand in, Lee announced that he was going to build six theaters on 48th and 49th streets—he had quietly assembled the property for them—and he also acquired the Century Theater on 62nd Street. That magnificent house, which had been born "The New Theater" (once managed by Lee), would augment the Winter Garden as a Shubert house for big musicals.

There was a kind of irony in this purchase. When Lee bought it, he went to some pains to acquire the property immediately adjacent to the huge theater, and he took Arthur Klein with him to visit both acquisitions.

They looked at the ring of boxes, the magnificent rococo treatment, the handsome marble, the gleaming chandeliers, and Lee said with firm pride, "They don't build theaters like this every day." He looked about him reverently. "They had the biggest budget to build a theater that anybody ever had, and even then, they went over." He shook his head in admiration. "This building will stand like a monument."

Klein admired the building on cue, and then asked hesitatingly why Shubert had acquired the property next door. Was he planning to enlarge the already vast house? Lee did not deign to answer; he merely studied Klein with infinite compassion.

Five years later, Lee ordered the "monument" demolished and on its site and the "property next door" built the Century Apartments. It is a large, deluxe building, on one of New York's most valuable sites, and it still stands.

For many years, particularly during the Depression, it housed many Shubert minions. When tenants were very, very hard to find, Lee would broadly hint to a director, an actor, a musician, a manager, that "it would be nice if they lived in the Century." Lee himself had an apartment there for a long while. So did numerous relatives. It was one way of keeping the place rented.

Another Shubert concern was that explosive monster—the motion picture. There were now as many motion-picture theaters as legitimate houses in so-called theatrical districts. And Lee was disturbed that they were not contributing to the Shubert incomes. True, he was a major force in Marcus Loew's empire (and a major shareholder too), but that was not the same.

At one luncheon, at the Hunting Room of the now-defunct Hotel Astor, he was sitting with Loew, comparing notes and complaining about inflation. He was building the relationship in preparation for his invasion of Keith, but his thoughts were on motion pictures. He wanted to know more.

He confessed to second thoughts on his relationship with Samuel Goldwyn. Originally, Lee Shubert was one-third of Goldwyn Pictures, but the two men had not gotten along. Lee would always refer to him

165

with respect, but always as Mr. Goldfish, Goldwyn's real name. (There is perhaps room for rejoicing in the fact that they *didn't* get along; the English language has survived all kinds of maltreatment, but the combination of Goldwyn and Shubert might have been the camel-killer.)

Although he referred to him with respect, Lee's private opinion of Mr. Goldwyn is best summed up in one line. "He always has to have one extra opinion," Lee told an associate. "After he has his *final* final opinion, he always gets one more."

Loew tried to patch things up between the men, but it never happened. Shubert was fascinated by the logistics of motion-picture exhibition. You needed one picture a week, every week, compelling an annual production of fifty-two films. (Theaters ran a film for one week only. It was a custom that would last for several more years.)

In addition, if you had a second theater in the area, you needed another film for *that* house, and if you had sufficient need (sufficient two-theater towns), you would be required to supply a hundred and four pictures a year—one a week for two chains. Only Paramount, under Zukor, had this kind of output, and this troubled Loew, and it troubled Shubert. Lee hated all monopolies except his own; Keith had it in vaudeville, and Paramount was rapidly attaining it in motion pictures. Too bad about Goldwyn, he told Loew, but we ought to think about this. Mostly he was thinking about Keith, and how Loew could help him. They planned.

Vaudeville, real estate, motion pictures, stock issues—enough to fill the life of the average man, but Lee was not average. The "void" in his life left by Justine Johnstone's departure had to be taken care of.

Down from Worcester, Massachusetts, came the Swanson sisters, Beatrice and Marcella—as if on cue. Handsome, bent on show business, they quickly found employment in the Shubert revival of *Florodora* as part of the sextet, and Lee noticed them, liked them, and started seeing them. Their names decorated a host of "Messrs. Shubert Present."

Florodora was one of fifteen Shubert productions that year. It was lavish, sumptuous, and, miracle of miracles, presented by Jake! Perhaps the presence in the sextet of the Swanson sisters had something to do with Lee's sudden magnanimity in allowing a Shubert production to be a solo effort by J. J.

He did grumble to the press that although he wanted to hold the line on ticket prices, *Florodora* was a terribly expensive show. (One way to tell J. J. that Lee was still in charge and watching budgets.) When the newspapers asked if the Shuberts were planning vaudeville, Lee had no comment. Marcus Loew said the Shuberts might, and E. F. Albee, boss of the Keith Circuit, said it was sheer nonsense.

166

Beatrice and Marcella Swanson.

Jake agreed with Albee, but not for the record. He too thought that vaudeville by Shubert was an insanity. It resulted in a typical scene between the brothers.

The dialogue was carried on between intermediaries; the reigning Shuberts did not speak to each other. (It is a rather fascinating fact that although their offices were on the same floor in the same building, they did not meet face-to-face. In later years, after they had built the Sardi Building, their offices were two hundred feet apart, diagonally across 44th Street, and still they held no conversations. On various occasions, they felt it incumbent on themselves to deny the fact that they were not on speaking terms—in the press, and in personal conversation. Jake referred to "those sons of bitches across the street." Lee, always more temperate, would say, "Try to find out what my brother thinks." Lee could afford to be more magnanimous—he called the shots. But one fact becomes crystal clear; they *tried* to avoid each other. Married by contract, married by joint interests, married by consanguinity, they carried on their personal enmity—Lee secure, Jake trying to prove. They established ground rules; they avoided conflict over girls, almost divvying up the various availabilities from the various choruses; they distrusted each other in all matters, except money, and every once in a while even that became a problem. For the people that worked for "the Shuberts" it was an omnipresent fact—the brothers did not talk to each other, except through intermediaries.

The chief intermediary at this time was Jules Murray, then general manager for the Shuberts. Murray, a stocky, hunchbacked individual was called upon to do the roadwork (and the necessary diplomatic editing) between the brothers.

Lee had hired Arthur Klein. He was signing contracts with actors and acts. He was holding endless meetings with Marcus Loew and William Morris.

Jake was making money. For both of them. And telling Jules Murray, "Tell my brother, what the f—k do we need with vaudeville?"

Murray would go down the corridor, enter Mr. Lee's office, and say, "Your brother does not quite see eye-to-eye with you about the vaudeville venture."

Lee would counter, his black eyes blinking, his voice, as always when he was crossed, reedier, "Tell my brother that we are proceeding with vaudeville. Last time we would have made millions if Erlanger had not interfered. I do not want *him* to interfere!"

Murray would race down the hall, enter Jake's office, and say, "Mr. J.J., Mr. Lee agrees with you but feels that after you have studied the possibilities, your own enthusiasm will grow."

Jake would bellow, "You tell that son of a bitch, my brother, that the answer is no, finally, positively, no!!"

Murray would return to Lee's office and state, "Mr. Lee, your brother wants you to reconsider."

Lee would raise his eyebrows and shift in his upright position in the small chair. "I have made the decision. You may inform my brother."

Murray, seeking his own time, would eventually inform Jake. "Your brother has taken all your objections into account and is proceeding accordingly."

"So, no matter what I say, the stupid son of a bitch is gonna be an idiot, hey? Then let him be an idiot, and you make sure you tell him what I said—don't leave a word out!"

Murray, by this time thoroughly winded, would wend his weary way back to Lee, translate the last diatribe from Jake into acquiescence, and Lee would smile benignly. "Fine. I knew he would agree."

Joe Gaites, who succeeded Murray, was a deeply devout man, dedicated to the principles of Mary Baker Eddy and Christian Science. Mr. Gaites had spent one whole afternoon plus half of one night playing Western Union between the sixth floor of the Sardi Building (Jake's) and the fourth floor of the Shubert Theater (Lee's). After more than a dozen "visits," the comparatively simple matter at hand had been resolved, and Joe Gaites was discovered seated at his desk, his head lowered, his hands folded on the desk-top, repeating in a prayerful monotone, "There—are—no—Shuberts. There—are—no—Shuberts. There are—no—Shuberts."

But there were. And they were trying to solve certain casting problems in their own patented way.

The Shubert's biggest breadwinner for a decade had been Al Jolson, still was Al Jolson, and suddenly, now, maybe wasn't going to be Al Jolson anymore. The crisis arose out of Shubert bookkeeping. Shubert peccadilloes in accounting had already become a legend in the business, rivaled only by Shubert contracts.

In the Jolson case, it is difficult to comprehend how the Shuberts, for all their avarice, would risk their top star's friendship by petty chiseling. He had made millions for them, and was in for a percentage of the profits—profits which somehow were always eaten up by costs. An accounting was submitted to Jolson, and he discovered he had been charged $400 for costumes for a certain musical number. He knew the costumes had come out of the Shubert shop, and had cost $50. Jolson did not get down on his knees and sing "Mammy." He reared back and swore that when his contract ended, he was finished with the brothers.

The Man with All That Glue. Eddie Cantor, in *Make It Snappy*.

They instantly began a wooing campaign to seduce Jolson back into the fold.

If Jolson needed any convincing that the accounting was not a "mistake" (as Lee had assured him), it came from Eddie Cantor, another very important star. He too was in for a percentage, and he too discovered that the Shuberts were a charitable institution—they never made a profit, not at least by the statements they faithfully submitted. He asked for an audit, and he was informed that the Eddie Cantor account had been charged with, among other costs, "$1,900—glue."

Now, since $1,900 worth of theatrical glue would have built all the sets from Noah's Ark to Expo '67 with enough left over to erect a summer cottage for Lee, Cantor became "mildly" suspicious. He charged into his attorney's office and sought ways to break his contract. He swore that he would never work with the Shuberts again.

Faced with the threat of the loss of two major stars, the Shuberts sought insurance, and after much searching, they zeroed in on a young performer who had caught their eye at a Sunday night "concert"—Georgie Price. To cover the tragicomic opera which is the saga of George Price's Life with the Shuberts requires a break in the narrative. But to truly savor the Shubert spirit and the Shubert way of doing business, the story, covering as it does a span of years, deserves to be told as a unity. So—The Affair Price, the tale of The Man Who Was Going to Be Built to Replace Jolson.

Price, who was doing very well in vaudeville (and don't think the Shuberts, actively preparing their raid on Keith, didn't take this into consideration) was approached by Lee. He was offered a one-year contract to perform in *Cinderella on Broadway*, a revue J.J. was preparing. As a stop-gap salary assurance, they moved him into *The Midnight Rounders*, a Century Roof production, supervised by Jake, and then began the real flirtation.

Price became a "member of the family." He spent a great deal of time in Jake's apartment—for dinner, after the show, Sunday breakfast. (Jake, at this time, was in an apartment over the Central Theater, across from the Palace on Times Square.)

So, when the time seemed Shubert-ripe, Jake asked Ed Bloom, one of their managers, to open negotiations with Price for a long-term contract. "Keep it our option," he told Bloom, "but don't lose him. Five years is what we want. And don't go over three hundred and fifty a week." Bloom made the offer. And then Bloom displayed his Shubert training.

J.J. and Jolson, Paris, 1921. This was the reconciliation that changed George Price's life.

He moved Price into a new and more sumptuous dressing room, which he was to share with Clarence Harvey.

Clarence Harvey was a long-time Shubert regular, and a general suspicion prevailed among his fellow-actors—this since the Equity Strike —that Harvey was a pipeline into the Shubert office. If the suspicions were correct, he would be reporting back to the brothers on Price's activities.

Price, who had fought his own way up through the theatrical jungle, liked the new dressing room and had heard about Harvey; he determined to test the potential of the new dressing room.

With Bloom's offer of $350 per week in hand, Price arranged with a friend to have a telegram sent to him at the Century Theater. The wire read:

ANXIOUS TO HAVE YOU STAR IN MY NEXT PRODUCTION
GUARANTEE LONG-TERM, COMMENCING 750 PER WEEK
PLEASE REPLY SOONEST ZIEGFELD

Playing his hunch on Harvey, Price left the telegram, face up, on his dressing table. To make sure the message was delivered, he sought Harvey's counsel that night. "What do you think I ought to do?"

The show entrained for Boston, directly after closing that night, and predictably, the next day, Ed Bloom appeared in Boston. He wanted to see Georgie Price.

"There comes a time in every performer's life," said Bloom, "when he becomes 'wanted.' Georgie, it's happening to you. Your talent is finally proving itself. And Georgie, I want you to know that Mr. J.J., himself, loves your records."

This last was enough to set Price's antennae tickling. Phonograph records had been introduced, and had happened. "His Master's Voice" was gracing thousands of store fronts, and phonographs were moving into middle-class American homes. Georgie Price was one of the three largest-selling artists in the field, rivaled only by Caruso and "Cohen on the Telephone."

Bloom went on to offer $500 a week for a five-year contract. Price refused the offer, stating his undying love for J.J., and Bloom was back the next day, asserting that any move at this crucial time in Price's careers could be wounding. "You stay with people who care about you, Georgie," he advised, assuming, for the negotiation, J.J.'s surrogate role. "The Shuberts will make you as rich as Jolson." He paused meaningfully. "Mr. J. J.," he said with emotion, "is planning his own record company."

Price declined to sign a contract at $500. Nor did he mention costumes or glue. By now, he was depending on Clarence Harvey as a communications medium. He confided his concerns to Harvey that night, and, sure enough, the next afternoon, a solicitous Ed Bloom was back.

Bloom omitted any reference to record companies, but did raise the offer to $750 per week, forty weeks guaranteed, and he had other goodies to dangle. Featured billing for the first year, star billing for the second year (name over title), and solo star billing thereafter. One other item Price stipulated—if the Shuberts asked Price to work in any Sunday night "concert," the fees were to be negotiated and were outside the contract. Bloom agreed, and Price signed. He was sure that he had covered every possible contingency in the contract.

With the signing of the contract, love filled the air. Jake became Price's spiritual and social father. He introduced him to a girl, and married him off in style. All the time, Price was working in *Midnight Rounders*.

It was in Detroit that Daddy Jake suggested to Price that he accompany Jake to Europe on his next trip, coming up shortly. Price demurred. He didn't have that kind of money. Jake's eyebrows shot up. "Who mentioned money? You'll be my guest! You and that nice little wife of yours come along."

The Prices began to make plans. There was an apartment to sublet, there were many things to do. In the meantime, there had been another visit from Jake. He was closing the show, and wanted Price to play out the remaining eight weeks of his first year's guarantee in vaudeville. Price consented. One week later, a visit from Bloom. "Mr. J.J. is planning to leave for Europe in two weeks. He would like you to sign this release form on the contract." Bloom smiled genially. "After all, you can't perform here when you're seeing Europe, can you?"

Price hesitated. He was still not rich enough to pass up five weeks of salary. But then he shrugged. How could he refuse to cooperate with a boss who was taking him to Europe? He signed the release, and returned to New York. The Shuberts helped him sublet his apartment to Mistinguette and Maurice Chevalier, who were coming into New York on a Shubert booking, and Price and his wife did the necessary shopping for the grand tour.

The week before sailing, Georgie went up to the Shubert office, was greeted warmly by their transportation man, and was handed his tickets. As Price was opening the envelope, Ben Mallam, the Shubert ticket man, asked him for $750. Price looked at him in bewilderment. "In a minute," he stuttered. "I want to see Mr. J.J."

When finally admitted to that worthy's office, there was a short interchange of how-are-you and won't-Europe-be-fun, and Price decided to slide into the subject with delicacy.

174

"How much money do you think I ought to take with me, Mr. J.J.?"

The Continental expert leaned back in his chair. "First, you ought to have a letter of credit from your bank. Then, Georgie, you should take two thousand dollars in pounds, maybe another two thousand dollars in francs."

Price, whose bank account was just under $500, stared at him. Finally, he managed to stammer, "Mr. Shubert, there seems to be a misunderstanding. I thought I was going to be your guest. Mallam even asked me for the steamer fare."

Jake stared at him uncomprehendingly. "Guest? What guest?"

"But you said—" began Price.

"I never said 'guest,' " said Jake truculently. "Why would I say a thing like that? Georgie, my boy, I just wanted you should see Europe with me."

Dazed, Price went back to his wife to try to explain why they couldn't go, and found out that a promised European tour is not so easily un-promised. The following Monday, the George Prices, J.J. Shubert, and Muriel Knowles sailed for Europe.

So, for the next six weeks, while J. J. was shopping the European theater for plays and musicals (partially financed by the money he saved on George Price's "guarantee"), George Price toured Europe too, wondering how he was going to pay back the money he had borrowed to be J.J.'s guest. And in that six-week period, events were going on in New York which were going to drastically affect Georgie Price.

Lee had taken personal charge of the Jolson matter. If Lee was a past master at negotiation, Jolson was an expert at being difficult. Jolson was undeniably one of the great entertainers of all time, but as a human being—Hollywood biographies to the contrary—he was an unpleasant, arrogant man. And (1) he was angry with the Shuberts, and (2) he knew he had them over a barrel. He was twice as nasty as usual.

Lee finally came up with a deal that met Jolson's terms. Jolson was understandably wary about the words "net profits," and Lee, in desperate need of his star star, offered Jolson a guarantee plus a percentage of the gross. Jolson accepted it.

A few blocks away a terrible fight occurred between Ziegfeld and Cantor, and when the news reached Shubert, Lee was quick to act on it. He re-signed Cantor.

When Price returned from Europe, he was one of the most superfluous commodities in the Shubert catalog. Daddy Jake, European guide, became unavailable, and Lee was impossible to see. Price was told that there were no plans for a show to star him. What the Shuberts wanted was a way out of their contract with Price—at no cost to them.

Finally, after four desperate weeks, Price received notice from the Shubert office. He was ordered to report to the Central Theater (vaudeville). The marquee had his name cunningly concealed in a type size equivalent to the sign manufacturer's logo. He was not billed, he was not featured—he was almost anonymous. And his dressing room, strategically placed on the third floor, was easily confused with a broom closet.

Frantic phone calls to Lee, to Jake, to anybody, elicited no response. In desperation Price went to see a friend of his, a young attorney, David Segal. After listening to Price's story, Segal ordered photographs taken of the marquee of the Central, clipped copies of the newspaper ads, and wrote a letter to the Shuberts.

They were, the letter stated, in breach of contract. They had not lived up to the billing clause, they had not given Mr. Price his contractually stipulated place in the newspaper advertisements, and therefore he could not appear until they, the Shuberts, lived up to the terms of their contract.

The reply from Willie Klein was curt. By failing to appear, Price had breached the contract, and they no longer recognized any obligations.

Price was close to total panic. His career was in jeopardy, his finances were shaky. What to do?

One of the more prestigious law firms in New York was the George Medalia office, and on Segal's suggestion Price told Medalia the whole sad tale. Medalia wrote a very strong letter to the Shuberts and filed suit for $300,000.

The Medalia letterhead and the suit worked. Price was instantly invited to a meeting in Lee's office. He arrived with attorneys, and Lee beamed on him, while Willie Klein shuffled papers. "It's that brother of mine," said Lee. "Georgie, you know how we feel about you. Do you think we would treat an artist of your caliber this way? You know better. It's just that sometimes my brother does things without thinking."

Medalia smiled. "Then you will live up to your contract?"

Lee was his most charming. "Shuberts always live up to their contracts."

Price interjected, "I want it in writing."

Lee's expression was hurt and incredulous. "From us?"

The stipulation that the Shuberts would live up to their written contract was put into writing, and then again, came the waiting. Price had been idle for nearly twelve weeks (remember, the contract only guaranteed forty weeks out of fifty-two), when finally he received word from Ed Bloom. Price was to open in a new Shubert production in Boston, *Spices*. In great excitement Price called Bloom. When do we open? When do rehearsals begin?

"Rehearsals are going on, and you open next week."

The billing was up on the marquee—*SPICES*, starring MAE WEST, JIM HUSSEY, and George Price. Technically, it complied with the contract. The newspaper advance ads handled billing in the same way. Technically, the Shuberts were complying. Price's dressing room was an inaccessible little cubbyhole on the third floor. Price was determined to be cooperative. He said nothing, moved his belongings into the room, and reported to Bloom on stage. "Well, Ed," he said, "what do I do?"

Bloom smiled. "When the curtain goes up, Georgie," he said, "you're on stage—in blackface. Then when the curtain comes down at the end of Act One, you're on stage, without blackface. Kind of in whiteface." He chuckled. "Then when the curtain goes up for Act Two, you're on stage again, in blackface."

Price smiled. "That doesn't sound like too much to handle," he said, and then thought he might negotiate a little. "The makeup change would be easier if my dressing room were closer to the stage."

"You'll have time," assured Bloom.

"Fine," said Price. "Okay! I'm in blackface, Act One and Act Two opening. In whiteface, end of Act One. What are my numbers? Where are the routines?"

Bloom stared at him. "Numbers? What numbers?"

Price was patient. "Well, when the curtain goes up, and I'm on stage, what do I do?"

"Do? You don't do anything, Georgie. You just stand there."

The message began to come through. The contract did not specify how Price was to perform. Only that he *would* perform *as directed by the management*. And that contract was paying Price $1,000 a week, and Price needed every penny of it.

"You mean the Shuberts are going to pay me one thousand a week to do a silent bit?"

"I got my orders, Georgie."

For six months, Price went on in a bit part, his name on every marquee the show played and advertised in every newspaper advertisement. No one heard him or saw him on stage, and each day it took more and more courage for him to face his fellow actors, the grinning stagehands, and the expectant Bloom. When would he quit? God knows he wanted to, but he couldn't afford it. What could he do?

177

It went on for six months. Business began to slack off, and as soon as they closed *Spices*, the Shuberts moved Price into a touring version of Jake's *Passing Show*. And they completely reversed their field.

Now, instead of having Price do absolutely nothing on stage, the Shuberts were determined to kill him with work. He appeared in thirteen scenes, had eleven costume changes, sang eight songs, and did a stand-up monologue. His dressing room was still the smallest available, and the most remote from the stage. He ran all the time.

And then the Shuberts introduced one more wrinkle—this *Passing Show* tour was a series of one-night stands, with sleeper jumps between towns. Just as the contract stipulated that Price would perform "as directed by the management," it contained a small clause stating that the artist "would travel as directed by the management."

"At the direction of the management," said the notice on the call board, "members of the company will report to the railroad station at 11:00 A.M. George Price and the crew will report to the freight yards at 3:00 A.M."

For the next few months, Price, guaranteed "star billing," traveled in boxcars with the scenery—a unique theatrical personality, whose travel arrangements were being made by Railway Express.

It became a game. In the colder months, one needed a blanket, a thermos of hot coffee or soup, woolen socks, two sizes too large, to be slipped over shoes. In the summer, there were box lunches to be purchased, lightweight sleeping garments, and always the necessity to be *on time* at the freight yard at some unearthly hour. If Price had reported late, it would have been breach of contract.

One might ask why Price put up with it. He was a recognized talent, a man who had established himself as a performer. Surely there were other avenues in show business which would have supported him. Why didn't he just quit?

Perhaps he didn't want to. To him, it was a war, and he wanted to win it.

Second, there is the terrible insecurity which is part and parcel of every actor's existence. It is one profession which lives with unemployment. Even as the actor is playing in a hit, he knows that hit will end its run, and his next play can be five weeks of rehearsal, one night of performance, and closing notice. There is no guaranteed continuity of income for performers, except in a long-term contract with a *financially responsible* producer. This Price had.

Finally, the power of the Shuberts must be kept in mind. They sat astride show business and their displeasures could be ruinous for a performer. The unspoken blacklist, pressure on other producers who needed Shubert theaters and Shubert routings—the brothers had weapons. Somehow, even as they victimized him, they protected Price.

He was developing an ulcer; he had dropped fifteen pounds, and once a month he had to face a solicitous Bloom, asking, "You want to quit, Georgie?" Price suddenly had an idea. From Vicksburg, Mississippi, he placed a call to the theater in Jackson, their next port of call. He learned that the theater was completely sold out for the next week.

Price knew enough about theatrical economics to realize that with good houses Monday through Friday the basic costs would be covered. The profits came in the Saturday performances. He decided to play his hunch. He performed faithfully through the Friday night show in Jackson, and on Saturday morning, he called the company manager, Jim Early, to tell him in a very hoarse voice that he had come down with laryngitis. He could not go on.

There were a host of phone calls to and from New York, but the box office refunded all the receipts for the two Saturday shows. On Monday, as they were beating their way north (eventually to New York), Price made a miraculous recovery, which lasted until Friday night.

On Saturday, he called Early again to report that he was ill—again. Faced with a second consecutive week of returning advance sales, Early panicked. He insisted on calling the Shubert office that Saturday morning directly from Price's hotel room. He cautiously reported his bad news, and in a few seconds Lee Shubert was on the phone, asking to talk with Price.

"Georgie, I heard you're sick," said Lee, in his best bedside manner. "I want you should see a doctor—the best doctor in town—and see him at once, and you send the bill to me."

It was too much for Price. "Sick?" he shouted indignantly, "Sick?" He shook his head in disbelief. "I am being killed! I have ridden in boxcars! I have needed search parties to find my dressing room! They have called me out at two in the morning to board a train that didn't leave until noon! They have driven me crazy trying to get me to quit, and let me tell you something, Mr. Shubert, *I'm not quitting!!*"

There was a stunned silence at the other end; you could physically feel the disbelief. "Who's doing this to you, Georgie?" asked Lee solicitously. "Why didn't you call me? Why didn't you come to me if you were having problems?" Before Price could reply, Shubert was talking again. "I will not stand for such treatment for an important performer," Lee attempted to thunder. "I will have Bloom in my office in five minutes, and before he leaves he will regret such behavior—particularly such behavior with a man as close to me as you are." He paused. "You believe me, don't you, Georgie?" Price spluttered. "So, do me a favor, Georgie," said Lee, "a personal favor. You go on today and tonight, and believe me, everything will be fine. All right, Georgie?"

Price said all right. Shubert insisted on giving his personal instructions to Early, and Price performed that weekend. On Sunday night, when the travel notice went up on the board, Price had been assigned Early's private compartment on the train. This went on until the show closed in Norfolk, Virginia, some weeks later.

Price glanced at the call board on his way back to the hotel, and there it was—in Shubert black and white. "Company entrains at the station at 11:00 A.M. Price and work gang report to freight yard at 3:00 A.M."

George Price came back to New York in the baggage car with the scenery and a pint of whiskey. He had just completed thirty-six weeks of the forty guaranteed by the Shuberts in the third year of his contract. They still owed him four weeks of salary. Price called on Lee Shubert to see if he could get that money.

Lee was his genial self. "Sunday night," he said, "you will work the concert at the Century Roof and double into the Central."

"Great!" replied Price. "How much per performance?"

"How much?" asked Lee, his expressionless face cherubic in its guilelessness. "I don't understand, Georgie. This way you can work out the contract."

"My contract excludes the concerts," said Price. "What are you going to pay me?"

"You son of a bitch," said Shubert softly. "You little son of a bitch."

A fee was finally agreed on, and now Price persisted in asking for the money due him. Eventually, Shubert wrote him a check for four weeks' work, the check drawn against the Shubert Benefit Fund account. Price performed at the Century, doubled into the Central, photostated the check, and deposited it, careful to retain the photostat.

This soap opera, starring George Price, might give the impression that he and the Shuberts were engaged in a war to the death. It was—to Price. To the brothers it was a minor skirmish in their daily scheduling. At this point in the Perils of Price, the Shuberts had invaded vaudeville (which resulted in reactivating the White Rats so that Keith now had a union on *his* hands), scared the hell out of Equity (almost precipitating a second Equity strike), continued their pavane with Erlanger and the remnants of the old Syndicate, and fired Arthur Klein, who had headed their vaudeville operation with the accompanying loss of almost $4,000,000. It is important to realize that this remorseless struggle with Price was really not very important to the Shuberts. It was just a matter of no-principle. Arthur Klein, whose Shubert salary had come from eight different companies, depending on Lee's whim of the moment, was back with Keith, and now, because of Price's phenomenal record sales, he sought out Georgie and offered him the headline spot at the Palace. Now, most performers used to work a lifetime, just hoping for a place on the bill at the Palace. It was the Mount Olympus of the vaudeville arts. Headlining the bill? It was the equivalent of immortality. And the salary was equally staggering: $1,750 per week. Price went to see Lee Shubert.

"I am very tired of all the fighting, Mr. Lee," he said. "You must be tired of it too. Let's find a better way. I even have a suggestion."

Shubert was seated behind his small desk, his hands flat on the top, his Indian face inscrutable. "Somebody made you an offer."

"It isn't that," said Price. "You have no plans for me. I'm not well enough to travel freight any more. I'll take myself off your hands for this year—we'll wipe out the contract for this year if you promise me *personally in writing* that next year you'll star me in my own show."

Price opened at the Palace, headlining the bill, which also starred Nora Bayes, and played out the year in various vaudeville appearances. It was a happy year, and it was a happy George Price who returned to the Shubert office to get to work on "his own show."

He waited six weeks of the twelve-week grace period—and he couldn't get to see a Shubert. Price had been assembling material and talents, things he felt would go, new touches, new songs, new sketches.

Finally he was ordered to report to the Imperial Theater for rehearsals of *A Night in Spain*, another of J.J.'s potpourri revues. When he arrived at the theater, he was greeted by Ed Bloom, whose first words were: "What are you doing here, Georgie? There's nothing in this show for you."

Price ran back to Lee Shubert's office. Lee was aghast. "You go back there and anything you want to do, do! It's your show."

Things were finally ironed out with Bloom, and Price brought in a suitcase full of ideas, routines, sketches, songs. The show rehearsed, then trained to Detroit, and prepared to open. J.J. appeared for opening night. The show was long—most first nights are—and made a little longer when Phil Baker, feeling little or no pain that night, played twenty-eight minutes in his opening eight-minute monologue, directing most of his jokes to a friend in the audience. J.J. called a meeting of the cast right after the final curtain.

"There are some people," said Jake, "who think I like to spend $200,000 so they can hold personal conversations over the footlights."

Baker looked at him. "Don't start with me," said Baker, who was rooming with Price. "I'm not Georgie Price. I won't take your s—t."

J.J. reared back. "You and that Price think you're so God-damned smart. I'll show you two momsers who's boss."

Bloom intervened, while Baker was yelling, "Shove your show!" and the cast was reassembled in the morning for some of Jake's "personal supervision."

Baker, sober now, promised to "talk to J.J." on Price's behalf. And J.J. needed talking to. He had systematically begun to emasculate the Price performance. The best song spot was removed. The sketch was cut. The other sketch given to another performer. It was brutal, damaging to the show, and demoted Price to a small part.

He determined to try to make peace with Jake. And it didn't work. Jake's hide was as tough as an elephant's and his memory was long. He hated Price. Week after week on the road, he destroyed Price's role. Convinced that when the show came to New York, his material would be restored and the show restaged, Price bided his time. But now they were in New York, and J.J. remained adamant. "I'm going to show you," he told Price balefully, "I am going to teach you a lesson." Price had underestimated Jake's vengeance.

With opening night staring him in the face, Price fell back on the one weapon that had ever won a battle for him with the Shuberts. The morning of the opening, he went to his doctor, and all of a sudden he could not sing. His doctor called Lee Shubert to inform him that he had "instructed Mr. Price not to sing. He might never sing again if he tried to, with his throat in this condition."

Shubert hit the ceiling. And Price, knowing that a Shubert doctor would be at the Price apartment insisting on an examination, left for Saratoga.

One week later, backed by lawyer and witnesses, Price reported at the theater. "I am ready to work," he informed the stage doorman.

"You can't come in here," said the doorman. "You are barred from the theater."

Price's attorney filed suit for one day's wages, and Willie Klein answered by claiming breach of contract. On the following day, Price reported again, again was turned back, and his attorney filed suit for a second day's wages. The courts were going to be busy, unless some way out could be found. Lee Shubert called a meeting.

"My brother believes, and I agree with him, that you were not sick and that this damaging thing you have done you did deliberately."

Price (doggedly): "I want the twenty-six weeks of salary still due me."

Shubert (reasonably): That is very difficult, Mr. Price. My brother will not allow you in any theater we run. I have tried to persuade him . . ."

Price (interrupting): "I want what you owe me."

Shubert (stony, voice rising): "My brother says he will see you in hell first."

Price: "Then you will have trouble."

Shubert (quietly): "I think we can handle your kind of trouble, Georgie. And I don't threaten so easy."

Price: "Not me, Mr. Shubert. Trouble with the government."

Shubert (leaning forward): "Government? What kind of talk is this? What kind of trouble?"

Price (his moment): "This." He shows Shubert a copy of the photostated check. "I don't think you are supposed to pay performers out of a so-called charity fund."

Shubert (excited, and beginning to stutter): "Now, don't move, Georgie. Don't g–g–get excited. You just sit in the ch–ch–chair and we'll talk."

Willie Klein was called in, looked at the "check," whispered in Lee's ear, and "in writing" settled the George Price contract with a check for $26,000. Price got in his final lick. He refused to sign the release form until the check had been certified at the bank. It ended his association with the brothers.

Price stayed in the theater until just before the "crash." He entered Wall Street, became a successful broker, opened his own office, and forgot about show business. But he never forgot the Shuberts.

Ten years after the contract was "settled," Price, with his three-year-old son and new wife, were in Florida, and J.J., always the patsy for any child other than his own, insisted on taking the Price boy for an outing, deluging him with gifts in the process. Price, telling the story, shook his head in complete wonder. "How could you figure him?" He corrected himself: "Them."

Chapter Ten

The Shuberts formally announced their plans for a vaudeville empire as a Christmas present to Keith in December of 1920. There followed a whole series of seemingly unrelated events, all of them part of a magnificently conceived plan in the mind of Lee Shubert. True, there were a few items that escaped his attention and gave him some minor woes, but the concept was beautiful.

Although they controlled more theaters than they needed, many of the houses were unsuitable for vaudeville. To build a solid vaudeville chain, they started acquiring theaters in cities where they felt they needed protection. Their first two moves were the acquisition of the Strand in Louisville and the Academy of Music in Baltimore.

The Strand was an old Shubert "possession," but it was under lease to Keith, who, quite understandably, was not enthusiastic about giving up his lease to a publicly proclaimed rival. It took some Willie Klein maneuvering, a short litigation—and the Shuberts had the theater.

The Academy of Music was a Klaw-Erlanger theater, and less than two weeks after that had been acquired, they leased, from Erlanger, the Forrest Theater in Philadelphia! What was going on?

It was enough of a ripple to rouse the dormant-for-four-years American Artists Federation, formerly the White Rats. They held a meeting in anticipation of Shubert vaudeville, which meant many more jobs. They hailed the brothers as saviors; Keith had ignored them, locked them out, given them no union status. Perhaps with *two* chains, they might have a union. Keith sent an emissary to Lee Shubert.

The gist of the message was: "You are going to lose your shirt; Keith has twenty million set aside to fight you, and in addition, you are creating a situation where only the actors will profit."

Shubert's reply was admiringly meditative. "Twenty million is a lot of money." He refused to discuss anything else.

It wasn't only Keith and the vaudeville performers who were alerted by the Shubert announcement. Equity had been having its own problems with the brothers. In addition to protests against Jake's physical violence, there had been an ever-growing series of complaints coming into the Equity offices that members of the union were being discriminated against in subtle ways by the Shuberts.

The brothers hotly denied this, but then some microscopic boiler plate in Willie Klein's contracts was brought to light by a formal complaint. Willie Klein had been the chief negotiator in the original Equity-Producers' agreement. It was he who had hammered out the various clauses, architected the basic understanding, directed the legal papers that were so solemnly signed by the Producers' Association and Equity. One of the basic points in that compact was the stipulation that performances would be limited to eight per week. But when that same Willie Klein drew the Shubert contracts with performers, he buried, in microscopic print, the right of the Shuberts to demand a completely illegal ninth performance, with no compensation, for Sundays.

When this came to light, Equity met, and demanded that the Producers' Association oust the Shuberts from membership since they had violated the contract. There were hasty skull sessions in Lee's office, and placating announcements that the Shuberts and Equity would work out their differences; finally, Equity and Willie Klein met, and the Shuberts were forgiven, and they promised never to do it again.

There were two other pressing problems facing the Shuberts at this time. Arthur Klein was "preparing" vaudeville, and the Messrs., mostly Jake, were readying some thirty shows for the upcoming 1920-1921 season. When it is appreciated that in today's theater, David Merrick, who, at least insofar as his voiced opinions about critics are concerned, is anxiously getting fittings for Jake's mantle, had managed a total of fifty productions in the first fourteen years of his theatrical career, the enormity of the Shubert undertaking of thirty for one season may come into sharper focus. It was a stupendous full-time job, to which neither brother could give full time.

They had done some systematic "raiding" to assist Arthur Klein in his endeavors, signing contracts with performers like Will Rogers, Jack Benny, Nora Bayes, Eddie Cantor (!), Al Jolson (!), Eve Tanguay, Mae West, the Marx Brothers, and even Walter Huston, doing a dramatic sketch as Old Kris Kringle.

In addition, they planned innovations: abridged versions of certain dramatic plays (starring Ethel Barrymore, Marie Dressler, John Barrymore, or Clifton Webb) or highlights from the musical stage—*Florodora, Maytime*, and other near-hits from Jake's repertoire.

It was an ambitious undertaking, complicated by a number of factors. First, Keith was bidding, dollar for dollar, for the best acts. This drove the prices to astronomical figures: Will Rogers, who had been getting $1,500 a week to star in Ziegfeld's *Follies*, was paid $5,000 a week by the generous Shuberts. It was an actor's paradise.

Second, the Shubert chain numbered twenty-two theaters. Because of travel problems and booking problems, their standard vaudeville contract stated that the twenty-two-theater guarantee would be played in a twenty-four-week period. This was one of Klein's major errors. Originally, it had looked like a lovely economy. You had the act for twenty-four weeks, played it for twenty-two and were off the financial hook. In practice, what it meant was that a hit bill could not be held over. You lost your actor or paid him a premium to hold him beyond the contracted twenty-four weeks.

The other major problem for Klein was inherited. Despite shrewd Shubert theater bookings, many of the houses in which they were planning to play their vaudeville were too small to pay for the salaries the Shuberts were offering. This had helped precipitate their acquisition of certain houses in road cities, and explained the Shubert decision to convert the Winter Garden to a vaudeville house. (This last almost resulted in bloodshed. The Winter Garden was Jake's baby!)

But Klein plowed ahead, making his contracts, planning his bookings and his publicity, fighting off Keith counteroffers, and sitting in nightly with Lee for strategy meetings, followed by supper in the company of the Swanson sisters. He also attended Lee's infrequent press conferences—quietly.

The brothers had not received a particularly good press for many years—not since they had donned the shining armor of the Trust Busters and reaped favorable comment until the time that they became their own trust. But the vaudeville announcement was greeted with enthusiasm. *Variety*, the bible of vaudeville, had never been too enthusiastic about the Shuberts, possibly because Sime Silverman hailed from Syracuse and knew something.

But when Lee made the first announcement, *Variety* played it big and quoted Mr. Shubert extravagantly.

"If I spend every dollar I have got," he said, "I am going through with this. I have a lot of money and if I lose most of it I will still have enough. . . . I'll show that bunch there are others in the business. We're in the show business, and vaudeville is as much in the show business as anything else."

What about Erlanger?

"Mr. Erlanger runs his business, and we run our business—which is very good, by the way. I was associated with Mr. Erlanger in Advanced Vaudeville some years ago, and I tell you this—without Mr. Erlanger's interference, it (vaudeville) will be very soft for me."

And what did his brother think?

"This is a Shubert decision."

So, chronicled *Variety*, the Shuberts will open up a new audience for "class" vaudeville.

• • •

186

While Lee was holding press conferences, Jake was mounting shows, and the Messrs. were presenting. It was a totally undistinguished season for them, despite two attempts with Helen Menken, one with Jeanne Eagels, and two Romberg musicals. The first, *Blushing Brides*, didn't do well at all; the second was *Blossom Time*, an all-time hit.

Jake, on one of his European scouting trips, had seen a successful German operetta, loosely based on the life of Franz Schubert. Perhaps he believed Franz to be a relative, or perhaps because he liked it, Jake bought it, brought it back with him, and then decided that the score was not suited to the American theater-going ear. Logically, that has to mean he liked the book.

The libretto had been manufactured by A. M. Willner and H. Reichart in Vienna, and Jake turned it over to Dorothy Donnelly for adaptation to the American audience's taste. Romberg (who else?) was asked to prepare a new score—also for the American audience.

The plot line went like this. Franz Schubert is in love with Mitzi. He writes "Song of Love" just for her, and asks his best friend, who happens to be a tenor, to sing it to her. (It became the hit song of *Blossom Time*.) Mitzi (are you ready?) promptly falls in love with his best friend. Franz Schubert learns of their love, and determines to bury his heartbreak in a (you guessed) symphony, which he also decides to leave (you guessed again) "unfinished." At the premiere of the Unfinished Symphony, Schubert (Franz) is ill, close to death's door, and he writes (you can't guess!) "Ave Maria." Curtain. Not only was this story line remote from Schubert's life; it was remote from anybody's.

But Romberg came up with a lovely idea. To musically tell this Viennese hasenpfeffer, he determined to use Schubert's own melodies. Miss Donnelly wrote attractive lyrics, and the show's score was powerful enough to carry that book.

The rehearsals were moist. Jake was personally supervising and he invariably cried at two spots—when the duet sang "Song of Love," and when the whole cast sang "Ave Maria." During one run-through, Jake, wet-eyed and tremulous, still managed to lose his temper.

"Hold it!" he bellowed, "hold it!" And he charged down the aisle toward the pit. He glared at Romberg, who was conducting the orchestra. "That beautiful song. That place where they sing 'Song of Ecstasy.' You wrote it, didn't you?"

Romberg replied that he had had a small assist from Franz Schubert, but yes, for the purpose of the show he had written it.

"Don't lecture me," Jake roared. "That God-damned song is beautiful and I want to hear every God-damned word. Understand?"

Romberg, dumfounded, nodded. Jake went on. "So, why is the God-damned orchestra playing so loud I can't hear the words?"

"But, Mr. Shubert," protested Romberg, "only the fiddles are playing. That's all. Just the fiddles."

Jake glared at him suspiciously. Finally, he shrugged triumphantly. "Only the fiddles, hey? Well, tell the f——ng fiddles to play on just one string! I want to hear the words!" He marched back to his seat, and stared at the silent Romberg and the stunned string section. Finally, he broke the unbelieving silence. "So, what are you waiting for? Time is money, gentlemen, and this time is *my* money!!"

Blossom Time was an instantaneous hit. It ran for nearly two years on Broadway, and spawned road companies like a pregnant shad. It made nothing but money for the Shuberts, and it was a never-ending source of tears for Jake. He would walk into remote theaters, sit in an empty seat in the back row and cry bountifully whenever "Song of Love" or "Ave Maria" was performed.

Blossom Time confirmed what the brothers had surmised from *Maytime*. An operetta was a happy way to make a lot of money. One must understand the Shubert definition of a "*lot* of money." Lee was sitting in his office, late one night, discussing the show-producing proclivities of a young man from the grocery business who had inherited a prodigious fortune, which he was quickly losing on Broadway.

"I am happy that he inherited a lot of money," mused Lee philosophically. "I mean a *lot* of money." He paused for stress. "When I say a lot of money, I don't mean a *lot* of money," he continued. "I mean a *LOT* of money!" It was clear when he said it, and it's clear now.

How did operettas make money? Well, for one thing, they didn't need stars. A company of *Blossom Time*, which J.J. shoved in for one night at the Ambassador, left on tour, advertised as "direct from Broadway" (they were). He hired amateurs, and would-be's, never-was's and old-line retainers. In many cases, their nearest and dearest didn't even know they were on tour, it happened so fast. The Shuberts had scouts at music schools; "Ma" Simmons, Jake's effeminate musical casting director, had friends at the Met, and when a young singer was not quite good enough for Gatti-Casazza, he or she was more than good enough for the Shuberts. Such casting cost next to nothing. It was not like a revue, where if you didn't have Jolson, you had to have Cantor. This was real low-price casting, and it made no difference. *Blossom Time* sold out.

Furthermore, the operettas fell into a pattern. Somehow, they all played in palace halls, or in other period settings. The costumes covered ankles, lower limbs, thighs, permitted décolleté, but were not revealing. Almost anybody, anyone, with any kind of shape, could wear them. Jake was denied normal casting advantages, but could always take comfort in the money he was saving. Girls whose ankles, shins, thighs, etc., required covering came cheaper.

So, an operetta could be cast for peanuts, and you could tour them indefinitely, with no raise in pay. Miraculously, when the Shuberts would throw the pick-up cast into the Ambassador for the one night which gave them the "direct from Broadway" stamp, the audience never noticed! The Shuberts decided that in an operetta, the audience came to see the show; in a revue, they came to see the performer. Jake became very partial to period pieces.

Lee liked them—as musicals. His bookkeeping appreciated them. But he never wanted to do them as dramas. "Audiences," he once pontificated, "don't like plays where people write letters with feathers."

Lee's dramas that year (without quill pens) were all near-disasters. He stayed true to his favorite formula: buy a Hungarian play, which has been translated into German, and then into British English; have same "adapted" for Broadway—you get four writers for the price of one. He tried it with the Jeanne Eagles epic, *In the Night Watch*, a melodrama which will not be described, but which was translated into English from the French translation of the Hungarian original.

In addition, Lee assumed the direction of a musical, *The Rose Girl*, which, by coincidence, featured Beatrice and Marcella Swanson. Lee's direction was difficult to comprehend. It included such odd suggestions as: "Would it be better if we switched Act One with Act Three?"

On one occasion, he interrupted the male lead, Charles Purcell, in the midst of an aria. "Right here," said the elder Shubert, "I would like to have an exceptionally witty line." There was a long pause, and at last, Purcell said, "As, for instance?" Lee stuttered, waved an expressive hand, and was saved by the orchestra.

The Rose Girl played three respectable months at Shubert's behest, and then vanished, and lo, the Swanson sisters reappeared in *Make It Snappy*, starring that man who would never work for the Shuberts again—Eddie Cantor.

In September the Shuberts opened their vaudeville chain, with appropriate publicity cymbals. The reviews were all favorable; the shows were good, often spectacularly so. For ten weeks, the brothers and Keith fought a booking war. If the Shuberts had Nora Bayes at the Central, on Times Square, across the street at the Palace, Keith booked Sophie Tucker. If the Shuberts played Will Rogers, Keith countered with Clayton, Jackson, and Durante. It was a financially bloody battle, the kind Lee Shubert least enjoyed, and at the end of the initial ten weeks, he knew he was losing.

Many of his theaters were too small; even when sold out, they could not make him a profit. And with a ruinous price war for talent as part of his commitment against Keith, the smaller houses not only didn't pay—they lost. Money started to pour down the drain in larger and larger amounts. And Jake screamed. *His* shows were making money; *his* productions were supporting Lee's folly.

Lee was already examining escape hatches. The ever-resourceful Willie Klein resurrected an old lawsuit, this one against Keith. Reactivated, it gave Lee Shubert a handle to hang his ego on.

Way back in 1914, when the Keith Theater Building was being erected in Syracuse, Lee Shubert had been approached by Paul Keith, brother of the vaudeville boss, and a large shareholder in the tightly held family company which controlled the business. To avoid conflicts of interest with the Shuberts, Keith suggested that the Shuberts stay out of vaudeville in Syracuse, and allow none of their theaters to be leased for vaudeville by any other company. In return, Keith would pay Shubert 50 percent of the profits in the Syracuse theater. The Shuberts discontinued vaudeville at the Grand Opera House. But after Paul Keith's death, according to Shubert, Keith refused to honor his brother's verbal agreement, and now Lee was asking Willie Klein what the chances were to collect the profits of the past six years. Willie was willing to try.

Klein, Arthur, was privy to the conversations and the legal strategy sessions. And now, anxious to do something better for Lee than his vaudeville venture, he came up with an invaluable piece of information.

Through a friend in the Keith booking office, Klein had learned the identity of the trustee who held the late Paul Keith's 33 percent of the company that controlled the business. And he had heard rumors that the legatee, E. H. Robinson, was willing to sell. Lee leaped at it like a starving leopard.

The sheer chutzpa of the idea enchanted him. If Keith made money, he would have to pay Lee Shubert part of his profits!! In addition, Lee would have a lovely pipeline into Keith's office. As a large shareholder, he would have access to Keith's books, would know exactly what Keith was paying actors and acts, and would hold a competitive advantage of incalculable value. He almost kissed Klein, Arthur, at the audacity of the possibilities. Klein went to work.

The executor-trustee for the Paul Keith shares was one Clark Day, then head of the Brooklyn Rapid Transit Company, and Klein started making pilgrimages to Brooklyn. Eventually terms were arrived at, and under the name "Diamond," Lee Shubert, for $650,000 became Keith's partner. Neither Keith nor *his* partner E. F. Albee knew it! It was beautiful.

Of course, Keith was informed that a "Mr. Diamond" had purchased the stock, and he spent a lot of time and a lot of money trying to find out who "Diamond" was, but the secret was very well buried. Periodically a representative of a Wall Street law firm which represented the mysterious Mr. Diamond would call at the Palace Theater Building and examine various aspects of the Keith business. And, naturally, checks were issued to "Diamond" and cashed, but no trail ever led to Lee Shubert.

The news that his Wall Street representative was giving Lee (from Keith's books) did little to cheer him. Keith was making money, buying entertainers for less than the Shuberts were paying, and was totally untroubled by the Shubert raid. On all counts, the vaudeville venture was a disaster; it threatened to become a debacle, and Jake wasn't helping matters at all.

"Tell my brother, the great vaudeville impresario, that if he didn't have my Winter Garden tied up with his crap, I could maybe make the Shuberts some money."

Arthur Klein, who was being paid five hundred a week to run the vaudeville operation, was finding Lee more and more remote. It had been customary for Klein to come to Lee's office at night, join him with the Swanson sisters for supper, share Lee's nocturnal roamings, and on one night of each week, receive his check. It had been. Now, it was changing.

Klein gradually became aware that Keith's difficulty in tracing "Diamond" could be explained—each week, it seemed, he was paid by a different corporation, each check solemnly signed by Lee Shubert, and each week the check was being more grudgingly bestowed. "This is coming out of my own pocket," Lee told him solemnly, "and Arthur, my boy, I hate that." Klein began to send out feelers. He did not think his Shubert association was long for this world.

Jake, thoroughly disgusted, was "preparing" for the new season. And now, Lee was determined to take some of the heat off Lee Shubert. The opening gun had been a vague clue in the leasing of various Erlanger theaters. Now came the salvo.

The on-again, off-again merger was on again. Erlanger and Shubert would pool bookings. Productions would continue independently, but the shrinking road (those damned motion pictures!) and the "insane demands of stagehands, actors, and musicians [those damned unions!] are making play production too costly." Equity reacted. It called an emergency meeting. Merger meant one buyer, and lower salaries.

Buried under the publicity was a short financial announcement. The Shubert Theatrical Corporation, a Delaware company, had been organized. It was capitalized at $25,000,000, and "almost 100 percent of the stock [was] held by the Messrs. Shubert." Lee had found time to spend with Bill Phillips. He had watched Joe Schenck organize United Artists with Chaplin, Pickford, Fairbanks, et al., seen Pickford marry Fairbanks in the Hollywood wedding of the century, and then, frozen out of the deal, watched Schenck "go public" with the stock. Schenck, who had begun at Palisades Amusement Park, made millions, as did his partners. Lee Shubert was content to buy several thousand shares, at Phillips' urging.

Phillips was instrumental in a second Shubert "investment." Henry Flagler was in the midst of his vast development project in Florida, and at Phillips' prodding, Lee went down with him to see Miami. It became a place he loved. He couldn't stay out of the land boom, and he made a lot of money speculating in lots, many of which he never saw. He did not object to the financial reward, but what forever endeared Florida to Lee Shubert was the sun.

Sallow-skinned, pale, ashen—these were the descriptions of Shubert until the early twenties. But when he returned from his first visit to Florida, he was instantly dubbed "the Broadway Indian," or "the Pharaoh of Shubert Alley." The ruddy, almost mahogany color was flattering to him. He looked younger. He liked it. There were no sunlamps yet—when they were introduced, Lee would have one of the first ones manufactured. But to keep that magic color, on sunny days Lee would drive to Central Park in his open Hispano Suiza and lie back on the seat, trying to keep his Florida tan. (The chauffeur would take his nap too.)

On other occasions, he would take sunbaths on the roof of the Shubert Theater. Every day at noon, he would march out onto the roof, either oblivious of, or not paying attention to, the fascinated onlookers in the windows of taller buildings. But his final answer to keeping a year-round suntan was his magic face lotion, concocted by his barber and himself.

Lee liked to be shaved twice a day—at 11:00 A.M., and then again at 7:00 P.M. He maintained a resident barber and, in one of the many rooms off his office, a barber chair, which he occasionally also used for naps. Since maintaining a resident barber is expensive, and since Lee Shubert did not like to waste money, the resident barber was also his valet. All his life he hired his valets from a barber shop—the

Plaza Barber Shop, to be exact. It made no difference to Lee whether or not the man had a valet's skills—he *could* shave him.

Assisted by the creative talents of a valet-barber, Lee concocted his face lotion. The recipe begins like a salad dressing. Olive oil and vinegar. Then add witch hazel. Now, the crowning touch, the color additive— iodine! It was a vile-smelling concoction, but it kept Lee coppery and, presumably, antiseptic.

Lee was very proud of his "face lotion" and mysterious about its ingredients. He honestly feared that some commercial company would steal his formula. But he would press bottles of it on close friends, assuring them, "It's good for you, and you look not only better, but healthier and younger."

It should be noted here that Lee had three valets during his Broadway career—all hired from the barber shop. They came to have tremendous influence on him, and thus on the theater. They voiced their opinions to him—often, he sought them. They were on terribly intimate terms with the King of Broadway, and became play critics, performance raters, talent scouts and advisers. One close friend of Lee's swears that the only man Lee ever feared was Peters, his last valet.

One night Shubert and his barber-valet were driving up to the Bronx to take a look at Anna May Wong, the Chinese film actress, who was starring in a production concerned with gang wars and racketeers and other Shubert plot details. On their way north, the barber asked Shubert, "Is that Wong dame really Chinese?" Lee assured him she was. "I think she's a phony," said the barber-valet. "She doesn't walk like any Oriental I ever saw."

This intrigued Shubert. "What do you mean?" he asked curiously.

"You know," was the reply. "The way Chinese walk—kind of funny."

"Stop the car and show me," ordered Shubert.

The valet-barber-chauffeur dutifully pulled the car to the curb, and held the door for Lee. Then he proceeded to walk up and down the sidewalk, taking tiny, mincing, bound-foot steps. Lee watched him in total fascination, nodding slowly. He couldn't wait for them to get to the theater. They watched the performance, and every time Miss Wong crossed the stage, Lee elbowed the Oriental expert. When the final curtain came down, Lee rushed backstage.

In Miss Wong's dressing room, he blurted out his critique. He admired her performance, but she didn't walk like a Chinese! Mystified, she demanded an explanation. And in the tiny dressing room, Lee Shubert minced back and forth across the room, showing her how an Oriental walked. Miss Wong, first amused, then furious, threw her

193

shoe at him, and quit. It took a day for the company manager to calm her down.

But this was the kind of influence his valets had.

It wasn't only barbers who helped make Shubert judgments. For many years, Jake's casting director was "Doc" Hunt, who only worked a half-day casting Jake's epics. The other half of his time was spent in his chosen profession. He was a chiropractor! Some of Jake's aides at the time swear J. J. thought of him as just a part-time casting assistant and never knew that Hunt was a chiropractor.

During the time that Lee had been changing his color, Jake had tended store in New York. He was not pleased with much of the merchandise, and sent a steady barrage of memos to Lee on the money being lost in "your vaudeville." There were moments of pleasure at *Blossom Time*, where Jake could lachrymosely luxuriate in "Ave Maria." But the bulk of time was spent planning next year's productions, and engaging in an epic fight with Romberg. Romberg publicly announced that he was finished with the Shuberts and that he "was going to go into production, to make some of the money the non-talented people who live on creative talents like parasites, are reaping."

Jake felt it necessary to hold a press conference, in which he deplored the emergence of "get-rich-quick Charlies" into show business "who think it so soft to produce a successful show." He fulminated against uncooperative unions, artists, playwrights, composers, and when the conference was over, with no evidence in the reporters' minds as to why it had been called, one press representative said, "That man is his own worst enemy." Franklin P. Adams, better known as F.P.A., a young reporter on the *World*, gruffly ad-libbed, "Not while I'm alive."

On Lee's return, Jake took off for Europe, accompanied by "Ma" Simmons, his shawl-wearing casting director. They were going to look for properties. Lee told Jules Murray to be prepared for a new collection of crying violins. "Show my brother a one-flight-down restaurant and a man who goes around the tables playing the fiddle, and he has found another Romberg."

The elder Shubert held *his* press conference—to announce further expansion of the Erlanger agreement, to say that "greedy actors, unions and composers, particularly stagehands," were threatening the business, and that he would shortly have an announcement of a second vaudeville circuit. He did not bother to deny suggestions that he and Erlanger, along with Dillingham, Golden, Ziegfeld, and the Selwyns, would shortly enter film production. Nor did he confide that he was already greasing the ways to slide out of vaudeville, discreetly, with no fanfare and, hopefully, without anyone noticing.

He would get out of *Shubert* vaudeville only. He would remain Keith's partner. As "Diamond" he would hold the Keith stock for several years, selling it finally, when it looked as if the boom was at its highest, for $1,700,000, a tidy profit for the Messrs. This, in addition to the profit-sharing checks that Keith was remitting. To try to pad the Keith contribution to Shubert income, he asked Willie Klein to start the suit against Keith in Syracuse.

There were the "normal" Shubert litigations; and there was a long-range problem he was going to have to play a major part in solving. When the vaudeville decision was made, the brothers had entered into a lot of contracts with actors. Their "guarantee" was staggering—over $73,000 a week. They wanted to hold on to some of those acts and actors for their own revues and cabaret-type entertainments. Others they would want to pay off. And there was a third group they wanted no part of and, if necessary, were prepared to give the George Price treatment to. Willie Klein was going to have to figure out the outs.

The "normal" Shubert legal tangles provided Klein with a rich and varied legal background. There were always the Shubert contracts, an endless source of legal research. Then, there was Jake. Jake enjoyed litigation. He would invite it—by hitting someone; he would encourage it—by intransigence; he would initiate it—by breaking his word. This summer, it was an automobile accident, and his chauffeur was charged with being drunk. Suit: $5,000. It was settled out of court. The chauffeur was not drunk—merely terrified by Jake.

Lee was suing Keith, and also suing Arthur Hopkins. He claimed he had an arrangement with Hopkins wherein Lee owned 50 percent of *The Claw*, a Hopkins production starring Lionel Barrymore, which had been sold to Hollywood. Lee settled it—out of court. Together, the brothers sued the Longacre Company, charging that exorbitant rents were being extorted from the Shuberts on their lease on the Astor Theater. It was laughed out of court. By this time, no court in New York would believe the Shuberts could be overcharged. One of Jake's dancers, Virginia Richmond, claimed that a chandelier had skulled her when it fell from the set of a Shubert production. She contended that her skull was worth $25,000. Jake denied this hotly, and Willie Klein settled—out of court. George Price was settled out of court, Eddie Cantor was settled out of court, and Arthur Klein, high priest of Shubert vaudeville, also settled out of court.

Klein had been promised a share of the "Diamond" deal, but Lee patiently pointed out that he was personally paying him for losing Shubert money and that he didn't owe him anything.

The Syracuse case, $1,000,000 against Keith, was not a satisfactory (to Lee) Shubert course of action. Lee, in deposition, repeated the story of the Paul Keith 50 percent of the profits deal. E. F. Albee denied the story, as detailed by William Rubin, Willie Klein's nominee to represent the Shubert cause in Syracuse. Albee claimed that the original offer made when Paul Keith was alive had been for 25 percent of the profits; when Paul Keith died, the offer was not renewed.

"At that time," said Albee, "Lee Shubert threatened a lawsuit, and I told him not to get excited; he would be taken care of. He has been. We lived up to Paul Keith's 25 percent agreement."

The case died. Lee did not feel it advisable to inform Albee that he was their partner.

Lee managed to keep Willie busy on other fronts. The New York *Daily News* had just commenced publishing. Every producer and production company sent a press representative to the *News* to see how they might be mutually helpful. Lee Shubert "invited" the *News* to send a representative to call on him. They didn't.

Shortly after the paper began, James Whittaker, their drama critic, referred to the Century Theater as a "mausoleum." As soon as Lee had been provided with a definition of the word, he barred Whittaker from Shubert theaters, and withdrew his advertising, some $30,000 worth annually, from the *News*.

They, in turn, instituted a survey of Shubert press relations through the years in the form of a feature article, and Lee hastily restored advertising and Whittaker's seats. Willie Klein, very busy now, suggested that Lee go to Europe, and with the senior partner gone, it was Jake's turn.

In Chicago, the *Evening Post* ran a series of articles on theater health violations. They picked the panicky time of the flu epidemic to point out that absolutely nothing was being done by theater owners to protect the audience against contagion, and they lambasted the Shuberts in particular. Jake promptly sued for $100,000. In addition to the suit, he issued a J.J. diatribe against the newspaper, which promptly sued the Shuberts for $500,000 for libel. Willie Klein managed to get both suits dropped.

Mercifully, summer was at hand, and in those pre-air-conditioned days, many theaters closed. The Shuberts could look ahead. Jake was in rehearsal in Atlantic City, in a ballroom near the Pier, with a new musical. At the Garden Pier Theater, a company was performing, and Jake requested permission from the company manager to "take a look at the show on stage," on a day when there was no matinée.

The company manager was a young fellow called Ray Whittaker (no relation to the New York *Daily News* critic), who had worked for the Shuberts that past winter in a Philadelphia vaudeville house. He gave Jake permission to use his stage.

Two days later, again on a non-matinée day, Whittaker, who was using a large dressing room as his bachelor apartment, was awakened by the tinkle of a rehearsal piano and the sounds of drama. He walked into the theater, and there was J.J. conducting another rehearsal. Whittaker was incensed.

"What are you doing here?"

"Rehearsing," said Jake blandly. "You told me—"

Whittaker interrupted. "I gave you permission to rehearse one day. Don't you think you ought to ask before you trespass on another's man's property?"

Jake started to bluster.

Whittaker told him to continue his rehearsal and left.

Two weeks later in New York, Whittaker hit Ray Long of the Shubert office for a job. Long suggested that he see J.J. Whittaker hastily told him the Atlantic City story. Long decided that perhaps it would be better if he, Long, went to see J.J.

In J.J.'s office, Long told him about the job request and identified the applicant.

Jake was typically unpredictable. "Hire him," he snapped. "I want a young man like that taking care of *my* property." Whittaker was sent to Kansas City to manage the Shubert house there.

And Jake prepared for the new season.

Gallagher and Shean were a song and patter comedy team who became a household word. The song, "Oh, Mr. Gallagher, Oh, Mr. Gallagher!" the big number in their act, was almost a second national anthem.

They had signed a contract with the Shuberts, assured that they would star in a Broadway production in 1922. They were looking forward to settling down in New York; they had toured for years. The Shubert contract was typically full of Willie Klein fine print, and Gallagher and Shean discovered they were going to play vaudeville—on tour. They were not happy.

Simultaneously, they were offered leads in a *Ziegfeld Follies*, at $1,500 a week; the Shubert contract called for $750 a week. Righteously indignant, the team signed with Ziegfeld and went into rehearsal. Now it was Lee Shubert who wasn't happy. He had Willie Klein sue to enforce their contract. It resulted in the most preposterous trial in theatrical history.

Klein based his case on two points. First, that Gallagher and Shean "were unique and extraordinary"—as stated in their contract—

Gallagher and Shean. The only actors who went to court to prove they were no good.

and therefore they could not be replaced. Second, the contract gave Shubert the right to tour the team in vaudeville.

Gallagher and Shean claimed that the vaudeville booking was in violation of their agreement, and furthermore, they "were *not* unique and extraordinary"—they were just ordinary. To prove their contention, they brought in witnesses—performers, directors—who solemnly testified that Gallagher and Shean were dull, trite, journeyman talents. Will Rogers, one of their best witnesses, stated that "Gallagher and Shean are a pair of bums." He went on to add, "I can't sing any better than a crow, but I do their routine better than they do."

The Shuberts, to be sure, had *their* expert witnesses, all of whom paid glowing tribute to the unique and extraordinary talents of Gallagher and Shean. Lee Shubert, to emphasize the point, solemnly told the presiding officer, Judge Delehanty, "that these actors make more money a year than you do." The judge received this in silence, although he had a lot of questions for Lee—questions which Lee stammered and stumbled through.

The proceedings were enlivened by a visit from twenty girls from Flo Ziegfeld's *Follies*, come to court, they stated, to testify that Gallagher and Shean were not "bums, but perfect gentlemen." They were not called to the stand, but they added to the Alice-in-Wonderland quality of a trial where two actors were swearing that they were run-of-the-mill, "nothing" performers, and the leading producer in the country was contradicting them.

Eventually, Judge Delehanty rendered his decision, and a gifted but, unfortunately, unidentified scribe wrote his story for the New York *Daily News* in the form of the Gallagher and Shean trademark song. This is it. (If you don't know the melody, find someone who does— and sing along.)

GALLAGHER AND SHEAN HAM ACTORS—BUT WIN!
Not So Good, They Agree with Court's Ruling

Supreme Court Justice Frank B. Delehanty handed down a decision yesterday in favor of Gallagher and Shean . . . in the suit of the Shubert Theatrical Co. to restrain them from further playing in the Ziegfeld *Follies*.

"Oh, Mr. Gallagher! Oh, Mr. Gallagher!
When the Judge said, 'Case is closed and I decide,
That the judgment, it is clear,
Goes to these defendants here,'
It made me feel so good, real tears I cried!"

"Oh, Mr. Shean! Oh, Mr. Shean!
I think I understand just what you mean;
But I said 'No tears for *me*,
I will leave all that to Lee' "
"But that's heartless, Mr. Gallagher!"
"NO, that's business, Mr. Shean."

Both Gallagher and Shean were on the stand under questioning by their attorney and cross-questioning by counsel for the Shuberts. Both Gallagher and Shean seemed to find difficulty in setting dates of their conferences with Shubert representatives leading to the signing of the contract under which the Shuberts sought to restrain them in this action from playing in the *Follies*.

"Oh, Mr. Gallagher! Oh, Mr. Gallagher!
When you were on the stand you talked so dumb!

You didn't know a thing
At the lawyers' questioning.
Your memory was simply on the bum!"

"Well, Mr. Shean! Well, Mr. Shean!
I can't say you yourself were awfully keen.
When he asked you, 'No or yes?'
All you said was, 'Well . . . I guess.' "
"Were we stupid, Mr. Gallagher?"
"Yes, like foxes, Mr. Shean."

There were present in the courtroom, ready to testify in behalf of
the defendants a group of *Follies* girls. They came in a half hour
after the beginning of the court session and created a distinct stir.

"Oh, Mr. Gallagher! Oh, Mr. Gallagher!
When the *Follies* girls came in so neat and sweet,
I cannot help but mention
That you didn't pay attention,
Forced the lawyer all his questions to repeat."

"But, Mr. Shean! But, Mr. Shean!
They were each and every one a lovely queen.
And as in their smiles we basked,
Who cared what the lawyer asked?"
"Ah, I get you, Mr. Gallagher!"
"Yes, I thought so, Mr. Shean."

Lee Shubert, on the stand, was caustically interrogated by Justice
Delehanty, who demanded to know why the manager failed to insert
in the contract the exact nature of the work which Gallagher and
Shean were to perform. Shubert found difficulty in explaining to
the court's satisfaction.

"Oh, Mr. Gallagher! Oh, Mr. Gallagher!
I thought I'd die when Lee was on the stand.
His story never showed
That he'd hired us for vaude,
And the Judge was forced to ask, to understand."

" 'Now, Mr. Shubert. Now, Mr. Shubert!
Why don't your contracts state just what they mean?'
The Judge seemed gosh-darned mad
Mr. Shubert seemed in bad."
"I felt so sorry, Mr. Gallagher."
"You're another, Mr. Shean."

Justice Delehanty rendered his decision after finding that the plaintiff had failed to prove either of his main contentions; first, that Gallagher and Shean were unique and extraordinary as a team, and second, that the contract he held provided primarily for the employment of the team in vaudeville instead of a full-sized production.

"Oh, Mr. Gallagher! Oh, Mr. Gallagher!
The Judge's first point was 'They're not unique!'
He agreed with Mr. Lederer
There are lots of actors better-er
And that our success is just a lucky streak."

"Oh, Mr. Shean! Oh, Mr. Shean!
He also ruled the contract doesn't mean
That we'd signed in vaude to show,
And so now we stay with Flo."
"That's fifty-fifty, Mr. Gallagher."
"*Seven*-fifty, Mr. Shean."

The court's decision yesterday permits the Gallagher-Shean team to continue with the Ziegfeld *Follies* at a salary said to be $1,500 per week instead of with the Shuberts, at the contract salary of $750 per week.

"Oh, Mr. Gallagher! Oh, Mr. Gallagher!
Judge Delehanty's set the legal price for pork:
With fifteen hundred beans
Placed each week in our jeans
We're the most expensive hams in all New York."

"Oh, Mr. Shean! Oh, Mr. Shean!
Mr. Shubert looked so mad his face was green—
He hired us as an entr'act
But we slammed him on the contract."
"Positively, Mr. Gallagher."
"Absolutely, Mr. Shean!"

Gallagher and Shean stayed with the *Follies*, and Willie Klein appealed. Jake was livid. "If I had been on the stand," he said, "instead of my brother, we would have seen something different." (The court of appeals saw something different, and Gallagher and Shean found themselves back in Shubert bondage. Lee 'n' Jake promptly slapped them into a *Greenwich Village Follies* and—all Broadway could see it coming —sent them out on tour.)

Jake was having an exceptionally good season. He already had three gilt-edged musical hits: *Sally, Irene and Mary; The Greenwich Village Follies;* and *The Lady in Ermine. Dancing Girl,* which Jake had personally supervised *and* staged, was going to make a little money. Meanwhile, Lee was doing a series of turkeys, and backing out of vaudeville like a reluctant crab.

Jake held a press conference in which he explained the secrets of successful production, and grew angry only when he was asked to explain certain failures. The purpose of the meeting was to inform the press that "a successful, high-type, sophisticated revue which was done by the Society of Illustrators is going to be expanded into a sparkling Broadway-type production by the Shuberts. We are calling it *Artists and Models.*" He also took a few free swipes at Romberg, who was producing his second failure.

The reporters faithfully reported Jake's announcement, enraging him with the heading, "Shuberts announce change of policy; to be sophisticated." Jake ordered the car and took off for Boston.

J.J. enjoyed automobiles. He liked driving out on jaunts, and his chauffeurs were always at the ready. And he particularly liked driving to Boston. The chauffeurs didn't.

Jake's temper was royally democratic; he would lose it with anyone, and he had no trouble losing it with chauffeurs. He liked to drive fast when he was going somewhere, and he would back-seat drive like a Grand Prix winner. "Watch where you're going!" he would bellow, and the chauffeur would flinch. "Who does that son of a bitch think he is?" Jake would scream, as a car momentarily blocked their passage. "Pass him!" Jake had absolutely no doubt that he owned the Boston Post Road, and he thus regarded all other traffic as trespassers.

On one occasion, on impulse, he ordered the car into Shubert Alley and peremptorily informed the driver they were going to Boston. Jake was in a black(er) mood, and the first attempt the chauffeur made at small talk was ended when Jake barked, "Shut up! Keep your God-damned eyes on the road!"

It was a rough trip. Traffic was rather heavy, and Jake kept giving orders. "I don't want to get to Boston tomorrow—I want to be there today." The chauffeur started to turn in his seat, and Jake bellowed, "You keep your eyes on the road, or I'll fire you!" It went on like that for the entire first hour of the trip. Every time the chauffeur instinctively turned his head to reply to a barked order, Jake would react. "Why are you keeping on looking at me? I'm so interesting you can't watch the God-damned road?" Or, "You want to get me killed?" Finally, Jake ordered the rear-view mirror turned away so that he could not be seen in it.

Rigidly staring straight ahead, the driver suggested that it wasn't safe to turn the mirror up. Jake screamed that there was a mirror on the outside of the car and the driver could damned well use that! "I don't need a spy for company!" Jake told him.

When the poor chauffeur noticed that he was running low on gas and would have to stop, he was petrified. When he started to slow down, Jake instantly demanded an explanation. As the driver gave him the reason, Jake issued his final order. "All right, but I don't want to hear another word out of you for the rest of the day," said Jake. "Keep your mouth shut, your mind on your driving, and your eyes away from me. Understand?" The miserable man nodded. By now, staring ahead was a conditioned reflex. He pulled into the gas station, ordered the tank filled, paid the bill, and drove resolutely to Boston, never turning, never saying a word, relieved at the silence from the back seat. He was convinced that Jake was buried in deep thought; he hadn't kibitzed once.

He arrived at the Shubert Theater in Boston to find the switchboard alive with lights, and a greeting party of four standing on the curb. He stepped out of the car, opened the back door, and no one exited. He peered in. The rear of the car was empty.

It seems that Jake had utilized the stop to visit the men's room, and the poor chauffeur had driven off without him. Completely terrified at the prospect of what was awaiting him, the chauffer raced back to pick up his boss. And of course there was Jake seated in the gas station, instructing the owner on how to improve business. Instead of truculence and the expected temper tantrum, Jake merely suggested that it might be a good idea from now on if the driver checked to make sure he had his passenger.

But Jake liked driving, and he liked Boston. It was away from New York and Lee; in Boston, Jake could play king, and he enjoyed that; and in Boston, he could buy property.

Long before 1910, Jake had started the regular visits to Boston. He stayed at the Ritz, and between girls and fights over various things, he started investing in Boston real estate. William K. Bean, a Boston realtor who worked for Cabot, Cabot and Forbes, was the Shubert agent in Boston, and it was he who scouted properties for Jake, and he who managed them after Jake bought them.

Bean was puzzled by the fact that the Shuberts never seemed to sell property; they just bought it and kept it, and watched it go up in value. Bean personally sold them fifty-seven assorted properties, from theaters and theater sites to office buildings and apartment houses. In 1954, the Shubert holdings in Boston were "appraised" at $10,000,000—and Boston is not famous for high appraisals.

Lee had never approved of Jake's investments in Boston. He watched them go up and up in value and in later years took a lot of ribbing because Jake's shrewdness was making both of them money.

One case in particular. Jake insisted on buying two pieces of property at $15,000 apiece. Lee fought him bitterly, predicting total loss, tied-up cash, waste of money. Under the unwritten law which governed their actions, Jake could make the final decision out of New York, and he opted purchase. Five years later, Jake turned down $125,000 apiece for the buildings. Bean, running into Lee at the theater, needled him.

"What do you think of the Stuart Street property now, Mr. Shubert?"

Lee gave no answer.

Back in New York, Jake could not control his glee over the triumph. "Ask my God-damned brother how he likes Stuart Street," he ordered. "And tell him I want an answer."

Lee listened impassively, and then said softly, "Tell my brother I am pleasantly disappointed."

Bean ran afoul of Shubert legalities some years later. He had suggested a refinancing plan to Jake and been enthusiastically told to go ahead. Since the Boston properties, like so many other Shubert ventures, were buried in a myriad of corporations, many of them dummies, it was a sizable job to get new mortgages, which left cash in Shubert hands, and properties well protected. (The dummy corporations need explanation. Jake's reputation for shrewd buying had become a legend in Boston, and it was good business to conceal the identity of the purchaser until the deal was closed. There are those who say Jake enjoyed the cloak-and-dagger routine because he could also conceal the ownership from Lee, until it was too late for Lee to object.)

At the conclusion of this fairly Herculean task, Bean submitted his bill for commissions on the mortgages and for his other services, and Jake refused to pay. It went into the Boston courts, and the Shuberts won. Jake proved to the court's satisfaction that no such companies—his own dummy companies!—existed!

It was during the Bean suit that Jake complained about a director who had decamped to Ziegfeld. "One thing you can't count on in this world," he said bitterly, "is gratitude."

Jake's *Passing Show of 1922* was not well received. It starred two Shubert stand-bys, Willie and Eugene Howard, and it faithfully followed the formula that had made it Shubert bread-and-butter for ten long years. But the audience didn't buy. Jake instantly put the 1923 version into work, replacing the Howards with George Jessel and otherwise attempting to spark the production.

Little hieroglyphics were appearing on the wall, but Jake couldn't read them. The Shuberts, in spite of Jake's protests, had entered into a three-way deal to build the Music Box Theater. Their partners were Sam Harris, a tasteful producer, and Irving Berlin. And the *Music Box Revue*, a smart, fast-paced revue was a hit. George White's *Scandals* featured "new" talent and new approaches.

Perhaps it is unjust to say Jake didn't see the signs. Perhaps that is why he went downtown to see the Illustrators' show that he had announced. But his 1923 *Passing Show* did no better than his 1922 version, and Jake left for Europe.

Lee kept the Erlanger-merger kettle boiling by issuing and denying statements. They would make films; they would not. They would book intelligently. Everyone was in. No, only a select few. It went on and on, achieving two things. First, it kept the Shuberts in the news, and second, it aroused Equity.

The hard-won five-year contract that had been hammered out in 1919, after the bitter strike, was up for renewal, and both sides were planning strategy. Erlanger and Ziegfeld wanted to refuse to sign a new contract with Equity. They based their argument on the new "cooperation" between the managers—that is, the Shubert-Erlanger agreement. Where could the actors work if everybody held out? They were joined by Sam Harris.

Lee Shubert thought differently. The Shuberts produced twice or often three times as many shows as any individual producer. And unlike most of their associates in the managers' group, they owned theaters. They not only made money on productions, they made money on their real estate. They lost money when theaters were dark, and they lost it two ways. Lee Shubert didn't want a strike, and he didn't want dark theaters. Obviously, he had no reluctance to smash Equity; he hated unions, but as a practical man, he was prepared to live with them. If breaking Equity was going to cost Shubert dollars, he chose the other way.

The whole series of ploys that were the projected merger with Erlanger were a threat to actors. Announcements that one legitimate theater in every major city was going to be converted into a motion-picture house didn't make the performers feel any better. It even provoked the Motion Picture Theater Owners' Association to attack the plan as an attempt "to gouge the public." Shubert replied that if the actors struck again, and if the stagehands supported the strike, he would convert *all* his theaters into motion-picture houses.

But behind the scenes, Shubert was having talks with Equity. He kept pushing them to modify their closed-shop clause so that he could go to his own colleagues with something in his hand in exchange for which he would write a new contract, and avoid a costly strike.

Meanwhile, behind Lee's back, Keith was propagandizing the other members of the producers' group to freeze out the union and break it, once and for all. He was successfully fighting off the vaudeville artists, and he did not want them getting any ideas. In addition, by this time, if Lee Shubert was *for* anything, Keith was against it.

Lee was made aware of Keith's maneuvers, and paid little attention to them. He had passed his fiftieth birthday, without celebration, and was trying to get things into an orderly arrangement. All the time he had spent with Phillips was going to pay off. He had carefully covered his flanks in vaudeville by making side deals, unconsummated, with Erlanger. He had bought into Keith; he was expanding the Shubert operations, and carefully, oh, so carefully, segregating the components of his empire into those that were controlled by him (and Jake) and those that were corporate.

There was a large real-estate operation in New York under the corporate umbrella "Trebuhs," or Shubert spelled backward. The prize theaters in the chain were in corporations he owned, with J.J. as a partner. Leaseholds were in the name of Shubert Theatrical, and various "rights"—in theatrical properties or in real estate—were allocated to "Sam S. Shubert and Lee Shubert."

His personal life was in order. He was seeing a great deal of Marcella Swanson, and she was appearing in a procession of "The Messrs. Shubert Present." Peggy Hopkins Joyce, one of America's more beautiful blondes, whose eyes kindled at the sight of diamonds, was seen frequently on Lee's arm at openings. (There was much debate in knowledgeable circles concerning this relationship. Lee was not the kind of man who made expensive gifts. Peggy Hopkins Joyce was a collector. How did Lee get around it?) In addition, a custom that would last for the bulk of his life had begun. Lee liked girls. He usually liked them at about noon. At fifty, he liked them, and at seventy-five, he would still like them. The routine was the same—when you have an empire, you have protocol. The "girl" for the day would call at exactly 11:00 A.M. If she was put through to Lee, the assignation was arranged—she appeared at the Shubert office, was ushered in, and performed. If, when she called, the message was "Mr. Lee is in conference," the date was off, and she was free to do as she pleased.

Peggy Hopkins Joyce. A frequent Lee Shubert companion. She loved collecting jewelry.

Otherwise, the date was on. It in no way interfered with Lee's fidelity to Miss Joyce or Miss Swanson. That part of his life was arranged.

Jake had his own arrangements. They were usually impromptu. For some reason, J.J.'s retinue of courtiers always included a large contingent from the homosexual fringe. Melville Ellis had been replaced by "Ma" Simmons. The "chorus boys" in Jake's productions were generally called "Les Girls," or " 'Ma' Simmons' girl friends." One theory for Jake's predilection for the twilight sex was security. Unlike Lee, Jake maintained his chorus as a harem—he would take the whole corps out for dinner with himself as the only male male present.

Strangely, both men were faithful in their fashion. No matter who the girl of the afternoon was, Lee would always be there for his night-time semi-permanent liaison. And Jake, in his own way, went home to his "companion." They each had a dividing line beween their extra-curricular activities and their commitments.

Lee kept Willie Klein occupied. Although the bulk of Klein's time was spent in clearing out the troublesome vaudeville contracts, he was actively concerned in the secret Equity negotiation, and in the run-of-the-mill Shubert litigations. The De Koven estate won a judgment for $10,000 on the old Lyric Theater deal, and Klein promptly appealed. He was busy appealing the Gallagher and Shean verdict. He was defending Jake on two assault counts. He was fighting two theater leases. And with cunning foresight, he was dreaming up an errand for the other Klein—Arthur.

Willie had broken down their contract list to three categories: want to keep, don't want at all, may have to pay. (Obviously, they wanted Gallagher and Shean.) The staggering concept that they might have to pay performers not to perform was sacrilegious to Lee. He reached back in memory and remembered how Erlanger had gotten out of the first vaudeville venture in which the Shuberts were involved. Keith had assumed the artists' contracts, and the Shuberts had promised to stay out of vaudeville for ten years. (They hadn't. They had leased the Music Hall to William Morris for the Harry Lauder tour in 1911 for $4,500. Originally, Morris had offered 27 percent of the gross as rent, but Lee didn't think Lauder would pull that kind of audience. When Lauder topped $35,000 per week, Lee was grief-stricken, until he discovered that Morris was performing one more time a week than the contract called for and demanded that the deal revert to percentage, not the flat price. It was settled by Willie Klein—out of court.)

Now, it was Lee's suggestion that a deal be made with Keith. The Shuberts would turn over all their "acts" to Keith, and he would pay them; in return, the Shuberts would permanently resign from vaudeville. Klein, Arthur, was delegated the privilege of calling on Keith. Keith refused to see him, and finally little Arthur sat down with E. F. Albee.

Albee, who in his youth had achieved a nationwide reputation for the profanity of his pungent dialogue, had been converted. He had met a man of the cloth, gotten religion, reformed, and forsworn all profanity. He listened carefully as Klein presented Lee Shubert's offer, and then, face red, veins distended, he fought for control. Finally, he could no longer control himself. He smashed his fists down on the desk top, shattering the glass which protected the wood. "Tell Mr. Shubert," he began, "that I will see him dead before I bail him out of—" he paused and shook his head. "I have thirty million dollars with which to bury Lee Shubert," he started again, and again he paused. He looked up imploringly at heaven. "Forgive me, Lord," he said. Then he turned to Arthur Klein. Pleasantly, he added, "Tell Lee Shubert to go f——k himself." Klein got up to leave. But Albee had a postscript. "And tell the son of a bitch"—eyes raised, piously—"Forgive me—that he owes me forty dollars for the damned glass top of my desk!"

Willie Klein continued negotiating out of contracts, and Lee collected his "Diamond" checks from Keith, and worried about how to get more. Jake got busy with "next season."

He made peace with Romberg and presented a number of properties that Romberg might do a musical with. Among them was the two-time loser *Heidelberg*, one of the early Shubert-in-New-York-by-Sam productions, which had bombed and which the Shuberts had persuaded Mansfield to try in their second attempt as *Prince Karl*. Romberg promised to think about it. (He had joined Jolson, Cantor, et al. in the "I won't work for the Shuberts again club" and had, with them, attained charter membership.

Jake had also acquired the Lehar operettas and was going to present them to New York. But right now, he was more concerned with introducing *Artists and Models*, his "sophisticated" revue, to the impatient audience.

What the Shuberts called *Artists and Models* had begun in the Village as a smart little amateur show, staged by the Illustrators' Society. A Shubert scout had seen it, recommended it to Lee and J.J., and Jake bought it. His changes in the show were elementary: first, throw out what we bought; then, make all the boys artists, and all the girls their models; then, we build a show around it.

Artists and Models, 1923. J.J.'s palette.

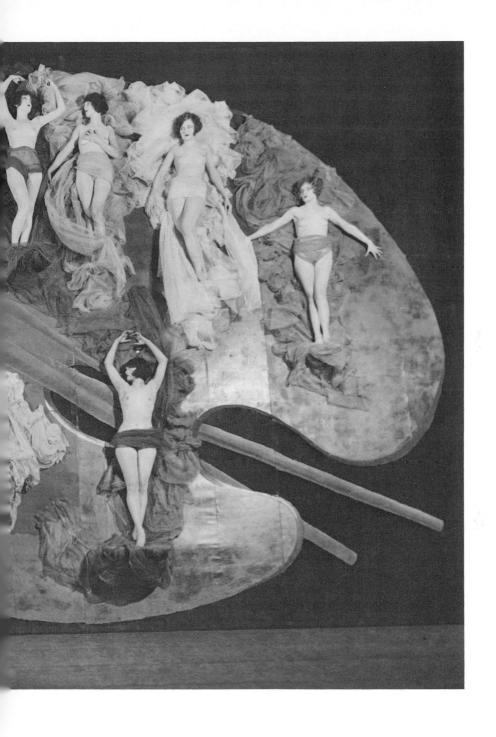

Artists and Models, 1923. Some of J.J.'s nudes that sold so many Shubert tickets.

The show had been built by Jake's "staff," and when he walked into dress rehearsal and watched the goings-on, Jake blew a fuse.

He wheeled on J. C. Huffman, his long-time director, the man J.J. had endlessly "personally supervised." "When I say *Artists and Models* what the hell do you think of?"

Huffman stared at him uncomprehendingly.

"You see a whole lot of men with hands on their hips, holding paintbrushes, making living tableaux with girls all full of clothes? Is that what you see?"

Huffman still had no answer.

"You never been in Paris?" was the next question.

Huffman mumbled that he had been to Paris.

"You think everybody in Paris walks around with his God-damned hand on his God-damned hip, like some God-damned faggot, asking girls to take poses?"

Huffman resumed silence as a wiser course.

"Now you're talking," said Jake to the silent Huffman. He scrambled down the aisle and up on the stage.

Purposefully, the creative Shubert walked up to the first show girl, grabbed her dress by the bodice, and ripped it down to her waist. The girl screamed, and covered her bared breasts with her hands.

"That's what an artist does," roared Jake. The girl screamed again and ran offstage.

"No broad who won't show her tits can work this show," yelled the Continental Shubert. "And that's final!"

He stalked out.

A number of girls quit, and were quickly replaced by more flexible thinkers. The replacements were all trained Shubert chorines who knew the routines by heart. Jake was not a great devotee of the dance, and Shubert choreography was elementary.

On August 20, 1923, *Artists and Models* opened at the Shubert Theater. That same night, the Shuberts opened *Home Fires* at the 39th Street Theater, and hardly anyone heard about it. *Artists and Models* was the theatrical sensation of the new season. It was not sophisticated, although some of the skits were clever; it was not as well produced as a *Scandals* or a *Follies*; but it was bare.

As soon as the word was out, the lines started forming, and the tickets became collectors' items. A strange thing happened in the audience. For the first time in a long time, single seats were selling as well as pairs, and they were being bought by men. Bald-headed men, men with full heads of hair, men, period. It was a throwback to old burlesque days.

214

Frank Fay was the star of *Artists and Models*, and that comedian, whose face was a promising leer to begin with, and whose exquisite sense of timing could convert the Lord's Prayer into a suggestive piece, helped make the show a box-office smash.

It also provoked a nationwide barrage of publicity. And of protest. Newspaper after newspaper took a dim view of "nudity" on the stage. Ironically, there was nothing new in it. There had been "living curtains"—undraped girls set in various set pieces—and there had been "tableaux"—undraped girls holding various poses. But Jake's show had the girls moving and taking part in skits, and it had shock value. Jealous rivals called it "dirty" and started planning ways to present undressed females in *their* productions. An antinudity backlash was the inevitable result, and censors started examining shows all over the United States.

One of the first victims was the Shuberts' own *Ted Lewis Frolic*, which was closed by the mayor of Philadelphia, as being "suggestive," "salacious," and "offensive." The Shuberts went into court and secured an injunction against the mayor's action, and ticket sales zoomed. Having failed in his first move, the mayor now revoked the license of the Shubert Theater in Philadelphia, and Willie Klein had to go back into court and fight that action. He won again, and the otherwise undistinguished show became a sellout.

The August 23rd issue of *Variety* devoted a great deal of space to the brothers. There were two editorials dealing with Shubert affairs and a fistful of news items.

The lead editorial was on *Artists and Models*, which *Variety* viewed with alarm. It was nude, they said, and it was vulgar, and the legitimate theater was better off without that kind of entertainment. On that same page, they reported the events in Philadelphia.

The second editorial was in the form of an open letter to Lee. "Where is Shubert vaudeville, Lee?" is the way it began. They went on to quote Lee's press conference of two years before where he had vowed to spend every dollar he had to crack Keith. "You gave your word, Lee," said the editorial, ". . . are you broke?"

On that same page was an insignificant little box detailing that Klein Brothers, a minor vaudeville act under contract to the Shuberts, had been forced to pay $1,000 to secure their release from that contract so that they could perform for going circuit.

Finally, there was another needling item, stating that tickets for *Artists and Models*, which could not be bought at the box office, were available at the ticket counter of the Ambassador Hotel—said ticket counter being a Shubert concession.

It can be stated that the August 23rd *Variety* did not bring joy and delight into the hearts of the brothers. They read it and they fumed and they roared at their press department, sending Claude Greneker into emergency sessions with various editors. And finally, the Shuberts determined to sue.

They hit *Variety* with a suit for $100,000, claiming libel. And of all that *Variety* had printed, what particular phrase did the Shuberts find libelous? The little box about the Klein Brothers!

In September, *Variety* noted the suit, and beside the story covering the Shubert allegations, they reprinted the Klein Brothers box. Like so many other Shubert "libel" suits, it was allowed to die away.

In October, Willie Klein filed a more meaningful suit. It was for a whopping $10,500,000, and it was against Keith. It charged Keith with restraint of trade, called his vaudeville operation a monopoly, and claimed triple damages. The Shubert allegation went on to note that they had lost $3,500,000 in vaudeville because of Keith's monopoly, and they then demanded the $10,500,000. (No, there was no mention of their ownership of Keith stock.)

The following day, Klein filed a second suit, this time against Keith personally, charging "terrorization" and demanding damages.

Keith was enraged. The Shuberts charging "restraint"! He raised hell with his attorneys, but for publication, he issued a terse statement. "It's an easy way to make money," he said. "But then, so is burglary."

Chapter Eleven

When it arrived 1924 was a happy year. Half of America was singing a nonsense song, "Yes, We Have No Bananas," and the other half was singing "California, Here I Come," which Al Jolson had interpolated into *Bombo* to make money for the brothers Shubert on the road.

The twenties were roaring, all except for Calvin Coolidge, taciturn in the White House. And no one roared louder than Jake and Lee—not in 1924.

Time had seen changes in their lives. Both parents were dead, and so was Joe W. Jacobs. Joe Rhinock, their partner since 1908, had found himself leasing theaters to Keith at the very time the Shuberts reinvaded vaudeville. He tentatively offered Lee his resignation, and Lee snapped it up. Rhinock was never invited back. Arthur Klein, the Shubert major-domo in the vaudeville fiasco, was back working for Keith. In Lee's mind, little Arthur had become the villain of the vaudeville debacle. Not only did Lee refuse to speak to him, but on one occasion, when he saw Jack Pearl, a Shubert comic, talking to Klein, Lee stopped talking to Pearl!

By 1924 the brothers had become the dominant force in the legitimate theater. They were producing about one-quarter of the plays in America. They controlled 75 percent of the theater tickets in the country. And Lee was playing a vital role in the affairs of Marcus Loew. It was a delicate role.

Loew's theater chain was huge, and he was having trouble "stocking" it with pictures. A little arithmetic convinced him that if he combined the efforts of a group of independent producers he would be free of the Paramount octopus. Louis B. Mayer was making about twelve films a year. Sam Goldwyn was making twenty. Joe Engel, under the name Metro, was manufacturing twenty. Totaled, they came to the magic fifty-two—a picture a week, first-run.

Loew determined to merge Metro and Goldwyn pictures, under the corporate name Metro-Goldwyn Pictures, and then throw the Mayer output into the bag. Mayer, almost as rough as the Shuberts when it came to making a deal, balked. He wanted his name on the company title; otherwise, he wouldn't play. He won his point, and the firm was organized as Metro-Goldwyn-Mayer. Louis B. had no stock, but he was on the masthead. The Goldwyn part of the arrangement didn't last very long. Whether or not Lee Shubert, with his dislike for "Goldfish," played any part in the decision can't be ascertained. But Goldwyn left his name on the company, and hung his hat in his own Samuel Goldwyn Pictures office. MGM was born, and Lee Shubert sat on its board.

To keep Lee's mind on his own affairs, the Vaudeville Actors Guild sued the Shuberts for damages, which they estimated at more than $5,000,000. The guild charged that the Shuberts had conspired with Keith to agree to stay out of vaudeville! It was salt in Lee's wounds, and Jake did not make it any easier. Nothing ever came of the suit.

The five-year agreement signed between Equity and the producers in 1919 was coming to an end. A bloc of the producers, including Erlanger, Ziegfeld, Dillingham, and Harris, had stated that they would not renew the agreement. Behind scenes, Keith was urging the producers to stand firm, break Equity, and once and for all do away with unions of actors. It was anticipated that the Shuberts would spearhead the drive to crush the union.

Lee Shubert remained noncommittal. He was away part of the time, and in his own offices his assistants and cadre were marshaling their strength in anticipation of the war with Equity. On his return, Lee quietly informed them that he would carry on his own private negotiation with the actors. It would be good for everybody, he announced to his stunned colleagues. He did not want a strike.

In his own group, only Willie Klein and Jake knew why. Other Shubert employees warned Lee that he would be called a rat, a turncoat, a traitor. He was adamant. And he resumed his long, protracted sessions with representatives of the union.

It was a thoroughly outraged Producers' Association that met with Lee Shubert a few days later. Word of his Equity meetings had leaked, and Erlanger demanded to know what was behind this independent dealing by Shubert.

Lee was controlled but could not conceal his sense of triumph. He had, he informed the producers, "worked out with Equity an understanding"; the actors would drop their demands for a closed-shop clause, and the entire negotiation could be handled amicably. Now it was Shubert's turn to be outraged. To his consternation, the producers, en masse, flatly turned down his suggestion. The concession he had so laboriously extracted from Equity was scornfully pushed aside. The producers were out to smash the union, and were not interested in any forthright negotiation.

Shubert was furious. He stalked out of the meeting. From that first Equity strike Lee had learned a painful lesson. The Shuberts, like all producers, paid a "tax" on each production into the treasury of the Association. But no matter how *many* productions a man may have brought in, he still had only one vote. Lee was not about to be stung twice in the same pocket. He was not about to permit the possibility of being outvoted. There were reasons he could not disclose that made it imperative for Lee Shubert to avoid a strike.

When Equity learned that Erlanger, et al., had turned down their proposal, as submitted by Shubert, they called a membership meeting. Erlanger submitted "the Producers' Plan," which was rejected out-of-hand by Equity, and the twelve hundred actors present voted the strike, as of June 1. It was now May 23. President Emerson informed the membership that the producers were "stubborn and short-sighted." They refused to see reason, he went on, except for Lee Shubert. He electrified the meeting with the announcement that negotiations were going on, and would continue to go on, with the Shuberts, hinting strongly that the brothers might resign from the Producers' Association and form a new group.

The anti-Shubert bloc refused to believe this. Producers started taking "positions"—the same tired positions they had assumed before. The Belasco Theater would convert to film. Klaw and Erlanger were going to enter film production for their own theaters. Ziegfeld was going to do his shows in London. Equity remained unimpressed.

One day later, Equity announced that they had signed an agreement with the Shuberts.

A furious Producers' Association met in emergency session. There were bitter words, vituperative accusations, harsh threats. Erlanger was livid with rage.

"You made a side deal," he accused Shubert. "You sold us out so you could make private terms with the damned union. Well, you won't get away with it."

"I think this whole thing is a frame-up," agreed Sam Harris.

The Shubert faction present—the meeting was not graced by the presence of either brother—hotly denied the accusation. They tried to point out the logic of avoiding a strike, but they were shouted down. The Shubert faction walked out when Erlanger made a formal motion that the Shuberts be expelled from the Association.

The next day, the die-hards went into court to seek an injunction against Equity. In the motion, they flatly stated that the Shuberts and Equity had entered into a secret agreement—in effect, a conspiracy in restraint of trade.

Lee Shubert issued his reply. "This move is not aimed against Equity, no matter what the motion says. It is a deliberate attack at the Shuberts. It is aimed at us. But I am not worried. This injunction will not be granted, I feel certain, and justice will triumph."

Judge McCook reserved his decision, and plays began to close.

Dillingham's semi-hit, *Stepping Stones*, closed its run. Katharine Cornell, starring in *The Outsider*, was served the strike notice, but Lee Shubert secured his own injunction against Equity! He had, he said, signed the agreement with the union, and he owned half of *The Outsider*. He demanded that Equity honor its contract. *The Outsider* stayed open and sold tickets.

The Shuberts formally quit the Producers' Association, leaving it ineffective and meaningless. The shouting went on—the charges, the countercharges, the warnings, the viewing-with-alarm. The strike was settled on the same terms that Lee Shubert had initially recommended. He was hailed by the press as "the sane man in an insane world."

Results? The Shuberts were free of group control. They had fought through alone, and were independent. They would stay so for thirty years. Why? Why had Lee Shubert worked so hard to avert a strike in his theaters and in his productions?

The answer came on June 25, 1924. The financial pages carried a headline: "Shubert Theaters Float Stock Issue."

Now Lee's determination to keep his affairs on an even keel, his conviction that nothing must rock his boat, came clear. Now it was evident why he had smashed the Producers' Association, why he had made his own deal with Equity, why he felt it necessary to brutally point out who was really dominating the theater in the United States.

The stock issue had to be attractive; it had to hold the aura of steadiness, dependability, and reliability if it was going to assure the cooperation of the Wall Street bankers and the public who would buy Shubert stock. Nothing must disturb the cash flow into Shubert theaters, and nothing could be allowed in any way to taint the offering. To guarantee this, Shubert was prepared to fight ruthlessly. He had. He had crushed all opposition.

It is impossible to *know* what went on in the minds of Lee and J.J. on the day they sat down in the board room of J. & W. Seligman & Company at 54 Wall Street. But surely there must have been the light-headed exhilaration of triumph. There they sat, the two short figures, the sons of the pack peddler who had fled to Syracuse. They were millennia away from cigar making and newspaper peddling, from charity and charity donors.

They sat in the headquarters of one of America's leading investment houses, listening to the guarantees that were being made. Bill Phillips, a Seligman partner, had done his work well. The largest theater company in history was going to issue stock. In effect, it guaranteed the Messrs. $4,000,000 for an interest in their theater business, the money aimed at "consolidating their holdings." It left the Shuberts with more than 50 percent of their own company, freedom to run it, and someone else's money to run it with.

What remained unsaid in the stock offer was the fact that almost *all* their real estate was held out of the new company. Theaters that Lee and Jake *owned* were leased to the company. No mention was made of "ice," of ticket-brokerage partnerships; and no reference to the contents of Lee's vault appears.

Even without these vast sums, the statement they issued is impressive. In the formal letter signed by Lee, one can sense the fierce pride in the brothers' accomplishment. "The business was established by Mr. Sam S. Shubert, Mr. J.J. Shubert and myself about twenty-five years ago, practically without capital. Except for $300,000 capital put in a few years later [Cox? Untermyer? Freedman?] the present business and assets have been built up entirely out of earnings. In addition, profits drawn out of the business have been the foundation of the personal real estate investments, worth several million dollars, of myself and Mr. J.J. Shubert. The business is the largest of its kind in the world."

It went on. The Shubert circuit consisted of eighty-six first-class theaters in New York, Chicago, Philadelphia, Boston, and twenty-seven other major cities. They could seat a hundred and thirty thousand ticket buyers a night, and their box office ran very often at $1,000,000 a week. In addition, they "booked" seven hundred and fifty theaters as one-night-stand houses, or better, constituting, as Lee delicately phrased it, "about 60 percent of the entire high-class legitimate theater in the U.S. and Canada." He defined "legit" as plays and musical attractions, as distinguished from burlesque, vaudeville, and motion pictures.

When they booked, Lee explained, they took from 30 to 50 percent of the receipts. If box-office returns fell below a minimum, they could force out the attraction, and replace it. No long-term losses could happen to a Shubert. (He did not really reveal that in many cases when returns were borderline, and a "hot" attraction seemed imminent, or a Shubert production wanted the house, the box-office personnel were told to inform would-be ticket purchasers that there were no tickets available in the half-empty house. That usually dropped the gate to below the minimum.)

He gave a list of some of the producers who booked through the Shuberts, and it included the Theatre Guild, Winthrop Ames, Brady, Comstock, Gest, Hopkins, Sam Harris, William Morris, and some forty others. Occasionally, they would lease an idle theater for motion-picture exhibition.

That accounted for more than two-thirds of their income. The rest came from their own productions. "They occupy about 20 percent of the total time on our circuit."

He listed some profits from their latest ventures. As of February 1924, *Artists and Models* had earned $196,000, *Bombo* with Jolson, $445,000, and *Blossom Time*, an astounding $700,000! "In addition to our own attractions," Lee added, "we frequently purchase part interests in attractions of producers who book through us." (If you want a decent booking, cut us in.)

There were thirty theaters in New York, half of Broadway's seating capacity. Seven of the fifteen houses in Chicago were Shubert theaters, but they booked three of the others.

Lee paid tribute, with no mention of names, to Jake's production facilities: the largest scenery inventory in the world, the largest costume inventory in the world, the largest equipment inventory in the et cetera. It enabled the Shuberts to produce more economically, Lee claimed, since other producers "buy new equipment for each production," or "lease from us."

He proudly informed the fascinated audience that "something which might be a major catastrophe for a less responsible firm does not affect us. Last year, when the entire sets and costumes for a Canadian production of *Blossom Time* were lost in a train wreck, our show opened on time. From our large inventory of sets and costumes in New York, replacements were rushed to Canada in time for our curtain."

He philosophized about the "stability" of his business. "The 'high-class legitimate theater business' to a great extent serves the relatively well-to-do and is less affected by a business depression than is the motion-picture business, which to a great extent serves those of limited means. In bad times our balcony and gallery patronage falls off somewhat, but our orchestra patrons come as usual; they then have more leisure[!] to attend the theater and feel greater need of the relaxation and amusement which the theater offers." He remarked that radio and motion pictures supplement theatrical income. "We sell for cash the motion-picture rights to many of our productions. . . .

"Theater operations differ from most other businesses where, if a mistake has been made and losses begin to develop, the situation may have to be nursed for months or years until it can be worked out. In theater operations, losses can be stopped almost at once by requiring an unsuccessful attraction to vacate the theater. We know every day whether any particular attraction is falling behind; we know this at a glance by comparing its box-office receipts with those of the rest of the Shubert circuit, reported by telegraph from all over the country."

He added admiringly, "The theater is a cash business." He then listed their past five years' earning record, which, except for 1922, was well over $1,000,000 a year. "In 1922," Lee explained, "the Winter

Garden and other important theaters did not contribute to earnings, being subleased at cost to a separate vaudeville enterprise."

The stock sold out.

On the 29th of June, Lee Shubert left for Europe. He was nearly five million dollars richer, as was J.J., than he had been—the market value of the stock had increased by nearly 60 percent. He was going to sign "important" properties and new shows for the company.

Before he left, he took out some additional insurance. For some inexplicable reason he listed Ohio as his place of birth. And, to be sure, he remained, for insurance purposes, two years younger than he was.

And Jake got busy with his season. He put three musicals into rehearsal while preparing two others for later presentation that year. *Dream Girl*, an operetta by Victor Herbert—his first Shubert production and his last show on Broadway—was laden with one of the worst books ever written for a musical. It was a minor hit, carried by Herbert's score and his reputation. Jake's *Passing Show of 1924* was a bad and tired show, and it ran. His 1924 *Artists and Models* was greeted by such reviews as "Even more daring and vulgar than last year's." It sold out.

"The Shubert luck!" groaned the kibitzers.

Lee returned from the Continent in time to supervise some "Messrs." and to present a few "Lee's." None did will. In fact, for five long months, nothing the Shuberts touched worked. Lee saw a lot of the Swanson sisters and a little of Peggy Joyce.

He liked his dates late in the evening, after the returns had been phoned in from across the country. In several of the Shubert buildings —four, to be exact—there were speakeasies, and when they weren't padlocked, Lee liked to visit them. He particularly liked the Montmartre, run by Clifford Fischer. Fischer's lease was on a percentage basis, and although Lee liked Fischer, he unilaterally determined that he would renegotiate the lease. Fischer refused.

One night, with the Montmartre jumping—customers dancing, the orchestra blaring, waiters bringing food and drink to the tables— and a happy Fischer estimating profits, twenty-five workmen entered and, wordlessly, started taking up the carpet. Fischer intervened, and the foreman explained that Mr. Shubert needed the carpet somewhere else, and right now! Fischer reached Lee by phone, and Lee said blandly that he had examined the lease, and the carpet was not included. Eventually, Fischer and Lee patched things up.

Then, after the five barren months, the Shubert luck hit again. The season into December had been just so-so. Jake's hits were making money, but Jake's losses and Lee's were canceling out the profits. On

A Lot Richer. A very satisfied Lee Shubert sailing for Europe the day after the Shubert stock issue sold out.

the 2nd of December in 1924, the Messrs. Shubert presented *The Student Prince*.

It would become the all-time theatrical moneymaker. It would pour millions upon millions of dollars into Shubert pockets. To this day, somewhere in the world, even as this is being written, a tired tenor will be singing "Overhead the Moon Is Beaming," and a stalwart bunch of Heidelberg students will raise the make-believe steins in "The Drinking Song." *The Student Prince* was a gold mine.

Luck? Or was it stubbornness—Shubert stubbornness? Or was it miserliness? Remember *Old Heidelberg*? They had produced a "version" of the play in 1902. It was a flop. They tried it again with the great Richard Mansfield, their first "star." This time they called it *Prince Karl*, and it flopped again. They resurrected it and presented it to Dorothy Donnelly and Sigmund Romberg as the plot for a musical operetta.

When Donnelly and Romberg turned in the script and the score, the brothers were unhappy. Lee had it read to him, and his brow furrowed. "Why can't we change the ending?" he asked Romberg. "People don't like sad endings in musicals."

Romberg explained that the story line was sound and that the score was keyed to it.

J.J. was not nearly so mild. "The music is too highbrow," he told Romberg. "Who goes to the theater for opera? A man wants opera, he goes to the Met. You call this music music?"

Romberg was insistent. When it came time for casting, he had another run-in with Jake. Romberg demanded trained voices. Jake was incredulous. "You mean pretty girls can't sing?"

Romberg got his trained voices; and then stated he wanted forty men in the singing chorus. Jake hit the ceiling. "Forty men singing that crap? Who needs it? Twenty men is enough, and that's final."

When they went into rehearsal, there were forty male voices in the singing chorus. And the brothers stayed worried. The music was not the sound they had expected. And that unhappy ending!

The Student Prince tells the story of Prince Karl, who, incognito, comes to Heidelberg in 1860 to attend the university. He is accompanied by his tutor, Dr. Engel. He meets Kathie, the waitress at the inn, and they fall in love. But their love is doomed; he must return to ascend the throne. Two years later, he comes back to Heidelberg to say farewell forever to Kathie and to tell her he is marrying a princess. They part.

"In a musical, people expect the hero and the soprano will be kissing for the final curtain—or, anyway, dancing," said Jake.

"In Drinking We Will Honor Graduate!" The student chorus in the original Shubert production of *The Student Prince*, 1934. Howard Marsh, as Prince Karl, seated right.

Richard Mansfield As Prince Karl. This was the second Shubert attempt.

"People pay money for tickets so they can walk out of the theater satisfied," said Lee.

They brought Brady to see the show, and they brought Morris Gest, and both agreed with the brothers. A sad ending is no good.

Romberg stuck to his guns, and during the Newark tryout, it came to a head. Unable to make the ending happy, Jake started trying to conceal the fact that it was *un*happy. He began giving suggestions to Huffman to brighten it up.

"The music plays against it," said Huffman. "And anyway, it would be ridiculous."

"My money says it's ridiculous to end this way!"

Jake took over. And Romberg blew. "I will not permit my music to be perverted," the composer shouted.

"Permit?" Jake's eyes narrowed. "In *my* theater, *you* won't permit? And what is perverting? Who is perverting? I am trying to protect my investment!" Jake shook his finger under Romberg's nose. "I don't want to hear no more about God-damned perverting, either!"

"The ending stands," said Romberg.

That did it. "Throw this man out of my theater!" shrieked Jake. "Throw him out before I kill him. And take his name off the marquee too!"

Romberg went to see Howard Reinheimer, his attorney. And Reinheimer served his ultimatum. The name goes back, and the show is played as written. Jake ranted, and cursed, and threatened, but Romberg's name was back on the marquee, and the ending remained unchanged.

The show came into New York, and it was with trepidation that the Messrs. presented. The next day they "knew it all the time." They had hit the jackpot. And while Jake strutted, Lee smiled quietly; they would have a very good statement, and the stock would go up. But even Lee did not yet realize how big a moneymaker he had. Not even Lee.

One month later, the Messrs. brought in *Big Boy*, with Al Jolson, and six days after that, *The Love Song*.

The Love Song followed the favorite Shubert pattern. It was the kind of idea which would have instant appeal to Lee, and to J. J.; and, in addition, it met Lee's specifications for a "good buy in a play."

The conversation was never recorded, but somebody must have said, "Remember *Blossom Time*? Based on Schubert? How about something based on Offenbach? You get all that snazzy French music for free, with the can-can thrown in, and you make up a story. How about it?"

So, the credits read: "Based on Offenbach's life and music."

227

For Lee, the credits go on to read: "From the Hungarian and German by Eugene Ferago, Michael Nador, James Klein, and Carl Brettschneider. Adaptation and lyrics by Harry B. Smith. Offenbach's music selected and arranged, and original music composed by Edward Kunneke."

It was Lee's favorite kind of billboard. But unfortunately, *The Love Song* wasn't *Blossom Time*, although *its* libretto is as much true-to-Offenbach as *Blossom Time* was true-to-Schubert, Franz.

Big Boy was a hard-luck show, jinxed from the beginning. It ran for a short time—Jolson was stricken ill, the play closed. The Shuberts revived it; it ran another hundred and sixty performances, and they moved it to Chicago. In Chicago, it did the biggest business of any show in the history of the city. And then Jolson was hit by the flu. The show closed down again. The flu epidemic in Chicago closed three shows in two weeks. Jolson, Cantor, and Leon Errol. The only one that made the Shuberts sad was *Big Boy*.

But the Shubert luck was holding. It was now Lee's turn. Jimmy Gleason, a veteran actor, had written his first play, *Is Zat So?*, and in partnership with a neophyte producer, determined to become a neophyte producing company. They had no money of their own, but they sold "stock" in the production and went into rehearsal. Gleason starred, partly directed, rewrote, produced, did not paint scenery, but did run out of money in New Haven.

Frantic, he called Lee Shubert, for whom he had worked. Lee drove to New Haven, liked the play, advanced $10,000 to bring the production into New York, and took a Shubert-sized slice of the producing company, plus an option on a second Gleason play—this one written with George Abbott. (The "desperation dollars," those last few thousands that mean the difference between a production and a fiasco, are usually accompanied by large quantities of the producer's hide. The Shuberts became adept at this facet of show biz; they had a mental trophy room where various producers' skins were mounted.)

Is Zat So? opened at the 39th Street Theater (Shubert-owned) and was an instant success, one of the big comedy hits of the season.

There were a lot of other things to keep Lee busy. In addition to his faithful attendance on the Swanson sisters—he was beginning, by this time, to concentrate on Marcella—and on Peggy Joyce, he found time for other companions from his favorite sex. There was a noisy episode in his assignation room shortly after *Is Zat So?* opened. It involved a young girl, under twenty, and the affair was hushed up discreetly. Lee went to Florida.

They had acquired property on 49th Street and Eighth Avenue, and on West 44th Street. This meant two more Shubert theaters to be built soon. In Florida, Lee set about finding a site for a Palm Beach Shubert Theater. (Why waste a vacation on rest?)

He explained the sudden slump in box-office attendance as "temporary." No, it was not radio. How can an audience enjoy hearing what they can't see? "Radio," said Lee, "is a novelty, and when the novelty wears off, people will return to the theater." But hadn't Mr. Shubert just said that it wasn't radio causing the slump? "When?" he asked. "When did I say that?" Just now, he was told. "It's a novelty," he said, ending the interview.

Jake was providing his own news. He barred John J. Daly, the critic for the Washington *Post*, from all Shubert theaters in the capital. Since there were no other theaters in Washington, Jake was putting Mr. Daly out of business. Jake disapproved of Daly's review of *Artists and Models*.

Daly had written, "*Artists and Models* is a blend of old-time burlesque and vaudeville, with vulgarity and coarseness streaking every number . . . cleverness fell by the wayside to let vulgarity and commonness takes [*sic*] its place. There are some lovely, exquisite scenes and a great finale, but the acts have dirt behind the ears, and evidently, everything has to be tainted to get by in *Artists and Models*."

The *Post* bought tickets for their critic, daring Jake not to seat him, and Jake threatened with the old Shubert bludgeon, "we will remove our ads." The *Post* said okay, remove. And Jake backed off. Mr. Daly returned to the Shubert free list, and Jake went hunting for new game.

He had no trouble finding it. He was going to work on a new edition of the *Greenwich Village Follies* and he asked his music director, Max Meth, how many men he was going to use in the pit.

"Twenty-two, Mr. J.J.," Meth assured him.

Jake left the show in the hands of "Ma" Simmons and J. C. Huffman and took off for Europe. Lee, burned mahogany by the Florida sun, attended rehearsal. He went backstage to see Meth.

"Max, why are there so few men in the pit?"

"There are only twenty-two parts in the orchestration, Mr. Shubert."

Lee mused on this. "Well, you still have a whole day and a night. I want thirty men in the pit."

"But . . ."

"I want thirty men in the pit. Get the parts."

Meth could see thunder over 44th Street. When Jake returned and found his orders had been changed, he would go into a tantrum. But how did you tell Lee? Meth decided to share the buck, since he knew he could not pass it. He went to see the company manager.

"Mr. Lee wants me to write eight new parts overnight, rehearse the men and open with thirty men in the pit."

"But Mr. J. J. said twenty-two," said the manager.

"*You* tell Mr. Lee."

They both went to see Lee.

He was genial, but adamant. "Time, gentlemen," he said, "is money. And time is fleeing. You better be getting the new parts for the orchestra, yes?"

They tried tactfully to explain that they had a small problem, and it wasn't a time problem. Finally, he ordered a letter written to Meth, authorizing the augmented orchestra, and he signed it.

"You see," said Lee, as he handed the letter to Meth, "I want this show to be as big as a *Ziegfeld Follies*. I went to the *Follies* and I counted—they have thirty men in the pit. Now we will have just as big a show."

The men stared at him. *The Greenwich Village Follies* was a tasteless, cheap revue. And that's what the critics said when it opened.

Jake came back from Europe and started to check receipts and bills. He smiled fondly at *The Student Prince*, mused happily at *Artists and Models*, sneered at Lee's turkeys, and then shot bolt upright in his chair when he saw the tallies on *The Greenwich Village Follies*.

He summoned the bookkeeper. "What the hell is this?" he demanded, waving a sheaf of bills.

"What is what, Mr. J.J.?" asked the bewildered man.

"Never mind!" Jake yelled. "Get Scanlon in here!"

Eddie Scanlon, Jake's right-hand factotum, came in. "What the hell are these?" Jake demanded.

Scanlon's mind raced. These—bills—what bills? Bills that angered Jake—POW! *The Greenwich Village Follies!*

"Well, Mr. J.J.," he began.

"Don't 'well' me!" shouted Jake in his angry conversational way. "I don't have to be 'welled.' What's going on in my office? Huh? Tell me who's doing things in my office without my approval?"

Scanlon temporized. Jake screamed. Finally, Meth and the company manager were summoned.

Jake sat behind his desk, eyes lowered, face flushed. "Who put thirty men in *my* pit?"

Neither of the men spoke. Silently, Meth handed him Lee's letter.

Jake read it once, and his face contorted, then he read it again. Silently he put the letter down on the desk top. He stood up and came around the desk menacingly, until he loomed in front of his employees. His face was red with his attempt at self-control, and then he couldn't hold it any longer. He raised a short, pudgy arm and wagged his finger under two noses.

"Who the hell do you work for?"

The men remained silent.

"Do you work for me, or do you work for that son of a bitch, my brother?"

Neither man spoke. (In theatrical parlance, they had just heard a blasphemy. No one—no, *no one* called Lee Shubert a son of a bitch —not out loud.)

"It was your job to say to yourself, 'Who do you work for? Mr. J.J.? Or that son of a bitch, Mr. Lee?' Then, you would have known how to tell him. But you didn't say that to yourselves, did you?"

The men shook their heads.

"Next time, remember!" Jake shouted, turning back to his desk. "Now, get the hell out of here. And I don't want no next times, either!"

Meth paused in the doorway. He coughed. Jake looked up. "Should I get rid of eight musicians, Mr. J.J.?" he asked tentatively.

Jake looked at him, and then scowled into the desk top. "No," he said. And he absorbed himself in his papers. The session was over.

Lee's next windfall from the trip to see Jimmy Gleason in New Haven came with the opening of *The Fall Guy*, the play that had fallen into his lap when he bailed out *Is Zat So?*. It opened to excellent critical notices and was the first Shubert-produced play to be listed as one of the ten best plays of the season by Burns Mantle. Lee was a success and he left for Europe.

Again, there were signs on the horizon. Maxwell Anderson and Laurence Stallings had written *What Price Glory?*, which not only got good notices, but was having a profound effect on contemporary playwrights. The salty dialogue, the "realism" of the approach to men at war, as opposed to the sugary romantic themes of prior war plays— these new techniques were having repercussions. A whole host of "realistic" drama was waiting in the wings. Since, in many cases, the dramatists were not sufficiently gifted, they sought "realism" in shocking stories of "realistic" lives of prostitutes or "realistic" portrayals of adultery.

Audiences were shocked, as desired, but so were censors. In the first cries of "Reform the theater!" the censors started attacking anything *they* didn't approve of. Honest plays like *Desire Under the Elms*, by Eugene O'Neill were hit, along with the trash. One critic, defending the O'Neill play, stated that it "was as shocking as a course in psychology, designed for finishing-school classrooms."

But new forces were emerging in the theater—new ideas, new thinking. The Shuberts didn't see it. The American playwright was becoming more and more important. The imported play somehow lacked the vitality, the brashness, the sheer young vigor of the American playwright—of O'Neill, Anderson, Sherwood.

And the American musical was beginning to shape itself into form. The revolution had started when George M. Cohan wrote his chauvinistic, impudent first plays. *Forty-Five Minutes from Broadway* was not just another musical—not even in 1906. It was an American musical. The Shuberts didn't see it.

They kept importing their Mittel Europa operettas, "Americanizing" them, and their ears were insensitive to the fact that George Gershwin and Jerome Kern and Richard Rodgers were writing "different" sounds, and integrating their songs into the fabric of the show. There were story songs, and mood songs, and they moved the plot.

It would be another five years before the change, already in the air, would happen on the stage. But the Shuberts would never see it. The *Passing Show* and girlie revues and old-line operettas were beginning to show age wrinkles. The audience was more sophisticated, more demanding. The Shuberts didn't see it.

In England, Lee started making news. He acquired six theaters in London—the same London where he had sworn he would never produce again. He announced plans to produce "European drama in London and then import the production for the Shubert theaters in America." He also pointed out to his stockholders that English theaters were different. Unlike American houses, there were "intangible assets in the loyalty of customers to the tradition of certain theaters." Lee could always tell an asset from an elbow.

He showed up in Berlin, and the papers said he had made a gigantic merger with UFA, the German film producers. This gave Jake a chance to hotly deny it in New York. It was a false rumor. Lee went on to Vienna and took a lease on the Theater an der Wien, to present German versions played in Vienna!

Jake was picking up another theater in Chicago and building the

Rialto in St. Louis. He was getting ready for *his* European tour, and for the new season.

He was also becoming an educator.

Shubert road companies of successful operettas were literally creating a shortage of singers. Jake determined to solve the problem by raising his own crop. (There were distinct financial advantages. You could hire a girl with little or no experience for an absolute minimum.)

Jake announced the establishment of a Singing School at the Century. It would be headed by Dorothy Francis, a well-known singing actress, and Harrison Brockbank. The Shuberts already had a dancing school for chorus girls, Jake added proudly, unaware that among the cognoscenti it was known as "Jake's harem."

"I expect to develop several singers out of this new school," said J.J. "Stage-door Johnnies are not popular around the Century and they are not encouraged. The young women of the company are too intent on making good as vocalists to pay heed to midnight clubs and auto rides and distant roadhouses."

Now he could go to Europe.

Lee had returned in time to watch the Messrs. present four turkeys in a row, to which he added a fifth, presented by Mr. Lee. Actually, they were all Lee's doing. Three of them starred Lionel Barrymore, who had never enjoyed such a run of luck in his life.

Lee also issued the first report to the stockholders, and it made him happy. A dividend of seven dollars a share, profits over the million mark, and in addition to the theaters acquired out of town, the Shuberts had acquired a half-interest in the Selwyn, and would book the Eltinge.

Two Shubert alumnae of the *Passing Show* were signed to Hollywood contracts, and Lee told Claude Greneker, the head of his press department, "Maybe now people will learn [hint to Greneker] that Ziegfeld isn't the only producer who discovers beautiful women. I found Nancy Carroll, and my brother found Joan Crawford before she was Lucille LaSueur!"

These repeated trips to Europe were not merely pleasure jaunts. It often seemed that there had to be more than two Shubert brothers—one always was "in Europe," one was "presenting" and acquiring, and a mysterious third was "en route."

All producers tried to cover the European scene. They looked for properties, they looked for props, they looked for performers, they looked for ideas and techniques (Jake would bring into the United

Lucille La Sueur (Joan Crawford). Miss Labor Day in *The Passing Show of 1924.*

States the revolving stage), and they looked for costumes and designs.

This last was most important. The revue of the mid-twenties was not the thinking man's show. It was not topical, it was not sharp, it was not intimate. The *Little Shows* were about to happen; some of the *Music Box Revues* were heading in the new direction. But the staple revues—the *Scandals*, the *Follies*, *Artists and Models*, Earl Carroll's *Vanities*—these were cut from the same piece of wedding cake. Ziegfeld always had more taste and wit and a better nose for comedy, but to half-closed eyes, the shows all had the same look.

They were lavish, spectacular, colorful, and filled with lovely girls in fantastic costumes—feathers, jewels, incredibly expensive fabrics. The producers vied with each other in the concoction of these costumes and their grouping on stage. The prized show-girl costumes were almost always created by Parisian designers. (Often, they were "borrowed" from the designer, without the designer's permission.)

American customs duties on imported costumes were prohibitive. The usual dodge to avoid the excessive tax was to send the costumes in uncompleted form into the United States, rush them to a costume shop, complete the sewing, and get them on stage. In other words, the costumes would be commissioned in Paris, designed, executed, and then the Parisian house would loosely baste them together. In that form, they were able to get through American customs as "material" as opposed to "garments."

When Jake, this spring of 1925, arrived in Paris, he was sent to see the *Folies Bergère* by his Parisian scout. It was an exceptionally lavish show, and had stunning props and costumes. Jake instantly assigned a costume designer to duplicate the ones he had selected.

What Jake didn't know at the time was that George White, planning his next *Scandals*, had seen the same *Folies* and had ordered the identical costumes. Jake hated White, to begin with. When White had started as a hoofer, Jake had dropped him from a show because Jolson had asked White out. On another occasion, when Jake needed White for a tap-dance specialty, they had not been able to agree on terms. Jake had flatly stated to White, "There ain't a hoofer alive who's worth a hundred twenty-five a week."

But these were only preliminary to Jake's real hate. That happened when White produced his first *Scandals*, and it was a hit. The Shuberts could hate Ziegfeld, dislike Earl Carroll, and have enough left over for White. Jake would growl, "So what's the tap-dancer going to do when he has his first flop? He's getting old for dancing, isn't he?" Or, "I remember George White when I fired him, which I will be glad to do again after he goes broke."

Jake and White learned of the other's activities at about the same instant, and the race was on. Who would get in first? Both men ordered their French designers to work a twenty-four-hour shift every day until the cutting and basting were completed. Both men were frantically trying to gauge the shipping schedules so they could load on the fastest boat. And Jake added one other fillip.

He cabled Lee to inform him of the possible problem and suggested that something be done to insure Shubert victory. The Shuberts, by this time, had considerable muscle. Lee called a strategy session with Greneker, Ray Long, his overall general manager, and Jack Morris, his personal executive secretary and trusted right-hand. The orders were simple. The Shubert costumes were to get through with dispatch; White's costumes were to be delayed in customs until after *Artists and Models* had opened.

Again, fate's fickle finger was working for White. One of the key men in the customs shed in New York was a close personal friend. He cabled White about the Shubert shenanigans, and White made his own arrangements. The costumes for the *Scandals* arrived, were cleared and rushed to White's costumer in New York for completion. And somehow, the Shubert costumes were "lost" for several days.

White opened his *Scandals* on June 22; the Shuberts couldn't get on stage until June 24th. Lee was in New Haven when White's revue opened to good notices, with special plaudits for the costumes. He went into a rage that would have made Jake envious. He fired off three telegrams to the New York office. Morris, Long, and Greneker were fired summarily.

Then Lee proceeded to tell everyone in New Haven what he thought of his three trusted lieutenants. Word got back to New York, and the unemployed trio were furious. To fan the flames, White planted an item that Long was suing for $100,000 worth of defamation of character and that Morris and Greneker would join him in the suit. The *Telegraph*, still anti-Shubert, gleefully printed it, and told the story.

Lee had calmed down by the time he returned to Manhattan. The men were rehired, and Lee turned his mind to other things.

Chapter Twelve

The Shubert circuit was growing daily. They took over the Cosmopolitan Theater on Columbus Circle, at the foot of Central Park—this from William Randolph Hearst. At the same time, in a deal that was not announced, they (Lee and J. J., not Shubert Theater Corporation) bought from Hearst his motion-picture studio at Second Avenue and 127th Street. The unreported price was a half-million.

Hearst's best box-office stars started appearing in MGM pictures right after the sale. Marion Davies and Lionel Barrymore joined the roaring lion. It was a typical Lee Shubert tie-in deal.

At the same time, he was dickering with George M. Cohan to take over the Cohan Theater in Chicago, and with Selwyn and Harris to take on their two houses in the same city. They closed with both "rivals" and then bought the Sam Harris Theater in New York for a million. Lee announced that their box-office receipts and "production economies" had resulted in a six-months' net of almost seven dollars a share, and said, "I anticipate better news for the shareholders when we issue our final statement."

The brothers were keeping Willie Klein busy with more than deeds of sale. The Twin Oaks Club sued the Shuberts for $50,000, claiming that Shubert actors, hired to work after-curtain in the night club, had been intimidated by Shubert management and didn't show, causing cash refunds and other damages. They stated that the Shuberts had deliberately put pressure on the performers because the Messrs. were going to open their own restaurant. Jake hotly denied it, pointing out that two Shubert properties, *The Moulin Rouge* and *The Plantation*, had been padlocked by the government for Prohibition violations, and said, "we are still trying to get them open so that we can rent them to law-abiding operators. Who needs a restaurant?"

Jake, the educator, was full of announcements. He was going to get "writers and composers and lyricists to write songs and sketches, and then get actors and scene designers, and try out productions on the road before bringing them to New York." Wasn't this the usual custom? Didn't most producers start with a property and then cast it? "Not always," said the producer. "We sometimes tell a writer that we want something for an important actor and then he goes to work. Anyway, it's new for us."

He announced that he was suing Fred Clarke, a producer, for stealing material from Jake's *Artists and Models* and from *Gay Paree*.

"We want copyrights respected," said Jake, who even then was being sued by no less than three European firms for violation of copyright.

To make his campaign against the press transcontinental, he explained that he was suing "that nice rich young man, Cornelius Vanderbilt, who owns the Los Angeles *Illustrated News*, for attacking our productions."

He did not "announce" that he had sued his neighbor in Westchester, seeking an injunction to keep the neighbor from burning leaves, which blew smoke into Jake's yard. The man promised to burn leaves only when the wind was right.

His most noteworthy achievement came when a theater owner in the Middle West sent a complaint to Shubert headquarters, objecting to the profanity and "vulgar" language of the Shubert company managers. Jake dictated a letter to be sent to all managers, cautioning them to watch their language; to think twice before saying anything which might offend people. He closed by reminding them that they represented the Shuberts and the Shubert reputation. It is a collector's item.

It wasn't only the Shuberts suing; it was also people suing the Shuberts. Otto Eurich, an Austrian producer, filed suit for $16,000 plus damages, naming Lee and J. J. His attorney's brief states, "The Shuberts have acted in bad faith, from beginning to end."

Eurich had produced the original version of *The Blue Paradise*, and had then entered into an agreement with Jake, who wanted to do the show in the United States in a patented Shubert version. They did produce it, and never sent any money to Mr. Eurich in royalty payments. World War I got in the way of communication, and finally, Eurich managed to reach the brothers, seeking payment.

They sent a representative to see him, offering him fifteen hundred in kronen, which he refused. He went to see his attorney, who started action. The Shubert representative returned to Vienna and offered four thousand in dollars, which was also refused. They then went to see Eurich's attorney.

He indignantly turned down a "gift" of fifteen hundred American, to settle the case. Willie Klein suggested the bill be paid, and the arguments forgotten.

This was Willie Klein's Vienna year. Bobby North, a one-time performer for the brothers, had graduated to the status of Hollywood producer. From the Shuberts he had purchased a property called *The Blue Pearl*, and he had paid $10,000 for it.

On *his* Viennese tour, North ran into Hans Bartsch, a German literary agent, who was very upset with North.

"How could you do this, Bobby?" Bartsch asked sadly. "How could you make a picture when you didn't have the rights?"

"What are you talking about?" replied the indignant North. "We paid ten thousand dollars for those rights!"

Bartsch didn't believe him. "Who did you pay the money to?"

"I paid Lee Shubert," said the angry North.

Bartsch stared at him. "Lee Shubert?" He shook his head, more in rueful awareness than in anger. "The son of a bitch, he did it again! He didn't own the rights!"

Bartsch brought suit, Willie Klein defended, and Lee settled— out of court.

Lee left for Europe—"to look over new plays and playhouses, and we may acquire new theaters while I am in Europe. Optimistic? I certainly am! Our earnings for the year should show about twenty dollars a share!" It was June of 1925, a very prosperous Shubert year.

He was going to shop for plays. He had to. The Shubert "first-class" chain numbered nearly a hundred theaters. In addition, they were booking more than five hundred one-night and split-week houses. And despite their own tireless production efforts and the product of more than forty "affiliated" producers, they could not keep their theaters lighted. There simply weren't enough plays to go around. Even with proliferating road companies of their hits, the squeeze was being felt, and it would get worse.

Before he left, one tiny item appeared in the theatrical news. "Lee Shubert is joining Joe Schenck, Mary Pickford, Douglas Fairbanks, Sid Grauman, etc., as a 'business consultant' to their United Artists Company." It was a straw in the wind.

He also announced his London season. *Is Zat So?*, the Gleason windfall, *The Fall Guy*, picked up in the same package, and, of course, *The Student Prince* would head the list. Lee had already shown his gratitude to Gleason by personally handling the sale of the motion-picture rights of *Is Zat So?*.

Lee had sold the play to William Fox for $90,000, and shortly after, the Authors' League had accused him of "under-the-table dishonesty" with Fox. They stated that First National Pictures had offered $150,000 for the rights but that Fox and Shubert had a working understanding. Lee denied it but, significantly, did not sue *Variety* (this time) for the usual grounds of libel.

Surprisingly, *Is Zat So?* and *The Fall Guy*, both wisecracking comedies in the American vernacular, caught on in England. *The Student Prince* was panned! Perhaps its advance build-up had been too great, perhaps the production was not gaited to British tastes, or perhaps it was too soon after World War I and there was little joy in London for Heidelberg *Weltschmerz*. Whatever the reason, the play was roasted.

Within a week, Lee was quoted in the London press and requoted in the United States. "London producers simply do not know their business. They will have no place in the theater if they do not mend their ways," said the Fox of Broadway in a magnificent fit of sour grapes.

He returned to the United States in time to see Bill Phillips float another public-stock issue in the theatrical field, and this time Lee Shubert was an "organizer," a "director," and a "major stockholder." The formation of United Artists Theater Corporation was announced by Joe Schenck. "We need theaters to exhibit the superior pictures made by United Artists," said Schenck. "This merger of talents—creative and business—will benefit everybody, the public most of all." Schenck was not quite right. Most of all, Lee Shubert would benefit; he was finding a way to keep theaters working. And he was wedging himself into solid, influential positions in the film industry.

Jake was doing his part to keep theaters in business. To open the season, amazing J.J., in the space of seventeen days, brought in three personally staged musical epics: *June Days*, *Gay Paree*, and the *Big Boy* revival. All were respectable box-office successes, and all received the usual Shubert reviews—the critics found them lacking in originality and taste.

June Days was a musical set in a girls' school, where the man who "inherited" the school falls in love with a student. Take it from there.

Gay Paree was an imitation *Artists and Models*, with girls, comedians, and girls.

While Jake warmed up another show in the bull pen, Lee produced two Lee's and Messrs. brought in three. Even Noel Coward couldn't help —his *Hayfever* ran less than fifty performances, and Lee's *Man with a Load of Mischief*, starring Ruth Chatterton, ran two weeks.

Princess Flavia, a musical version of the Zenda story, was one of Jake's most ambitious production efforts—lavish, opulent, and overbudget.

The most distinguished event in the history of *Princess Flavia* came when the brothers talked to each other. Not really *to* each other, but it was the closest they had come to doing it in years.

What had happened was this. While Jake was casting the Zenda piece, he determined that the male lead would be played by Harry Welchman, an English musical-comedy favorite, and he had brought Welchman over. As noted, the play was going well over the prepared budget, and when Lee returned from Europe, he was told that the show was in trouble. His eye scanned the budget, and then the cast list, and when he spotted Welchman, he got very upset. He had seen Welchman in London and disliked his work, his voice, and to this he now added his salary.

Poor Romberg, who had written the score (while preparing *The Desert Song* for other producers!) was conducting the orchestra when Lee entered the Century Theater. He told "Ma" Simmons to inform his brother—Jake was standing next to "Ma"—that he would like to see some cast changes and some economies.

Jake blew. He turned to the empty theater, ignoring the awed multitudes on stage. "All persons who have no business with this production will leave the theater at once." No one moved. Romberg, feeling that perhaps something heroic was expected of musicians at times like this—after all, the band played on the *Titanic*, musicians stopped riots with "The Star-Spangled Banner"—was about to signal the orchestra to play—anything—when Jake, voice trembling like a ship's horn, shouted to the empty theater again. "No one is allowed in a J.J. Shubert rehearsal without an invitation. All people not connected with this show, get out. Rehearsal will not continue until the theater is clear."

The house was deathly silent.

Lee, his voice rising higher in pitch, and commencing to stammer, as he always did under stress, said, "Mr. Simmons, you will p-p-please inf-f-f-orm my b-b-brother that I d-d-do not ap-p-prove of his l-l-leading man."

Jake's anger made his face as red as his brother's skin lotion had made Lee's. "There will be no rehearsing in this production until all strangers are removed," he intoned in a roar.

Lee Shubert turned on his heel and walked out of the theater. Welchman stayed in the play, and it was not a hit, but it sold tickets fairly well, and then went to Chicago to play out a season.

The *Desert Song*, produced by Schwab and Mandel, was a hit-hit. It played on and on, and J.J., instead of merely resenting Romberg for the money Romberg was (at last) being paid, now began to view him with a deep distrust. Why hadn't Romberg given them the play? What had happened to loyalty? Hadn't they practically raised Romberg?

They had hired Romberg, put him on weekly salary (small) and seen him turn out hit after hit, do patchwork on other shows, play piano at rehearsals (to augment his salary), and conduct the first few weeks of a production (to further bolster his income) before sending him back to his Muse to write another show. And in these pre-ASCAP days, it was the Shuberts who owned the songs! Yes, Romberg owed them a lot.

Jake put *A Night in Paris* into rehearsal, starring Jack Osterman, Jack Pearl, and Norma Terris, and became his own self again. Rehearsals were chaotic. Huffman was directing, and Jake, in addition, was "personally supervising."

Osterman, a clever comedian, was a reasonably mild man who got belligerent only when near a bottle. Then he believed he had selected the wrong profession. He felt he should have been a fighter, and more often than not, he thought he was and indulged in role playing. The show had been having its own troubles when Jake marched in, as was his custom, to take over the "polishing." Words led to more words, and eventually to anger. Jake pushed Osterman, and Osterman told him to stop pushing. Jake ignored him and started again to explain something to Huffman. Osterman stood there, waiting for Jake to apologize. Finally, he walked over to one of the chairs for the cast and sat down. No sooner was he seated than Jake whirled on him. "Who told you to sit down?"

Osterman did not like being yelled at. "My ass," he replied sweetly. "It's tired."

Jake rushed at him, and cooler heads stepped in between, edged Osterman out of the theater, and got Jake back to supervising. Osterman moved into a speakeasy handy to the theater and, over a few shots, meditated on the vagaries of producers. By the third drink, he felt it necessary to straighten Jake out. He went back to the theater, and walked into the wings.

Jake was standing to one side, intently watching a dance number. Osterman walked up to him, tapped him on the shoulder and said, "Mr. Shubert, I want to talk to you."

Jake ignored him. Osterman tried again. "Mr. Shubert, I . . ."

Jake waved him away. Osterman was persistent.

The number ended, and as Osterman started to open his mouth, Jake turned and, without a word, slugged him. "That was for before!" said Jake.

Osterman was an ad-lib comic. "And this is for now," he said, and drilled a right flush to Jake's jaw, putting him through a flat.

Osterman's distinction is shared only with Walter Catlett—they are the two actors who slugged Shubert. Jake didn't fire him. He needed him for the finale.

All of these Shubert revues were more or less copying the formula which had made *Artists and Models* a success. There were certain cliché snigger words in the United States guaranteed to provoke whistles. Paris, pronounced Pa-ree, was sure to raise an eyebrow. Greenwich Village, that den of iniquity, home of "artists" (snigger word), made nice people leer. And the Shuberts were opportunistic about their titles as an advertising device. They put a "Follies" after "Greenwich Village"; and they did *Gay Paree;* and when the size of the business astonished

242

even Jake, they went right back to Paris, pronounced Paris for the new show, and produced the same kind of mélange, calling it *A Night in Paris*.

But it took Jake to produce his next *Gay Paree*, another flaccid set of skits, blackouts, songs, and girls, all living the riotous Bohemian life of Left-Bank Paris, and to select as his comedy star Chic Sale, the Midwest outhouse comedian! Continental was the word for J.J.!

Lee was busily defending "art" in the theater. Jake's undraped shows were being imitated, and Ziegfeld, who presciently was beginning to sense the end of the era of the *Follies*, issued a statement that he was going to eschew nudity. "It is," said Flo, the discoverer of the Ziegfeld girl, "vulgar."

Lee Shubert, queried by the press, stated, "I hope Mr. Ziegfeld keeps his word, but I doubt it. I point out that in every great museum there are statues and paintings and other works of art that are full of nude female figures."

He was also busy with the announcement of the statement of earnings for the Shubert Theater corporation. They had doubled their last year's profit.

He also announced the plans for an office building on property owned by the brothers on West 44th Street, between Broadway and Eighth Avenue. He said, "We had planned a theater and restaurant, but now we are going to put up a central office building for theatrical people. It will be called the Shubert Building." It was never called the Shubert Building. Some say that Lee was persuaded that if they *did* call it the Shubert Building nobody in the theater world would base there. Others said viciously that if the Shuberts were going to consolidate their offices in the new building (as Lee had stated), then no other tenant's money was safe. It was just a number on a building until Sardi leased the space for the restaurant. It is still called the Sardi Building.

In September, just as the new season was swinging into high gear, Lee was slapped with a summons. Although it concerned money— $1,000,000 worth—for once, it was not the money which was Lee's primary concern.

Lee Shubert was a very complex human being. Socially insecure, he masked his insecurity well. He liked women, and admired those with style and dash—and feared them. He was a social animal, but restricted his socialities to small groups; at large parties, he was shy and inarticulate. He was a vain man, and a proud one, and he cherished his own vision of his own reputation—that of a moral man. (There were armies who disagreed with him.)

The kind of drama he liked was indicative of the feelings of the

243

man who posed as a cherubic Egyptian Sphinx. He liked plays with what he called "a moral." A "bad woman" reformed. A wayward child saved his father. A family was reunited. A girl, hell-bent on sin, was kept honorable by marrying her seducer. Time after time, this kind of schmaltzy plot was a "Mr. Lee Shubert Presents."

He almost never used profanity. Men who worked with him for over twenty years never heard anything stronger than "son of a bitch" from his lips. He disliked people who were profane. He was "moral."

How to reconcile this pious stance with his own activities with the opposite sex is part of the complexity of the man. It was as if he were a college sophomore of the twenties, with the female world divided into "nice girls" and "the others." He enjoyed, in his two accomodations off his office, hundreds of "the others." (On one trip to Hollywood, a private party was thrown for the elder Shubert. Half the beauties in filmdom attended, and Lee remarked to an old employee, now in the Hollywood party circle, "I had eleven of them!")

And that is why he was so perturbed with the summons which had been served on him. You will recall a "noisy" episode in his office in early 1925. Now, nearly two years later, he found himself accused of "violent . . . assaults. As a result thereof, the plaintiff became pregnant with child, and . . . was delivered of a child on the 25th day of October, 1925."

The girl had been just under twenty when the alleged assault took place. Lee was fifty-three.

It was a mess. No one in the Shubert organization knew of the situation, except for Willie Klein, who had been hastily summoned. It was specifically kept from Jake. What to do?

Lee's reactions were surprising, and divided. His pride did not want to see him exposed to the kind of sensationalism this sort of suit promised. At the same time, he was not prepared to admit paternity; nor would he deny it. There was a lot at stake—his own fortune included.

Klein handled the matter with beautiful dexterity. The girl had filed for $500,000, and her mother for an equal amount. Klein negotiated well. A financial agreement was made between the girl and Lee Shubert, by which he paid a weekly sum to her for the support of the child. This out of the way, both parties agreed to terminate the pending action and submit the matter to an arbitrator—Judge Victor J. Dowling, presiding justice of the Appellate Division of the First Department.

When the matter reached the arbitrator, the statements revealed that Lee had been paying $200 a week. The arbitrator awarded $75 a week to the girl for the rest of her life, with a confusing exception relating to marriage within ten years. A similar award was made to the child—a boy.

The matter was so settled, the arbitration was signed, and all papers were ordered sealed. The story never reached the newspapers. The arbitration was in Nassau County, and only after the case was disposed of, was Jake informed.

Its effect on him was, as always with a Shubert, unpredictable. Perhaps somewhere deep in the truculent brother's mind was a sense of superiority—one item where he could *prove* he had something Lee did not have. The knowledge that Lee *might* have a child produced a strange series of reactions.

Jake "discovered" his son.

For the first time in many years, he began to be interested in his boy, the same son whose paternity he had once so viciously denied in the boy's presence. John was just entering his first year at the University of Pennsylvania. A shy, retiring young man, taller than a Shubert, he found himself surrounded by his father. And, it must be remembered, Jake was a very busy man. But suddenly, he had time for John, and interest. And perhaps thoughts of continuity were beginning to trouble the man who had just passed his half-century mark. He began to invite John to New York, to see him in Philadelphia, to bring him into the Shubert orbit. He took pride in "the first Shubert to go to college."

But he was still Jake. Intermingled with the sentimentality were sieges of cruelty, savagery, sadism, bullying. Not even his heir could tell how Jake would feel from moment to moment.

When Jake went out after a show, he was almost always accompanied by a bevy of girls from the chorus. And almost never was there a male from the company invited. Occasionally, the house manager or a conductor might be invited, but Jake liked to rule in lonely sovereignty.

On one such occasion, in Philadelphia, he "invited" Max Meth (the conductor who had been trapped with eight extra musicians) and John to join him. John was subdued at the table, as his father held forth on business, life, and the theater, with an occasional ribald remark to one of the girls. Meth wanted to leave early, and as was Jake's custom, there were separate checks. (Jake did not like to waste money.)

Meth picked up his check, and as he started away from the table, he left a fifteen-cent tip. Jake summoned him back.

"You make so much money on me?"

Meth didn't understand.

"Fifteen cents you leave for a tip? It's too much."

Jake handed Meth back a nickel. "Don't be such a big spender." He turned to John. "He thinks money grows on trees, this fiddler," he told the boy. Then he turned to the girl sitting beside him. "So does my son. Did he ever work for a nickel?" He turned back to John. "Did you? Did you ever work in your whole life?"

John shook his head.

"My son has a rich father," said Jake sarcastically. "When I was your age, I was managing a chain of theaters." He pointed his finger at John. "Don't let me catch you leaving tips."

Lee was still trying to cope with the shortage of material for the theater circuit. True, he had leased certain theaters to United Artists. But booking attractions in the first-class houses was difficult. He had been lucky with a revival of *What Every Woman Knows*, which he had personally presented in association with William Brady, and which had given Helen Hayes her first Broadway starring role.

But the rest of Lee's season was disappointing. The upcoming Shubert presentations were not much better. They were fated to have only one real hit, *Countess Maritza*, and two other musicals that would have respectable runs—*Katja* and the Chic Sale *Gay Paree*.

Countess Maritza was a Hungarian epic with music by Emmerich Kalman, and featured a relatively new Shubert star, Odette Myrtil, later to become a Hollywood star. Miss Myrtil, an accomplished violinist, played the role of a fiddling gypsy and won the audience with her fire and her skill.

One night Lee asked Miss Myrtil if she had made any plans for Sunday. Since he had made no passes other than a few fatherly "feels," Miss Myrtil felt secure. No, she was free.

"I would like you to meet a very interesting man—a friend of mine," said Lee expansively.

On Sunday, Lee, Miss Marcella Swanson, Odette, and the gentleman attended the Sunday night concert at the Century Roof. Mysteriously, Lee and Miss Swanson disappeared. Miss Myrtil's escort invited her to join him for a drink. They drove to an expensive apartment, and when the chap had distinct difficulty finding the makings for the drinks, a dawning suspicion arose in Miss Myrtil's mind. It was obviously not his apartment, and Lee had not vanished by chance.

She was not happy when the "proposition" was put to her. The gentleman was enamored, he would like to "set her up in an apartment," and he would make her a great star. Now let's go to bed.

Miss Myrtil said she was already a star. She then went on to inform him that she was French, that she was female, that she believed the male-female relationship should be based on romantic attachment, a wooing, a love affair—and not treated as a business deal.

Countess Maritza, 1927. Odette Myrtil and Harry K. Morton. J.J. loved violins.

The gentleman wordlessly reached for his wallet, and carefully placed a $1,000 bill on the coffee table. Miss Myrtil departed.

The next day, Lee Shubert called at the dressing room. "Well, Odette, how did it go?"

Miss Myrtil glared at him. "What are you? A producer or a procurer? You ought to know better. I walked out!"

Shubert stared at her uncomprehendingly as she recited the events of the evening, culminating with the "down payment."

"You're a very foolish girl," he said.

Although *Countess Maritza* was a lavish, sprawling production, it was attended by the usual Shubert cost controls. One of the featured dancers approached "Ma" Simmons, asking for "bloomers for the second act."

"Why can't you use the bloomers you wear in the first act?" asked Simmons.

"They don't match the costume."

"Who'll know?" asked "Ma."

"I have the dance with all the kicks in it," explained the girl.

"I'll ask J.J.," said "Ma."

The weighty problem was brought to Jake, who decided against a second pair of bloomers. He used Shubert logic to reach his conclusion. "If," ruminated Jake solemnly, "she's got legs where an audience knows what color her bloomers are, it don't make a damn bit of difference what color her bloomers are."

Prior to *Maritza*, Miss Myrtil had played in *Vogues* and in *The Love Song* for the Shuberts, and after the long run in *Maritza*, she felt she wanted a vacation. She had not seen her family in France for several years, and now, as a star, she wanted to visit them in glory. She went to see J.J. and made the request for a three-week vacation. Two weeks for the round trip, and a week with her mother in France.

Jake smiled benignly and assured her that she could take the time off. "We'll put in your understudy," he said.

"But she doesn't play the violin," protested the actress.

"Well," said the impresario of musicals, "you're not leaving for two weeks, are you? She can learn!"

Miss Myrtil was to have additional Jake musical lore during the following season. The Shuberts never gave up trying to fabricate another *Blossom Time*. They tried with Offenbach and failed. Next, they determined to do George Sand and Frédéric Chopin, with music by Chopin, adapted by . . . and they called it *White Lilacs*.

Miss Myrtil was to play George Sand, and the contrived plot dealt with the love story of the glamorous pair and their eventual separation. When the play didn't look too good, Jake came up with a brilliant suggestion. Chopin would write a serenade which George Sand would play on the violin. It would give the second act a lift, he assured them all. Stunned, Odette said she didn't believe that George Sand played the violin.

"Who'll know?" barked Jake.

"I will not play the violin," said Odette.

"Then why did I engage you?" asked Shubert.

The number did not go in.

There were a number of clouds on the Shubert horizon. The theater had changed in many aspects, but one of the most significant was the emergence of American playwrights. Where once there had been a mere handful of American originals in any given season, with the bulk of production going to European "tried and tested" dramatists, now the situation had shifted. The logical development was a guild of dramatists, who would band together to protect their properties, their rights, and their position in the theater.

The Shuberts fought them.

Note has been made before of the growing smut in the theater. Realism had become an excuse for vulgarity. The hue and cry for censorship organized itself into action. A play jury system was instituted to screen plays. The Shuberts fought it. It never worked. The Shuberts suggested self-censorship, and that didn't work either.

Lee took the opportunity to deliver a statement on censorship, which included a rap at playwrights. The *Morning Telegraph* of February 4, 1927 reported: "The authors of plays are the ones who should be held responsible for the condition of the stage as it is at the present time, because if they did not write plays that are being criticized, they could not be staged by any producer." Right? Right!

Of course, Lee could also say, in arguments with the organizers of the Dramatists' Guild, "The Producer is more important in the theater than anyone else, including the author. I don't care how many plays a playwright writes, who could see them if there wasn't a Producer? Who would know about a playwright unless a Producer invested his capital in it? That is why I say the Producer should *share* the copyright with the author." Right? Right!

249

But censorship was inevitable. Honest plays were hit as hard as the trash. *The Captive*, a serious work, the first play to touch on lesbianism, was affected. So were *Sex* by, and with, Mae West (the brothers were minor backers), and *Virgin Man*. Miss West was fined and went to jail for a week. So did the author and producer of *Virgin Man*, the saga of an unkissed Yale man who fails to be seduced by the fleshpots of New York. Both plays were trash.

The most shameless of the shows was a revue called *The Bunk of 1926*. It was ordered closed, with attendant publicity, but a court injunction secured by the producers kept it open. Even then, with all the publicity, it was so bad that it didn't sell tickets. Being banned in Boston didn't help. During the close-the-show, "injunct"-to-keep-open shenanigans, the producers saw a large sale coming up—they wanted to move to a larger theater in anticipation of same.

Moral Lee Shubert, who publicly deplored the revue, privately served an injunction against the producer to prevent him from leaving *his* Broadhurst Theater. A buck is a buck.

While Lee was getting injunctions, he thought he ought to do it on a wholesale basis. He asked Willie Klein to get one against the Dramatists' Guild. "We want to deal freely," said Lee. "We want to give the public any play we think they might like. Why should one group control the American theater?"

He went on. "We have not dealt with any member of this monopolistic organization for over a year." (He did not say that the Shuberts were the *only* producers not dealing with the guild.)

Arthur Garfield Hays, representing the guild, stated that it was a labor union with all the rights of collective bargaining.

"Monopoly," warned Lee solemnly, "is bad for the public and bad for the little fellow who is the backbone of American business."

Less than two months later, he would announce that the Shubert Theater Corporation controlled 75 percent of the theaters in the United States, and nearly 80 percent of the first-class theaters in the United States—which obviously must have been good for the public and America's business spine.

In between announcements, the Shuberts signed the Dramatists' Guild agreement. Lee was nothing if not flexible.

He also announced a sketch-writing contest with prizes, bought the National Theater on 41st Street, and the Cort on 48th. He fulminated against Governor Al Smith, who had sponsored a padlock bill to seal theaters which presented offensive material, claiming the law was "confiscatory and illegal."

Jake sailed for Europe, proudly announcing that he "would take the cure at Vichy," which led to several bad jokes. And Lee, with Bill Phillips, announced a second stock issue, this one for $7,500,000. It would gain the brothers another $10,000,000 or so in stock sales and give the company additional working capital. Lee still personally controlled his company; he still owned personally the more valuable *leased* assets of his company; he had taken out nearly $20,000,000 in cash for himself and his brother in the two deals.

One other item took up valuable Shubert time. For the nth time in as many years, the Law wanted to protect the public against ticket scalpers. Ice again.

This time it was Federal District Attorney Tuttle for the people. The investigation brought out some interesting details. There were two "systems" by which brokers got tickets to theatrical attractions, explained John A. Sullivan of the Sullivan Theater Ticket Service.

The "concession" system was organized so that the broker paid a fixed fee each month to the producer for the privilege of buying tickets at box-office prices. This fee varied from $50 and $100 a month all the way to $1,000 a month, depending on the box-office business.

Then there was the "commission" system. This formula provided for the broker to pay a fixed fee per ticket. Sullivan went on to say that every theater in New York operated on one or the other system. Except for the Shuberts. They used both!

The "concession" payment went to the Shubert Theater Corporation. The "commission" payment went to the individual theater. There were rumors about Shubert ownership or partnership in certain ticket-brokerage firms, but this was not examined too carefully. (It was rumored that Lee had 50 percent of Tyson, McBride, Sullivan, and an arrangement with Leblang.)

The Supreme Court of the United States ruled finally that the New York law limiting the markup of a ticket speculator was unconstitutional. Now Lee could have it both ways. House seats, delivered to speculators with an agreement on the split of the profits; "concession" and "commission" agreements; and the profits of the ticket firms which they owned all or part of. All kicking into the Shubert pockets.

Jake returned from Europe and assured worried America that "we are still way ahead of the rest of the world theatrically," and maintaining their shuttle pattern, Lee left to "look over the European market and examine the London situation for the next season."

The most important theatrical event of the year had gone unnoticed by everyone. It was a sixteen-performance revival of a sentimental Jewish play, starring George Jessel. The title was *The Jazz Singer*.

251

Chapter Thirteen

Lee commenced his attack on the 1927–28 season by calling in George White. The senior Shubert had not forgotten the costume fiasco, and with the theater situation as uncertain as it was, he was determined to kill two birds with one theater. He would net some money on White, and fill a theater with an attraction, and get White in the Shubert stable.

White was using Erlanger theaters and Erlanger road-bookings for his attractions. Lee thought he ought to be a Shubert attraction. He offered White a 65 percent to 35 percent split of the gross—the larger fraction for White.

White expressed interest, but carefully spelled out to Shubert that Ziegfeld enjoyed a 70–30 divvy with Erlanger, and that Honest Abe had made the same arrangement with White. The black-eyed Shubert blinked reflectively and came up with an astonishing offer. "If you will book with us, I will give you seventy-five percent of the gross, and I will advance you a hundred thousand dollars as an investment in your show. I will do better than that." He leaned forward in his chair behind the small desk, firmly planting his hands on the edge. "I say to you, Georgie, that I will pay you personally a thousand dollars per week per show."

White studied the proposal, and then replied, "It's a ridiculous offer, Mr. Lee. You have to lose money on it. You can't make out."

"I want the deal."

"It doesn't make any sense," protested White.

"If I want to be foolish, let me," said Lee impassively. Then, in seemingly casual by-play: "You got somebody in mind to star in the *Scandals*?"

Light dawned on White. He had been talking to Ed Wynn, who, joining a large club, had sworn never again to work with the Shuberts. He had fought them bitterly in the first Equity strike, and had been "punished" by the brothers in their own inimitable style. No bookings, no routings, the worst theaters—anything they might plan. Now White could understand Lee's offer. It would give him Wynn.

"Nobody in mind yet," said White easily. "But, Mr. Lee, Erlanger has played straight with me. I would be unfair if I just walked out on him. If he ever double-crosses me, I'll be back."

White went directly to Wynn's attorney, Joe Bickerton. He wanted Wynn for his next production, *Manhattan Mary*, and had been exploring the situation with Bickerton. On behalf of Wynn, Bickerton had been jockeying the price. Ziegfeld wanted Wynn for a *Follies*, and was offering $2,000 per week. White knew this. "I will advance $150,000 into Wynn's account at the Guaranty Trust if you sign the contract today." Bickerton stuttered, made a phone call to Wynn, and the deal was closed.

They had been in rehearsal for less than a week when White received a call from Abe Erlanger. White was informed that Wynn was under contract to Erlanger, could not perform for White, and White would have to shut down. White demanded to see the contract, and Erlanger blew. "My word is good enough," he said, and ended the meeting.

Wynn denied the contract. White confronted Erlanger with this, and Erlanger was adamant. Wynn would play for him, and only for him. Then he made an offer. "You can have *my* contract with Wynn for twenty-five thousand dollars." (No, it was not only the Shuberts who behaved like Shuberts.)

White studied Erlanger for a moment, and came to his decision. "All right. You won't show me the contract, so I have to take your word. You prepare the release. I'll be back with a check."

White went directly to Lee Shubert's office. "You know about Wynn?"

Lee nodded.

"You still want the deal? The hundred-thousand-dollar deal?"

Lee nodded again.

"Then write me a check for twenty-five thousand dollars—and make it payable to Abe Erlanger."

Shubert didn't even blink. He ordered the check.

White went directly to Erlanger's office. The release was ready. "I want a receipt for the check," said White. Erlanger flushed, but had his secretary prepare the receipt. White leaned over the desk. "Hold your hat when you see the check," he cautioned, and handed Shubert's check to Erlanger.

"I hope the check is good," said Erlanger. "And I hope he steals you blind."

White booked through the Shuberts from that day on.

Bringing White into the Shubert fold did not please Jake. Jake hated all other producers, particularly rivals in his "musical field." He hated Carroll and he hated White and, most of all, he hated Ziegfeld.

When Max Meth left the Shuberts (temporarily) to conduct *New Moon* for Romberg, and then to do *Whoopee!* for Ziegfeld, Jake felt he had been stabbed. Eventually, he rehired Meth, and a revelatory interview took place.

"Did you like *Whoopee!?*" Jake asked.

"It was a nice show," replied Meth.

"What made you like it? What the hell did Ziegfeld do?"

"Well," temporized Meth, "the scenery was beautiful. Urban does great sets. And the costuming was gorgeous."

Jake glared at him. "My costumes aren't gorgeous?"

"I didn't say that," protested Meth.

"My costumes come from Woolworth's?"

Meth remained silent.

Jake stood up and came around the desk, pointing his finger under Meth's nose. "My sets are junk, eh?"

"Mr. J.J.," said Meth. "I never said that. You asked me if I liked the show and why. I told you why."

Jake mused over this and resumed his seat behind the desk. "Is Ziegfeld a nice man to work for?"

"He's very nice."

"And I suppose I'm a bastard?"

"I didn't say that," said Meth.

"I'm nicer than Ziegfeld!" Jake shouted. "You understand? And my costumes are gorgeous!"

Meth was leaving, and Jake's voice rolled into the corridor after him. "And so are my sets!"

Jake used his gorgeous sets and costumes in a revue called *Padlocks of 1927*, which starred Texas Guinan, of night club fame, and featured a sultry singer, Lillian Roth, and a slick-haired dancer named George Raft.

It was not a hit, but it provided one minor sensation for the season. Miss Guinan made her entrance on a horse, and the horse got stage fright, resulting in a valiant effort to fertilize the Shubert Theater.

Jake, watching from the wings, wanted to punch the horse. "He thinks he's a God-damned critic!" Jake muttered.

He came right back with a Romberg hit, *My Maryland*, an operetta concerned with the doings of Barbara Frietchie from the poem of the same name. It had been a smash in the hinterlands, and despite tepid critical reception, it was a hit in New York. One of the big songs in the show was "This Land Is My Land." Manny Seff, assigned to the publicity chore by Greneker, tried to persuade Representative Emanuel Celler of New York to propose a bill naming Romberg's paean the new national anthem, to replace "The Star-Spangled Banner." Jake approved but Congress didn't.

While Jake was lavishing love on "Shoot if you must this old gray head," Ziegfeld was opening a show that revolutionized the musical theater. There are two stories in circulation. One has it that Ziegfeld

Texas Guinan—and the impulsive white horse. They both appeared in *Padlocks of 1927*.

had read Edna Ferber's *Show Boat* and fallen in love with it. He had brought it to Irving Berlin, who turned it down. He then approached Jerome Kern and Oscar Hammerstein II, and they too fell in love with it. When the piece was ready, Ziegfeld was enjoying a period of no money. They had to wait a year. That's one version. The second has it that it was Kern and Hammerstein who brought the idea to Ziegfeld. It makes small difference. The work was a landmark in the theater.

Kern's score was amazingly tuneful, but, more important, even though the authors called it "a musical comedy," it wasn't. It was a musical play. The songs and the lyrics were integrated into the action. The first, fitful attempts of the earlier years had come together in this one magnificent effort. It was musical theater raised to a new art form, and it was the first in a series of illustrious musicals that climaxed with *West Side Story*. Jake didn't like the show.

The season was strange. There seemed to be a restlessness in the air. Even though the country was going through an era of unprecedented prosperity, the amusement business was hurting. Some said it was the attractions. Others blamed it on radio. But the theater was having a bad time, and so was Hollywood.

The motion-picture factories were facing serious problems. The independents, in particular, were struggling to survive the slump. No one was hurting more than the Warner brothers.

To find a new "gimmick," a publicizable something that would lure customers' dollars into the box office, they determined to take a flyer on a new invention that had come out of Bell Laboratories—synchronized sound for motion pictures. It was Warner blood money that they dug into to make the first part-talking picture.

The subject the Warners chose was *The Jazz Singer*, by Sam Raphaelson, which George Jessel had starred in for a season, plus sixteen revival performances. The now-familiar story of the rabbi's son who becomes the singer of popular songs seemed tailor-made for the screen experiment. The Warners secured the rights and approached Jessel to repeat his starring performance. Jessel said he didn't want to be anybody's guinea pig.

The money pressure on the Warners was intense. They had tied up another packet of dollars in the property, and they had to get to filming or they would be forced out of business. They were just about broke. They went to see Al Jolson. Jolson, always a gambler, decided he would gamble on this one. They hacked out terms, the Warners could not meet the salary demands, they offered stock instead, and eventually a contract was signed. They made *The Jazz Singer*.

It opened on Broadway in October, and Lee Shubert was in the first-night audience. Its reverberations have not yet finished. A new form had been born, and it would revolutionize the entire entertainment industry. Careers would end, new careers would be born. Playwrights who couldn't get arrested became Hollywood's darlings. Every film studio wanted to make motion pictures that talked, and Warner Brothers, a few short months ago on the verge of business extinction, became an important force in filmville.

The long-range repercussions would go on for years. Keith-Orpheum, the Shuberts of vaudeville, would be pushed to the wall by the combined assault of radio and talkies. They would see vaudeville die, they would need sound in their theaters, and to get it they would be married to Radio Corporation, forming R.K.O. The broker on the marriage was Joseph Kennedy, father of the late President, and when the crash would force R.K.O. into receivership, Joe Kennedy would become the receiver and a film maker.

More tellingly, the legitimate theater would reel and shudder under the onslaught of the talking picture.

Twenty years before, when the silent era was born, the stage had been forced into readjustments. The road, as it had been, vanished. The small touring and repertory companies that had brought live theater into every town in the country were out of business. Their stock performances of broad comedies and chillers were better performed by the movies and at a cheaper price. Only the big attractions—and they played split weeks more often than not—provided stage entertainment, and expensively.

The Broadway stage had been forced to explore new directions. Broadway went for adult themes, some censorable material, and the splashy musical revue and operetta. Now the talking picture would carve out its own area—carve it out of the living theater. In these first days, when cameras were bulky and equipment ponderous, they would do the intimate comedies and dramas and, of course, the small musical. In a year, they would be producing musical extravaganzas that dwarfed anything Broadway might offer. And they could sell tickets for a fraction of the price of an orchestra seat.

Movies could take a straight play and open it up, giving it size and scope, and star-cast it with box-office names in the plural.

The revolution in Hollywood was equally drastic. The big box-office names, the manufactured stars who had had no stage experience, were soon to be dumped into the discard pile. Broadway actors found themselves in a sellers' market. Directors who knew words and dialogue commanded astronomical salaries. There was an exodus west to the film studios.

What would the theater do? Its potential was what it had always been. It had electricity, and it had talent—the magic of live actors touching the heart and the mind with the skill of artistry and the words of inspiration. It had the illusion of tearing out the wall and having audience and creators share together in a precious living experience. And that was not Jake Shubert's stock in trade. He would never admit it.

One short month before *The Jazz Singer* opened in New York, they buried Marcus Loew. Lee, who had been dry-eyed at his father's funeral and at his mother's, wept. Their relationship had been close and warm and respectful. The haberdasher and the furrier who had become theatrical czars understood each other.

A few years before, Loew and his wife had gone to England to meet with the companies which were distributing MGM pictures in the British Empire. Their "distributor" was a lord of the realm, owning vast estates in Dorset. He invited his "associates" from America to spend the weekend with himself and her ladyship at their country place.

The "house in the country" was a castle; the grounds were literally miles of park; deer browsed beneath the trees; it was a picture postcard —particularly to the middle-class millionaire Marcus Loew. In a moment of expansiveness, he told his host, "When you and your wife come to America, you must spend a weekend with us." Loew and his wife lived in a modest, comfortable home in Arverne, just outside of New York.

A few months later, Loew received a cable from his British distributor, announcing the date he and his wife would arrive in New York, and assuring Loew that one of the things he and her ladyship looked forward to most was their weekend with him and his good wife. Loew went into shock. He had never anticipated that his spontaneous invitation would be accepted. And where would he entertain them? At the house in Arverne? With herring for breakfast? What to do?

At the Hunting Room of the Hotel Astor, he spotted Lee Shubert. He walked over and confided his dilemma. Shubert was all ideas. He had seen a magnificent house on Long Island. It was for sale—a palatial estate, where a man like Loew ought to be living.

"Why should I live on Long Island, when you live next to your office?" asked Loew.

"Ah," said Lee. "You're a motion-picture magnate; I am just a poor theater man."

Loew insisted that Shubert accompany him at once on the inspection tour of the estate. Lee summoned his car and the man drove out. The place was lovely—a huge, rambling mansion, with extensive grounds, gardens, and a pool. It was perfect. There were only two drawbacks. First, it had not been lived in for many years, and needed decoration and furnishings. Second, during its period of vacancy, the shrubs and flowers had gone to seed. And time was pressing.

Again, Shubert was full of suggestions. "You got a film studio, no? And they got a prop department, no? So when did you need a film studio more?"

The next day, a prop man and a set decorator were on their way from Hollywood. They looked the place over, got on the phone, and the day after that, a trainload of props, furniture, china, silver, ancestral portraits, and greenery was shipped out from California, accompanied by sufficient bodies to put everything in order, and with skilled household help to run the large establishment.

His lordship and her ladyship arrived, were met at the boat by Loew, driven out to "my place in the country—on Long Guyland." The weekend went off perfectly—the stage butler was divine, the household ran like a stage set, and no one noticed that a good part of the garden was stage shrubbery.

Intoxicated with the success of the house and the décor, Loew determined to buy it. And he did. He and his wife moved in, minus staff, and soon he had found his favorite place in the house—one small corner of the vast drawing room, where he would sit at the table each night and play solitaire. Then, he would wander up the baronial staircase to the master bedroom and climb into the monumental bed, and feel lonely.

One day, not too long after he had acquired the estate, he ran into Lee Shubert again at the Hunting Room.

"You made me a lot of trouble," he told Shubert. "Trouble?" asked Lee perplexedly. "You had a problem. I helped you solve it. Now you live on an estate, like a prince. How did I make you trouble?"

"The house is too big," said Loew simply. "I can't book anyone for weekends. Who likes playing one-handed pinochle?"

Perhaps this, as a part of their shared experiences, was what made Lee weep as he delivered the eulogy at Marcus Loew's funeral. He didn't weep long. He was one of the first to explore the possibility of purchasing the Loew family stock—he wanted MGM. He never got it. He also tried to buy the tidy holdings in MGM of Arnold Rothstein, a notorious gambler of the era, and failed here too. Schenck bought the family share, and took practical control of MGM. Schenck did *not* weep at Loew's funeral.

· · ·

Lee was busy with real estate and with production. A new theater on West 47th Street, a warehouse in which to build and store scenery and costumes on Greenwich Street, the corner adjacent to 63rd and Broadway, and plans for a twenty-eight-story hotel on Times Square.

He was less brash in announcing the third annual Shubert Theater Corporation statement, on August 24, 1927. Earnings were down to less than ten dollars per share. But his sorrow was assuaged when he looked at his productions for the troublesome season.

While Jake was doing a *Greenwich Village Follies* and a new *Artists and Models*, and trying *White Lilacs* with Chopin, Lee was having his best time in years.

He had his flops, to be sure, and Marcella Swanson appeared in one of them—*Mixed Doubles*, a tasteless farce which opened and (mercifully) closed quickly. He made it up to Miss Swanson by giving her a respectable run in *The Madcap*.

And So to Bed, a sequel to the diary of Samuel Pepys, was a hit; *The Silent House*, an English thriller, was a bigger hit. By this time, Lee was leaning heavily on the advice of other people in his selection of properties. He had endorsed the idea that Manny Seff, attached to Greneker's publicity staff, should do the European "scouting" for "Lee's side." (The Shuberts had almost formalized their tacit understanding. Their employees recognized the division, and knew that they worked "on Lee's side" or "on J. J.'s side.") Seff had worked for the *Herald Tribune* before joining the Shubert publicity staff, and had covered the European theater for the *Trib*. Now, he served the same function for Lee and Jake, in addition to normal press agentry.

(His duties did not end there. The Shubert "revues" boasted some of the worst sketches to come to Broadway. And they were rewritten, "fixed," "doctored" by an assortment of Shubert employees. Seff found himself rewriting routines, and wound up writing a whole play, *Blessed Event*, which became a hit, was sold to Hollywood, and took Seff there, where he became a successful screen writer.)

Well before this, one night, wearing his press agent's hat, Seff was sitting on-stage at the Casino Theater, talking with Irene Dunne, then starring for the Shuberts in *Luckee Girl*, and the curtain went up. Jake was in the wings, and hissed "Don't move!" Seff sat at the table in pretend-animated conversation with Miss Dunne for the whole first scene, vanished from then on, leaving a slightly puzzled audience. Who was the man with the heroine?

Jake used to read every play that "Lee's side" recommended and that Lee bought, and hated every one of them. Lee had taken an option

Irene Dunne in *Luckee Girl*, in which she starred for the Shuberts. That is Irving Fisher with Miss Dunne.

on *Cynara* in London, and Jake saw the first act, hated it, and told Seff to forget the option.

"But in the second act, it has that great seduction scene," said Seff, knowing his customer.

"Seduction scene?" said Jake, eyes narrowing. "Pick up the option!"

Jake starred Jeanette MacDonald in *Angela*, which didn't make it, and Lee had his moment when he opened the new Ethel Barrymore Theater, Shubert-built, and brought Miss Barrymore under Shubert management.

He was proud of the affiliation, and you can be sure it was a "Mr. Lee Presents." As a matter of fact, it began as "Mr. Lee Shubert Presents Ethel Barrymore in *Kingdom of God*." When Miss Barrymore saw the marquee thus spelled out, the first lady of the theater informed the manager there would have to be some changes in the billing. "If he's *Mr.* Lee presenting," she said, "then Mr. Lee Shubert will be presenting *Miss* Ethel Barrymore." The marquee was changed.

The Barrymore season was critically acclaimed and only fair financially, but Lee came back with John Drinkwater's *Bird in Hand*, which would run five hundred lucrative performances. It was Lee's biggest solo hit.

Jake kept trying. He did *Boom Boom*, with Jeanette MacDonald and a Werner Jannsen score, and it didn't go. Marcella Swanson was featured, but the most striking part of the show was a handsome young juvenile lead that the Messrs. presented. His name was Archie Leach, and his good looks stole the reviews. He is better known as Cary Grant.

Jake tried again with *A Night in Venice*—Jake was covering the Continent in his attempts to find a winner. He had done *A Night in Paris*, and *A Night in Spain*; perhaps he would have better luck with Venice. He didn't. In Paris he had seen an act which enchanted him. The Dodge Sisters, stripped to the waist, did a dance in which one was the hunter, the other a bird, and were real attractions at the *Folies Bergère*. Jake booked them.

On opening night of *A Night in Venice*, the girls did their act— but in full costume. Percy Hammond found the show "tasteless and unfunny," and went on, "One thing I do regret. The Miss Dodge who was the hunter should have been given a gun."

Jake barred Hammond from the theater.

Busby Berkeley had staged the dances in *Venice*, just as he had for *Pleasure Bound*, a show born to trouble. It was another of Jake's "revues," and had been brought into the world a number of years before as a straight play, designed to star two Jewish comedians. It had never been good enough to come into New York.

Boom Boom, 1929. That's Jeanette MacDonald with Stanley Ridges.

Boom Boom again. Archie Leach (Cary Grant) with a bevy of *Boom Boom* girls.

In a series of contortions, it became *Well, Well, Well!* a Shubert musical with a book line that didn't work. Jake began therapy on the sick show—his own therapy. Usually, it consisted of adding "acts"— vaudeville turns, blackouts, or just plain specialties. The show soon lost its "line" and was just plain revue. Title: *Well, Well, Well!* starring Phil Baker and Jack Pearl.

Nothing went well, well, well with it, and in Pittsburgh Jake changed more of the now nonexistent story line, changed some of the star performers, and changed the title to *Pleasure Bound*.

By now, neither Pearl nor Baker was quite sure of what he was doing. Just at this time, Douglas Fairbanks, Sr., offered Pearl a dramatic role in a new picture he was planning. The money was good, but more important to Pearl was the opportunity to play a character role. Scratch a comedian and you bleed a Thespian with a capital *t*.

Pearl had been with the Shuberts for almost ten years—since they had bought his contract for their vaudeville excursion. And he had been particularly close with Jake. The relationship had transcended business; as with Price, some years before, Jake enjoyed playing adviser to Pearl. He had voluntarily torn up Pearl's contract with a few years to go, to pay him more money and to grant him that special Shubert clause containing the words "unique and extraordinary." (The new form stated that in case of any dispute, the matter would go to arbitration. Willie Klein was not about to have a second Gallagher and Shean field day in court.)

On fire with the golden opportunity to become the great dramatic star that he felt was his destiny, Pearl went to see his friend Jake Shubert. J.J. flatly refused to release him from *Pleasure Bound*.

"Why do you want to walk out on a hit?" asked J.J.

"But it's not a hit. It isn't even a show any more," protested Pearl.

"What the —— does a God-damned actor know?" bawled Jake. "You stay in the show!"

"I quit!" said Pearl.

"I'll sue you until you're dead!" said Jake.

Pearl quit, Jake sued to enforce his contract, and they went to arbitration. No one yet can figure out why, except that perhaps the Shuberts wanted to test the arbitration system. Under the contract, each party could name one arbitrator, and the court appointed a third, impartial referee.

The Shuberts named Bill Phillips, by now working full time with Lee. Pearl, knowing Eddie Cantor's "warm" feelings for Jake, named Cantor. The referee was the president of American Car and Foundry.

From the beginning, Cantor was less interested in settling the Pearl case than he was in settling the Cantor grudge with the Shuberts.

He demanded that a midnight performance of *Pleasure Bound* be held for him and the other arbitrators so that he could see for himself whether Pearl's talents were "unique and extraordinary." The Shuberts indignantly refused.

The rehearsals went on, with no Pearl attending, and finally the arbitration decisions came in. The Shuberts had a binding contract for Pearl's services, which were "unique." Reluctantly, he returned to the play, only to discover that Jake was making still more changes. One of his first "new ones" was to cut Pearl's big tickler in the first act.

They argued back and forth, and finally, Pearl, losing his best line and his temper in one afternoon, heaved a chair across the stage. It bounced, skidded, and slammed into Jake's leg, opening a nasty gash in his shin. Jake screamed like a stuck pig. A doctor was called, and Pearl kept trying to apologize for what had happened, but Jake ignored him.

"Get Mrs. Pearl here," Jake told Scanlon.

Eventually an agitated Mrs. Pearl appeared, and Jake summoned her to his chair of pain. Dramatically, he rolled up his leg to reveal the bandage. He held his hands wide apart. "A cut this big!" said Jake sorrowfully. Now he rolled a baleful eye at Jack Pearl, miserable in the background. "If *I* didn't need a second act, I'd put him in the hospital!" said Jake.

Despite Jake's efforts, *Pleasure Bound* bombed.

Lee did not let his stage successes go to his head. He kept his feet on the ground, and kept assembling same. They bought property on West 51st Street and on East 53rd Street. (Lee felt that one day the theater would move from the West Side to what he always called "the fashionable East Side," and he started as early as 1928 assembling property on that side of town.)

With six theaters in Chicago, they announced plans for two more, plus leasing the Wood. Ironically, Lee bought the B. F. Keith Theater in Boston, undoubtedly chuckling to himself that they had bought it with Keith's own money—the profit from the stock sale. It was the sixth Shubert theater in Boston.

In Philadelphia, they built and opened the Forrest Theater, their fourth house in that city. It produced a wonderful contretemps. Somehow, in designing the theater, plans for dressing rooms were omitted! How this went through all the hands it did, from architect to Shubert office to contractor, etc., without being picked up is inconceivable. But it happened. The theater was completed before anyone noticed that there were no provisions for dressing rooms.

The Shuberts were forced to acquire additional property (at a rousing price), to build a tunnel, and provide the longest walk for actors from stage to dressing room that has ever existed. The onus for the architectural boner was placed on Lawrence Shubert Lawrence, Sr., a nephew exiled to Philadelphia.

Lee's mournful remark, made as a confidence to a Shubert employee, was: "You know—I've got a brother—J.J.—he's an idiot, but not intentionally." Then he shook his head in surrender. "But I got a nephew, Lawrence—he's an idiot *intentionally*."

J.J. completely exploded when he learned of the mistake. He fired Lawrence at once, and, of course, Lee rehired him—at once. This would be a pattern for many years. There is an apocryphal tale that Lawrence waited until J.J. had sailed for his European tour, and cabled him aboard ship:

DEAR UNCLE JAKE DON'T WORRY IF THE SHIP SINKS YOU DON'T OWN IT LOVE LAWRENCE

To make sure that Willie Klein kept in practice, the brothers arranged the usual litigations. Dorothy Donnelly, the librettist who, with Romberg, had given them *The Student Prince*, died suddenly, and her estate sued for an accounting on royalties. Settled—out of court. This settlement had to be made out of court because the estate's attorney had served an order to see the *personal* books of Lee and J.J.

A fellow called William Cunningham, Jr., sued Joe Cook, the comedian, and the Shuberts for $100,000. He had been sitting in the theater, minding his own business, and laughing at Cook's creations— the show was *Rain Or Shine*—when Cook fired a pop-gun, and the cork hit Mr. Cunningham in the eye. He wanted recompense, and even though the play was in a non-Shubert production, in a non-Shubert theater, Cunningham figured that if he would sue anybody, it might as well be a Shubert. The case was thrown out of court.

An unnamed female patron sued the Shuberts for $5,000, claiming that she had been scalded by the hot-water tap in the washroom of the Broadhurst. Klein solemnly proved that there was no hot water in the tap. He could have proved that there *never* was hot water in any tap in any Shubert theater.

Jake insisted that Klein sue radio. Who in radio? Anybody in radio. Radio was using songs from Shubert shows with Shubert permission. Klein announced that he was going to sue the radio industry, and then didn't.

Jake, nearly fifty-three years old, slugged another actor. This time it was Guy Robertson, in rehearsal in Asbury Park, New Jersey. Jake decked him with a right to the head, and Robertson sued. Jake defended, alleging that hitting an actor during a rehearsal was not assault. Lee intervened. The show had been thoroughly blocked and was about to go out on what was left of the road. He persuaded Robertson to return to the cast. Jake didn't slug him again.

Instead, he slugged his chauffeur.

Driving from his Westchester home, Jake was in his usual hurry. The chauffeur, an Englishman, was paying attention to business and *not* turning his head, but he still didn't please the savage Shubert.

"I ain't got all day," said Jake. "Get a move on."

The chauffeur replied that he was doing the best he could; the traffic was heavy.

"Don't give me no excuses," growled Jake. "Get a move on. Go faster."

The chauffeur refused.

Jake began to roar. "You drive this damned car like I tell you to drive," he shouted, "or I will get someone who can."

"I keep asking you to leave earlier," said the Englishman. "This way you're always in a hurry, and I say it's dangerous."

"No back-talk!" said Jake. "I won't have no back-talk. Speed up!"

"When we get to New York, Mr. Shubert," said the driver, "I quit."

"You quit?" bellowed Jake incredulously. "You are going to quit?" He lunged forward. "Pull over. I want to talk to you."

The car pulled over to the roadside, and driver and Jake got out. Shubert was in a fury. "You quit, hey? Well, you're fired! You're fired before you can quit."

"That's fine with me," said the driver.

"It's fine with him!" said Jake to the world at large. And then he hit him. The Englishman dropped, rubbed his jaw, slowly climbed back into the car and drove J.J. to New York. There he "resigned," went to his attorney, and sued for $5,000. Willie Klein settled—out of court— and Jake left for Europe. Manny Seff had cabled great excitement about a Reinhardt staging, and Jake wanted to see it.

Lee kept busy buying property—on 49th Street and First Avenue and assembling more brownstones as potential sites on West 47th and West 46th. By this time, the Shuberts owned or leased all of the block bounded by 44th and 45th streets between Broadway and Eighth Avenue, except for the two hotels. Almost a city block in the heart of Times Square. And they were rapidly pushing north!

Only a short time before, Lee had publicly fulminated against playwrights in general, who were then, to him, the least significant force

Archie Leach. Cary Grant went into the lead in the Shubert's second "adaptation" of *Die Fledermaus.* This one was called *A Wonderful Night*, and Mary McCoy played Adele.

in the theater. Now, he announced publicly that the Shuberts were going to finance authors to produce their own plays so that "the creative people can not only be paid for their work, but also share in the profits." Empty theaters could make a Maecenas out of Lee.

The first of these "new" ventures was a Zoë Akins play, *The Furies*, "produced" by John Tuerk but which was a Shubert piece. It did not do so well, nor did the next few "patron of the arts" Shubert productions.

Lee was forced to pay Al Jolson $40,000 for four weeks' work in Chicago. Phil Baker was ill, the show had to go on, and Jolson took the forty. The only actors enjoying anything near that fee were Cantor, who was getting $5,000 a week from Ziegfeld, and Marilyn Miller, who was being paid six.

Lee had offered Jolson five, then six, and finally surrendered at ten. "You are now the highest-paid actor in the world," he told Jolson joylessly.

"I'm working for the richest producer, ain't I?" asked Jolson.

Lee smiled thinly. "With actors like you, I won't *stay* rich," he remarked.

In his new role as the Playwright's Protector, Lee felt called upon to defend Eugene O'Neill, whose *Strange Interlude* was being attacked as vulgar and obscene. The prosecutor pointed out that Mr. Shubert's concern was pecuniary—the play was booked into a Shubert theater.

It was fortunate for the reigning Shubert that in the war on obscenity in the theater, prosecutors had been changed in midstream. Otherwise, it might have been emphasized that when the original finger was pointed at *Strange Interlude*, Lee had decided it was immoral, saying "the Theater Guild hides behind art."

As the theater owner, he didn't want to do any more than that. But a citizen's suit was filed against *Strange Interlude*, and the citizen doing the filing was, amazingly, Willie Klein!

(As a matter of fact, only one other citizen's suit appears in the history of the censorship drive, and that too against the guild. This time, the play was *Volpone*, the Ben Jonson masterpiece, and the suer was Sam Weller. Sam Weller was a member of the press department of the Shubert Theater Corporation and editor of the *New York Review*, the Shubert house organ.)

Lee Shubert, public, and Lee Shubert, private, were two different men.

.   .   .

Overriding the entire theatrical scene was the impact of the talking picture. The road was doomed. The *New York Times* editorialized on it. Brady came to Lee Shubert and told him if he didn't get into motion pictures, he would be ruined. Lee then publicly denied that he had made an agreement with Brady to go into motion pictures. There had been rumors that Lee was buying something called Voca-Film.

A few weeks later, he was able to deny that he and Brady were setting up American Talking Pictures, Incorporated.

Jake had summoned Seff to London to explain all his excitement at Reinhardt's *Die Fledermaus*. After all, the Shuberts had produced two versions of *Fledermaus:* one called *The Merry Countess*, the second called *The Night Birds*. And they had produced both without bothering to negotiate the rights, which had given Willie Klein a few problems when the widow of Johann Strauss sued for royalties. What was so special now?

Seff insisted that Jake must see the show for himself. Not only was the entire production lively, gay, tuneful, and artistic, but Reinhardt had introduced a "revolving stage" which enabled the show to have an incredibly attractive pace and flow. Jake sat up. After all, he had gotten the idea of "the runway" at the Winter Garden, from Reinhardt. Maybe lightning would strike twice. They went to Berlin.

Jake saw *Die Fledermaus and* the revolving stage, cabled for Watson Barratt, the Shubert set designer, to get to Berlin at once. This time, he would not only "steal" the music, he would copy the whole production, including the revolving stage. And he did.

While Jake was in Europe, they had moved the Shubert offices into the Sardi Building. Not *all* the Shubert offices—just Jake's! The original understanding had been that with their need for space they would consolidate all their departments in the new structure. Their press department had been in a brownstone; production spread through three buildings. Now, it would all be tidily under one roof.

The instant Jake sailed, Lee had "Jake's side" moved out, lock, stock and barrel. He remained in his happy quarters in the Shubert Theater, where he could look out the turret windows at the sixth floor of the Sardi Building, and chuckle.

When Jake returned, he was forced to swallow the deal, and to change his vocabulary. From that day on, Lee became, instead of "that son of a bitch down the hall," "that son of a bitch across the street." It was an all-Shubert street.

With Jake safe in the new building, Lee went to Europe. Before he left, he announced, "We have had a bad theatrical year, possibly because of the talking picture. But I am not worried. The actors who leave the stage for this passing fancy will return to the stage where their living is."

Jake was on fire with what he had seen in Berlin. He could hardly wait to produce the third Shubert version of *Die Fledermaus*. Barratt had faithfully reproduced each Reinhardt staging, copied décor and costume, re-created the revolving stage, and Jake hired people to stage it. He would only supervise, and add the new title *A Wonderful Night*.

For the role of Max (Eisenstein in the original), Jake decided to cast the good-looking juvenile lead he had hired for *Boom Boom*—Archie Leach (better known later as Cary Grant). Now, *Fledermaus* is an operatic operetta, and Max is a singing role. Grant had the best looks on Broadway, and already was showing the incomparable charm that makes him so unusual a personality. There was one drawback. He could not sing.

Jake waved away the problem with complete aplomb. He instructed his director to make sure that on every occasion that Grant was called upon to vocalize, he would be standing in front of the male chorus. Grant would mime singing—mouth open, eyes gleaming with song—while from behind him a member of the chorus would do the actual singing. And so it was. Grant, electrifying the audience, was a star.

It was possibly the most beautiful production that had ever come out of the Shubert shop. It was a lovely show, the critics adored it, but somehow not the audience. One possible explanation exists. Two days before the opening of *A Wonderful Night*, the stock-market crash of 1929 shook America. By the time Jake's show hit the street, more than $12,000,000,000 worth of America's wealth had vanished.

It was the thunderclap that ushered in the storm of the Great Depression. Fortunes vanished, rich men threw themselves out windows, and poor men wondered where the next day's bread could be found. The richest nation in the world staggered under the onslaught, and the most productive manufacturing plant man had ever seen limped, shuddered, and threatened to grind to a halt. A great panic was in the air, and a great confusion. The Depression that "could never happen" had happened.

Chapter Fourteen

The Depression didn't register. At first, people just did not believe it. It was a temporary slump, it would soon be over, the market would go up. Actually, for a few weeks after the first disastrous crash, theater attendance increased. There was a need to relax, to laugh, to believe that everything was the same. Stock-market jokes were inserted into all the revues, and the stand-up comics put "topical" material into their routines. It was not long before it stopped being funny.

Just before the tumble, Lee had picked up three more theaters—the Majestic, the Royale, and the Masque. Two weeks after that, he announced another hotel to be built—it would not be. *Nigger Rich*, a melodrama as tasteless as its title, was brought to Broadway by Mr. Lee, and closed quickly—it was notable only for the fact that it gave Spencer Tracy his first starring role in the theater.

Then Lee hit for three in a row. It started with *Young Sinners*, and followed with two blockbusters. *Death Takes a Holiday* was his second production to appear in the Ten Best Plays, and then came *Topaze*, adapted from the French of Pagnol by Benn Levy. Frank Morgan gave a transcendent performance as Topaze, and the show just ran and ran and ran.

Lee had not wanted to do *Topaze*, or *Death Takes a Holiday*, or, for that matter, *Bird in Hand*, but Seff had prevailed upon him to "try." Jake, to be sure, didn't like, on principle, *anything* Lee was producing. "As soon as my brother hears a play with words in it he don't understand," Jake told Seff, "he thinks it's got class."

Topaze happened during a Shubert economy drive, and J. J. was a staunch believer in economy. When he first read *Topaze*, Jake hated it. But he couldn't find anything specific to hate. So he read it again, and reread it, and finally, he came up with his critique. "In the third act," said Jake, "they say Topaze is worth twenty-five million dollars. Who would believe it that a silly schoolteacher could make that much money in so short a time? Nobody should write plays like this with figures like this without any experience in the money world. You got to make the figure believable. Make it fifteen million." It was done.

Jake was running into problems in his new domicile in the Sardi Building. He was the only overnight tenant in the building, having designed a garishly gloomy apartment for himself atop the new structure. Everyone else went home at night.

Did it pay to heat the entire building just to give heat to Jake?

"Vas You Dere, Sharlie?" Jack Pearl (left), who learned that J.J. Shubert was a Bible expert.

Spencer Tracy (right), as he looked when making his debut with the Shuberts in *Nigger Rich*, 1929.

Not to Jake's thinking. Still, it was at night that he liked to read plays, and it began to be a "coldly" realistic problem. He solved it by getting a battery of electric heaters which were placed in his bathroom, and there he would sit to the wee hours, reading.

Jake actually did read plays. Whether he truly grasped their meaning or not is another matter. Lee didn't even read them. They were synopsized for him by trusted assistants, or they were read *to* him. During these readings the author ran one paramount risk. He would sit down in Lee's office, with the Indian-headed Lee in the chair behind the desk, flanked by three or four stone-faced Shubert aides. He would get no encouragement from their lack of expression. He would begin to read—with expression—playing all the parts, feeling all the wit, emotion, and force he had put on paper. And then he would look up, to spy behind the desk a sleeping Shubert. Lee invariably dozed off. One did not wake Lee Shubert. Lee Shubert awoke. The author would read louder. He would shout. Lee would gently snore. Occasionally he would rouse himself, smile, look attentive, and then off he would go again, sound asleep. To an author, it was torture. He would finish, look expectantly at the aides—and of course, they would have *no* opinion until they had heard one from Shubert, who hadn't heard the piece at all. One of them had recommended the play; otherwise there would not have been the reading. But who? The author never knew.

It wouldn't only straight plays that lulled Lee. He could go to sleep to music with equal ease. When disillusioned Rodgers and Hart returned from Hollywood, a Shubert scout arranged for the men to play their score for Lee. It was *On Your Toes*.

Rodgers seated himself at the piano, and Larry Hart, small, small-voiced, and large-cigared, stood in the bow of the piano, singing the lyrics. This took place in Lee's apartment—the office was too small for a piano. Rodgers was playing the soft melody when he became aware of the fact that Hart was singing the tender "Small Hotel" in a louder voice than he had ever used before. He looked up questioningly, and Hart gestured with the cigar.

Rodgers stared at Lee, who was fast asleep in his chair. Rodgers played louder and louder, finally with the pedal full down all the time. Hart, whose loudest voice was soft, was trying to bellow above the piano. Lee slept. (And yes, he would invariably wake up in time to get the wired and phoned box-office returns from the Shubert circuit.)

Jake continued his nocturnal reading in his bathroom. Not only did he read plays, but he read the Bible. And he could misquote from it endlessly. He fancied himself an authority on the Bible, and this led to a strange argument with Jack Pearl, after Jake and Pearl had kissed and made up. Pearl quoted a line from the Bible, and Jake said he had misread the line.

Pearl was stubborn. "I tell you I read it in the Bible," he said.

"You never read that in no Bible," said Jake confidently.

"I read it in the Bible," said Pearl flatly.

"What Bible?"

Pearl stared at him. "What do you mean 'what Bible'? There's only one Bible. *The* Bible!"

Jake nodded triumphantly. "Then you're leaving things out! *I* read the *un*abridged edition!"

The Willie Klein department was its usual busy self. Jed Harris —né Jack Horowitz, and who, as Horowitz, had worked in the Shubert press department—went to court to enjoin the Shuberts from enjoining Walter Winchell from attending any Shubert Theater. Harris wanted Winchell's presence and plugs, and Harris won.

Lee bided his time, and then sued Harris. He claimed Jed had a contract to book *Front Page*, a smash hit, into a Shubert Theater, and in violation of the contract, Harris was going into Erlanger's Times Square Theater. Harris won again, and this time Shubert was angry. When Horowitz had first started to become a producer, Lee had encouraged him, given him office space, and gotten the promise of Shubert booking in exchange for it. He had been had by Harris.

The critical acclaim that had greeted *A Wonderful Night* had not gone unnoticed in Berlin. Mrs. Strauss prepared to sue for the royalties on her late husband's music, and Reinhardt, who had a writer's credit on the libretto, wanted to sue for at least his royalty, since there was no way he could sue for the piracy of his own production.

Willie Klein and Jake came up with an interesting countercharge. First, they contended that the Strauss copyright had expired. So why should the Shuberts pay any royalties?

And if it *hadn't* expired, their claim continued, *A Wonderful Night* was really not adapted from *Fledermaus* at all. It had been taken from an earlier play, *Le Revillon* (from which *Die Fledermaus* had been adapted). Thus, if either Shubert contention was upheld, there was no need to pay script or libretto royalties.

This out of the way, they announced that a Shubert representative was going to see the widow. A week later, they issued a guardedly optimistic statement that talks were progressing, and finally, righteously proclaimed they would pay "royalties to the widow." They had aced out Reinhardt.

Lee sued Edna Leedom for $50,000—again, that favorite Shubert sum—for leaving the cast of *Lovely Lady* to marry the heir to a brewery. She was under Shubert contract, and Lee wanted to enforce it. He couldn't; love triumphed.

Lee and Jake, who had contributed $50,000 apiece to the United Jewish Appeal, sued to prevent a Jewish troupe from showing its wares in their Shubert-Riviera Theater. They lost.

Mrs. Ella Gray Discola sued Shubert Theater Corporation and Lee Shubert for $680,000, charging fraud and conspiracy in the deal when Lee had purchased from her the Central Theater at 47th and Broadway. She claimed that she had been told that the property was worth only $800,000. Who told her? Her attorney.

Subsequently, she learned that Shubert had "given" her attorney $12,000, and her attorney's secretary $8,000, to forget or never know that the true value of the property was $1,480,000. She was suing Shubert for the difference, and her former attorney and his secretary, too.

Willie Klein, on behalf of Lee, denied the allegations and moved to have the venue changed from Westchester into New York. He got that done, and then beat the suit. Like many another great man, Willie Klein never lost a big one.

On April 26, 1930, Lee sailed for Europe to open his London season with the shows he had imported from the *last* London season: *Death Takes a Holiday*, *Topaze*, etc. At departure, he said it was the best season in the history of Shubert enterprises. He was lying in his teeth.

The company had lost nearly $1,000,000, and Jake tried to cover the story by denying that the Shuberts, the Warners, and Paramount were going to merge their activities into a $365,000,000 company. He also denied that the Shuberts and Warner Brothers were going to produce thirty musical films, comprising the choice musicals in the Shubert catalog. "If the Shuberts want to produce musicals, the Shuberts will produce them, on stage, or on film," stated Jake loftily. "We don't need partners."

The Shubert relatives had been pretty well absorbed into the organization. One branch was in the ticket business. A brother-in-law got most of the insurance, a sizable item which the brothers cut with him. Nephew Lawrence was building theaters without dressing rooms in Philadelphia, and Milton, his half-brother, was assigned to "Lee's side." One large group of cousins were in various box offices; a smaller group ran the concessions.

Jake, who had the family devotion of the tiger fish (which eats its kin), did not approve of any of this. But his pet dislikes were Milton and Lawrence. Neither nephew had inherited Shubert drive, native intelligence, acquisitiveness, or anything else worthwhile. Lawrence, however, *was* charming. He was amusing, fun to be with, occasionally drank too much, and in the main did an almost adequate job. Lee had tried to make him a producer, on the theory that anybody could be a producer, but after Lawrence "produced" *The Man Who Corrupted Hadleyburg* (setting back Mark Twain considerably), they "taught" him box-office and theater management, sent him to Philadelphia, made him tack a "Lawrence" on the far end of his name, and let him be.

Milton was a larger problem. He had not even inherited what Lawrence had. He wanted to be a producer, but didn't quite know what the job entailed. Lee's connections got him a job in Hollywood at Warner Brothers, but Milton didn't make it, even there in Lotusland where no-talent producers with connections were the backbone of the business. So, he wound up on "Lee's side."

Periodically, J. J. would fire Lawrence and Milton, or any other one of the relatives, but Lee, as head of the family, would calmly rehire them. The only times Jake was smitten with deep family emotions came when intermittent ticket scandals resulted in investigations involving Jake and Lee. Jake and Lee were never indicted. But oddly enough, the man who was indicted always turned out to be a cousin! Then, Jake was grateful, and *mishpochah*. There are some who say that blood relationship to the Shuberts is what drove the relatives to ticket-scalping and "ice," and that Lee and Jake never knew anything about it. And there are those who think the earth is flat.

Lee returned from London, facing ever-darkening economic skies. Ziegfeld was about to go bankrupt. Arthur Hammerstein, uncle of Oscar II, already was; Erlanger was struggling. The national paper loss in stock values was now at about $25,000,000,000. Hoover was struggling to combat "it" in Washington; Jimmy Walker was making jokes about "it" in New York; and the new governor of New York, Franklin D. Roosevelt, had an eye cocked on the White House.

It was the state of the theater that puzzled Lee most. Plays that had every right to run were living very short lives. In every other slump, as Lee had pointed out in his stock prospectus, the theater had retained its loyal audience. Now that, too, seemed to be deserting. He examined the possibility of cutting prices and voted against it. Like many other men in business, he felt that sooner or later the market would come back, and with it his audiences. (Incidentally, one knowledgeable estimate from his own broker rates the loss in his personal stock portfolio at over $10,000,000. J. J. shared the account, fifty-fifty.)

But what about the immediate present?

They had made some money with a series at the Jolson Theater, where they revived some Victor Herbert operettas, and so Jake was planning revivals of his own operettas. His big new show for the year was *Nina Rosa*, by Romberg, and he had toured it, polished it, and now he was about to bring it in.

When he came to rehearsals the week before opening, he noticed there had been a change of drummers in the orchestra pit. He summoned Max Meth to his side. "Where is Joe?" demanded Jake.

The show was a big production with a thirty-six-man orchestra and a cast of a hundred and fifty, and they had had a number of problems with it in Chicago. Jake had gone to Europe, swearing Meth to absolute fidelity to the show as it had been blocked. Meth had promised, only to find that Lee had sent Milton Shubert in to "take a look." Milton was full of ideas—none good. Meth had fielded them as well as he could, making minor changes, resisting the major ones.

Jake returned, caught the minor alterations at once, and raised hell with Meth. Now he wanted to know about the drummer, Joe. Meth had allowed the drummer to leave the show to join another production more geographically convenient to his home.

Meth explained, and Jake looked at him in contempt. "No drummer," he said, "no Meth. You're fired!"

Romberg stormed up to Jake. "No Meth, no Romberg! I am going back to Hollywood!"

They raved and raged, and finally Jake agreed to let Meth conduct the opening. "But I don't want to talk to him," he told Romberg. "If he comes near me, I might kill him."

Nina Rosa opened and just about made it. Nothing else the Shuberts produced did. Not even Ethel Barrymore in blackface, playing in *Scarlet Sister Mary!* It wasn't until the last day of 1930 that the Messrs. managed to get another respectable entry in the Broadway sweepstakes.

Lee had been to Europe earlier that year and seen a French musical comedy that he liked a little for its plot and a lot for its male lead, Oskar Karlweiss. Through Shubert intermediaries, he advised Jake to see and buy the piece and the star. Jake made the trek to Vienna and liked the show. He too liked the male lead. There was a slight difference: Jake liked Walter Slezak. (Karlweiss had been granted a week off, and Slezak, his understudy, had taken over.) Jake bought the show and signed Slezak to play the lead in New York. Back in the States, through the Shubert communications system, he informed Lee that the piece and the star now belonged to the Shuberts.

Lee went to a rehearsal and saw king-sized Walter Slezak playing the role that slim Oskar Karlweiss had impressed Lee with. Lee shook his head in puzzlement. Finally, he returned to his office and sent for Jules Murray.

"My brother is a fool!" he told Murray. "He hired the wrong actor. You tell him to fire this big man and get the little man I saw."

"What was his name?" asked Murray.

"I don't know his name," said Shubert, "but he was a little fellow and very slim. This is not the same man."

Murray dutifully crossed the street to the Sardi Building, took the elevator to the sixth floor, and went in to see Jake. "Mr. J. J.," he began, "your brother thinks that there is some mistake in the casting of the male lead in *Meet My Sister.*

"Sure, there is," snarled Jake. "Sure there is. *He* thought of it." Then grudgingly he added, "I like Slezak."

Murray tried to explain that it wasn't Slezak; it was the other fellow. The more he explained, the more confused the conversation became. Jake finally dismissed him. "My brother made a suggestion; I accepted it. Now he wants to welsh on his suggestion, hey? Well, you go tell the son of a bitch across the street, I am holding him to his suggestion."

Murray delivered a censored version of Jake's reply, and Lee, determined to get to the bottom of this, came to see Slezak at the theater. He introduced himself, and then asked, "You have gained weight?"

"A little," said Slezak. "Not very much."

"When I saw this play in Europe," Lee said slowly, "I could swear you were smaller."

Slezak did not understand.

Lee went on. "He—you—were much thinner."

Slezak was nimble-witted. "Oh, you must have seen my understudy!"

Shubert was satisfied. Slezak opened in *Meet My Sister* and went on to his successful American career.

Earl Carroll had opened his new *Vanities* one month after Jake's *Artists and Models* was panned. The *Vanities* was its usual lavish, musical girly show, and was promptly haled into court on an obscenity charge. Jimmy Savo, that wonderful little pantomimist, had a sketch where he played a shy window dresser changing the undergarments on female mannequins. The censor found the scene objectionable.

What Jake found objectionable was the big production number that was the highlight of the show. It was an underwater ballet, featuring the Carroll girls. The Shuberts had used exactly the same device in *Artists and Models*, and Jake felt he had been damaged—$100,000. He sued.

In court, Carroll *and* Jake each claimed that they had bought the rights to the number from the *Folies Bergère*, which had conceived the effect. Neither man could prove anything, and the judge decided Jake had not been damaged. He threw the case out, and on the same day Carroll won the obscenity trial.

Lee was forced to announce that the year-end statement for Shubert would show a net loss, as opposed to the more-than-a-million profit of a year ago. But he stated staunchly that although his competitors were dropping their ticket prices, he was going to hold the line across the nation. Immediately thereafter, he dropped the ticket scale in Cincinnati from a $3 to a $2 top.

. . .

Lee was studying the scene. Strange things were happening in America, and he drew mental charts as the returns came in each night from his nationwide chain of theaters. A sickening downward plummeting in attendance and in receipts—that was the graph.

He could see other pathological symptoms. There were apple stands along Broadway, where men in Chesterfield overcoats, turning up the velvet collars against the piercing cold, were peddling the apples at a nickel apiece.

There was also a soup kitchen on Broadway and a malaise in New York—the New York of which he owned so much. Men who had been rich a year ago were trying to borrow money from him. Actors, who had been so independent just a short time before, could be hired for fractions of their former salaries. And though there were almost as many plays produced in those first years of the Depression as had been presented in the golden days, there were hardly any hits. The audience just wasn't buying. And there was a rash of plays that stayed open for only three or four performances. The Depression theater audience lacked curiosity—at least about the sort of plays that were being presented.

And they were becoming a shopping audience. They didn't just "go to the theater." They would not order seats in advance of the opening, and they would not pay a scalper. (In addition to a loss on his shows and his theaters, Lee wasn't even getting the "ice.") Grey's Drug Store, on Times Square, was the pacesetter for the low-price ticket. Joe Leblang and his wife, Tillie, would pick up the unsold seats at 7:30, and, before the 8:30 curtain time, move them out at cut-rate prices. Shubert had the tickets "delivered" to Leblang! (Rumor had it that Leblang had an "understanding.") Lee had a saying that "when a theater seat is empty for a performance, there is no way to ever get back that lost income." So he tried to sell the seat for what he could get, and smart ticket buyers waited at Leblang's for Lee's tickets. Now, *all* theatergoers were smart.

Other producers were slashing prices, from the standard $3 top to $2 and even to $1. Some made it, others didn't. Then, instead of cutting price on new shows, they tried revivals of shows that had been successful some years before. It didn't work. The next step was to take a more recent hit, recast it, and put it on at low prices. Occasionally, one ran fifty or sixty performances; others just didn't make it. Half of New York's theaters were dark, and half of New York's theaters were Shubert houses. And the road was dead. And 75 percent of the road was Shubert.

Lee examined it all very carefully. He came to the reluctant conclusion that their only real moneymakers had been the English imports, and the shows he had *bought* into. Jake was no longer making Shubert profits; he had been a loser for four years. Where had their recent money *really* come from? Deals like the *Street Scene* arrangement. (When William Brady ran out of money in the middle of *Street Scene*, Lee, for "friendship's sake," had taken half the show for less than a quarter of the investment. Friendship. It had made a small mint (and was Lee's first association with a Pulitzer Prize play). And, of course, money came from the percentage of the gross when a theater was rented, plus the profits on the "house seats" (if any), reserved for the theater owner. Lee Shubert determined to open a new branch of his business.

If Brady was hurting, as Gleason had hurt, then others would need money and assistance to bring their shows to Broadway. To get that money from the man who had it—Lee Shubert—they would have to agree to book Shubert Theaters, accept Shubert road showing, give the Shuberts more than the backer's standard percentage, and Lee could set the odds. (Very soon, Lee discovered that he didn't have to put up all cash. A two-week guaranty of performers' salaries—the by-contract Equity Bond—could be signed by Lee Shubert and count as a cash investment. No cash need be posted; Equity accepted Lee's signature. The advance against the theater rental—part of every show's budget—could be waived by Lee (it was *his* theater) and counted as a cash investment in the production. Lights, props, sometimes complete sets and costumes could be "rented" from the Shuberts, and again this was reckoned into Lee's "investment." The cash was small, the percentage large. It was a good Shubert deal.)

He determined to become the first theatrical pawnshop—a place where a producer could hock his show and Lee could negotiate the amount of the loan and the price for it. No, it was *not* a Shubert Theatrical Corporation project. This belonged to Lee and Jake.

Jake announced cut-rate performances of the revivals of *Blossom Time* and *The Student Prince*, and the "triumphant return to Broadway" of Al Jolson, starring in *Wonder Bar*. Even Jolson couldn't run. Perhaps it was the fact that he could be seen for a quarter in motion-picture theaters. Publicly, Lee Shubert blamed it on "the strikes, which had turned people's minds away from enjoyment." Privately, he told Joe Gaites, who had by now joined the organization, "Tell my brother it's a lousy show." He prodded Gaites for Jake's reply.

281

"Mr. J.J. says, 'People don't appreciate a good clean show any more,'" Gaites reported.

"I think the music stinks," said Lee. "Tell him I said so."

Gaites transmitted, and Jake was furious. "Since when does the son of a bitch know anything about music?"

Gaites censored the reply, but transmitted its gist.

Lee smiled quietly. "Maybe I am not a music expert like my brother," he said quietly, "but all the empty seats in the theater agree with me."

They were forced to close their New Haven theater. The last disastrous season had cost them $40,000. (The Shuberts had a hundred first-class theaters, and more than five hundred split-week theaters. In only one house they had sustained a $40,000 loss. Elementary arithmetic is eloquent.)

One of Lee's favorite anecdotes was his blue-suede-shoe story. "You take blue suede shoes," he would say. "A man makes one pair and it costs him maybe five dollars. He sells them for ten dollars. So, he made five dollars. But, if he makes a *hundred* pairs, he's in business." Here, his little black eyes would twinkle, and the creases in his face would wrinkle into a leathery smile. "People say to me, 'Mr. Shubert, why are you so stingy in a deal? What difference can a hundred dollars make in a large contract?' Well, if I save a hundred dollars each on a hundred theaters, *I'm* in business—I have made some very nice money."

Now he could lose some very nice money.

But he was going to trim the losses. He hotly denied that he was disposing of his London theaters, and then sold five of the six for over $2,000,000, netting a handsome half-million for himself and Jake—personally. The London houses had always been segregated from the corporate holdings. The Great Depression had not yet crossed the Atlantic to England, so Lee could take his profit and run.

He used that profit to consolidate his West 46th Street holdings by buying, at a distress price, the Chanin Theater, which the Shuberts had been leasing for many years.

He kept making brave announcements about the future, but in June of 1931, Broadway was rocked. Lee was forced to ask his bondholders to waive the due interest. The request was part of a proposal that Lee had worked out with Bill Phillips, whereby the real estate of the corporation would be transferred to a new corporation. This, they stated, "would avert quick liquidation" at sacrifice prices. They sweetened the blow by proposing to issue "adjustment bonds" at 6 percent to replace the bonds on which they were defaulting the interest payment. The suggested formula was that for each $1,000 debenture bond they would issue a $1,000 "adjustment bond," plus ten shares of Shubert Theater capital stock.

The stockholders protested. They didn't like it at all.

Lee pressed. He urged immediate acceptance. Failure to move quickly would mean receivership, he warned, and disastrous liquidation. He started to cut back costs within the Shubert organization. Expensive shows were eliminated. Jake's activities were curtailed. And he ordered the payroll cut. Lee assigned David Feinstone, one of his assistants, to the chore of slicing salaries and firing people.

Feinstone did the dirty job, and returned with a neat report on monies saved, people dispensed with, etc., etc.; for this he received Lee's thanks. He was on his way out of the office when Lee called him back. "Take a hundred dollars off your paycheck too," said Shubert. "We're all together, aren't we?"

There was a little bit of the sadist in Lee, and this kind of "joke" he enjoyed. Although the Shuberts had fought the *New York Times* relentlessly, Lee was personally fond of Sam Zolotow. Lee was a lonely man. And Sundays, from his office, he would call Zolotow and talk with him for hours. In the course of such conversations, he would "leak" news items concerning Shubert doings. Zolotow would print them, and Lee would call in Greneker and rake him over the coals. "Where would a newpaper get inside information," Lee would demand, "unless someone in your organization told them?"

Greneker would point out that his "organization" now consisted of himself, Jimmy Proctor, who had replaced Manny Seff, and such pick-up press agents as the occasion warranted.

"So it has to be you!" Lee would say softly. "I don't tell that much to Proctor."

Greneker never learned the source of the "leaks."

Mixed with this special kind of cruelty in so complex a man was a softness and a kindness. When Charles Dillingham, a producer Lee esteemed, went broke, Dillingham continued to live at the Astor for many years, the bill being paid each month by Lee Shubert.

When Dillingham died, Bob Christenberry, the manager of the Astor, approached several Broadway figures to raise the money for a large funeral. Shubert demurred. "I want to do it alone," he insisted in his little voice. "I want to give him the kind of a sendoff he would have liked." He did.

The Shubert handout list was huge. Unemployed actors, writers, backstage employees, musicians—all through the Depression, they would file into Lee's office, and were hardly ever turned down. In those dark days, Broadway was crowded with panhandlers. Lee would walk up the street with a friend, and as any supplicant approached, Lee would literally race the friend to the beggar. It had to be *"his"* panhandler.

He did not restrict his largesse to friends. Al Woods, who had been so successful as a producer-manager, went broke. He was on his uppers, facing eviction from the Beacon Hotel when a friend of his went to ask Lee for help.

Lee turned him down. "Al Woods always tried to make a rough deal with me," said Lee. "Whenever he knew I needed an attraction, he would gouge me. I pass."

The friend went to Zolotow, asking him to intercede. Zolotow was familiar with the story. When Woods reopened *Shanghai Gesture* (which had started at the Martin Beck Theater) he had gone into the Shubert Theater at Lee's request. And Woods had been able to muscle for himself a percentage of the house profits, an unheard-of arrangement for the Shuberts. Lee had to have the show, and so he signed, but he did not forget, or forgive.

Zolotow called on Lee. He repeated the request, and again, Shubert was adamant. "I will not be taken for a soft man," he told Zolotow. "I cannot forget what this man did." Zolotow argued, gave up, and left. It wasn't until several weeks later that Zolotow learned that Lee had sent $100 to Woods the instant Zolotow had left, and did so every week thereafter. Lee didn't want to be known as a patsy.

Old-time chorines who had lost their looks or their lovers were put into backstage jobs or hired as ushers. Some were even made assistant cashiers in the ticket windows. And it wasn't only Lee. Jake too had this sentimental streak during the lean years.

The theater critic in St. Louis perhaps best summed up Jake's charity. "We admire Mr. Shubert's loyalty," he wrote. "But we do wish he would pension his overage chorus girls to some other cause than the St. Louis Municipal Light Opera Company."

It must not be assumed that all at once they had become the purely benevolent Shuberts. They were still their avaricious selves. Catherine asked for more money from Jake, and he savagely turned her down. She pleaded destitution, and he remarked, "She was broke when I met her; let her get a job."

Arthur Hammerstein's estate was sold at bankruptcy auction in Westchester, an auction that no one seems to have heard of except the Shuberts. Lee made the journey and bid in Hammerstein's interests for less than $700. What he bought included the producer's rights in *all* Hammerstein productions, plus the writer's royalties belonging to Hammerstein by right of purchase. Among the Hammerstein properties picked up for this sum were *The Firefly* and *Rose Marie*. The Shuberts subsequently sold *The Firefly* to MGM, (small-world department) and the Shubert share of the purchase was over $20,000. And they still retained all stock, amateur, and performance rights in the property.

Erlanger, still punching, had noted Aborn's success with the Victor Herbert season for the Shuberts, and promptly hired Aborn to produce a Gilbert and Sullivan series for him. No sooner did that announcement appear than Lee Shubert called in Aborn. He offered Aborn a *Shubert* season with Gilbert and Sullivan. Aborn declined; he had enjoyed life with Jake and wanted no more.

Twice more, Shubert made offers to Aborn, and each time Aborn declined. In no time, the Shuberts announced their own Gilbert and Sullivan festival for the Jolson Theater, plus a second company which would tour, miraculously arriving in Boston and Philadelphia one week before the Aborn-Erlanger Civic Light Opera Company had been scheduled to appear.

Neither company did well (predictably) and the Messrs. closed down in Boston, temporarily surrendering the Savoyards to Erlanger.

They sued *Life* magazine on a libel claim when *Life* referred to them as "lousy producers." (This was the old *Life*, not the Henry Luce publication.) They went to trial, and Justice Schmuck (*sic*) soberly decided that the word "lousy" when applied to a person's work was not libelous.

Winchell quoted the decision, and noted, "To say that the Shuberts are lousy producers is no longer libel; if anyone calls them the best producers in town, *that* might be libel."

They beat Ted Healy on a salary suit, and tried to mount a new season's productions. Priestley's *The Good Companions* could run for only eight weeks, but Lee managed to feature Marcella Swanson in it. Their biggest hit—and that was no hit—was *Everybody's Welcome*, starring the Ritz Brothers and Harriette Lake, better known now as Ann Sothern.

They fought a claim by Arthur Hartley that the Messrs. had welshed on an agreement to finance a musical revue, *Brighten Up*, which would feature Lita Grey Chaplin and Georges Carpentier, the French prizefighter. Hartley wanted $250,000, and the Shuberts didn't want to give it to him.

Carpentier had been a box-office draw in Paris, and Jake imported him. But aware of the ex-fighter's unreliability, Jake insisted on a curious clause in the contract. It stipulated that if Carpentier arrived at rehearsal a half hour late on four occasions, the contract was voided. Hartley tried desperately to keep Carpentier punctual, and he succeeded.

But Shubert scouting reports on the show indicated that it was a disaster. It couldn't make it.

Willie Klein called Manny Seff to his office. (This was Seff's last Shubert assignment. *Blessed Event* was about to open and take him to Hollywood.)

Klein started things with: "You have attended the rehearsals of the show, every day?"

Seff indicated that he had.

"You watched the clock carefully, and Carpentier was late ten times. You will testify to that." No question, this; it was a legal declaration.

Seff refused.

"I will have you fired," warned Klein.

"I can't testify your way," replied Seff. "It's perjury."

"Get out," said Klein coolly.

Someone else in the Shubert office did so testify, and with Carpentier in breach of contract, the producer could not deliever the agreed-upon package. The Shuberts won their case.

On October 9, 1931, the Shuberts filed suit in the United States Court of Claims, seeking $268,000 in damages. They alleged that this was the loss they had incurred, due to federal condemnation and destruction of Poli's Theater in Washington, D.C., a Shubert leasehold.

On October 20, 1931, Catherine D. Shubert, divorced wife of Jacob J. Shubert, filed suit in New York against J. J. Shubert for "adequate support."

John Shubert called on his mother and begged her not to sue. "There is enough dirt on the Shubert name already," he told her. "Let's not pile on any more."

She would not hear him.

"I will take care of you," he promised. "You will not have to worry. I will personally see to it that you have everything you want. Just stay out of court. We've been in enough courts."

She refused to listen. The case was taken under advisement by Supreme Court Justice Aaron J. Levy.

One day later, on October 21, 1931, Messrs. Gerson, Beesley, and Hampton, of Chicago, filed claim for $5,000 against the Shubert Theatrical Corporation. They petitioned the court for "protective measures" to insure the creditors against possible further losses. They were asking for a receiver to conserve Shubert assets pending bankruptcy.

The Shuberts did *not* contest the petition! Willie Klein admitted that Lee and J. J. had lost $3,000,000 in 1930 and 1931, and on behalf

The Incredibly Lovely Miss Ethel Barrymore, starring for Mr. Lee Shubert in *The School For Scandal*. Even she couldn't save the Messrs. from the black days of 1931.

of the firm agreed to a receiver's being appointed by the court, to take over the assets of the company.

Federal Judge Caffey appointed the Irving Trust Company of New York and Lee Shubert as co-receivers. They were to report back to him in twenty days. The panicky stockholders, $18,000,000 poorer than they had been one day before, called for an investigation.

The world's largest theatrical company had gone broke. Or had it?

Why hadn't Lee and Jake fought the receivership? Why hadn't they avoided the $5,000 suit? It was a bill easily paid or, conceivably, bought off for $1,000. Why didn't they try? One possible explanation can be found in the frantic strategy meetings that had been going on around the clock between Bill Phillips, Willie Klein, and Lee Shubert.

Chapter Fifteen

They had come to the conclusion that the Shubert Theater Corporation was not salvageable. Play production was a quick way to lose money; half their Manhattan theaters were dark; those theaters they owned personally were valuable only as real estate; those they leased were losing Shubert money; outside producers were broke; and so were the angels who had helped finance Broadway production.

The banks and insurance companies that by foreclosure proceedings were becoming the Shuberts' rivals in theater ownership were ignorant of the ins and outs of theatrical operations. Their ineptitude would eventually mean trouble for *all* theatrical business.

And the boys with the quick cash—the racketeers, the bootleggers, the muscle boys—were moving in.

It was a good time to get out. That's what Klein said and that's what Phillips said, and Lee, a sunburned spider, sat and listened. He neither agreed nor disagreed. He listened. Finally, and for his own reasons, he consented. He did not agree.

The bankruptcy—that's what it was—stunned Broadway and it stunned Wall Street. Panicky stockholders called for a meeting. Ugly rumors were started and repeated. The Shuberts had committed a giant fraud. Meanwhile, there were plays in work, plays in rehearsal, and plays coming in to New York for opening.

Everything they brought in failed, except for Lee's production of *Cynara*, the play with the second-act seduction. It was a miserable season. It led to bad jokes. "The only hit the Shuberts have is Sardi's." "See a Shubert production early; it won't be there later." "What does Lee say to Jake? 'Brother or no brother, I want Ziegfeld!' "

There were other headaches. They stopped production on eight shows, most of them Jake's. And promptly, they faced an Equity suit for almost $10,000 for actors' salaries. They dropped eight unprofitable leased theaters—six in New York, and one each in Boston and Philadelphia. The total loss sustained in the eight playhouses during the past year was a staggering $327,000.

They proposed a reorganization plan to Judge Caffey, and he did not approve it. Instead, under enormous pressure from the infuriated stockholders, he empowered an investigation of Shubert finances. He specifically instructed the investigation to examine charges that the Messrs. had commingled company and personal funds to "enrich themselves as individuals." He named, to head the investigation, Charles Evans Hughes, Jr., son of the Chief Justice.

In the same ruling, he extended for six months the joint receivership of the Irving Trust Comany and—Lee Shubert!

Why would the court appoint as co-receiver of the assets of a bankrupt company the man who, while not specifically accused, was certainly tainted with the suspicion of criminal actions? It could not have happened in steel, or automobiles, or matches, or insurance, or banking. When Insull's empire collapsed, the court did not name good Sam to unravel the puzzle of his utility complex. Why then Shubert?

Part of the answer lies in the intricacy of theatrical operations. How do you make a theater profitable? How do you decide which play to back, which play not to? How do you determine that a play, with encouragement and shrewd investment, is worth keeping open—that it will catch on? How do you make a theater contract, determine the accuracy of a budget, negotiate with an author and an actor, get the right director, get the sets built, put the show on? Who determines the advertising budget? What papers to expend it on? Who makes the instant decisions when changes are indicated? Who hires a composer? A "doctor"? Who runs a show?

In mass-production America, the theater was an anachronism. Each play, each musical production, presented its own unique problems. There were no rules, no guidelines, no standards by which "plays" could be judged, monies ascribed, returns anticipated. It was a special field, and it needed a specialist. It had to be Lee Shubert if the investors were to recoup anything. And he knew it.

Second, Lee and Willie Klein had worked well. The Shubert empire was a labyrinthine maze of interlocking corporations, some personal, some in partnership with the corporation, some leasing to the corporation, some partially owned by the corporation. To sort it all out, they needed a Shubert. And Lee knew that too.

Where was Jake? He was not a co-receiver; he was not even named on the board of the proposed (and rejected) reorganization plan. He was not producing—not since *Marching By*, a fourteen-performance musical which Jake "personally supervised." It led to many a tired joke. "All Shubert shows this season should be called *Marching By*. They pass in review—all panned."

Suddenly, this arrogant, truculent, difficult man had become superfluous. He had retrogressed thirty years. Once again, he was "the other Shubert." His power and his money he still enjoyed; but his raison d'être, his drive, his satisfactions—all these were being denied him. Lee was preparing musicals; a garment-district graduate who had gone mysteriously into the ticket business, Harry Kaufman, was helping Lee plan. And musicals! Jake's domain! It was bitter to swallow, and doubly so for a man like Jake.

True, he was an equal partner. Letters of agreement, beginning way back in 1919 and renewed in 1922, guaranteed that he and Lee would equally share the fruits of their labors. But this was not power, and it was power Jake needed. He *had* to strut into a theater, coat over his shoulders, lapels held together with his pudgy left hand, and shout orders to cast and crew. He had to sit for hours, "planning" his productions. He had to walk into Sardi's and head for *his* table. Now, all of it was denied him.

Instead, he became a virtual recluse, an embittered, unhappy, antagonistic man, entombed in the Sardi Building. He buried himself in his memories, and he luxuriated in mapping out spectacular musicals he would never produce. He had been passed by, and he could not admit it. He would fight it again and again and again; he would become more violent in his angers, more unpredictable in his moods. Always irascible, he was now nearly impossible. Only Muriel Knowles, who had been his assistant and companion for more than ten years, could stay with him and give him the comforts of companionship he required. Girls he still had, and that too helped. Girls came cheap during the Depression.

Circumstances had compelled the brothers to see each other. Their huge investments required it. Their meetings were curt, formal, most often attended by lawyers, always by Willie Klein. Jake had been forced to agree to every suggestion made by Lee—certainly not graciously, not even courteously. He had been beaten down.

In the middle of December a wave of rumors hit New York. Lee Shubert was ill. He had been taken to the hospital. The first wave of news suggested that he had collapsed—a nervous breakdown brought on by the pressures of his crippled business. The *Telegraph* reported that he was withdrawing from Shubert enterprises; Jake would take over, subject to the stockholders' approval and the court's. Next, Lee Shubert in "critical condition."

None of it was true, except that Lee had gone to the hospital. He was fifty-nine years old, and his prostate was acting up. That was it. The operation was successful, and the only gossip left for the Sardi set was what effect it would have on his "girls."

While Lee was recuperating in the hospital, Jake launched a gigantic suit against two music publishers, who had been supplying Shubert music to be played on the radio. (Jake hated radio. In the first place, they were using what he liked to call "his material" and not paying for it. Secondly, a lot of ex-Shubert performers were making a lot of money in the advertising medium. Cantor was a big star; Jack Pearl, with his "Vas you dere, Sharlie?" had become a national celebrity. Joe Penner, a minor Shubert comic, coined a household phrase with "Wanna buy a duck?" Al Pearce was knocking on doors across the country, and Sam's old flame Julia Sanderson was a leading singing star. Jake didn't collect a dime from any of them. So, he hated radio.) Jake lost the suit, and since he instantly began planning another one, he found himself trapped into listening to the radio. He kept score on how often Shubert tunes were played. Obviously, to do this, he had to become a radio fan.

The week before his ex-wife's suit for support was to come up in court, Jake was visited by his son. John was twenty-four, a tall, shy, troubled young man. Bound to his mother, awed by his father, he tried to be a bridge between them and to be himself at the same time. His hatred for his father confused him. He wanted to like him, wanted to know him, but there were the years of estrangement, the years of Jake's ambivalent moods, the terrible rages, the accusations. Now, it was doubly difficult. John Shubert wanted to keep his father and mother out of court. That was what he had come to see Jake about.

Jake's own feelings about his son were muddled. He was proud of his "college boy." (John was attending Harvard Law School. He would not finish.) He liked his looks, the way his slow smile fleeted across his face. He hated Catherine, and he hated John for being her son.

This confusing mixture of emotions made the inarticulate man even less communicative. These two men could not talk to each other—ever. Their relationship was painful and awkward. But John felt he had to keep the support case out of court.

He began by reiterating what he had told his mother. There was enough scandal already. Jake, initially pleased to see the boy, froze. This was an interference he would not have. He stared down at the desk top, fat hands clenched on the edge, so that the knuckles were white. He cut John off after a few sentences.

"She signed an agreement, and the State of New York said it was fair; tell her to go to hell!"

John winced. He tried once more.

Jake cut him off. His voice swelled. "I say tell her to go to hell! I won't give her a dime, and if you don't shut your mouth, you won't get a dime either!"

John left.

On February 11, 1933, Catherine Shubert appeared in court before Justice Levy, pleading destitution, and seeking support from Jake. She had used up all the funds stipulated in the divorce settlement, "most of it to support Mr. Shubert's son." She claimed she was penniless, and asked the court to amend the divorce agreement.

Jake's reply was legal. He invoked the statute of limitations—the divorce was fifteen years old—and he asked the court to deny Catherine's motion. John Shubert did not attend.

On April 7, Justice Levy dismissed the suit, and Catherine carried it to appeal. She and Jake were shaping John's life for him.

These were bitter times for the Shuberts. The bondholders and the stockholders were pressing for action. They compelled Lee to merge his booking office (the road) with the Theatre Guild and the remains of the Erlanger routings into one office, the American Theater Society, headed by Marc Heiman of Syracuse and Erlanger. The Messrs. retained 50 percent of it. More pressure, and more nasty rumors. Eight Shubert companies, in one way or another affiliated with the Shubert Theater Corporation, were added to the receivership.

The bondholders demanded a complete audit, claiming fraud. To illustrate the claim, they pointed to several deals they questioned. The Jason Corporation, Shubert-owned, originally bought the Central Theater from Shubert Theaters, sold it to Trebuhs, Shubert-owned, and then Trebuhs resold the theater to Jason. The deals showed Trebuhs with a $50,000 profit, all on paper, and all, the stockholders alleged, for the puffing of the statement.

In addition, when they sold their stock, the Shuberts claimed their stage equipment was worth $1,750,000. On what basis? The appraisal was made by Bill Brady, a close Shubert associate. Now it was alleged the equipment was worth only a fraction of the appraisal.

They also pointed out that Lee Shubert had been granted lifetime leases, at one dollar per year, on several apartments; J. J. Shubert "and others" enjoyed similar privileges.

They cited various other suspicious transactions; stock transfers, real-estate deals, payroll entries. They demanded the investigation speed up. Justice Caffey so ordered.

Lee stated that he had cut Shubert payrolls by 50 percent, including "my own and my brother's salary." Some cynic suggested a Lee 'n' Jake benefit. He pleaded with Equity to allow Sunday showings with no change in salary minimums. It would "provide work for actors, and give producers a chance to reactivate their theatrical activities." Equity said that Sunday performances were a closed issue. Lee threatened to curtail his "production plans" unless he could see a profit "for the creditors and shareholders," by Sunday performances. Equity ignored him.

There was a barrage of new anti-Shubert jokes. The best of them went this way.

"Well, I just saw Mr. Shubert," said the fledgling director.

"Which one?" asked the cynical unemployed actor. "Ess Aitch? Or Eye Tee?"

And it revived some old ones. Back in 1925, Fred Allen was walking by the Shubert Theater and crossing Shubert Alley one day when an irate producer came storming out of the building.

"What's the matter?" asked Fred. "You look upset."

"Oh, what a miserable son of a bitch," groaned the producer.

"So's his brother," agreed Fred amiably.

Word of this yarn, probably apocryphal, got to Jake. Instantly he barred Allen from the use of Shubert Alley, owned one half by the Messrs., the other half by the Astor estate. If Fred wanted to cross from 44th Street, by Jake's edict he would have to walk around the block. Allen enjoyed it.

Sam Langford, the great Negro prizefighter and a warm and lovable man, was the doorman at the Shubert Theater. It was his job to "bar" Allen—and Fred, much as he loved Langford, tried to make it as difficult as possible for Sam. He would wait for his chance, and if he thought Langford was busy, he would make a break for the Alley. Usually, he didn't make it because Langford was alert, but when he did, he would shout up to the turret office, "Hey, Lee! Tell Jake I did it! I used Shubert Alley." Langford would feel chagrined, and try to duck Jake for a couple of days.

One night, Langford was exclusively watching for Allen, and when he spotted Fred, the ex-fighter hurried toward him. As Langford drew near, Fred delicately lifted a foot, held it in his hand, and began to *hop* through the Alley.

Puzzled, Langford watched him. "Now, Mr. Fred," said Sam, "I don't want no trouble. You know you're not supposed to be in here. Why are you hopping around like that?"

Allen paused, balancing on one foot. "I'm only using one foot, Sam," said Fred, "so I'm really only using half the Alley. Tell Jake it's Astor's half." And he hopped on through.

Eventually, Jake withdrew the ban.

It wasn't all jokes. The stockholders insisted that, in addition to the American Theater Society, the Shuberts organize a second joint-booking office with Erlanger to avoid "the ruinous duplications, the extravagant costs and the expensive competition" of the booking war.

This second office would handle all attractions which could not be profitably handled by ATS.

The Capitol Theater Corporation in Albany sued Lee for $21,000 for rent due, plus interest. They were awarded a judgment.

The Shubert production schedule listed a scant five shows for the entire 1932–33 season—none by Jake. Lee got one hit out of the five productions—*Autumn Crocus*, which introduced Francis Lederer to America. Ironically, it was Lee who brought the country its national Depression anthem.

Lee's one musical—for the season—was a revue that tried hard and just barely missed. It was *Americana*, and a lot of thought that had gone into it was dissipated by indifferent casting. It was *Americana* which pioneered "formal" ballet in the musical theater when Lee had Charles Weidman and his dancers do the show. It should have been an event and wasn't. There were some good songs and some good skits, but *Americana* never quite jelled.

The "big moment" in the evening came when a sad-faced little man, Rex Weber, came out in front of the curtain and sang "Brother, Can You Spare a Dime?" It soon was the dirge for Depression-down New Yorkers, and through Jake's love, radio, it swept the country. It became the Depression classic.

If the theatrical season was as drab as the news of the day (and it was), there were occasional excitements—for newspaper readers. Jimmy Walker, the colorful mayor of New York, resigned in the face of the investigation ordered by Franklin Roosevelt, governor of New York State and soon to be elected President. Walker's connections with Lee Shubert were more than casual.

Jimmy Walker, in a strange way, was a political Jake Shubert. He was born for the twenties. Dapper, witty, trivial, superficial, he had been a hoofer, a songwriter ("Will You Love Me in December as You Do in May?"), a politician, and in 1926 he was elected mayor of New York City. He loved people—particularly "important" people—and he loved the glamour and importance of being mayor of the big city. A Catholic, married to a devout Catholic, he was, paradoxically, the gay blade of the twenties, personified.

He liked girls and action and champagne. All through the "dry" era, it was Mayor Walker at the Central Park Casino, an elegant and exclusive nightspot, drinking the champagne that was "available," dancing up a storm on the floor, epitomizing the Roaring Twenties. He visited every posh speakeasy, he hobnobbed with those he emulated—

The David Belasco Funeral, 1931. Left to right: Lee Shubert, George M. Cohan, Mayor James J. Walker, David Frohman. The man directly behind Lee is William Morris.

the rich, the successful, the jet set of the pre-jet age. At his side, almost constantly, was lovely Betty Compton, a young actress, seen in many Shubert shows.

The nasty "Tin Box" scandals broke in the early days of the crash, and Walker was coming up for reelection in 1930. The Shuberts, as stated before, were a-political. (There is no record of Lee or J.J. ever having cast a ballot. They couldn't care less. Nevertheless, New York politics was important to them. Every judge, every senator, every representative, every important ward heeler was on their "free" list. They needed the insurance of influence in the right places in case of crisis. So, Walker was important to them.)

Jimmy Walker loved Betty Compton. But there was no way he could be free to marry her. It was an impossible situation, and when word came that the liaison would become an election issue, there was more at stake than a marriage. Whole political dynasties might be affected. It was determined that Miss Compton would legally "marry" someone to remove the possible election onus of the relationship from the shoulders of the Catholic incumbent.

It was arranged. Maybe Lee "arranged" it. Miss Compton, as much in love with Walker as he was with her, and determined to protect his career, consented to marry a Shubert employee. Rumor had it that the man was paid $10,000 for his services. Another rumor had it that Lee Shubert put up the $10,000. If he did, it can be assumed that Lee thought the mayor would be grateful.

The resignation of Walker, the election of Roosevelt, the subsequent Bank Holiday—all had their repercussions in Shubert affairs. Jake, in complete disgust, had gone to Europe, returned from Europe, decided to go around the world, had gone around the world, and returned again. He had not had a single production. Each time he showed in New York, the news was bleak.

The receivership—Lee's, not Jake's—was operating at a loss, while Lee desperately struggled to keep the theaters alive. He announced that the "receivers" (it is difficult to estimate the extent of the Irving Trust's participation) would have to borrow $113,000 to continue through the year (the date was October 14). This was in a plea to the court to extend the receivership. They needed time, they said, to try to raise the money. They had *told*, they reminded the court, all interested parties that $500,000 were required. So far, they had only raised half of that. The rest, Lee Shubert stated—the difference between $250,000 and $113,000—had been "personal loans from my brother and myself, some of it including loans on our life insurance."

297

While the court pondered, the New York Stock Exchange moved. They took Shubert stock off the board. What it meant was that the Shubert Theater Corporation was broke. But were the Shuberts?

Willie Klein replied to a reporter, who asked the question. Willie's response was cynical. "Are the Shuberts broke? I do not think so. No, I have no idea how much they are worth. But one thing I can assure you. Neither one of them will ever be buried in Potter's Field."

Neither one would. On every European trip—usually two a year per Shubert—they had observed the London theatrical scene, taken in Paris and the *Folies Bergère*, hit Vienna and Berlin, seen Rome and Budapest. Oftentimes, in the "good old days," Jake had grandly hired people, in city after city.

Although discovering talent, acts, ideas, composers, etc., was the primary function of the Shubert brothers' European tours, there was another reason. Somehow, no matter what the convolutions of the routing, one or the other brother made Switzerland. That is the happy land of watches, chocolate, skiing—and numbered bank accounts, anonymous to the world, and lucrative to the frugal Swiss and the equally frugal depositors.

There were no more frugal depositors than the Shuberts. And the theater was a cash business. Every gimmick Jake ever bought or "borrowed" from the *Folies Bergère* and every "new Romberg" he imported were a by-product of the European hegira, with Switzerland as its mecca. What Lee and Jake truly loved about the Alpine paradise was its numbered bank accounts.

While Jake was on his world tour, Lee and Willie Klein and Bill Phillips were staving off disaster. They twisted and squirmed, they sacrificed properties, they bargained out of leases, they borrowed money, they paid token payments, and all of this they were compelled to do under court scrutiny.

Their plan was coldly practical. They would abandon all non-theatrical properties which could not support themselves. They would further slash overheads. They would make every effort to persuade mortgagees to postpone interest payments, amortization payments, and taxes. Somehow, they would raise funds to prepare for the new season. They estimated this at nearly $200,000. Without attractions they would collapse.

Incredible as it may seem, there were only three Shubert companies playing anywhere: *The Student Prince* and *The Blue Mask* on the road, and *Cynara* at the Shubert Theater in New York. *The Blue Mask* would never reach New York. The outlook, those days in late 1932, was bleak.

They only partially listed losses in their productions of the 1931–32 season. *The Good Companions* (Lee), $20,000. *The Little Racketeer*, a bad musical (Jake), $15,000. Their Gilbert and Sullivan war with Erlanger (Jake), $2,628.

Grudgingly they determined to abandon the Greenwich Street warehouse, the Copley in Boston, and two Philadelphia properties, both nontheatrical.

The Shubert Theater Corporation had leased fourteen theaters from the brothers or from subsidiary companies controlled by Lee and Jake. They would disaffirm the leases on five of these and on three additional houses. This would protect the corporation against another loss of over $300,000.

In the past year, the brothers had personally advanced to the corporation $500,000, secured by a second mortgage on the Central Theater; $25,000 in cash; $35,000 to pay the rent of the Lyric in Boston; and $100,000 to meet various crises—all secured by notes. And now, the corporation was broke again. Could they advance more?

And how long could it go on? Lee sat there and waited for Jake to return; this was going to be a joint decision. The plan was liquidation of the Shubert Theatrical Corporation. Throw it on the auction block, sell off its assets, pay off (it would be a pitifully small percentage) pro rata on debts, and forget it.

There were certain receivership obligations which would be paid off before anything was paid to the creditors. For example, there were those personal loans by the Messrs.—*those* would be paid. There were legal fees; Willie Klein would be paid. There were receivers' fees; Lee and the bank would be paid. What was left of the assets, if anything, would then go to the creditors.

Jake didn't argue. He had plans cooking in his curly head—plans which were partially initiated by John Shubert, and greatly motivated by the fact that the corporation in receivership had added Milton Shubert and Lawrence Shubert Lawrence, Sr., to its board.

John Shubert had returned to Cambridge after his abortive attempt to keep his parents out of court. He was in his second year at Harvard Law School, and for two months he was unable to work. By May, he had decided that he was through with the law. May was the month that the court of appeals refused to reverse the decision against Catherine Shubert for "support."

Hobbled by his mother's emotional leash, equally bound by his father's financial leash, young John was facing an important decision.

He had to find ways to support his mother, he believed. And he had to find a career. He went to see his father.

There must have been deeper motives. Perhaps he thought he could "change" the Shubert image. (He was only twenty-four.) Perhaps he believed that he would find himself—he was lost, and always had been —in his father's world. Perhaps he wanted the financial solidity his father's business assured. He had a discussion with Jake.

Jake approved. It was a wedge on Lee and the nephews. And it is safe to assume that Jake thought he was slugging Catherine in another way: he would take over her son. John was given a job on "Jake's side." The heir apparent had moved it. Jake was full of plans for John. He would start by assisting in production and direction. At the top. As J.J. Shubert's son should. The young man was swept up in a cloud of excitement.

He went back to Cambridge to tell his mother the news, and to his amazement she heartily agreed with him. He would take care of his patrimony. *Her* son would one day run the empire, live in a castle, like the prince he was—and who would share the glory? She had her own plans. Queen Mother to the Shuberts.

At Harvard, John had become friendly with a first-year law student, Fred de Cordova. The mutual liking was heightened when the boys discovered that Fred's mother and Catherine were schoolgirl friends. John called Freddie and told him of his plans. Impulsively, he asked de Cordova, already a theater buff, if he wanted to join him. De Cordova accepted on the spot.

Ten days later, John was ensconced in the Sardi Building, and de Cordova was the assistant stage manager at the Parsons Theater in Hartford. Some people think that the move to join the Shuberts was the tragic decision in John Shubert's life. He had surrendered his right to be himself. A psychiatrist might say that Catherine and Jake had done that for him twenty-odd years before.

Jake was playing father to the hilt. He more or less assigned an experienced Shubert manager, Eddie Duryea Dowling, to be the crown prince's squire. Jake helped John "decorate" his office, and when it came to decorating, Jake could be a menace. Although he assured every visitor to the Sardi rooftop apartment that "the furniture ain't props; [he] picked every piece in a furniture place," it still looked like a production number for a heavy German melodrama.

He was expansive with de Cordova. He had come up to Hartford to look over the theater and the production, and he called Fred over.

"Son, how much you been living on?"

De Cordova replied, "Twenty-five dollars a week, Mr. Shubert."

"Your mother with you?"

Fred nodded.

"Ain't it tough to make out on that?"

De Cordova grinned. "It is, Mr. Shubert. But you won't believe this—we're saving four bucks a week."

"Your mother used to be an actress, didn't she?"

De Cordova shook his head. "No. She never was on a stage in her life."

Jake's tone became authoritative and condescending. "Don't be such a God-damned fool. Your mother used to be an actress!" Shubert called the manager. "I want you should give a hundred dollars to Freddie de Cordova, and fifty dollars to his mother, who used to be an actress. And you send the bill to me, care of the Shubert Benefit Fund. The whole idea of the fund is to help people of the theater!"

Jake, the expansive father, liked playing the benevolent despot. But his moods were uncertain, and most of the time, he was just plain despot.

Two years after the de Cordova episode, Jake thought John was ready. Jake was going to let him "really work on a show." John had served his apprenticeship and was invaluable to the organization in a way his father never recognized. He liked Lee, and Lee liked him. He was the one tangible bridge between the Messrs.

There were other values he brought to the Shuberts. John was a pleasant man, likable, shy, uncertain, courteous. Jake patently was none of these, and Lee, though polite and courtly, was, after all, Lee Shubert. In theater circles, that fact removed him from the common run of humanity.

On the last day of 1932, the Shubert receivers formally petitioned the court for permission to hold a public sale of the assets of the company. Gloom hit Broadway and the thousands of households that had invested in stock. A lot of Shubert employees were murdered by the announcement. Joe Gaites was in to the tune of $70,000. Frank Waters, the comptroller, was hung for $40,000. Almost every relative on payroll was hooked for part of the loss. It was brutal.

On January 10, 1933, Judge Caffey issued the order to liquidate the Shubert Theater Corporation. On that same day, in a move that stunned everybody, Lee Shubert resigned as receiver for the court. He stated that he was going to bid at the public sale, in an attempt to recover the assets of the company "I and my brothers built." The sale was set for February 11.

Lee's independent decision resulted in an epic fight with Willie Klein. Klein, Lee's attorney and friend for thirty years, privy to every Shubert decision and instrumental in their successful fight for dominance in the theater, had not been informed. The doughty little warrior's face darkened when he heard the news. An emergency meeting was called in Lee's office. Klein. Phillips. Lee. Jake. No one else. The brothers did not address each other. They did not have to.

Lee was behind his desk, the others sitting on the stiff, pull-up chairs in the dimly lit oval room. Willie started the discussion. "Why? All I would like to know is why. Pride? Somebody else might maybe own a Shubert theater?"

Lee stared at him enigmatically. "You know better," he said finally.

"Then why?" pressed Klein. "It's insanity. Who wants to pay money to buy guaranteed headaches? Theaters are a dead business. We got talking-picture houses in low-tax neighborhoods. We got a situation where people who buy theater tickets normally, can't. So who wants theaters? Who needs them?"

Lee said nothing. Jake was squirming in his chair.

Phillips joined Klein. "As an investment, they're risky. Unless you intend to convert them—which is expensive. Or tear them down—or build on the site later. The property, the ground, is valuable. But not with the theater standing on it."

Lee was impassive. "If I buy, I have no plans for tearing them down—or converting them."

"He likes empty theaters," said Klein. The skinny little lawyer leaned forward, emphasizing his agitation. "It is none of my business, Lee. It's your decision. And Jake's. But, as your lawyer, and as your friend, I have to say this. Money you've got. I don't know how much. And I don't want to know. But you and Jake are well fixed for the rest of your lives. You can live like kings, travel, go wherever you want. If you feel like producing a play, so, it's a hobby. Produce! Live! [Jake was squirming.] But you do this foolish thing, all you are buying is trouble."

"I don't think I would enjoy living that way," said Lee mildly.

"Unless," interpolated Phillips smoothly, "you are investing in land, Lee. Then, if you can hold on. When this mess is cleared up by Roosevelt, you tear down the theaters and go for office rentals. That's intelligent."

Lee never had a chance to answer. Jake was on his feet. His voice was strident. "What the hell do you two know? I tell you, when you tear down a theater it's like a death in the family."

Lee was staring at his brother. In his mind, there had to be the thought: Jake understands. He *knows*.

Lee was still looking at his brother when he spoke (they had never been closer). His voice was higher-pitched and his emotions were so strong the stammer was beginning. "We came here more than thirty years ago," said Lee. "We didn't have a guaranty. Nobody guaranteed us anything. First, it was Sam and me—and then, my brother"—Lee gestured—"joined me. We worked eighteen hours a day. Every day. Seven days a week." He stared at Phillips and Klein. "You think it was easy? Who was on our side? Who? You know, Willie. Nobody was on our side. Then,"—and Lee paused, his voice choking—"then, Sam died. It would have been easy to quit then. To sell out. It was tempting. We would have had lots of money—more money than we needed." He looked directly at Klein. "We could have lived like kings, and traveled. I came close." He did not look at Jake. "My brother came here." Again the gesture of the hand toward Jake. "My brother wanted to continue." He shook his head solemnly. "I am not a young man any more, and, Willie, you are right. I have all the money I need."

"You're sixty," said Klein. "Why are you buying trouble?"

"I am fifty-eight," said Lee with dignity. "And I am not buying trouble." He leaned forward in his chair, hands flat on the small desk, and his voice got louder, higher, and he was stuttering. "D-d-do you think we d-d-did it just for m-m-money? Just for the s-s-silly money?" He shook his head, still not looking at Jake. "I am not ashamed of the m-m-money we have made. I am not ashamed of the n-n-name Shubert on theaters. It makes me v-v-very p-p proud. B-b-but we d-d-did not c-c-come to New York to work and to let our work d-d-die." He was trying to be cogent and logical, and he was enormously emotional. "You understand, Willie? It should not just disappear."

The small room was terribly still.

Finally, Klein shook his head. His voice, Willie Klein's rasping voice, was very soft. "No," he said quietly. "I don't understand. And I violently, absolutely, positively disagree!" He paused. Then he cleared his throat. "But if you want, I will help you do this foolish thing."

Lee nodded. "Thank you, Willie. I thought you would help us."

Bill Phillips nodded.

Jake stood up. "Well, that's settled." He rolled toward the door, his pudgy figure erect, chest out, elbows stiff at his sides. "I don't expect you people who ain't never been in the theater to understand." He opened the door, looking back at Klein, and ignoring Lee. "I don't say this kind of crap very often," said Jake, "but I agree with my brother one hundred percent!" He left. He and Lee had never come closer.

303

In those thoroughly black days, one event occurred which must have cheered Lee. For weeks after the prostate operation, Lee had been the subject of much discussion. Could he or couldn't he? They were making book on it in Sardi's and Moore's and in the Astor.

One evening, some of the girls from a show and a few Shubert employees were sitting in Sardi's, enjoying a drink, when Lee's secretary (male) appeared. Would Miss —— please go up to Mr. Shubert's office?

The girl said she would be right up, and the secretary left. There was a lot of ribald comment, and the girl shrugged and left, promising to issue bulletins.

About a half-hour later, she reappeared in the Sardi doorway. She said nothing. Simply held up her hand, thumb and index finger making a ring!

On March 4, 1933, Franklin Delano Roosevelt was inaugurated as the 32nd President of the United States. He had inherited a frightened nation. On March 6th, he declared a Bank Holiday. Four days later, Lee Shubert, an officer and bondholder in two banks, was called upon to pay nearly $80,000 as the first assessment against the depositors' security.

On April 7, on the steps of the Sub-Treasury Building on Wall Street—the very site George Washington had stood on to deliver the first inaugural address—the assets of the Shubert Theater Corporation were sold at public auction. There was one bidder. Lee Shubert. He bought the bankruptcy for $400,000, in the name of Select Theaters Incorporated, a corporation newly formed by Willie Klein. He gravely deposited an earnest check for $40,000. The Shuberts were back in the saddle.

How does one explain it? Why did the Shuberts do it? That it turned out to be good business is academic. At the time it was done, it was *bad* business.

One theory states that they had a passion for the theater. Not a talent, perhaps; not a gift; not a poetic, semireligious understanding, which is the basis for so many theatrical careers. But a passion they had, and a lust, and a love. They lived for it. Maybe not at the beginning—perhaps it began as a quick way to a quick buck. If that is so, then they were trapped in their own quick bucks. Like the man who hired the whore, then fell in love with her, married her, and learned to worship her.

Howard Reinheimer, no fan, thinks that is the way it happened.

So does Max Gordon. So did the late Harold Freedman, the distinguished theatrical agent.

Before sentiment completely blurs the facts, it is important to remember that one of the terms of the Shubert offer was that those people who had bought the adjustment bonds would be paid first from the proceeds of the liquidation. The bonds had not sold so well. Only $300,000 worth had been subscribed. Lee had taken $200,000 of this sum. In effect, he had bought back the Shubert Theater Corporation, valued at $25,000,000 just four short years before, for $400,000, less the $200,000 advanced, or $200,000 net. The purchase may have been motivated by sentiment, but when Lee Shubert bought, he bought like a Shubert.

Almost at the same time as the sale, Jake left for Chicago. He claimed the move was permanent. He told the press, "New York is too sophisticated for me." The Shubert staff assured one and all that the move was temporary.

What really happened was that Jake wanted to do a show, and it was too expensive a show. Lee vetoed the idea. Lee had other plans. The Shuberts had eight theaters in Chicago, and Chicago was about to open its World's Fair. People who came to world's fairs, reasoned Lee, must have money. Let Jake create in Chicago and collect some of the money, and open some of the Shubert theaters.

On June 5, Lee told the press what Select's plans were. It was a surprising announcement. Voluntarily, he and Jake were giving one-half of the stock of Select to the debenture owners, the stockholders and the creditors of Shubert Theater Corporation. The formula was spelled out: ten Select shares for each $1,000 debenture; one Select share for each $105 in allowed creditors' claims; one select share for each ten shares of Shubert common.

"We still hold one-third of the common stock in Shubert Theater, and approximately ten percent of the debentures," Lee said. "We have, in addition, in the past few weeks, invested $850,000 in a second mortgage on a property [the Hotel Edison] about to be foreclosed. It was the only way we could save it. All the cash advanced to Shubert Theater Corporation by my brother and myself, prior to the receivership, we have written off. It is lost. Also, we have assumed responsibility for, or paid, hundreds upon hundreds of thousands of dollars for commitments we personally guaranteed. *None* of this is charged to Select." Under the formula, the Shuberts had absolute control of Select. They owned more than 60 percent of the corporation.

Lee's "theatrical hockshop" was in business. The Group The-

305

ater, an eager band of young actors and playwrights and directors, had hit Broadway two years before in *The House of Connelly*, a beautifully produced show that somehow didn't catch on. They had picked up a play by Sidney Kingsley that had been optioned four times before.

In the drab days of the Depression, four producers had determined that a depressing realistic melodrama of force was precisely what the public didn't want. So, four "skilled" producers did not bring *Men in White* to Broadway.

The Group fell in love with the play, took it out to its summer headquarters in Smithtown, Long Island, worked it, and worked it, and then, needing money to bring it in, invited Lee Shubert to take a look. He liked what he saw, quickly made an advantageous deal, guaranteeing the bond, the Broadhurst Theater for the fall, some cash, and a large percentage for the Shuberts. Then, he set off for California. He had invested in *Her Man of Wax*, a satiric fantasy about Napoleon, and he wanted to see it, where it was trying out in Los Angeles. That's what he told the papers.

The real reason for his trip was a letter from Billie Burke. Ziegfeld had died a few months before. His estate was a mess—mountains of debts, acres of unpaid bills, new ones coming in every day. His lovely widow, Billie Burke, had sifted through the wreckage, trying frantically to find ways to meet her ever-mounting obligations. She had known Lee Shubert, she had starred for him. In desperation, she wrote to him. Would he consider reviving the *Ziegfeld Follies?* It would keep "Flo's name alive," she wrote, "and I trust you to do the show as you would have done it with Flo, had things been different." Lee was intrigued.

Like everyone else who had ever met or worked with the charismatic Miss Burke, he adored her. He knew she needed money, and his own ego wanted to do the first post-Ziegfeld *Ziegfeld Follies*. He replied to Billie, telling her he would be in Los Angeles and would call on her.

Just before he took the train, he gave the go-ahead to John Shubert and to Jake. They could proceed with their musical *Hold Your Horses*.

Chapter Sixteen

The preparation of *Hold Your Horses* was possibly the happiest time John Shubert had ever known. Demonstrating unexpected wisdom, Jake left him alone to try to plan a show with a "different" look. It was Jake's production—never forget it—but he was letting John have his head.

The book, a Gay Nineties, Tenderloin confection, was by Corey Ford and Russell "Buck" Crouse, who were bright and witty; Robert Russell Bennett had written the score. A lot of talented young people were being cast, and the show was gaited to the talents of Joe Cook, the funny, funny eccentric comic, whose off-beat delivery and weird props had built him a steady Broadway following.

It was fun working on the book, and fun getting Russell Patterson, the illustrator, to design the sets. There were the normal problems in rehearsal, but they weren't being solved, and they were facing the opening in Boston.

There had been a parade of directors, some of the changes compelled by the "office," some by Cook, some by agreement between John and his co-workers. Jake had been chafing as the bad reports filtered back. Finally, he couldn't contain himself. He took off for Boston to see for himself.

He arrived to witness a scene of incomparable chaos. Seated in the dark cavern of the theater were Ford, Crouse, Jimmy Proctor, and a lighting man. This was to be the dress rehearsal, there was "new" material to be routined, a hundred people were milling around on stage, John was submerged in details, the orchestra was running through numbers, and everybody seemed to be talking at once. But there was no action.

Jake, instead of taking his usual place in the wings, had entered the theater proper, and in his Napoleonic-coat pose, was nervously pacing the aisles. Nothing was happening on stage, except the incessant chatter. From the pit, there were musical grunts. Jake paced. Finally, he could no longer restrain himself.

"Quiet!" he bellowed, "I say, quiet!"

He sailed down the aisle, was helped onto the stage, and the theater was still. Turning his back on the multitude on stage, he walked dramatically to the foots, holding up his right hand, palm out. The incredulous four in the orchestra of the theater watched him.

"Silence!" shouted Jake, "I want absolute silence!" He paused dramatically. "From now on, there is only one captain on this ship," he roared. "Only one captain! My brother and me!"

The half-captain took over immediately, "organizing" things. He issued a stream of orders—all pretty dreadful. John tried to interrupt him. "I think we ought to talk this over."

"Later, later," said Jake abstractedly. "All right," and he turned to de Cordova. "You got all the notes?"

De Cordova nodded.

"I want copies of everything in my hands. Everything! You understand?" He swaggered toward the stage door. "I am going to New York, but I will be back tomorrow with some more ideas."

The "creative" team held a council of war to map strategy. Jake was up to his old tricks. When in doubt, add girls, specialty numbers, and songs. He would be "adding," and ruining the show. They agreed to fight back, and John agreed to have a talk with his father.

Jake returned the next day, and a truck from the Shubert costume house was not far behind. Jake had a "present" for *Hold Your Horses*.

America's biggest hit song of the time was "The Last Roundup," and little doggies were getting along all over the country. Jake had secured the rights to the song and wished to interpolate it into *Hold Your Horses*. Roundup—horses—get it?

He gave this piece of good news to the writers, composer, lyricist, and John. There was a stunned silence. *Hold Your Horses* was set in New York in 1890 from start to finish—from the Bowery to Rector's to Coney Island. Two of the leading parts were Diamond Jim Brady and Anna Held. How could anybody imagine that a Western ballad about a dying cowboy would fit into the show?

Jake mistook the silence for awe. "A built-in hit song to start with," he said modestly. "That's pretty good for openers."

"I think it's terrible," said John. "How can you put a Western song into a Gay Nineties show? A New York show?"

"We'll work it in," said Jake comfortingly. "Don't worry, son, it'll fit like a glove."

Someone else tried to tell Jake that the song was a "sad" song— the cowboy died.

"We'll change it," said Jake euphorically. "Who says he has to die?" He stood up. "Well, I also sent up some cowgirl costumes for the chorus. You better get them fitted."

"I think the idea stinks," said John. "It will ruin the show."

Jake turned to him, his head lowering pugnaciously. "Ruin what show?" he asked caustically. "You little snotnose! In two months look who became an expert! What the hell do you know about shows? Who

308

taught you?" He turned to the embarrassed room. "My son, the *pis-cherke*, already knows more about shows than I do!"

Jake walked to the door, and opened it. "Go to work on the number like I tell you! Fixing shows you didn't learn in Harvard!" He left.

The number never did get in, but *Hold Your Horses* opened in New York on September 25th, didn't do well, and Jake was vindicated. "Not one song anybody whistles," he told everyone. "And they could have had a big hit."

One night later, *Men in White* came to the Broadhurst, was an instantaneous hit, and Lee liked the tickets it sold. Privately he told an assistant, "I'm glad my doctor isn't like Sidney Kingsley's doctor."

The Group had done a beautiful job. Luther Adler, Eddie Bromberg, Morris Carnovsky, Bobby Lewis, Sandy Meisner were all splendid, and two bit parts were played by Clifford Odets and Elia Kazan. Lee Strasberg directed brilliantly, and Mordecai Gorelik's sets were so clinical they smelled of iodoform. It would run for two seasons.

Men in White may have had the longer run, won the Pulitizer Prize and added more dollars to the Shubert treasury than *Hold Your Horses* lost, but *Hold Your Horses* was the most personally important play the Shuberts ever produced.

Whatever gains had been made in the tenuous relationship between Jake and his son were dissipated. John, who had hated his father and felt guilty about it, no longer just hated him. Now he had contempt for his taste and for his hypocritical stances.

"Don't argue with success, son," Jake would tell him, confident that his next production would be a hit. And John, who knew the show wouldn't be a hit, would nod. He went along for the ride, the cachet of being a Shubert, and he promised himself that some day he would take over the reins and make the name Shubert respectable on Broadway. He told that to a lot of people.

His chief stock in trade was his total likeableness. He had no real knowledge of the theater; he was an amateur, with connections. But he was the heir to a dynasty, and a regime. He might have learned with a father other than Jake. But J.J. Shubert was his father, and John, twenty-six years old, couldn't even tell him he had met a girl. He was afraid to.

She was twenty, blonde, shapely, petite, fun-loving, warm and pretty. Her name was Kerttu Helena Ecklund, of Finnish-American descent, and she had fallen in love with this most "hung-up" young man. If Jake suspected, he didn't say anything. Not yet. He himself had never avoided a girl because she worked in a show. A thousand assignations could testify to that.

But from the beginning, he had warned John to stay away from the chorus girls. They were not fit companions for the son of J.J. Shubert.

Hold Your Horses had one other dividend for the Shubert inner circle. Peggy Gallimore, another girl in the show, started to see Willie Klein. Eventually they would marry.

Lee used to say that it may not have been the best musical ever to come out of the Shubert office, but it was "the most marrying."

Lee's business wheeling and dealing proceeded. He had made his deal with Billie Burke to produce a *Ziegfeld Follies*. He had seen a performance of *Her Man of Wax* and decided to bring it into New York. He should have looked twice.

He also held a meeting with Pola Negri, the high priestess of vamp. A German play, *A Trip to Pressburg*, had attracted the interest of several producers over the years. It was eventually optioned by Lee, and he was determined to star the Polish siren in it. They signed an agreement, went into rehearsal, but the inherent bugs in the piece began to show, and Lee decided to close it.

For Christmas, Miss Negri presented him with a claim for $4,000 worth of salary. Lee had no intention of paying Miss Negri anything, but Willie Klein pointed out that the contract had an arbitration clause which was compulsory.

One month later, after the arbitration had begun, Lee and Miss Negri announced an amicable reconciliation of their disagreement: Lee was proceeding full steam ahead with *A Trip to Pressburg*, and Miss Negri was learning her lines.

Lee gave it another month, saw a rehearsal, and came to the conclusion that, in the main, he agreed with all the other producers who had optioned the German play, done adaptations, and neglected to produce it. He canceled the Boston booking, and presumably paid off Miss Negri.

During the "affair Pola Negri," Lee had opened and closed his California discovery, *Her Man of Wax*, watched Herman Shumlin direct Lee's production (with Crosby Gaige) of *Ten Minute Alibi*, and brought in his one hit for the year—*No More Ladies* was a success, and it featured Marcella Swanson.

He had also watched Willie Klein fight off a series of nuisance suits. It was "Let's-sue-the-Shuberts time" on Broadway. They were the only people who had money to sue for. Actors sued on nonexistent contracts; producers sued on nonexistent understandings; and whole crops of new litigants claimed to have written, created, composed various Shubert productions.

Lee felt honestly aggrieved. He never minded a lawsuit where there was a basis of fact. But to be accused of malfeasance when he wasn't guilty, this was too much! Willie Klein didn't lose one lawsuit.

They were still fighting the battle of survival as a company. It was almost impossible to keep the theaters alive. Lee, independently, came to a drastic decision. Where the theater was a loss, and where he and Jake had personally guaranteed the lease, they would have to negotiate the best possible settlement they could manage. Where the Messrs. had not guaranteed, they would abandon.

Their theater in Kansas City was one they were financially responsible for. Their manager there was the same young man Jake had hired way back in 1921—Ray Whittaker. He had helped Jake "discover" Joan Crawford, had run an efficient operation, had eventually met Lee, and now Lee called him to see what he could do about getting them out of the onerous lease.

Whittaker could see the handwriting on the wall. With the Shuberts abandoning, he was out of a job. He made a lovely (for the Shuberts) arrangement with the Kansas owners—the descendants of the men who had refused to buy Sam's oil portrait—and came on to New York with a gimmick designed to entrance motion-picture audiences. He went to see Lee Shubert, and was offered a job. "Come over here and work with me," suggested Lee. "I can't pay you much, but starve you won't. And after all, what the hell are movies?"

Whittaker accepted and became general manager, on "Lee's side." Eventually, he took over the real estate chore too. He arrived in time to find out what is was really like to work for the Shuberts.

Jake was a thoroughly frustrated man. He was not allowed to produce. He would go to the warehouse and caress his "gorgeous costumes." He would take endless inventory of tired Shubert sets. And he would look at the rest of what comprised Bill Brady's $1,750,000 worth of "equipment," and wonder why he couldn't use it. He was utterly miserable. His son was there, and they could not communicate. He had seen John with Eckie, and he had made his feelings known about that. He was chafing to be doing something.

It was just about then that Lee announced the first Shubert-produced *Ziegfeld Follies*. Jake was euphoric. At last, finally, at long last, America would see a Jake Shubert kind of "Follies." He would out-glamour Ziegfeld, he would out-dazzle Urban, he would out-musical anything that had ever happened before.

The instant Lee announced the *Follies*, a series of public gasps came from the profession. There were artistic gasps—"The *Shuberts producing* a *Ziegfeld Follies*? With sets from the warehouse and costumes from the closet?" More urgently, there were business gasps. The executor for the Ziegfeld estate sued at once. He claimed the Shuberts had no rights to the title or the show.

Lee produced a contract between Producing Associates, Incorporated (Shubert-owned) and Billie Burke Ziegfeld. Under the terms of the contract, Billie would receive $1,000, and she and the estate would receive 3 percent of the gross receipts.

The Ziegfeld creditors now entered the act. (And it was estimated that Ziggie had left about $500,000 worth of creditors.) What right did Miss Burke, or Mrs. Ziegfeld, have to enter into any sort of contract with anybody?

(Jake, all the while, was blissfully preparing "ideas." He was confident that Lee could work out the deal, and confident too that this opportunity was his chance to "show" people once and for all how great were the talents of J.J. Shubert.)

Miss Burke claimed that her husband had signed an agreement with her, whereby he gave her all rights to his properties. This was to repay her for monies she had personally advanced as loans to his productions. Where was the agreement? Miss Burke said she had lost it.

Lee left for Europe, and turned the matter over to Willie Klein. As usual, Klein was resourceful. The *Follies* would be presented "by Mrs. Florenz Ziegfeld," and what rapacious creditor would sue a poor widow? The show went into rehearsal, and although the name "Producers Associates" never appeared, it was a public secret that it was a Shubert show.

Before he left, Lee delivered a crushing blow to his brother's ego. Jake was informed he was to have nothing to do with the *Follies*! Jake went wild. Why? he demanded. There was a fierce interchange of verbal messages. Jake refused to buy Lee's lame excuse of "legal difficulties." He ranted and raved, and Lee was adamant. Jake would stay away from the show.

If ever there had been a scintilla of a chance of a rapprochement between the "sides" of 44th Street, it was forever killed. Jake had been humiliated, and all Broadway knew it and talked about it. And Jake knew—and all Broadway knew—who had so publicly shamed him. It was a tragic time for a fiercely arrogant man.

Never had Jake more fervently prayed for a "Ziegfeld" flop. Any rumor that indicated something in the show didn't work was to be cherished, talked about, sneered at. His prayers did him no good. They had come up with a pretty good revue. It had in the cast Fred Allen (restored to the Alley), Fanny Brice, Willie and Eugene Howard, Jane Froman, Vilma and Buddy Ebsen and a host of others. It had a good score and smart lyrics—"Yip" Harburg and Vernon Duke had done some of the numbers—it was smartly paced and looked good. It was a hit.

Jake's misery was not helped by the knowledge that Lee and Harry Kaufman had been very much present all through the production. But the final straw in Jake's bitterness was that the show had opened in Jake's very own Winter Garden. And the critical praise, the rewarding ticket lines, the handsome show—none of this did he have a part in.

For Jake, there were other displeasures. One of the first victims of the economy cutback had been Milton Shubert. Scheduled to produce "an English season," his production slate had been dropped. Now he was employed on "Lee's side," and preparing plays! Lawrence Shubert Lawrence was in Philadelphia. John was on "Jake's side," in New York, fooling around with writing a piece for the stage, smarting from the abrasive association with his father, and being told by Jake to "stay away from that blonde."

When Lee returned from Europe, and announced the purchase of seven new properties for next season, Jake had had it. He left for Europe. There was literally nothing for him to do. In his absence, Fred de Cordova moved into Jake's apartment with John.

Max Gordon, the veteran and distinguished producer, had bought the Sidney Howard adaptation of Sinclair Lewis' *Dodsworth* and turned it over to a brilliant, young director, Robert Sinclair. Gordon, who, with Al Lewis, had started with vaudeville dramatic sketches and had graduated to productions for Broadway, intuitively had the ability to surround himself with talent, and to let it function. (His relationships with men like George Kaufman, Moss Hart, Sidney Howard, and others were warm, personal, and trusting, and the plays they did for him were largely hits.) He was an old friend of Lee Shubert.

Sinclair, working with Gordon's designer, Jo Mielziner, had worked out a fluid, exciting production for the Walter Huston starrer. It required the use of a revolving stage, and that meant it required a theater with a stage depth that would accommodate it. They gave Gordon their plans, and he was excited with their concept. Not excited enough, however, to lose his sense of dollars and cents. His director might need a deep theater stage, but he needed a theater on 44th Street. That was the street that sold the tickets.

He called in his attorney, Abe Berman (who also represented Irving Berlin), and asked Berman to see Lee. He wanted either the Broadhurst or the Shubert Theater. They fulfilled the show requirements, and they were on 44th Street. And he reminded Berman that the Shuberts were in desperate need of an attraction for either house, and to drive for the best deal possible. Berman called on Lee.

There was a stiff negotiation. Berman was able to point to dark theaters all over town, with particular reference to dark Shubert theaters. Eventually he and Lee nailed down a deal—a very good deal for Max Gordon. Lee, not eager to reveal the terms to other managers, extracted Berman's promise not to reveal the terms of the contract, and Berman gave it to him.

Gordon was elated with the terms of the contract. And he was more elated when *Dodsworth* turned into a smash hit. Gilbert Miller, planning a production, ran into Max Gordon and casually asked him what the *Dodsworth* deal was. Gordon told him.

When Miller approached Lee about renting a theater for his show, Lee specified terms, and they were not nearly as favorable for Miller as they had been for Gordon. Miller told him so. Shubert was furious. He refused to give Miller the same terms he had given Gordon, and he called Berman to tell him what he thought of him. "You broke your word, Abe," said Lee, "and I will never speak to you again." Berman, pure as the driven snow, tried to protest his innocence, but Shubert hung up on him.

(A few years later, Berman and his wife were in London, and out on the town one night, they ran into Lee and Marcella Swanson, dancing at a club. Marcella nodded, but Lee stalked out of the room, remarking, "I do not want to be in the same room with that man.")

From the day that Lee stopped talking to Berman, Jake began to like Berman. "If Lee disliked you, that was the only reason Jake needed," said Berman. "I never did any business with Jake; in fact, I hardly knew him. But he told everyone how much he liked me—myself included."

Meanwhile, John Shubert had come up with an idea. And he approached his Uncle Lee with it. The season before, 1933, there had been a revival on the West Coast of *The Only Girl*, a Victor Herbert musical first produced in 1914, and it had done pretty well. The Los Angeles production had interpolated some of Herbert's best tunes from other Herbert shows into the score for *Only Girl*, and Lee was intrigued. He gave John the go-ahead.

With Jake safely in Europe for what promised to be a long tour —perhaps there was knotty business in Switzerland—John went into full stride. He had forgotten the Shubert spy system.

From their earliest days, the Shuberts trusted no one. True, there were formal memoranda on what was going on, exchanged between the brothers' "sides." In money matters, details were strictly the business of Lee and Jake, period. But beyond that, there was no faith. The books were audited. Two sets, a lot of people think—one for the Shuberts and one for the record. But it ended there.

They did not trust the house managers, even though a good number were relatives. They had perfected an almost foolproof "count-up" to protect themselves against defalcation. They did not trust their top executives, convinced that in a venal world venality was to be assumed and that their most trusted associates would make side deals. There was a strong rumor, and probably well founded, that phone calls were monitored. Each brother tried to have one or more plants on the other "side" so that they would be privy to what was going on before it was going on.

Jake was so convinced that he was being "spied on" that he made Boston arrangements to insure his privacy. In the building which housed Shubert headquarters in Boston, there was a small gift shop—antique store, and Jake made a "deal" with the owner. Jake would use the phone in the store rather than go through the switchboard in his own office. Every month or so, Jake would ask the owner how they stood financially. The man would bring out the phone bill and the arithmetic, and then he would deduct it from the rent. If there was a difference in Shubert's favor, he would pay that difference as his rent. If the phone bill exceeded the rent, Jake would let it carry over to the next month!

It was a shabby way to conduct the world's largest theatrical enterprise, but it's the way the Shuberts did it.

One of Jake's stooges informed him of his son's plans. The boys had been hard at work, the show was in rehearsal, and Jake's apartment in the Sardi Building was a bachelor's paradise. Jake had a magnificent liquor closet, and John had been a generous host. He had been seeing a lot of Eckie, and without the need of concealment they found themselves enjoying each other more than ever. There had been parties in the apartment, and laughter and gaiety.

There had been the normal number of show problems, some occasioned by a very dated book, others because a number of the chorus girls had been repetitively late for rehearsal. But the show was in its final days before opening, and, tired but happy, John and de Cordova returned to the apartment after a late rehearsal.

They were stunned to find a glowering Jake, sitting in the darkened living room. He rose as they entered and stalked dramatically into the dining room, and waved a hand at a six-week supply of empty bottles. "Explain yourself," he said to John.

Before John could speak, Jake was screaming. "All the time I have been away, you have been up here with your *nafkes*, hey? Playing around with your whores, having wild parties, sneaking behind my back! I'll teach you! I'll teach you a lesson you won't forget! You and your no-goods!"

He was waving his pudgy hand under John's nose. John tried to say something, but Jake wasn't listening. His voice rose to a shriek. "What is this show you're doing? Who told you to do a show? I'll break you into pieces, you go behind my back like that! What is this show?" His face was red and contorted, and de Cordova was terrified at the rage, the uncontrollable rage, that had taken possession of the man. De Cordova literally ran out of the apartment.

The next morning, he reported to the theater. John was tense, white-faced, and they hardly spoke. Rehearsal was held up; four of the girls were late. John exploded. He called the office and ordered two-week notices for the girls. They proceeded with the dress rehearsal. Toward the end of the dress, Jake appeared at the theater, and wordlessly he watched the finale. John dismissed the cast, and as he did so Jake stepped forward. "The cast is not dismissed," he barked.

Awkwardly, the actors and dancers clustered on the stage, and Jake made his way to them. He ignored John completely.

"Freddie," he said to de Cordova, "is it true that you gave notice to four girls?"

De Cordova said it was true.

Jake turned to the cast. "Which four?"

The girls stepped forward hesitantly.

Jake reached into his pocket, and took out the four pink slips. He waved them for the cast to see. Then, savagely, he tore them into shreds. "This will show you how much authority my son has in this organization," said Jake. "You're back in the show." He held his place for a beat, and then turned and walked out. It was his second public assassination of his son.

The Only Girl opened on the 21st of May, 1934, and closed after sixteen performances. Jake's rage was not appeased by its failure; Lee was planning another musical revue, scouted up for him by Harry Kaufman. And *Life Begins at 8:40* was destined to be another hit. Music by Harold Arlen, lyrics by E. Y. Harburg and Ira Gershwin, staged by John Murray Anderson, featuring the Weidman dancers, and Ray Bolger and Bert Lahr. It was a completely non-Jake show—and a success. Not really distinguished, but a success.

·　·　·

Lee's "hockshop" principle was working very well. He was getting percentages of a lot of plays. The negotiations on terms usually took a pattern. It went something like this for many a producer.

Almost always, it began with a pleasant session with Lee, who genially agreed to terms, ending the conversation with "Go see Weinstock and get the papers." Weinstock was then in charge of theater bookings for Lee.

The producer, pleased with the ease of the deal, would go off to "see Weinstock," asking himself why all these stories about the Shuberts. He didn't know that the minute he had left Lee's office, Lee was on the phone to Weinstock, laying down the terms he really wanted.

The producer would find himself involved in a brand-new and protracted negotiation. Most often, he would begin to get a little angry and come back to see Lee, which introduced him to Step Two, Shubert Contracts.

Lee would be concerned, apologetic, with a faint touch of embarrassment thrown in for effect. "Weinstock," he would say ruefully, "has to check these things out with my brother. My brother thinks the deal is too generous." (A lot of people think Lee and Jake encouraged the feud talk just for such situations!) "Go work it out with Weinstock."

Eventually, the producer would hammer out an agreement which Weinstock would promise to have on paper in a few days. Now would come the big meeting in Lee's office to sign the papers. Usually, the producer, wary by now, would bring his own lawyer along and read the contract word for word. Suddenly, he would come upon a never-before-discussed clause, upping something in the Messrs. favor.

On one such occasion, a producer discovered that there had been a radical percentage shift against him. He turned to Lee and demanded, "How did that get in?"

Lee beamed at him from behind the desk, every part of his mahogany face, except the eyes, smiling in good fellowship. "I guess it just crept in," he said.

"Let it creep out," suggested the producer. "You're not being fair, Mr. Lee."

There was a quick interchange of amused glances between Weinstock and Lee, and the producer knew he would never use the word "fair" again with Lee Shubert. Not in a business negotiation.

Herman Shumlin was luckier than most producers in his dealings with the Messrs. Shumlin had fallen in love with *The Children's Hour* and had sent the script to the Shubert office. Jimmy Proctor, who had handled publicity on *Ten Minute Alibi*, which Shumlin had directed, read the play and instantly became a one-man expeditionary force to persuade Lee to back it.

The Children's Hour, Lillian Hellman's first play, was a study of the tragic consequences of scandal and rumor, set up in a girls' school. Part of the structure of the play was its delicate handling of lesbianism. It was a hard play to finance and a hard play to put on. Fired up by Proctor, Lee agreed to back the play, and entirely with his own money.

Shumlin opened *The Children's Hour* at the Maxine Elliott Theater, and it was the dramatic blockbuster of the year. It ran for two years, and Lee Shubert's pawnshop had another winner.

Thoroughly disgusted with the life in New York and weary of travel, Jake determined to merge with big-league baseball. And with the Hollywood Bowl. He announced a series of summer festivals to be held in baseball parks, notably Fenway Park in Boston and Navin Field in Detroit. In the Hollywood Bowl, Jake said, "We will bring artistic productions of *May Time*, *Blossom Time* and other worthy pieces."

Lee, impressed with Robert Sinclair's work with *Dodsworth*, flim-flammed him into the chain gang with yet another version of *A Trip to Pressburg*. This time it was called *A Journey by Night*, and it spent one forlorn week at the Shubert Theater. They even had a flop with Tallulah Bankhead, which was a very hard thing to accomplish in the mid-thirties, when Miss Bankhead reading the telephone book could run for ten weeks. She could only manage nine with *Something Gay*.

That year, 1935, was probably the worst year in the history of the American theater. Not only had production cut back in number, but runs were shorter than ever. New phenomena were appearing on the scene. The Federal Theater Project was trying to be a stage WPA, and succeeding only partially.

Lee Shubert remarked grimly, "It took a miracle to save the motion picture. Silents were on their way to extinction, audiences were getting bored with them, and then came the talkie. What kind of miracle can there be for the stage?"

He was fighting doggedly to maintain his theatrical empire. It is estimated that more than 60 percent of the shows that were produced in New York were in one way or another partially financed by the Shuberts. Even with the minimal cash investment, prodigious amounts of Shubert capital were leaving the safe. And the risks were high.

Lee had other problems to contend with. He knew Jake was infuriated; he was encouraging John to find properties that he and his

318

father could do. He knew that this would be aggravated when Jake learned that Milton, his pet hate, was going to work on three shows. That would really do it.

The good news was sparse. The *Ziegfeld Follies*, Shubert version, was doing very well on the road, huge business in Chicago, record in Los Angeles, sellout in San Francisco. Lee was planning a second edition. And that was about *all* the good news.

There was a very embarrassing lawsuit, filed against them by Howard Reinheimer. On behalf of his clients, Otto Harbach, Oscar Hammerstein, and Herbert Stothart, Reinheimer sued "in the matter of rights and royalties" in the property *Rose Marie*, which the Messrs. had bought at that $684 auction. (Friml had no rights—he had sold his interest to Arthur Hammerstein.)

The Shuberts had been licensing *Rose Marie* in France, in the United Kingdom, in various parts of the United States—as a matter of fact, all over the world. And they had taken in thousands upon thousands of dollars.

Reinheimer wanted the "rights" question clarified. Just what rights did Arthur Hammerstein have? In the days when the composers and the author signed their contract with Arthur Hammerstein, there was no standard Dramatists' Guild contract. Each contract was drawn separately; radio, TV, and talking pictures had not yet appeared—who owned those rights? Just how would each contract be interpreted?

His second suit was on the "royalties" due his clients. Here, Reinheimer flatly accused the Shuberts of outright theft. He claimed their statements were fraudulent and they had cheated money from the authors.

The "rights" to musical properties were part of the Century library, in the Sardi Building—on Jake's "side." It was the library's job to issue statements. This had been done only sporadically in the case of Harbach, who complained to his attorney. Reinheimer wrote to the Shuberts, asking why there had been no recent accounting, and received no reply.

Purely accidentally, Reinheimer learned that *Rose Marie* was playing in Omaha and that, for some puzzling reason, it had been leased to the Omaha impresario by Tams-Witmark, a sheet-music publisher. He wrote a curt note to the Shuberts, asking for an explanation.

By return mail, he received a check for Harbach and a totally unexpected royalty check for another of his clients, Sigmund Romberg, for royalties more than three years late for *Nina Rosa*. Harbach's check seemed rather small to Reinheimer. It was for $30! Attached to the check was a voucher. It listed the Omaha rental at $500, less 10 percent to the agent, less material rental, $150 (the music arrangements for the orchestra), less producers' share (50 percent of the remainder—$150 to the Shuberts), leaving a net of $150. Twenty percent was due Harbach, and the check was for that sum: $30.

On a hunch, Reinheimer checked Tams-Witmark on the terms of the deal. Tams replied promptly. They had acted as agents for the *Nina Rosa* deal in Omaha, where they had arranged a lease for *$1,000*, kept their 10 percent, and had forwarded $900 to the Shuberts. In addition, they had prepaid the $150 for the music arrangements!

Reinheimer wrote to the Messrs. outlining the above and claiming an incorrect accounting. Return mail brought a correct check and a polite letter apologizing for the "unfortunate mistake," and which went on to ask for the return of the first check. Reinheimer kept it. It made quite a souvenir.

Reinheimer withdrew both suits; they were settled "out of court" by Willie Klein. It was a costly suit for the Shuberts. A host of other authors wanted to know about the Shubert statements, and several filed suit, notably Emmerich Kalman, who filed for monies on *five* separate shows. He didn't sue both Shuberts—just Jake.

In addition to sheer nuisance suits that resulted from this saving of less than $100, it cost the brothers another plum. Some years later, when the Dillingham-Ziegfeld estates were to be auctioned, Lee drove up, confident that he would steal another trove. When he arrived, he found Reinheimer there. The attorney, alerted to the sale, which was held in Westchester, had pooled the resources of Oscar Hammerstein, Irving Berlin, Jerome Kern, and others and they had put up about $25,000 to bid against the Shuberts.

The authors feared clouding of the rights and loss of royalties. Reinheimer worried that the sum raised was insufficient. MGM had purchased film rights to many of the properties coming up for auction, and Robert Rubin, MGM's chief attorney, quickly joined the pool. He pledged up to $50,000.

The Shuberts stopped bidding at $40,000 and the valuable estate went to the group and MGM. It is interesting to speculate whether this would have occurred had it not been for one small, petty Shubert swindle.

Lee had two hits out of three tries. *At Home Abroad*, by Howard Dietz and Arthur Schwartz, starred Bea Lillie, Ethel Waters, and Eleanor Powell, and was directed by Vincent Minnelli. It was a hit. Then came a social-problem play which wasn't, and then it was time for the

At Home Abroad. That is the inimitable great lady of comedy in the tutu—
Miss Beatrice Lillie. The violin is being played by James McCall, and obviously
Reginald Gardiner is upset. Winter Garden Theater, 1935.

second Shubert, Jake-less *Ziegfeld Follies*. Fannie Brice was back, and Josephine Baker came on from Paris to join the cast. There were two comedians, Bob Hope and Ken Murray, and Lee drove to Boston to see the show.

Ken Murray had a stand-up monologue, which led into a sketch, and Lee grew fidgety as he watched the routine. When the curtain came down, he went back to see Murray.

"Ken," he said, "I don't like your opening monologue."

Murray was upset. "What's wrong with it, Mr. Lee?" he asked. "The people are laughing like crazy."

"I know," agreed Lee, "but I think it's dirty."

"Dirty?" asked Murray. "I have done that monologue for ten years!"

"I still think it's vulgar," said Lee stubbornly.

"But I did that bit on the Paramount stage the week before we started rehearsals," protested Murray.

"I know, I know," said Lee soothingly. "But on *my stage*, you can't say 'ess—aitch—eye—tee'!"

By now, Murray was thoroughly confused. He just closed his eyes, and shook his head to clear it.

"In the Paramount," Lee continued easily, " 'ess—aitch—eye—tee' you can say. But on my stage, you can't." Then he seemed to relent. "On *my* stage, you can say "eff—you—cee—kay.' " He was a shy man and could not bring himself to say the words—he spelled them.

If Murray had been confused a sentence before, he was totally disoriented with this last. "I guess I just don't get it," he said.

"Don't you see, Ken," said Lee, and now, in his own way, he came up with a piece of priceless theater wisdom: "When a man pays four-fifty instead of fifty cents for a theater seat, his sense of humor walks out of the bathroom into the bedroom." He slapped Ken on the back. "Change the monologue."

It is too bad that Mr. Murray never came into New York with the *Follies;* it might have been rewarding to see how he used "eff—you—cee—kay" in his monologue. Mr. Murray left the show because of a billing problem.

He and his agent, Louis Shurr, had made their arrangements with Lee. Bob Hope and his agent, the same Louis Shurr, had made their arrangements with J.J. *Both* contracts called for top male billing. Something had to give, and it turned out to be Ken Murray.

This second Shubert-bossed *Ziegfeld Follies* was much less Ziegfeld and much more Shubert. Mr. Lee had determined to bring box office to it, and one of his first moves was to try to persuade Gypsy Rose Lee, the reigning queen of burlesque, to play a lead. He called Miss Lee, left word that "Mr. Shubert" had called, and was mystified when there was no call back.

Miffed, he sent Harry Kaufman to Miss Lee's dressing room. Miss Lee, whose music arranger just happened to be named Shubert, had ignored the call. When Miss Lee learned that it was Mr. *Lee* who had called, and when she heard the word *Follies*, she almost broke the pen in her haste to sign a term contract at $250 per week. (She was earning $2,000 a week in burlesque.)

Her promised "brilliant costumes"—eleven changes in all—turned out to be right off the Shubert racks. She supplied her own. She shared a dressing room with Fannie Brice, and they split the cost of a dresser between them—Lee didn't supply one. It was only the compatability of the company that kept the show from being an enormously unhappy one.

Just before opening, Abe Cohen, the company manager, got into a dispute with the musicians. Under the Shubert economy drive, he was trying to push the orchestra to avoid overtime. The musician's steward quoted the union rules. Cohen, too long with the Shuberts and Jake, betrayed the experience. "F - - k the union!" he exclaimed.

The steward was outraged. "Nice thing," he said, "a hell of a way to talk. I'm going to Petrillo!"

"F - - k Petrillo!" suggested Cohen.

Abe, nicknamed "Franchot," was barred from the theater for twenty weeks.

The *Follies* opened and despite the seediness was a hit. This fact did not relax the austerity. Each night, the curtain came down at 10:50, and at exactly 11:10, no matter how many visitors might be backstage, Lee Shubert would personally turn out the lights. Complaints were fruitless. "Why should we waste electricity?" Lee asked. "Con Edison is on relief?"

Toward the end of the run of the 1936 *Ziegfeld Follies*, the show was in Detroit, and Miss Lee was mystified by a phone call from Twentieth Century Fox, telling her to report for "a few weeks' work." She explained that she couldn't; she was under contract to the Shuberts. Not any more, was the reply: we bought the contract. She reported—at $250 per week.

It wasn't till long afterward that Miss Lee learned that Mr. Lee, whom she describes as "fascinating—a cross between a wooden Indian and a hooded cobra," had sold her contract for something like $25,000!

The *Follies* success didn't help Jake's morale, and he wasn't even cheered when Milton's two productions were flops. He was tired of traveling and he was bored, bored, bored. He realized that the *Follies* would

Bob Hope and Fannie Brice (top). The Shubert *Ziegfeld Follies of 1936.*
Bobby Clark and Gypsy Rose Lee (bottom). *Ziegfeld Follies of 1936.*

run, shut down for the summer in those pre-air-conditioning days, and then would reopen in the fall. He decided to start a second company of the show in California. He did.

Then this erratic man went up to San Francisco with the *Follies* company, and called on Lou Lurie, the Bay City financier and theater buff. They had enjoyed lunch at Jack's and were waiting for the elevator to Lurie's office when they were approached by an old-time vaudeville acrobat, Buster Ferguson, who was now a latter-day Emperor Norton. He cadged his living in downtown San Francisco—much of it from Lurie—and today was pay day.

They entered the elevator, and Lurie said to Ferguson, "Do you know who's riding in the car with us Buster? This is the famous J.J. Shubert."

Ferguson, who did not have all his faculties, mumbled, "Know him well. Know him well."

"Oh, come on, Buster," remonstrated Lurie, "how would you know J.J. Shubert?"

Ferguson was patient. "There were three brothers," he explained. "Sam, Lee, and Jake. The good one died."

Jake laughed louder than Lurie and in the latter's office insisted on handing Ferguson a hundred dollars. How could this unpredictable man, at this peculiar time of frustration, have reacted so, when he could find no way to laugh with his own son?

He had made no reconciliation with John. They talked; Jake knew that John was seeing his mother and taking care of her; and he knew he was seeing Eckie. In Jake's mind, Lee had betrayed him, his son had betrayed him, everyone had betrayed him.

Lee was being harried by the Ziegfeld creditors and the Ziegfeld estate. With two successful *Follies* running (the first on tour) and making money, the Ziegfeld creditors wanted their share. They threatened suit. Finally, with Billie Burke, Lee bought all rights to the name "Ziegfeld Follies" for $27,500. The creditors were exultant over their deal. They should have waited to celebrate.

Disturbed by the fact that the only new shows produced by the Shuberts that were making money were *Reflected Glory*, starring Miss Bankhead, and *The Show Is On*, a revue starring Bert Lahr and Bea Lillie, late in 1936 Lee went to Florida. He wanted to be sure of his strength. He had finally consented to let Jake supervise a show.

It was by Lehar, and it was an old-fashioned piece. *Frederika* did not make it. Jake had broken his heart and his back on it. His feelings were not brightened when Milton Shubert came up with a minor success, *Swing Your Lady*.

Milton even started making announcements of projects. He claimed the rights to a Shaw play, and the rumor got out that the Theatre Guild was out, and the Shuberts were in, for all future Shaw productions. It wasn't so. The guild didn't want to do *On the Rocks*, and neither did anyone else.

Lee had been studying the situation. To his keen nose, it smelled as though the worst were over. (He would still complain, and still chisel, but he felt they had weathered the storm.) In the years 1931 to 1937, the worst years of the terrible Depression, he had salvaged his business, secured his position, altered his methods, and poured an estimated $5,000,000 into the theater. Perhaps he had to. God knows he and Jake had taken ten times that *out* of the theater. But they were not compelled to give it back. And yet, this funny little man—someone described him as a Japanese admiral of Jewish descent—had almost single-handedly kept the New York stage alive.

Even without the Shuberts, there would have been plays and theaters to show them in, to be sure. But not as many theaters, and not as many plays, and not as many jobs for the established talents of the stage, and no training ground for the new talents. Certainly, there was the Federal Theater, and from it came wonderful new eager people. But it was the Shuberts who provided the continuum, and it was the Shuberts who could have pulled out and abandoned the living stage.

This, more than the Alley, is their monument. And while the name "Shuberts" is used in the plural, it was Lee Shubert who *was* the Shuberts during those long years of trial, and it was he who sustained the stage, and kept New York its capital.

But now, he could sense the upswing. He announced sixteen plays for the upcoming season. He was bringing the Abbey Players over from Ireland. He had a number of exciting projects. With some well-hidden satisfaction, he announced Eddie Cantor's return to Broadway, after an absence of eight years. He knew that he would be financing 50 percent of the rest of Broadway's output to some degree. And he even let Jake announce.

Jake had come back from Europe with *Three Waltzes*, "the finest light-musical work I have ever seen or heard." He also had big summer plans. Jones Beach. Randall's Island. St. Louis. Louisville. "In all this," said Jake, "I will be assisted by my son."

The only Shubert *not* making announcements was John. On September 30, 1937, he eloped to Maryland with Eckie, and he announced it to no one. Nor did he tell his father. He was afraid to.

Chapter Seventeen

On September 18, 1937, the Shuberts had launched a second Broadway company of *The Show Is On*, run it for seventeen performances, and then shipped it on tour as "direct from Broadway," an old Shubert trick. Lee brought in the Abbey Players, as promised, but not Eddie Cantor, as promised. Instead, the Messrs. came in with a book show starring Ed Wynn, and *Hooray for What!* was a hit.

Jake went into rehearsal with *Three Waltzes* at about the same time that Lee's "side" went into the staging of *Between the Devil*. Both were fair, and if Jake didn't have a hit, he at least had the satisfaction of outrunning Lee's production by three weeks. The score was ninety-three performances for Lee—one hundred twenty-two for Jake. In the spring of 1937, Harry Kaufman had come to Lee, seeking his backing for a Rodgers and Hart show. They had conceived the idea of a comedy concerned with the adventures of a hoofer who gets mixed up with the Russian Ballet. And they had Ray Bolger to star in it. Lee liked Bolger, the idea, and even came up with the title—*On Your Toes*. He plunked down $1,000 as option money, and told the men to get to work.

They called in George Abbott to help, turned out a fast-paced book and a lovely, exciting score, including the novel idea of interpolating a ballet as an integral part of the story. Now it was time to play the score for Lee. And, of course, this was the one he fell sleep to, and then decided not to produce.

Undeterred by this, Rodgers and Hart went to see Dwight Deere Wiman, who instantly fell in love with it. Back to Shubert came the pair, offering to return his option money. Lee refused; he determined to play dog in the manger. If he wasn't going to produce it, and he wasn't, then no one else would.

They waited out the option, brought Balanchine in to choreograph the show, created stage history with *Slaughter On Tenth Avenue*, and made a lot of money for Wiman. Harry Kaufman was desolate. He kept pointing out to Lee what had been lost.

Shubert let him complain, until one day he said, "Harry, we're still partners in the show."

Kaufman was pleased, but puzzled.

Lee's eyes twinkled. "They're playing in *my* theater," he said. "We get our percentage."

"But we could have had it all," protested Kaufman.

"Being a pig can be stupid. A little is a little, a little of a lot is more, and all of nothing is smaller than a little," said Lee. The one important Shubert aftereffect of *On Your Toes* was that Lee *did* listen to Kaufman from then on.

In the early part of 1938, the box-office men went out on strike, picketing the theaters, and in other ways annoying Jake. Lee was in Florida. Jake summoned Lee's assistant, John Kenley, and ordered him to work in the box office. Kenley refused.

"You will work there," Jake threatened, "or you won't work anywhere."

"I can't do that," said Kenley.

"God-damned unions," muttered Jake. "Troublemakers! They think they own the theaters, the God-damned unions!"

Kenley, sharp-tongued and acerbic, and also very secure in his job on "Lee's side," replied sweetly, "They wouldn't need unions if it weren't for men like you, Mr. Shubert."

Jake glared him out of the office.

Jimmy Proctor was working up a Shubert release, a statement of policy in re the strike, and he wanted to clear the copy with Jake before handing it out to the papers. He was fighting the deadline, the newspapers were about to go to press, and he dashed up to Jake's office. The secretary would not admit him or even announce him.

"But this has to be cleared right now," said the exasperated Proctor. "What's so impossible about seeing him for a second? Why can't he be disturbed?"

"He's having his mind read," explained the secretary.

Whether it was a result of Jake's mind reading or not, the box-office strike was settled in two days, when the theater owners capitulated. Since the pay rise hit the Shuberts harder than all the other theater owners combined, they proceeded to try to crush the union. Other unions they dealt with were more easily handled, and so the Shuberts encouraged one to raid the Managers, Agents and Treasurers' Union in a takeover. This resulted in a plea for an injunction to stop the Shuberts from interference.

The Shubert press department was charged with the task of getting free space in the papers with their Shubert releases, and they had to "prove" that they had succeeded. Sometimes this was pretty difficult. The "proof" was a large cardboard, on which the printed items would be pasted daily, under appropriate mastheads. Then, as now, the *New York Times* was the target.

When the news ran low, and they couldn't get into print, the press department knew it had a friend in the *Bronx Home News*, which would print almost anything. They would shovel great quantities of filler material to the *Home News*, clip them, paste them on the board under the *Times* masthead, and proudly show them to Lee. Or Jake.

The brothers never read the copy; they just wanted to know there was a lot of it. The content wasn't important—just the quantity. If the board was reasonably full, and the *New York Times* logo was prominent, all was well. To the Shuberts, this was news fit to print.

But the real jitters hit the press department when somebody printed an attack on either brother or both, and this was not infrequent. Storm clouds would gather over 44th Street, and sooner or later, Greneker would be summoned to the throne room. Why do such things appear in print? Why didn't you stop it? Why haven't you answered it? Very often, the article printed sad, painful truth. Without real ammunition for a reply, the harried chief of the Shubert press would decide that the best thing to do was to maintain silence. To the Shuberts, this was treason.

On one such occasion, Lee demonstrated his thin skin and absolute hands-off policy toward Greneker. Danton Walker had printed an item, calling Greneker a "good press agent, whose press work makes him like the Shuberts." Lee resented the item. (It was not Greneker's press work; it was the Shubert charm and integrity that made Greneker like the Shuberts—that was Lee's opinion.)

He wrote a demanding, indignant note to Greneker.

He began by quoting Walker's line. He found it uncalled-for. He then "suggested" that Greneker write a reply to Walker, defending the Shubert position, and in Lee's very own words suggested how the letter might go—this in May of 1944.

He wanted Greneker to ask why Walker found it so hard to like the Shuberts. They employed more people than all the other legitimate theater people in the country. They gave benefits, contributing their theaters to such efforts. He suggested that Greneker suggest to Walker that Greneker found such attacks a symptom of a personal grudge Walker was carrying. He strongly intimated to Greneker that he tell Walker that he was not writing this on behalf of the Shuberts; the Shuberts were too magnanimous, had too much savoir-faire for anything like that. No (Lee hinted emphatically to Greneker), the Shuberts would *never* never ask me to do anything like that. I am doing this because of the esteem and respect in which I hold them. Lee concluded by stating that although there was no way for him to *make* Greneker write such a letter, he would like to see it before it went out.

He was seventy-one when he dictated that, late one night, to his

329

then assistant, Jack Morris. It leaves no doubt about who was minding the store.

In March of 1938, the Shuberts launched a $1,000,000 suit against Harms, Incorporated, a music publishing house, for allowing Shubert songs to be played on radio. It was the opening gun in their attack on ASCAP and the broadcast industry.

Jake, cheered by this frontal assault on radio (he had supplied lists and lists of Shubert songs played), was unusually genial when he arrived in Boston to host a press party to celebrate John Shubert's first co-production with the Messrs.

The Messrs. and John were going to present *You Never Know*, by Cole Porter. It had not been that easy to arrange. Milton had co-produced with the Messrs.; and Jake, from feelings of equity rather than paternity, thought the books ought to be balanced by John co-producing. It was so ordered. Jake still did not know of John's marriage, but he wouldn't have believed it if he knew. He was getting along a little better with his son, and had even scrawled "J.J. Shubert" on a pass to the theaters for Catherine.

Cole Porter lyrics were a little hard for Jake to understand. One number, "From Alpha to Omega," in the show he persisted in calling "From Alfalfa to Omega," and correcting him only made him angry. *You Never Know* was not a Jake Shubert kind of musical. For that matter, *You Never Know* wasn't really a Cole Porter kind of musical.

It was a vintage French farce plot, where the baron pretends to be his "man," Gaston (Clifton Webb), the better to carry on a flirtation with Mme. Baltin (Libby Holman), while Maria, Madame's maid (Lupe Velez), can ditto with M. Baltin. It's a very Mozartian plot, but unfortunately, unlike Mozart, it can be understood.

Eckie was dancing in the chorus, and Jake, unaware of his son's marital status, conducted a happy press conference, at his favorite hotel, the Ritz Carlton. John stood beside him.

The *Boston Herald* described J.J. as "beaming, proud, happy, relaxed and fat."

"You ask me if my son has come to me for advice about his first show? Where did you ever see a son going to his father to ask him anything these days? And if I gave him any advice, he wouldn't take it. He says I'm old-fashioned."

Jake waxed philosophical and fatherly. "He should have been a lawyer, where you decide on things. I'd like to see him get married and settle down."

330

"Would you like him to marry an actress, Mr. Shubert?"

Jake glared. He turned meaningfully to John, and then back to the press. "Being a theatrical producer, I couldn't say too much on that subject. But I think he can find as good a wife away from the stage as in the theater." John smiled.

"Are you backing the show, Mr. Shubert?"

"My son," said Jake proudly, "has money of his own."

John had almost *no* money of his own. In effect, he was living on an allowance. It came in the form of a salary from the company, but it was not generous. Jake's whip was an often-repeated threat. "I'll cut you out of my will, you talk to me like that!" It kept John compliant.

Everybody, including the Ziegfeld creditors, at last understood why Lee, instead of stalling, had paid cash money for the rights to the title "Ziegfeld Follies," when it was announced that MGM had bought the title for a reported $100,000. It was a tidy profit. The creditors screamed, but to no avail. Lee closed with MGM.

This also canceled the proposed new Shubert *Ziegfeld Follies*, which was going to star Gypsy Rose Lee. It killed her chance to get back some of the money Lee had extracted from her in their prior association.

In the middle of the summer, Lee made a trip to Philadelphia that resulted in a Shubert gold mine. Harry Kaufman had been insistent; there was a one-hour vaudeville-type show that Lee simply had to see. Afraid of another *On Your Toes*, Lee succumbed to Kaufman's enthusiasm.

This way, he would not have to have an audition. He could *see* what they were talking about. And this he preferred. Lee Shubert's mind was not really a producer's mind. Words meant little to him. Oh, to be sure, if someone said, "net cash!" or "profit" or "tax-free," he understood completely. But the subtleties, the nuances, the delicate shades of meaning—these he did not understand.

The "show" that Kaufman was so urgent about was a madcap, zany, impromptu, uninhibited, knock-down-and-drag-out, low-comedy, burlesque farce. Lee saw it, and he liked it, and he made an offer to the impresarios, Olson and Johnson. He asked them to extend the hour with more of the same so that they would have a two-hour show, and then he would book it into New York. They agreed. They kept the title: "Hellzapoppin." Lee was so pleased with the deal, he promised Kaufman "a piece of the action."

Just before *Hellzapoppin!* opened, the Shuberts went into partner-

John Shubert

Hellzapoppin! Olson and Johnson with some of the belles of the chorus. Mrs. John ("Eckie") Shubert is the girl at top right.

ship with their only major rival in theater operation—the United States government. The WPA Federal Theater Project was running as many as eight houses in New York, and one of their hit plays was *Prologue to Glory*. It was decided that the show would go out on tour, with the Shuberts booking it and they and the United States sharing in the profits, fifty-fifty.

When the story broke, it started a wave of Broadway humor. One wit suggested that Lee would probably be the next secretary of the treasury, at which time the country might go broke, but they could always buy it back at auction. (One actor said that he had always thought the Shuberts *were* the Government.) It even provoked an investigation by Parnell Thomas.

The representative from New Jersey, a precursor in thought to the late Senator Joseph McCarthy, had already called the Theater Project "a hotbed of Communism." Now he wanted to know more about the Shuberts. Were they part of a plot?

John Shubert's co-production opened on September 21, 1938; *Hellzapoppin!* opened the following night. *You Never Know* received so-so notices, and ran for less than ten weeks. *Hellzapoppin!* startled the critics by becoming one of the longest-run shows in history. It just went on and on and on.

Its success in no way altered the Shubert economy program. A highlight of *Hellzapoppin!* was a blackout, in which cups of dried beans were thrown out to the audience. One zealous Shubert money-saver suggested that they "use smaller cups with larger beans, whereby a saving of more than one dollar and fifty cents per week can be achieved." Lee vetoed it.

Paper cups became important in many Shubert activities.

On an earlier occasion, a show was in rehearsal in a Shubert house on 44th Street, and the stage manager called the producer's attention to the absence of paper cups.

"So, get paper cups from the Shuberts," said the producer.

One day later, the stage manager explained that the Shuberts would not supply any paper cups. The producer grew angry. *He* called the Shubert office. They were sorry. They had no authorization to issue a carton of paper cups.

The producer called Lee Shubert. "My cast is thirsty," he reported, "and your God-damned office won't send over paper cups."

There was a long, indignant pause on the other end, and then Lee replied, "You bother me with such nonsense?"

"I am entitled to paper cups!" insisted the producer.

333

A carton of paper cups was delivered, followed one day later by Lee Shubert. "I examined the contract," said Lee, "and nowhere in it does it say you are entitled to paper cups during rehearsal. Only after the show is open. However, I have okayed it."

The producer, forever after, insisted on a "paper cup during rehearsal" clause in all his Shubert contracts.

Paper cups on one occasion cost Lee a production he really wanted. For years, Lee had sedulously wooed the Lunts. He wanted the prestige (and the ticket sales) their names guaranteed. He reminded Miss Fontanne that he, Lee Shubert, had given her her first part on Broadway. He appealed to loyalty, to sentiment, to money. Finally, they capitulated; they booked their production of *Taming of the Shrew* into a Shubert theater.

The Lunts were outraged when they discovered that they were being billed three dollars a week for paper cups, under the production charges.

When *There Shall Be No Night* came along, Lee wanted it for the Shubert Theater; the Lunts took the show to the non-Shubert Alvin Theater. It was an expensive three dollars.

Hellzapoppin! was an enormously profitable show. Except for Olson and Johnson, the cast was almost anonymous, resulting in the favorite Shubert kind of payroll—low. Tom McKnight, who had written some of the sketches for the show, was walking past the theater one day, accompanied by Bobby Clark. McKnight looked ruefully at the long line waiting to buy tickets, shook his head disgustedly, and said to Clark, "You know, two weeks before this thing opened, Lee Shubert offered me 20 percent of the show for fifteen thousand dollars, and I refused. That goes to show you what I know about show business."

The comedian corrected him. "No, Tom," said Clark, "that goes to show you what Lee Shubert knows about show business."

While the war was crippling Europe, there was a truce in effect on 44th Street. Curiously, as the Shuberts retreated from active production, consultations between the brothers became more and more necessary. For more than a year now, John had been promoted to the post of intermediary, message bearer, censor. He was good at it. Lee liked him, he was Jake's son, and he could usually negotiate a compromise.

But when the brothers actually began to meet, there was apprehension in the Shubert offices. What would happen? How would things work out when the two men were face-to-face?

The first sessions were anticlimatic. They were completely and totally formal. Lee was polite, Jake was as polite as he could be, and the discussions were practically run by Robert's Rules. Then, as the staffs began to relax and it became a little less than sensational for the Shubert brothers to meet, the formality relaxed and the shouting began.

There was a strict protocol about the confrontations. Invariably, Jake came to Lee's office; Lee *never* went to Jake's. Invariably, the conversation would be punctuated by Jake's temper, and then, invariably, Lee's voice would rise, he would commence to stammer, and then they would arrive at a loud decision.

One of the decisions was to buy back theaters. There was a definite pickup in theater business. The war was in the air, and there was the incipient boom that always accompanies that kind of "good business news."

If the theater was coming back, then the Shuberts would hatch plans. And they would hatch them in Lee's office in the turret of the Shubert Theater.

There was one aspect of the office that requires description. The office proper was a circular room, twelve feet in diameter, painted, at one time, a French gray. Gray it was, and so was the waiting room outside. In this small room, Lee would sit for sixteen to eighteen hours a day, seven days a week, seeing people. Never did he refuse to see anyone. He explained this to Mike Todd one day. "The one person I didn't see would be the one with the good deal."

To accelerate the "seeing" process, there was a small foyer, also French gray, between the waiting room and the office. This foyer had *two* doors on one side, and a third leading into the office proper. In it sat Lee's secretary. To handle the daily overflow, Lee had developed a technique. He would come to the door from the waiting room. He would greet the caller warmly. If he was persuaded that "there was no deal," he would latch one prehensile hand on the caller's elbow while shaking hands. He would march the caller into the foyer area, and then expertly propel him to the door exiting back into the waiting room, explaining all the while why he was so glad to see him. The caller would find himself on his way, and Lee would be appraising the next customer.

If, on the other hand, there *was* a deal, Lee would make the same elbow grab, march the visitor into the office, sit himself down behind the desk, with the guest in the stiff chair before it, and listen to the proposition.

It was always a proposition. Lee once complained to John Kenley,

"Everyone who comes in that door wants something from me. If anybody ever came in and said, 'I got a present for you,' I wouldn't believe him."

So, nobody ever came in with a present.

Lee was seated in that office with Kenley one afternoon, shortly after Joe Gaites (the man who tried to tell himself "there are no Shuberts") had left the organization.

Shubert asked Kenley, "How much money does Gaites have?"

Kenley said he had no idea.

"He owes us seventy thousand dollars," said Lee sadly. "You and Gaites were friends; how much money does he have?"

Kenley replied, "Would you respect me if I told you?"

Lee thought about it for a moment. "No," he said finally, "but I wish you would, anyway."

(A few months later, dining with Gaites, Kenley brought up the subject of the Shuberts and monies due. Gaites was a philosophical man. "They gave me a tip to buy Shubert stock, and offered to lend me the money to do it with. So I bought seventy thousand dollars worth." He shook his head. "Willie Klein sold *his* stock. Jake got rid of a bundle of *his* stock. Nobody tipped me to sell mine. I was wiped out.")

Lee took a long cruise to South America in 1938, and in Rio he spotted an exciting performer. He signed Carmen Miranda for her American debut for the upcoming season. Jake was holding the fort in New York and keeping Willie Klein busy. They were flexing Shubert muscles at ASCAP, they were suing Jack Kirkland for $25,000, contending that he was violating their copyright on *Florodora*. They were fighting with Fortune Gallo, their associate in the operetta festivals that had been shut down at Jones Beach, and in Lee's absence Willie Klein pulled one of his favorite tricks. He settled a case out of court, while the jury was out deciding the award!

The Shuberts, through Klein, had probably been instrumental in writing the bulk of what is laughingly called theatrical law. Their "unique and extraordinary" clause was unique. Some of their legal battles had set other theatrical precedents. But the case of J. J. McSherry vs. Lee Shubert was one of Willie's pets.

McSherry had approached Lee with a tax-saving idea, and been promised payment. He didn't get it, and he brought suit to collect, asking for $1,000. His attorney made an impassioned plea, Willie Klein made *his* impassioned plea, and the jury filed out. Neither attorney was too certain what would happen, and in a quick meeting McSherry's lawyer persuaded his client to settle for $200.

It was done. A few seconds after the hastily scrawled agreement was signed, the jury filed in and announced that it had awarded McSherry $523. Lee was $323 richer than he would have been.

Lee returned with Miss Miranda, and in association with their goldminers, Olson and Johnson, the Messrs. presented *Streets of Paris* with a phenomenal cast. In addition to Miss Miranda, whose debut excited Broadway with the introduction of her torso and "The South American Way," the players included Bobby Clark, Luella Gear, Abbott and Costello, Gower Champion, and lots of others.

It was a rowdy, vulgar review, and Miss Miranda stole the notices. It was a hit.

Jake was trying operettas in the Midwest, and they were not going well. They closed the Wilson Theater in Detroit, which had been spring-boarding the touring companies, but they didn't really mean to do it. Jake wanted negotiating room with the unions. He forced Equity to agree to that ninth performance without additional salary, on the threat of closing other theaters in Detroit. And he forced the musicians to go along. Flushed with success, he went on to Chicago.

Claudia Cassidy, the theater critic for the Chicago *Tribune* had just came back from New York, where she had interviewed Lee. In the course of the interview, Lee had remarked, "My brother wants an eye for an eye and a tooth for a tooth—almost always *two* eyes for an eye, and *two* teeth." Miss Cassidy printed the remark and Jake arrived in Chicago in time to read it. It did not make him happy.

Jake had come to Chicago to take a look at a new Shubert production, designed for Broadway. It was titled *Three after Three*, starred Simone Simon, and was being handled for the Messrs. by Fred de Cordova. It was not a good show. Jake had his usual comments and suggestions and decided to change the title to *Walk with Music*—there was very little else that might help.

Walk with Music was beset by an abundance of tribulations. Lucinda Ballard, married to Howard Dietz, and a gifted designer, should have known better before taking on the costume chore for the show— she had dealt with Jake before.

She had been asked to work on a *Student Prince* revival with the rambunctious J.J., who invited her to "take a look" at the production on stage. The sets were sparkling and new, and so were the costumes; this was unusual for a Shubert production, where the proverbial admonition for the theatergoers was: "Don't sit in the first five rows unless you like the smell of mothballs." This was a fresh-looking show.

As Miss Ballard sat watching, a weird procession made its way across the stage—J.J., followed by people with boxes. Al Ostrander, who had designed the show, paled.

On stage, J.J. started opening the boxes, extracting paper garlands. Not just plain paper garlands—these were dirty, well-used, shabby paper garlands.

Ostrander, aghast, rushed to Miss Ballard. "Tell him," he said hoarsely, "you have got to tell him that these garlands are ghastly! They're corny, they don't belong, we don't want them. You have to tell him."

Summoning her courage, Miss Ballard approached Jake. She told him.

He stared at her uncomprehendingly. "But Miss Ballard," said the truculent Shubert, "I have always personally hung the garlands." He looked at her, and then his voice became a little bit harsh. "And I always will!"

Garlands there were.

Now, years later, *Three after Three* having been redubbed *Walk with Music*, they were going to "look at it" in New Haven. They looked, and unfortunately they had to listen. The show was not very good; the only kind things the reviewers could say referred to a few performers and the "look" of the show.

This was another Shubert co-production, this one with Ruth Selwyn. J.J. had been a quiet, polite producer all through rehearsals. Possibly he was overawed by Miss Selwyn, who attended each rehearsal dressed to the teeth and might have impressed Jake with her *grande dame* approach to the theater.

Directly after opening night and the New Haven reviews, Jake reverted to type, and Miss Selwyn found hers. There was a great screaming match, and everybody agreed the show had to be "fixed." The Shuberts started fixing. John, who had worked with Miss Ballard and Jo Mielziner all through the planning and who had brought his clean, delicate architect's eye to the sessions, stood with her when Jake started moving in the goodies.

The girls had already arrived. Jake's motto, as always, was "When in doubt, add girls." There they were, and now, out of the boxes came the costumes for the girls. They were all old, and once upon a time they had all been pastel. Now they were faded into dingy browns and tans. They did not belong in this show. Miss Ballard told John Shubert so. He agreed.

"You must tell your father," she insisted.

He shook his head smilingly. "It wouldn't do any good."

She knew *she* couldn't tell J. J. What to do? "Can't you say something to him?"

"No."

"But, John, what will the show look like?"

"A New England boiled dinner," he suggested.

And it did. Horrified at what the New York critics would do to the show and to her, Miss Ballard rushed to her contract. (She could not rush to her husband, Howard Dietz, because he was having *his* troubles with the other Shubert.) Triumphantly, she found a clause, which had been inserted at Jo Mielziner's suggestion—no changes without permission of the designer.

Triumphantly, she invoked her "no changes" clause and quit, taking the next train to New York. There, a few days later she was summoned to the Shubert office. Willie Klein was the summoner.

"You had no right to do what you did," said Klein sternly. "You walked out on a show."

"My contract says," began Miss Ballard, but Willie cut her off.

"Why did we give you that silly clause in your contract? So you would sign it! So, you signed it. Now, we are going ahead, with your costumes, our costumes, and your name on the show."

Miss Ballard was furious. "You will take my name off your show!"

"We bought your name," said Klein, "and we'll use it!"

When she tried to sue, there was no one to sue. Following a procedure they had introduced a few years back, the Shuberts had each play in a different owning corporation. When *Walk with Music* flopped, Miss Ballard could find no one responsible to be responsible.

Miss Ballard's husband, Howard Dietz, had no difficulty finding responsible parties—he had been a "friend" of Lee Shubert's for years. They sat on the board at MGM, and Dietz had done the lyrics for *At Home Abroad* for Lee.

They had disagreed about three of the numbers in that show—Dietz begging to take them out, Lee insisting that they stay in because "when I hear an audience laugh, I know something." They only laughed in Boston, and after opening, Lee had the numbers cut in New York.

While Jake and Willie Klein were traumatizing Miss Ballard, Dietz had been given the emergency call by Lee. *Keep off the Grass* was in trouble in Boston, and they wanted Dietz to write three numbers for the show. He agreed, subject to an inviolate, solemnly-sworn-to agreement from Lee that they would be dropped from the show if Dietz, and Dietz alone, thought it wise. Lee solemnly swore to it. (No more unsigned agreements.)

Dietz wrote the numbers, and learned to hate one of them—the

Life Begins at 8:40 (top). Ray Bolger, Luella Gear, Frances Williams and Bert Lahr, the Winter Garden Theater, 1934.

Keep Off the Grass (bottom). Jimmy Durante, Ilka Chase and Ray Bolger singing up a storm in the Shubert production, 1940.

"Debutante" song. When he asked Lee to take it out, Lee's reply was, "When we have a suitable replacement." It never came out, Dietz refused to be available for additional material, but inexplicably Lee persisted in sending royalty checks to Dietz at regular intervals.

There is one other Dietz-Shubert occurrence that merits recording. When Max Gordon produced *Flying Colors*, by Dietz and Schwartz, the show was capitalized at $100,000. Gordon was in for $25,000, Dietz assumed responsibility for $25,000 and Lee for $25,000. The remaining unsold fourth was owned by all three. Lee without discussion sold his part of the 25 percent left for $25,000, which in effect meant that he was a quarter partner with no investment. It was the way Rockefeller began.

Lee helped the banks out in October of 1939 by taking back the Belasco and Fulton Theaters. (He would subsequently get rid of the Belasco because it was, in his opinion, "on the wrong side of the right street.") But it was the first step at recapturing some of the lost properties. The good theaters they had never lost. Those had been owned by Jake and Lee and leased to the parent corporation.

When Lee announced the purchase, a member of the press raised the question of a Shubert theater monopoly in New York. Lee denied the charge with great indignation. He then added a significant postscript. "But, it would be better for everybody if one reliable, experienced firm books all the best local houses." He meant it, but only if the "experienced, reliable firm" were the Shuberts. As a matter of fact, they were "unique and extraordinary" in the field. There was no longer any competition.

The Shuberts' long feud with Winchell had eased somewhat when the columnist issued rhapsodies of praise for *Hellzapoppin!*, but it fanned up again when Winchell printed an item stating, "Lee Shubert's real romance is a former showgirl named Swanson who became an actress." Lee zealously protected his privacy. He left for Europe.

Willie Klein was facing a two-headed battle. In April of 1940, the brothers were being sued by Amedeo Passeri for a round $200,000. Mr. Passeri was trying to promote the New York Grand Opera Company and he charged the Shuberts wouldn't let him. This kind of suit Willie Klein, by this time, could fight off with one brief tied behind him. The other suit was rougher.

Jake, using the thin camouflage of his niece's husband, had bought Herrick's Ticket Agency in Boston, where the Shuberts controlled every theater suitable for a musical show. And they instituted their favorite

341

system—*all* tickets designed for ticket agencies were funneled through Herrick's. Some non-Shubert brokers had trouble getting any seats at all. And every producer coming into town was an automatic Shubert partner. The stink started, and had quick echoes in New York.

An attorney moved into the Supreme Court to test the validity of the ticket-brokerage law. He contended that the law had been "born, promulgated by, and passed" through the influence of "the Shubert interests." "It is," the charge went on, "one more part of a scheme to gain total monopoly of the theater." He added the damning phrase "just as they have in Boston."

It was a sticky mess. The two-pronged attack on the Shuberts continued for many months. Lee returned to find two states engaged in investigations of his activities. Klein was fighting off attempts to widen the investigation to cover theater bookings. Oscar Serlin was unable to make a deal with the Shuberts on *Life with Father*. He managed to book his own independent theaters by duplicating in many ways what the Shuberts had done thirty-five years before. Now the investigators were suggesting Serlin be called.

From a business standpoint, the theaters were doing well. The Shuberts had to produce only two shows for the 1940 season. Lee's hockshop supplied all the other entertainment they needed. Having struck pay-dirt with *Hellzapoppin!*, the Shuberts determined to sink another shaft with Olson and Johnson, and they called this one *Sons of Fun*. In addition to the two founders of the "no-sense" theatrical presentation, the show featured Carmen Miranda and Ella Logan. It ran for seven hundred and forty-two performances.

Their second stab was *Night of Love*, started by Jake in Chicago. It lasted two weeks there and one week in New York, and was notable for the presence of John Lodge in a bit. Perhaps Jake hoped to soften Boston criticism of the ticket scandal by using a Boston Brahmin; unfortunately, the show never got to Boston.

The Shuberts could afford it. More than 75 percent of Broadway's attractions were in one form or another Shubert "investments," partially, 50 percent, or otherwise—mostly on Lee's hockshop formula. Of those that had no part of the Shuberts' dollars, 90 percent were compelled to play Shubert theaters. It was a monopoly, in the truest sense.

As such, the Messrs. resented all other closed corporations. In the early part of 1941, they moved into high gear in their war with ASCAP. Not only had Jake been keeping score on Shubert tunes being played on the airwaves, he had John doing it and, without Jake's knowledge, John's wife. Every time Jake heard anything that had ever been played in a Shubert production, he added another check mark to his growing list—and he got angrier.

(Jake had now completely succumbed to radio. He enjoyed *all* of it—soap operas, quiz shows, music programs. And he indulged a second vice: he was a sucker for double-features. The sheer bargain of two for the price of one appealed, but in addition he was hooked on movies.)

In January, Jake announced the formation of the Performing Acts Society of the Theater, Incorporated, an association of composers and authors who would supply music for radio, in opposition to ASCAP. His timing was good; these were the initial days of the BMI (Broadcast Music, Incorporated) versus ASCAP war.

ASCAP, organized in 1914 to protect composers and lyricists from people like the Shuberts, was based on the principle that a creative artist's work when played for money should return some of the money to the creator.

With the radio explosion, ASCAP had become a collection agency, deriving income from broadcasters, who paid fees to the Society on a specially devised formula. These fees, in turn, were distributed to the ASCAP membership under a second formula. They were a music monopoly.

The radio interests, anxious to weaken the ASCAP strangle hold, had formed BMI, which they financed, encouraged, and supervised to a *great* extent. They used a *great* deal of music in the public domain— "I Dream of Jeanie with the Light Brown Hair" was played to death— and they purchased the rights to a number of music catalogs. One, in particular, was heavily laden with Spanish music, and BMI with the cooperation of the radio programmers is largely responsible for the Spanish-music boom that so dislocated the American sacroiliac. Of all the producers in the theater, only the Shuberts cooperated with BMI.

The Shubert contention from the beginning was based on their ownership of "grand rights"—the dramatic rights to a song, used in context with any portion of the play it came from. Since almost all their most successful music was written by ASCAP members and since ASCAP members were deriving radio income, the Shuberts wanted their cut. When they failed to get it, they went into business for themselves, inviting all other producers to join in the attack on radio and ASCAP.

Not at all certain that he was going to share in the ASCAP royalties being received by Friml, Romberg, et al., Jake raised the package price to the Louisville patrons who had been sponsoring a summer series of light-opera presentations. This was a small operation, out of the Shu-

343

bert warehouse, and in the main it had been supervised by John and Fred de Cordova. Now Jake raised the ante, and the Louisville people balked. They refused to pay Jake's price, and offered the entire deal to de Cordova. He explained that he would have to take it up with J. J. Shubert.

First, though, he discussed it with John. John Shubert was thirty-three years old by now, and was preparing a wryly titled show, *Johnny on a Spot*. (No, it was not autobiographical.) He couldn't care less about the Louisville operation. "It's less than we make on paper cups," he told Fred. "Take it—it's yours."

De Cordova came up to New York to meet with Jake, and found him behind his desk, glasses precariously perched on his nose, and in a seemingly benign mood. Fred explained that John was turning down Louisville and that it had been offered to him. "But, Mr. J.J.," he said, "I can't take it unless you give me the go-ahead."

Jake took off his glasses, came around the desk, and in his most fatherly tone said, "Would I stand in your way, Freddie? After all, you're like the family to me."

De Cordova started to relax, and then stiffened as Jake continued. "*But*, you buy *all* shows, *all* sets, *all* arrangements and *all* costumes from me."

Fred said he didn't think that was possible.

"You think you'll get costumes from Brooks?" demanded Jake. (Brooks was, and is, the leading costume house in New York.) "I'll take care of that right now. I'll call Jimmy Strook and no costumes. And where are you going to get music, huh?" Jake had worked himself up. "Everybody wants to produce! Everybody thinks it's such a soft job! What makes you think you can do it?"

De Cordova pointed out that he had done it all last season. Jake wasn't listening. "*Everything* you buy from me!"

Eventually, using John as ambassador, de Cordova worked out a reasonable arrangement with the Shuberts.

Lee was having other problems. Irving Maidman, then a real-estate broker, had learned that the 44th Street Theater, which the Shuberts had lost by foreclosure, was for sale. He felt it could be "stolen" for $200,000 and, he told Lee, "It's worth a million!"

"I know," replied Lee, "I have a million in it."

"But it's a steal."

Lee leaned forward on his desk, scratching himself vigorously with his letter opener. "If something costs a hundred dollars, Irving, and you buy it for fifty, if you don't need it, it isn't worth twenty-five. I don't need it."

"If you don't need it, buy it anyway," urged Maidman. "I know I can sell it to the *New York Times*."

"The *Times* isn't interested," said Lee.

It was sold to the *Times*, and the present plant of the newspaper stands where the 44th Street Theater, with the Nora Bayes Theater on the roof, once stood. It was one of the few times in real estate Lee guessed wrong.

Lee used to call Maidman "the dirt peddler." He had sobriquets for several people. Mike Todd was the *ganef*, Yiddish for "thief," Bill Doll, the wild publicist, was "the coal salesman." Some years before, when Doll had determined to produce a play, he rented a theater from the Shuberts, suffered his turkey, and wanted to get some money back on the guaranty. Eventually he did, but every time he ran into Shubert, Lee would ask solicitously about the coal business. For some reason, he confused Doll with the man who sold the Shuberts coal.

Lee learned that the woman he was sending $75 a week had married. He asked Willie Klein to go into court and seek a cessation of the payments. Willie fought him bitterly. He was afraid that this time the story would hit the papers. It did. And Lee lost. Why would he publicly air the garbage for so little money? It was completely uncharacteristic. He left for Florida to suntan his pride.

They were planning a big season. There would be a Gilbert and Sullivan Festival at the St. James. There would be two new revues. John had *Johnny on a Spot*, and business was booming. In Massachusetts, Governor Saltonstall signed a bill into law to control the Herrick Ticket Agency. In Boston, it was known as the anti-Shubert bill.

The year 1941 was dwindling to a close. The Messrs. had won far more than they had lost. Two events were happening over which they had no control, and each would have an enormous effect on the kings of the theater.

Seven blocks away, in the RCA Building, an experimental communications station was beaming something called television at some five hundred sets in the New York area. And in the Pacific, that marvelous shore duty called Pearl Harbor was about to enter the history books.

Chapter Eighteen

When World War II happened to the United States, Lee Shubert was approaching his sixty-ninth birthday. He insisted on registering for the draft. He was not motivated by patriotism. It was sheer vanity. He saw it as a way to establish his youth on the public record.

Jake was five years younger, and ignored the war. He had been fighting everyone for so long that Pearl Harbor was just December 7 to him.

The brothers were Jewish, although neither was a working Jew. The closest Lee came to a house of worship was when he drove by in a car, or when someone died. Jake occasionally attended services during the high holy days, but attended all funerals. However, as Jews, they disliked Hitler.

John commented, "If my father had had an education, he could have *been* Hitler." He was only half-joking. Pearl Harbor meant that John was going to have to tell his father about his marriage. And he was not looking forward to it. Nor was there pleasure in the offing when he knew he had to break the news to his mother.

His apprehensions were misfounded. Jake took the news with Shubert aplomb. If it was a fact, then pragmatically he would make the best of it. Catherine's reactions were predictably ambivalent. The part that clung to John as the expression of her own existence, and its meaningfulness, could never accept another human being to share him with. At the same time, the practical woman, supported by Shubert largesse and wanting one day to help rule the Shubert empire, would make her diplomatic concessions. She grudgingly accepted Eckie.

John opened *Johnny on a Spot*, which ran for four performances, and then left for Washington and the army. Eckie went with him, and before long John was named a major in charge of entertainment for Special Services, U.S. Army.

Johnny on a Spot opened one month and one day after Pearl Harbor. In that one fateful day, America's perspective had dramatically changed, and so had the theater. Plays born one year before, nursed for twelve months, cast with devotion, rehearsed with love and dedication, staged with affection, opened to a scared new world. They were out-of-date before they sold a ticket. *Johnny on a Spot* was an early war casualty.

Other Shuberts were affected by the war. Milton, the heir apparent on Lee's "side," went into the navy and, from that moment on, insisted that he be called "Commander," his naval rank. The navy commission revived his Anglophilia. Milton was, by inclination, a devotee of all things British—he even tried to use a monocle. Several years before, however, he was going to co-produce, with Gilbert Miller, an English edition of *Kind Lady*. Exasperated by the endless stream of irritating suggestions emanating from his co-producer, Miller barred Milton from the Scottish tryout theater. Instantly, Milton became a violent Anglophobe. He wouldn't even drink English tea. With his commission, and a British ally, it all changed. Once again, the "Commander" could practice with the monocle.

In January of 1942, the *Saturday Evening Post* ran an article by Robert Sylvester of the New York *Daily News*. He called it "Dream Street," defined his title as West 44th St. and devoted his story to the denizens of the magic slot, Shubert Alley, that was the shortcut from 44th to 45th Street.

The "King" of "Dream Street," said Sylvester, was Lee Shubert. His personal fortune was over $10,000,000; the Shubert empire was worth over $400,000,000. It wasn't. Only God, Lee, and Jake knew how much it was worth.

Lee approved of the *Post* story, with minor reservations. He liked being king, but objected to public airing of his worth. How could he negotiate a theater deal, pleading poverty to the adversary, if he was worth all that money? And who would pay for the paper cups?

And deals he was negotiating. They combined the Boston Comic Opera Company with the Jooss Ballet for a season of Gilbert and Sullivan dance, and kept the St. James Theater busy. Jooss had brilliantly choreographed his antiwar ballet "The Green Table," and its mood was right for the times.

In association with Clifford Fischer, they made a shrewd guess about audience preferences in wartime. They revived vaudeville with *Priorities of 1942*, starring Lou Holtz, Willie Howard, Phil Baker, and Paul Draper, and it was a huge success. When that worked, they came right back with another vaudeville show, *Keep 'Em Laughing*, which didn't do so well, so they replaced Gaxton and Moore with Gracie Fields and Argentinita and replaced the title with *Top Notchers*. It was the same show and didn't keep 'em laughing.

They booked their theaters shrewdly, kept Jake busy reviving *Blossom Time* and *The Student Prince* in various parts of the country, and Lee joined the army of "smart Broadway boys" who refused to invest in *Oklahoma*. He did, however, book it into a Shubert theater.

Driving back from Boston, where he had gone to see a tryout of *Oklahoma*, Lee remarked, "Who wants a musical with a funeral in the second act?"

The Shuberts proved their patriotism by providing, at no charge, the facilities for the Boston Stage Door Canteen and its larger counterpart in New York. Lee loved to walk into the New York version and even wait on tables. Jake would attend infrequently, assuring everyone that his son was in service.

When the rationing program occassionally made it difficult for the canteens to find butter, mysteriously Lee could make it appear. He supplied tubs and tubs of butter in New York, to go along with the thousands of seats he made available for servicemen all through the war.

Mrs. Richard Rodgers, then heading a Red Cross Blood Unit, wanted to solicit a "theatrical" blood-bank donation. Hesitantly, she approached Lee, seeking the use of the stage of the Majestic Theater as the "collection center."

Lee agreed—on one condition. She froze, expecting the Shubert bite. He named his condition. One, use the lobby—it was as big as the stage and more convenient. And two, he would make it available if he could provide food and drinks for all contributors.

They had made no public announcement, but slowly the Shuberts were retiring from "production." Like so many other entrepreneurs who had started as hockshops and graduated into respectability as "bankers," they were becoming the Rothschilds of Broadway, the Chase Manhattan of the indigent producer.

They were making financial investments in the majority of the plays that would come to Broadway; they were partners, fifty–fifty, in the only booking companies; they controlled the booking companies because they controlled the theaters in every key city; and Lee didn't even have to fall asleep at auditions—he just didn't have auditions.

At about this time, the Lee Shubert investment legend emerged on Theater's Main Street. "You put up half the money," went the Lee legend, "I will put up half. Put your money where your mouth is, and I will put *my* money where your mouth is."

It was not quite true. Under the terms of the Shubert investment formula, he wasn't really putting up half the money.

It was the Equity Bond, the theater-rental guaranty, the use of lights, sets, and costumes—all figured as a part of the Shubert "investment." He was for many years the only Broadway angel who was taking depreciation on part of his investment.

The war economy had begun to percolate through everyone's bank accounts. Everyone was working. There were limited ways to spend the fat war wages. More and more people had "luxury" money for the theater. Motion pictures were experiencing the biggest take they had ever known, and the theater, despite a dearth of anything really meaningful, sold out.

The ticket-brokerage business was entering its Golden Age. And the Shuberts controlled ticket distribution in New York, Boston, Philadelphia, Detroit, Chicago. (They also controlled the legitimate theater in those centers, plus Los Angeles, Baltimore, Cincinnati and Pittsburgh. In San Francisco, Lou Lurie controlled the legitimate theaters and booked through the Shuberts.)

Now, in addition to the legally set markup, there was a wholesale scalping operation in hit shows. A $5 seat might be bringing $25 on the market. Lee remarked mournfully that the "one thing you can't control in a theater is 'ice.'" A lot of people felt he condoned it because he couldn't stop it. A lot of other people don't think he wanted it stopped because so much of it was pouring as tax-free, unreported income into his bank vaults. And if Lee was getting any, then Jake was getting half of it.

In the middle of 1942, they favored Broadway with the rawest revue that had hit New York in many a year. They subtitled it "a revue-vaudeville-burlesque show," and it was mostly the latter. The title was *Wine, Women and Song*.

The censors fell on it with fervor. Before they were finished, the show *and* the theater were padlocked, and the Ambassador Theater stayed closed for almost a year, its license revoked because of the vulgarity of the presentation.

While Willie Klein was trying to keep *Wine, Women and Song* open by injunction, the Shuberts took another turn with Olson and Johnson in their patented *Hellizapoppin!* formula. This one was called *Count Me In*, and no one knows who the first critic was to say, "Count me out."

Hardly had the censor's axe descended on "Wine, etc." than Lee found himself facing another embarrassment. *Native Son*, the realistic dramatization of the Richard Wright novel, was revived at the Majestic Theater (Shubert) and the *Catholic News* deplored the play, terming much of it "objectionable."

349

Lee ordered the play closed; he was taking back his theater before they padlocked it. The instant Lee issued his closing notice, the protests began. The Dramatists' Guild led the counterattack and were soon joined by every important theater figure. Beset on all sides, Lee was compelled to back off. *Native Son* stayed open for the rest of its run.

The brothers renewed their feud with the box-office union, whose members, nationwide, were seeking a pay raise. The Shuberts refused to negotiate, were soon faced with a strike in all their theaters—in Philadelphia, New York, Boston, Chicago, etc.—and so his economic discretion compensating for the better part of his economic valor, Lee offered a fifteen-dollar-a-week raise for all employees who belonged to the union.

The union accepted, but in those "controlled" days the issue had to go to the War Labor Board. The board studied the case and arrived at a conclusion: they approved the raise—but made it retroactive to the last Labor Day, or approximately six months of back pay, to be donated by the Shuberts to their employees. Lee screamed like a stuck pig, and paid.

Lee had gauged the public ready for another *Ziegfeld Follies*, and the Shuberts put one, under Harry Kaufman's auspices, in work. It starred Milton Berle, who, ever since he had accompanied one of the 1920 *Florodora* sextet on stage, had wanted to star in a *Follies*. The Shuberts accommodated him in 1943, and the critics were not lavish in their praise. They found the show much more Shubert than Ziegfeld. Nonetheless, it was an instantaneous hit, and would run for two years—longer than any Ziegfeld *Ziegfeld Follies* had ever run.

Jake, who had been reviving *The Student Prince* all over America, brought an edition into New York, staged by "Mr. J.J. Shubert." In Chicago, where he had opened it, the reviewers found it "shoddy," which was one of the most generous of their adjectives, and in New York it was termed "a shamefully seedy revival of the tuneful Romberg operetta," or "another Shubert bankruptcy auction production." Louis Kronenberger, critic for *PM*, who had murdered the *Ziegfeld Follies* and Berle, stated that "the Shuberts are up to their old, penny-pinching tricks." The critical consensus was that it was a typical Shubert warehouse production, on consignment to the New York ticket buyers. Jake was livid —he had personally hung the garlands.

His resentments were mollified when Theater License Commissioner Moss gave the Shuberts permission to reopen the Ambassador. They took the padlock off with *Blossom Time*, another Jake-staged revival, and again, as much critical attention was paid to the antiquity of the costumes, sets, and props, as was paid to the show.

Now Jake was more than livid. He barred Louis Kronenberger of *PM* from all Shubert theaters. On the same day, he filed suit against *Variety* for $300,000; the charge—libel. Jake was judicious in his allegations. He wanted only $100,000 for what *Variety* had said about *The Student Prince*. But, for their comments on something called *Cocktails at 5*, he demanded $200,000.

Cocktails at 5 was Jake's version of a "Continental, sophisticated revue." It was total disaster in Chicago, where it ran one dismal week, and *Variety's* Chicago correspondent added gratuitously "that it combined the worst elements of the Shubert warehouse, cunningly collected for just one unfortunate show."

Jake wanted to bring it to New York, explaining to the world that "Chicago ain't sophisticated enough for this kind of smart revue." But he was outvoted. Actually, the show made *Wine, Women and Song* look like something by Louisa May Alcott. Foiled in his attempt to revive Broadway, Jake filed the suit against *Variety*.

Variety wryly commented, "We don't think our treasurer can count that high," and like every other Shubert vs. *Variety* litigation, it died away.

It had been a fairly long time since the Messrs. had barred a theater critic or taken on the press in other ways, and they decided to keep in practice. This time it was Lee, and he announced that he was taking Robert Garland of the New York *World Telegram* off the free list. He couldn't really "bar" Garland because there was a state law that said a ticket purchased must be honored. (The Shuberts had fought that, too.)

When Garland was informed that his down-front seats would no longer be available and that he would have to sit in the back of the theater, his only reply was that "maybe that's a better place to sit to see a Shubert show."

At this same time, the New Opera Company had brought in a successful revival of *The Merry Widow*, starring Jan Kiepura and Marta Eggerth. They tried to get bookings for a tour from the United Booking Office, only to be put off with repeated assertions that no dates were available.

Then, Lee announced a Shubert revival of *The Merry Widow*! It opened in Philadelphia, and Sam Zolotow, in his Sunday column in the *New York Times*, referred to "the Battle of the Widows." Zolotow stated that, after having failed to get its route from UBO, the New Opera production had gone to the West Coast for a successful four-city tour, and then come back to the New York City Center for four more weeks. UBO now was offering a tour, but by coincidence it consisted of cities into which the Shubert *Widow* would be booked first. The New Opera group decided to plan its own tour.

Zolotow concluded his item by reporting the Philadelphia opening of the Shubert *Merry Widow* as "one of the most amateurish productions to grace the Philadelphia stage in several seasons." Earlier, he indicated that the brothers were planning a second company to tour the South.

The operetta was in the public domain and anyone could produce it and avoid a royalty payment. Zolotow and the majority of the other theater reporters didn't resent the Shubert production, although they felt it was dirty pool. The booking question was another matter.

Lee was furious. He demanded that Greneker do something about it, and the Shubert press chief, already a veteran at the joustings, called Zolotow. He told the reporter he had been unjust, unfair, and had shown his antipathy toward the Shuberts. Greneker went on to state that he had read every Philadelphia review and could not find Zolotow's quote, which made Zolotow guilty of lousy journalism.

The Battle of the Widows went on, and Zolotow, who hotly defended what the *Times* had printed, was in the Shubert doghouse for quite a while.

During the box-office strike negotiation, the Messrs. had claimed no ownership in Detroit, which was an outright lie. Now they ordered the house manager at the Lafayette in Detroit to sue Petrillo for more than $500,000, asserting that Petrillo's union was featherbedding the orchestra in the theater.

The musicians walked out in protest, and the stagehands and actors honored the picket line. When the strike threatened to spread, the Shuberts settled—presumably on a theater they did not own or control.

There was no room for doubt about who owned what, when Lee became a censor. Lee Sabinson was producing *Trio*, a play that dealt with lesbianism. He had booked a Shubert theater in New York. Things were peaceful in the City of Brotherly Love, with no attacks on the theme of *Trio*, when the Shuberts announced that they were canceling the theater lease in New York. Now the bluenoses began to act in Philadelphia.

Sabinson went to see Shubert at once. Lee was candid with him. He was not going to have any theater of his padlocked, ever again. Sabinson's protests were useless. As in the case of *Native Son*, there was a large public reaction. This time Lee remained adamant.

Trio was forced to close in Philadelphia, while Sabinson frantically shopped for another theater. He finally made arrangements with the Belasco Theater (no longer a Shubert operation), and then, after a fairly successful run, when the theater's license came up for renewal, municipal government pressure compelled the theater owner to evict the show.

The *New York Times* remarked that there seemed to be two kinds of censorship in the theater: one was the Wales Act, on the statute books, and the second was a Shubert fist.

More immediately painful to Lee than the *Trio* mess was an edict by Commissioner Moss, forbidding eight theaters to sell any tickets to brokers. Moss was compelled to take the drastic step by the flagrance of "scalping" on hit shows. The general public found it impossible to purchase seats at the box office for any successful presentation. But, if the would-be buyer could ante up enough extra money, tickets were always available at the brokers. Very obviously, something was wrong, and Moss suspected the theater owners. Of the eight houses singled out for this special treatment, four were Shubert theaters and, of course, all eight theaters housed hits.

Although there was no specific charge filed against the owners of the eight theaters, the implication was pretty clear. The Shuberts issued a bitter denunciation of "Moss's Hitlerian action," threatened to file for an injunction, and then pulled in their horns and meekly went along with the order. They had fingerprints all over the tickets in question.

Propitiously, it was just at this time that Lee issued a blast at the 20 percent tax on theater tickes. That same week, he opened negotiations to buy out his partners in the Majestic, Royale, and Golden theaters, and then bawled out Danton Walker for printing that the Shuberts controlled all but a dozen of New York's houses.

One house where their control was getting thin was the 46th Street Theater. It was under lease to the Shuberts, and they had an option to purchase, but the owner and the Shuberts were not getting along.

The Messrs. had backed *Dark of the Moon* and booked it into the 46th Street Theater. Reluctant to pick up their buyer's option, the brothers stalled and stalled, until finally the owner, disgusted with the pace of the negotiation, made other arrangements. He sold the theater to the City Investment Company, which purchased the theater under the name of Amusement Properties, Incorporated.

No sooner did they have the theater in their possession than the new proprietors invoked the terms of the lease; they served notice on the Shuberts that they were taking over the house because the gross receipts

353

were less than $17,500 a week. Under the terms of the lease, the theater operation would revert to the owners whenever the receipts dipped below the stated figure.

Immediately, the Shuberts began purchasing enough tickets each week to make up the difference between their gross and the guarantee of $17,500. They were holding on to the theater, not only to protect their lease but to house *The Red Mill*, a revival they had booked into the theater from the same West Coast farm club that had given them *Song of Norway*.

(This was a fascinating Shubert ploy. Usually, when they wanted to evict a show for what promised to be a more profitable attraction, word went out to the box-office men not to sell tickets, to turn away customers, so that the show would fall below the stipulated minimum. Now they had reversed the process.)

They won the first round in court, but eventually the 46th Street became an independent house. *The Red Mill* went into the non-Shubert Ziegfeld Theater.

For the Shuberts, the war years were a pleasant blur. Business was good. Their production load was small. If there were problems with coal, or cream—well, they had friends. The navy survived Milton Shubert, the army put John Shubert in charge of the entertainment section, all of America welcomed Lee as chairman of the theater division of the March of Dimes.

A New York newspaper noted that in the period beginning with Jake's latest *Blossom Time* revival to V-J Day, the Messrs. had brought a measly five productions to Broadway. True, they were shareholders in almost everything else, but their producing days were just about ended. Perhaps they made a lot of money on these real-estate deals, but it was hit tickets which were becoming a major part of Shubert operations. Lee and Jake swore they didn't like it; they did little to change it.

If anyone around the theater didn't know this, they were made aware of it at the end of April in 1946. Milton was back in the saddle, or possibly, back on the poop deck, on "Lee's side." John was Jake's heir apparent. Business was good, and Rodgers and Hammerstein were producing a new Irving Berlin musical, *Annie Get Your Gun*, starring Ethel Merman.

The show, prejudged an outright smash hit, was due into the (Shubert) Imperial Theater the end of April. They started loading the show in on Thursday, April 25, when one of the main girders in the building suddenly buckled. The crew stopped work, the Fire Department and the building inspectors were called, and the Imperial was declared unsafe for occupancy. It would take two weeks to make the necessary repairs.

What was to be done with *Annie Get Your Gun*? A Rodgers and Hammerstein production of an important Broadway musical by Irving Berlin starring Ethel Merman was not inexpensive. It represented a large weekly cash outlay, and holding it for two weeks with full salaries for all, became a major economic factor.

Lee Shubert got busy. It was a hell of a way for a seventy-year-old man to spend his time, but with a prodigious burst of energy, invention, and phone calls, Lee managed to keep one show *in* Boston (and out of Philadelphia), to keep a second show *out* of Boston, and thus to make a theater in Philadelphia available for *Annie*.

Before this could be accomplished, it was late Friday night. *Annie*, under the managership of Morrie Jacobs, loaded on trucks and set out for Philadelphia. The Sunday editions of the papers in Philadelphia were "locked up." No line of print announcing the sensational musical could appear. It was a totally unheralded Merman appearance, in a Berlin musical, and a chance for all theater lovers, Berlin devotees, Merman fans to come to the box office and get seats.

It must be explained that the Shuberts had a monopoly in the Pennsylvania city. They owned every theater capable of presenting a legitimate play. And there was a well-lived fact of theater life in Philadelphia—no one could buy a good seat for a show on its way to New York, except from a ticket broker. There were *never* any choice seats available at the box office—not for a hit. There had been periodic "investigations" by the city authorities, and occasionally someone was raked over the judicial coals, but week in and week out during the "season," if you wanted to see a play on its way to New York, you called a broker, paid the premium, and sat in the orchestra.

Now, came *Annie*. There were no newspaper ads, no advance publicity of any kind. It wasn't until Saturday that the producers were able to start radio spot announcements, advertising the two-week run of the play. And a very bright reporter for the Philadelphia *Record*, Louise Lee Outlaw, got herself a brainstorm.

On Saturday morning, at 6:45 A.M., Miss Outlaw started the line at the ticket office of the Shubert Theater in Philadelphia. At 9:30, the window opened, and there were fifty-odd eager play lovers in the queue behind Miss Outlaw. Miss Outlaw requested two seats in the fifth row center for the following Saturday.

"The first nineteen rows are all sold out," she was told.

"Never mind Saturday," suggested Miss Outlaw. "Any evening."

355

"The first nineteen rows are all sold out for all evening performances," was the reply.

This was a rather astonishing phenomenon, to Miss Outlaw's way of thinking. The usual Philadelphia box-office reply of "Sorry, but we had a heavy mail-order write-in" could not apply. Where were the tickets? The legitimate brokers had none. Miss Outlaw chased her story, and no one had an answer. Greneker in New York professed himself "mystified." Lee Shubert said, "I can't understand it. Why, it's impossible unless someone grabbed all those tickets for himself. I haven't been able to reach Mr. Lawrence (nephew Lawrence Shubert Lawrence, Sr.) but when I do, and find out about what this is all about, I'll call you back." Lee didn't call back. Lee was having apoplexy, and attempting to give same, courtesy of AT&T, to Lawrence.

One unfortunate Shubert employee in Lawrence's bailiwick suggested to Miss Outlaw that "all the good seats for the show had been bought up by the New York people, the producers."

This prompted a call to Oscar Hammerstein, the co-producer, who was tracked down at his Bucks County farm. Hammerstein was amazed to get the news of the ticket shortage, and the Shubert explanation of why it existed.

"All the first nineteen rows for two weeks? We don't have that many friends!" he told Miss Outlaw. "Richard Rodgers and I have nothing to do with the distribution of tickets. Mr. Rodgers has not purchased one ticket for the Philadelphia run, and neither have I. The matter of selling and distributing the tickets is entirely in the hands of the Shubert office. You will have to get your explanation from them." He paused and then added, "No, I do not think I want to make any guesses."

When all attempts to get Lee back on the phone failed, the story went to press, and everybody on the "inside" giggled. It was fairly obvious what had happened to the tickets, and it was likewise apparent that someone was caught with his hand in the till. No names were being named, but it was embarrassing to be called Mr. Lawrence in Philadelphia that weekend.

Lee was on the phone with his nephew, his mahogany face redder than ever, his voice reedy as a boy's, and the stutter very much in evidence. "Get those God-damned tickets back, you hear me? I don't want to know anything except you get those tickets!"

Lee, accompanied by Whittaker, took the next train to Philadelphia. A flustered Lawrence met them at the train, and they walked to the theater, Lee delicately skinning his nephew step by step in a lovely dissection of his intelligence, his tact, his business acumen, and his sense of responsibilty. It was an awe-inspiring performance, and Whittaker kept wishing he were elsewhere—it is not amusing to see another man decapitated.

By the next morning, seven thousand "missing" tickets mysteriously reappeared in the ticket racks. For the first time in human memory, the average playgoer could buy tickets at the box office for a hit show in Philadelphia. If Lee had hoped to bury the scandal by getting the tickets back and personally ordering a special ad in the papers announcing that "select locations will go on sale Monday morning," he was being naïve.

It merely made more news when the tickets reappeared. The papers, particularly the *Record*, had a field day with the yarn. Lee had implicated his nephew in the disappearance; he tried to clear him the following day. "I never said that Mr. Lawrence gave the choice tickets to the speculators. If the tickets were given to speculators, they were given by the theater's treasurer. . . . Now that we have found out what the situation is, we will have to see to it that in the future the public will continue to be able to buy the good seats at the box office."

The affair *Annie Get Your Gun* died away. They did not fire the theater manager.

Lee hardly had time to assuage his damaged pride by buying some Broadway property and consolidating his East Side holdings, when he was in the papers again.

In the early part of August 1946, he was visited by some gentlemen from the Anti-Trust Division of the Department of Justice. They wanted to talk with him about Shubert Theater Enterprises and the United Booking Office.

Although they made no specific inquiries (yet) about the ticket situation, no doubt the Philadelphia incident was part of the motivation for the visit.

"Producers," explained Lee, "can use a Shubert theater in New York, and never once utilize United Booking. But if they use UBO on the road, then they must stay UBO for the life of the play."

The Anti-Trust Division callers promised to come back, and the press covered the story. The articles pointed out that the Shuberts owned seventeen theaters in New York, controlled the booking of an eighteenth, and that in Philadelphia they owned all the theaters, and all of them were UBO, and in Boston they controlled all theaters but one and *they* were all UBO. Translated into practicality, this meant that if a show wanted to play Boston or Philadelphia, it would have to sign a life contract with UBO (and shows *had* to play one or both cities). It was not necessary to add that if the play didn't sign with UBO, it might have trouble getting a New York theater. It was a very cozy setup.

PM went on to point out that as of August, there was a total of nine-

357

teen theaters showing attractions in New York, and of these, eight were Shubert houses. (Another three of their theaters—the Ambassador, the Winter Garden, and the Golden—were temporarily running films; the rest were dark.) Oddly, the five best-selling musicals of the season were *all* in Shubert houses. *Annie, Call Me Mister, Carousel, Oklahoma!* and *Three to Make Ready*—all were Shubert tenants. And every contract stipulated "house seats" for the theater owner—anywhere from twenty-five to seventy orchestra center seats per performance, which the Shuberts could sell, allot to broker or—.

The only other musicals in New York were two revivals, booked into independent houses. It was very coincidental.

Tired of being on the receiving end of all this attention, the Messrs. came to the conclusion that a counterattack was in order. They sued Columbia Pictures, with Trebuhs, their wholly owned real-estate subsidiary, doing the suing.

Columbia had just finished *The Jolson Story* and was going to open it at the Radio City Music Hall. The Shuberts didn't want it opened. Not unless they were paid, oh, a reasonable sum—like $500,000, for example.

Their reasoning went like this. They had employed Jolson for many years. He had appeared in eight separate Shubert hits at the Winter Garden, not to mention the Shubert theater they had graced with his name. But it was Jake's Winter Garden that was their major complaint.

They humbly petitioned the court that Columbia not be permitted to show any part of the Winter Garden, inside or out, or to use the name "Winter Garden," or to mention "Shubert" unless they received Shubert permission and paid "valuable consideration." In Shubert parlance, "valuable consideration" was at least $500,000.

In case this wasn't enough to influence the decision, they stated to the court that, some years before, they had commissioned a script called "Winter Garden," and that *The Jolson Story*, in part, was based on this exemplary script, Shubert-owned, and written by Ward Morehouse. Mr. Morehouse was embarrassed and taciturn.

A few months later, Judge James McNally threw the Shubert case out of court, and Lee sailed for Europe—his first trip since 1939. The war was really over.

He returned in July 1947, and Jake sailed on July 2 for *his* Grand Tour. Both men, presumably, visited Switzerland. Lee announced seven productions on his return, including a new *Ziegfeld Follies*. They would not produce a *Follies*, and they would produce only one of the other six. They were just about retired from active production.

The *New York Times* pointed out that in the last twelve months, the Shuberts had produced exactly one show—*Hidden Horizon*, another Agatha Christie British mystery. It was not successful.

Their colorful wars with the actors, the composers, the playwrights were gently coming to an end. Now they were bankers, and as bankers their battles would be with federal authorities, with producers, with unions, and, most of all, with mass media.

They had no respect for dramatists; but they needed them. They were completely flexible men when it came to principle—Lee could attack authors as noncontributors, fight battles to the death against the Guild, and then issue statements (in attempts to beat on Actors' Equity) terming the playwright the key to theatrical success.

They had less respect for actors. "To be an actor takes more nerve than skill," Lee said. Jake would cajole them, bully them, and when he felt it necessary, physically attack them. Together, the Messrs. would cheat them on contracts, lie to them about deals, sue them in court, and then woo them when they needed them.

Composers they never understood. Directors they fired and rehired, treated with contempt.

No, they had no respect for talent. They admired it and used it, and Jake had a damned good nose for smelling it out. But they never respected it. They never respected anything they could hire, buy, or sell.

Now that they were essentially real-estate operators, theatrical bankers, and were in the ticket business, they zeroed in on a brand-new enemy—the ticket broker. "They invest nothing," Lee told the *Daily News*. "They have no expenses. There are new brokers every day. Anybody goes and gets a license and he is a broker. If they would help sell tickets to mediocre successes [*sic*] it would be different. But they don't want to do that. All they want to do is sell tickets to hits at advanced prices. They're just a lot of parasites."

They had just financed and opened the newest ticket agency in New York, and in Boston their niece was suing Jake for her 25 percent of the profits of Herrick's Ticket Agency, owned by the Shuberts. They were very broad-minded.

Chapter Nineteen

By 1948, the Shubert offices had settled into a routine that was not nearly as interesting as in the heyday of their production activities.

Milton was on Lee's "side" and John was on Jake's, and the various employees of the two factions used to discuss among themselves what would happen after Jake died. No one ever talked about Lee's demise—it just didn't seem possible. Obviously, the Shuberts had thought about it.

They organized the Sam S. Shubert Foundation, which was reputed to have about $500,000 in hand, with the bulk of the Shubert fortune to go to it. They stated that it had already made sizable bequests to various organizations and individuals. Jake was president, but not on the board. Lee was on the board and so was John.

They had not grown any less cantankerous. They were still at war with the unions. Lee issued pronunciamento after pronunciamento blaming the unions for making it impossible for producers to work. Jake, ever the calm one, merely canceled thirteen productions in Cincinnati, eager to fight Petrillo on a featherbedding charge. It would be a Taft-Hartley test case.

The Shuberts entered into an agreement with WPIX, the *Daily News* TV station, granting WPIX the right to televise Shubert opening nights. It was early in the TV story, and the newspapers buried the item in the back pages. They devoted a lot more prominence and a lot more space to Lee Shubert's divorce. On September 2, 1948, in Reno, Mrs. Lee Shubert, the former Marcella Swanson, sued her husband (!) for divorce, charging mental cruelty.

Since no one knew they were married, the show world was, to put it mildly, surprised. There was an insistent buzz of cynicism. Where had they been married and when?

The affidavit which accompanied Marcella's plea stated that the marriage had taken place in Berlin in June of 1936. The cruelty was based on the fact that Lee had never set up a home for her and had never publicly acknowledged the marriage. He certainly had not.

The smart boys along Shubert Alley instantly came up with a number of theories. The first went along these lines. They had never been married, but now Lee was "tidying up the battlefield." He was no longer a young man, he wanted to legitimatize a relationship that had lasted since the twenties, he wanted to "settle" some money on Marcella, so he arranged a divorce without ever having been married at all.

To substantiate this, they pointed out: Guess who was Marcella's attorney in the Reno matter? None other than Willie Klein. True, he was not licensed to practice in Nevada, but he was "presented" to the court by Marcella's attorney, and attended the closed hearing.

One of the more interesting of the "sealed documents" made part of the record was "an agreement made the 15th day of July, 1948" between Lee and Marcella, and signed by them in the presence of Willie Klein. Under the terms of this agreement, Marcella was to receive $600 a month for the rest of her life, subject only to the condition that the payments cease should she remarry. *That* was on the record. The amount of cash paid to her as a settlement was not mentioned.

Again, the disbelievers built on the theory. They picked Berlin to be married in because it had been bombed out in World War II and there were no records available. No one asked to see a marriage certificate in Reno, and why would Marcella hire Willie Klein to represent her against Lee Shubert? It made no sense. No, this was a Shubert divorce, and a Shubert divorce had to have an angle. It was probably a convenient tax device for Lee to give Marcella money, do the nice thing, and make sure she waived all rights to his estate. Agreement July 15; arrive in Reno one week later. It was all too pat.

It is difficult to believe that Willie Klein would so flout the laws of Nevada, run the risk of a stupid exposure and conceivable action by the bar association just to make Lee look honorable. No, they had to have married.

In New York, Lee's divorce created a sensation. Bob Sylvester, a Broadway columnist for the New York *Daily News* ran his story on the divorce, and was in a restaurant the next day when Lee and Milton entered. Lee spotted Sylvester and called him over to the table.

"Some day," said Lee, already beginning to stammer, "some d-d-day, I'm going to knock your h-head off. You g-g-get m-me in m-m-more d-d-damn trouble!"

Sylvester, assuming that Lee was referring to the divorce story, defended it. "Mr. Lee, the divorce is news, and I had to print it."

"I'm not talking about that," said Lee. "It's that other thing you printed."

Sylvester was confused. "What other thing?"

"You keep telling everybody I'm seventy-three years old. Everytime you print anything about me, you make me five years older."

"But *Who's Who* says you were born in 1875," objected Sylvester.

"I'll bring you my birth certificate! I am sixty-seven—I will be sixty-eight my next birthday."

Lee was half a year away from his seventy-sixth birthday, and possibly he noticed Sylvester's hesitation. He dictated a memo to Greneker.

"Mr. Greneker—Herewith order form from *Who's Who*. You will note I have changed birth date to 1878. Have them send me bill. $9.75. LS."

Lee had decided to be, for the time being, just seventy. This was one step toward reality; after all, eight years before, he had tried to be forty-five, and register for the draft. The *Who's Who* order was mailed 9-20-48.

Nothing is sensational for more than three days in show business —not even a Lee Shubert divorce. It died away in the press. Lee was strangely lonely. He spent long hours—long even for him—in the office. His nephew Milton was in constant attendance, and when he wasn't seeing his uncle, he was seeing Marcella. Lee was troubled, and not only about his ex-wife. There were other problems.

Their long-term leases on the theaters immediately adjacent to Shubert Alley were expiring in 1952. Already, certain smart "operators" were approaching the Astor estate, which owned the land, making offers.

In between changing his age (again)—and getting divorced—and several minor affairs like a fight with the Dramatists' Guild, Lee found time for meetings with William Zeckendorf, a leading New York realtor. He was disturbed by rumors that not only were the "operators" after his theaters, but a motion-picture consortium was also in the act.

The motion-picture fellows were interested in acquiring the property—and more—in setting up, in midtown New York, a film manufacturing complex, which could take advantage of the talent in Manhattan. They were going to call it New York Film City, in imitation of Radio City. Jake was a picture fan, true enough, but not when it came to pirating *his* theaters. Lee didn't even like pictures; he always called a bad play "a cheap movie script." The Shuberts moved quickly.

On November 10, 1948, in what was called the single largest real-estate transaction in the country since Rockefeller Center, the Shuberts bought the Booth, Plymouth, Shubert, and Broadhurst theaters, together with the land under Shubert Alley. The price was reported to be between $3,500,000 and $4,000,000. Bill Zeckendorf brokered the deal.

Bob Sylvester, possibly in apology for revealing Lee's "true age," said that "they saved show business for the living theater—and for themselves." They now *owned* the block except for the two hotels at either end and the Sardi Building across the Alley on 44th Street, plus huge "protecting" chunks all the way to Eighth Avenue on the Sardi side. And unlike all other New Yorkers with streets named for them, as A. J. Liebling pointed out, the Shuberts worked *and* lived on their own domain.

.   .   .

Shubert Alley. Milton Shubert (left), an unidentified gentleman, Lee Shubert and John Shubert. That's the *New York Times* plant on West 44th Street behind them.

The Remarriage. Lee Shubert and Mrs. Lee Shubert (Marcella) after their divorce and remarriage—1948.

Lee had not seen Marcella, and he missed her. Zeckendorf, who had grown very fond of Shubert, suggested that Lee come to dinner; he and his wife would invite Marcella.

Lee refused. "Absolutely not," he said. "No, no, no."

"But this is silly," said Zeckendorf. "What can be wrong with a dinner party at our house, with you and Marcella as guests. After all, you're not exactly strangers."

Shubert wrestled with the idea. Finally, as always, he negotiated. "On two conditions," he said.

Zeckendorf stared at him.

"First," said Lee, "it must be perfectly clear to Marcella that I didn't ask for such a dinner."

Zeckendorf grinned. "It's my idea," he replied.

"Second," said Lee, "nobody must know about such a dinner."

He won both "negotiated" points.

Nobody heard of such a dinner. For the first time since the divorce, Lee and his wife were at the same table. He was stiff to begin with, then relaxed, became extraordinarily engaging. He was flirting with his own wife. He told funny stories, did some of his favorite imitations, tried to make a hit. He did.

They remarried shortly afterward, in a quiet ceremony in Florida. But they had little time for a second honeymoon. Ticket prices were coming back to haunt the Shuberts.

South Pacific, one of the colossal hits of all time, was playing at the Majestic Theater, Shubert-owned. The price of seats from scalpers had risen to astronomical proportions, and it was next to impossible to secure seats at the box office. There was a mountain of complaints on License Commissioner Murtagh's desk, and finally he launched an investigation.

Ticket investigations were nothing new in Shubert affairs; they had been going on for years. But the memory of Philadelphia and *Annie Get Your Gun* was still fresh, and the Boston suit was still in the courts. It was all very embarrassing.

The treasurer of the Majestic, the man "charged" with ticket distribution, was Jack Pearl, no relation to the comedian of the same name. He refused to give any information to Murtagh, and Lee was summoned. Lee was vague. He did not "bother with these details; they are in the hands of assistants." No, he really didn't know too much about the ticket situation. Righteously, he suspended Pearl.

Called before Murtagh again, Pearl still refused to answer questions, and Lee fired him. Pearl was taking the whipping, and "would be taken care of," went the word. A month after he was fired, he was re-hired as the treasurer of the Mansfield Theater. There was another uproar about this strange turn of events, but it all died down.

Shortly after the investigation had sputtered out, as all ticket investigations seem to do, Lee was asked what good had come out of the probe. He thought about if for several seconds, and when he replied, he was both grave and succinct. "None."

Lee Shubert was soon to be called on for the most skillful negotiating of his life. In Washington, the Honorable Emanuel Celler, chairman of the House Judiciary Committee, loosed a vicious tirade against the Shuberts. They were facing the most serious crisis in their history.

"The Shubert interests," blasted Celler, "have clamped a stranglehold on the theater. Theatrical people are afraid to testify." (One performer stated, "I'd never act again in the legitimate theater if you used my name.")

"I have checked," said Celler, "and I have found a malodorous picture. The Shuberts control 60 percent of New York, and 90 percent of legitimate theater elsewhere. They have allocated tickets to hit shows to 'pet' brokers, using kickbacks of all kinds."

He was talking about "ice," and the *South Pacific* scandal was what had provoked the blast. "In Boston," said Celler, "a sister of the Shuberts [he was wrong—it was Jake and Lee] has control of the brokerage agencies, and on hit shows it is almost impossible to get tickets unless one gets them through an agency."

The representative talked about "intimidation of producers!" "They are afraid to testify. They would be put out of business. They don't know where they could house their productions, either on the road or in New York, if they spoke out."

He put the Messrs. in good company, announcing that his monopoly investigation was going to look "carefully" at U.S. Steel, Dupont, the soap companies, with special attention to Lever Brothers, and at Pan Am Airways.

Celler was cynical about the taxes paid on marked-up tickets. "You can bet all the tea in China no income tax is paid on *South Pacific* tickets which sell for twenty-five dollars plus."

It was a very strong attack against the Shuberts. The implications were plain, and on 44th Street, painful. Milton Weir, Willie Klein's partner, was the Shubert spokesman.

A court of appeals had already examined such charges, in connection with the rental lawsuit over the Guild Theater, said Weir. The court found "charges of monopoly are merely conclusions and surmises, and rather weak ones at that."

"Representative Celler," Weir went on, "is wholly unfamiliar with the theatrical business. . . . His inflammatory statement has no support in fact."

Jules Pfeiffer, in Chicago, just a short half-month ago, had filed suit against the Messrs. for nearly $2,000,000, charging that the Shuberts were a trust in control of 95 percent of the second-class theaters in the country, and were keeping him from making a living. The Messrs. had paid very little attention to that suit. After all, they had been sued for $2,000,000 before, and on similar charges. Now they hastily prepared answers to the charges, and settled the Pfeiffer matter for $40,000.

There were rumors aplenty coming out of Washington. The attorney general was about to launch a suit against the brothers. The Department of Justice was investigating UBO. There was soon to be another antitrust suit filed in Boston, and another in Philadelphia.

From out of the woodwork of the past came a batch of unattributed quotes from disgruntled people of the theater. "They blackballed me, and I couldn't work." "They gouge on every contract." "I was in Lee's office when the payoff was made." They wouldn't testify, but they would smear—anonymously.

In the midst of the mess, the Teamsters' Union charged Jake with using nonunion labor to transfer properties in New York and refused to move the new season's shows into the theaters. Jake was fed up with being the only monopoly in the theater, so *he* sued the teamsters and seven other unions as a monopoly.

Celler came back ten days later with another blast. His reasoning went like this: Because of their ownership and control of so many theaters, and because they invest money in many productions (Lee's theatrical "banking"), the Shuberts have more than the average producer's interest in the disposal of tickets. For example: *South Pacific* at the Majestic, owned by the Shuberts. (Lee was beginning to hate the very mention of the show.)

"Lee Shubert has the right to purchase sixty of the best seats for his personal use every performance." Thus eight performances per week equal four hundred and eighty tickets per week, bought at the box-office price of $6.60 That comes to $3,168 per week, or $164,736 worth of tickets per year! The "best" seats for *South Pacific* were bringing $75 per pair from scalpers. And that was only one show playing in a Shubert house!

Lee had forty seats for every performance of *Kiss Me Kate*, twenty-five for *Happy Time* and another bundle for *Call Me Madam*. The total markup in tax-free dollars becomes astronomical. And how was the money divided? Did none of it come back to the Shuberts? All of it? Some of it?

"Who gets these tickets?" demanded Celler. "Do favored brokers procure them? Is there any accounting of them? What is paid for most of them? Who gets the proceeds? Is the admission tax paid? Is the income tax paid for the profits of their sale? What do the favored brokers pay for the privilege of disposing of these tickets? What are the kickbacks?"

While Celler was haranguing on Capitol Hill, the attorney general was filing an antitrust suit down the street. The ultimatum was stated clearly. Either get rid of the booking branch of the business, or get rid of the presentation branch. Either way, the Shuberts were to dispose of enough of their theaters to restore competition.

(The *New York Times* editorialized that the government contended that the Shuberts had destroyed the monopoly of Klaw and Erlanger only to create their own monopoly. More than forty years before, George Bernard Shaw had predicted exactly that.)

The attorney general's suit was detailed. "The defendants for many years have been, and are now engaged in a combination and conspiracy in restraint of interstate trade in producing, booking, and presentation of legitimate attractions.

"They compel producers to book their legitimate attractions through defendants.

"They exclude others from booking legitimate attractions.

"They prevent competition in presentation of legitimate attractions.

"They discriminate in favor of their own productions with respect to booking and presentation.

"They combine their power . . . to maintain and strengthen their domination in these fields."

The government then went into the Theatre Guild situation. The guild customarily presented "on the road" three guild productions and three "outside" productions through the American Theater Society, in which the Shuberts were partners. The outside productions were picked by a selection committee. Lee and Marc Heiman were two of the four bodies on the committee, and Heiman headed UBO, as a Shubert partner. It was very neat, thought the attorney general.

The attorney general went on to list the theaters the Messrs. controlled, pointing out that "nearly every key tryout town" was controlled by the Shuberts. They listed the cities and the theaters. And they concluded by pleading "that the defendants be 'perpetually' enjoined from acquiring any interest in the branch of business relinquished."

Remember, they had already suggested that the Messrs. "relinquish" their theaters or give up their share of UBO.

Milton Weir, on behalf of Lee and Jake, denied all charges as "totally unfounded." And then he began the grim struggle to protect his clients.

Completely undeterred by the government's move, Jake in association with Lou Lurie, bought the Earl Carroll theater-restaurant in Los Angeles! Lurie had called, suggested he had a "good buy" and asked Jake to send a check for $78,000.

"What's the good buy?" asked Jake.

"Whatever I say is a good buy," said Lurie. "Are you sending the check?"

"I'm writing it now," said Jake sourly.

"Good," said Lurie, "then I can tell you that you own half of Earl Carroll's on Sunset Strip."

Jake brightened. "I'll send it airmail," he said. "That's a good location."

Lee discussed the suit with the press. The government was wrong. And he would be glad to give up the theaters. There weren't enough plays to keep theaters alive, anyway. Then his face grew hard, and his voice was bitter. "Who will support the theaters when they are dark—six months every year? Who will do what we do?" It was a good question.

What disturbed him more than anything else was the press quotes of anonymous attacks. He told his secretary one night, "When we gave our word, we did it over our own signature. Who are these people who say these terrible things and are afraid to sign them?

"Where were they in 1931 and in 1933 and '4? Were they risking everything they owned, borrowing money on their own signatures, borrowing on their life insurance? Did they keep actors working, these producers who won't say who they are? Did they put plays on for nothing, these actors who say we blackballed them? We paid them. We kept them eating.

"They are like all other anonymous people. I wish the God-damned papers would print their names and make them say these things to my face.

"I am not ashamed of what my brother and I have done. I sign my name to it. He signs his. We know who we are."

Milton Weir was carrying the load for the Shuberts; Willie Klein was aging, and the younger partner spearheaded the counterattack. He was fighting off personal vendettas as well. Howard Cullman, the tobacco magnate and theater "angel," was a member of the League of New York Theater Owners, and he suggested that Weir resign as counsel for the league. Weir, said Cullman, was involved with an antitrust theatrical suit, which could embarrass the league. Weir ignored it.

He planned the fight against the Chicago suit, and won the first battle. His strategy was to try to isolate the suits, one by one, so as to lessen the overall effect of the monopoly charge against his clients.

In June, Weir presented the court with the formal denial of all charges made by the government against the Shuberts. The case would be decided in the courts. It was fitting and proper; the Shuberts, having feuded with everyone else of consequence—the press, actors, playwrights, Klaw and Erlanger, ASCAP—now were taking on the United States. And they did not let the size of the opponent trouble them. They continued their usual routines. Jake was reviving *Blossom Time* and *The Student Prince* wherever there was a stage and an idle violin. Lee was "banking," and they were even picking up additional theaters. Antitrust? Who? Not the Shuberts. They were trying to buy the other two-thirds of the Lyceum Theater, and Milton Weir was protesting. Not now, he counseled, not now. After all, we are facing an antitrust suit, and this is no time to be adding theaters.

Lee's reply was predictable. "We can always sell it if we have to; and how do you know we have to? If we *don't* buy it, we'll never find out."

Defending a government-filed antitrust suit would be a full-time job for most people, but the Shuberts were busy with other things. Lee was putting up one-third of the money for three Herman Shumlin productions, having a violent disagreement with Jake about a cheap comedy called *The Fifth Season*, and was becoming entranced with television.

Jake was fighting Lee about *The Fifth Season*, and fighting all the unions, the Chicago press, seven New York newspapers, Governor Dewey, the OPA, and dining-car waiters. Together, the brothers were assailing ticket brokers. More and more, Jake was bringing John into the business end of his "side." He was taking John along on union negotiations, and John was making the terms on the out-of-town theater bookings.

Lee did not really like *The Fifth Season*, a play set in the New York garment district. He smelled its commercial odor, and he thought it would make money. But when Jake set himself against it, and in no uncertain terms, Lee decided to proceed with it. It was a hit. "Sometimes," Lee remarked, "being stubborn can make a man a lot of money."

Lee's feuds lasted a long time. He started a ruckus at the league when Abe Berman, representing Irving Berlin, was treated as a member. Lee protested.

"This man is a lawyer," he said, "not a theater owner, and he only represents a man with one-half of a theater. I object to his being here."

It had nothing to do with the league; he still hadn't forgiven Berman because of the *Dodsworth* deal. And Lee owned the other half of the theater—the Music Box.

His dislike for Billy Rose was a different kind of thing. He thought Billy was a wheeler-dealer, and he just plain didn't like him. (It really had nothing to do with wheeling. No one ever *hondled* better than Mike Todd, and Lee adored Todd, occasionally even making money with him—not often, but occasionally.)

He thought Rose was cheap talent, he thought Rose was not really part of the theater, he thought him a "smart aleck," and perhaps he resented the fact that Billy was almost as rich as he was.

Al Lewis, who had been dealing with Lee for almost half a century, first as Max Gordon's partner, then with Sam Harris, and finally on his own, was producing an Irish musical, *Three Wishes for Jamie*, starring John Raitt. It was going to open on the West Coast and come on into New York. Lee had put up $18,500 for the show, and when he heard that Lewis, dissatisfied with the production, was going to close it on the Coast, he sent Jake out to "persuade" him not to.

Jake stopped off in Chicago, long enough to provoke a crisis. He suggested that the critics not attend opening nights, but come on the second night instead. "It will give the public a chance to decide," said Jake. "Theater is a business, just like a department store. We both take ads in newspapers, and when was the last time a newspaper attacked a department store? My shows they attack!"

A critic replied that theater critics call attention to plays, particularly hits. Perhaps, of late, Mr. Shubert wasn't having enough hits. That did it. Jake barred all critics from Chicago shows. Of course, he couldn't make it stick; he left for California, and the press department applied salve.

Jake took the "Chief" out to the Coast, walked into the dining car for dinner, and was warmly greeted by the steward, who seated him with a flourish. "Yes, sir," said the steward. "*you* don't need any menu! I know *your* order!"

Jake beamed in pride, and then was slightly puzzled when the steward served him a steak with lettuce and tomatoes.

The next day at lunch, the act was repeated. Jake entered, started to tell the steward his order. Again he was interrupted.

"You surely not going to tell me *your* order, sir? I know what you like!"

Jake grew sullen as he cut through the steak and the salad.

At dinner, the steward started his spiel, and Jake cut him off. "I *do* need a menu," growled Jake, "and what in hell makes you think I'm such a nut for steak?"

The steward smiled proudly. "I have served you before, Mr. Mayer." Jake glared. "You think I would forget a man like Mr. L. B. Mayer?" asked the confident steward. "You always order steak."

Jake stalked out of the dining car. True, there was only a faint physical resemblance, but perhaps the steward was seeing with an inner eye. The czar of MGM and J. J. might have been soul brothers.

In San Francisco, Jake went to see *Three Wishes for Jamie*. He met with Lewis after the show, and Lewis believed that Jake was in agreement. The show needed fixing.

But Jake was there as a Shubert, and not as a showman. He argued with Lewis. "Once you close a play, almost never can you reopen it. I want you to work on the play *now*, and bring it into New York." He didn't tell Lewis that this advice was the purpose of his mission.

That night, Lewis, Jake, and Lou Lurie, a major backer of *Three Wishes*, were dining together. Lewis was trying to persuade Jake to intercede with Lee.

"My brother is very impulsive," said Jake, "and then he gets stubborn like a mule. I will talk to him, but he is still hurting with those London turkeys he brought over."

Lurie shook his head. "Why can't you and Lee work together? You have an empire. If you can't work together, then close up shop and walk away with $65,000,000."

"Maybe more," said Jake aggressively, and then he grew morose. "Yes, we have an empire," he said. "And God help it if either of us or both of us die."

Lurie said, "There's Milton, and what about Johnny?"

Jake shook his head, staring at his plate. He seemed very tired in an instant. "Johnny hates this business, and this business hates Milton."

Against his better judgment, Lewis agreed to bring the show to New York. He went on ahead to make theater arrangements with Lee.

"I don't want to talk about a theater," said Lee. "You go into the Broadway."

"I can't," said Lewis. "It's wrong for this play."

"The Broadway," Lee insisted.

Lewis remained firm.

"In that case," said Lee levelly, "I want my money back."

371

Lewis left, went to see Tony Farrell, who had acquired the Mark Hellinger Theater, explained his predicament, and left Farrell's office with a check for $18,500.

The next morning, Saturday, Lewis went to call on Lee. He handed him his check, returning Lee's investment. Lee put it on the desk and stared at him, the black eyes hooded.

"I wish you luck with Billy Rose," said Lee.

"It's not Billy," protested Lewis.

"If you would rather do business with a Billy Rose than with the Shuberts, I wish you luck."

"It's not Billy Rose, said Lewis.

"I wish you luck, anyway," said Lee, and busied himself with papers on his desk. He did not speak to Lewis for more than a year. *Three Wishes* was an expensive failure.

A year later, Lewis and his wife were waiting their turn in the dining car of the Philadelphia train, en route to an opening, when they saw Milton Shubert and Lee seated. Milton called them over and asked them to sit down. Lee was stiff, and Al Lewis was uncomfortable. They started to talk.

"It wasn't only *Three Wishes*," said Lee. "It was the three hundred thousand dollars I lost with you and Sam Harris in those three shows, like *Face the Music*, and those other two—one was with the Fairbanks fellow."

"I wasn't in those shows," protested Lewis.

Lee glanced at him. "You're sure? I thought you had a piece of all Harris musicals."

"Of course, I'm sure," said Lewis, a naturally mild man but now getting angry. "You mean you've been angry with me for—for—it's got to be twenty years, and you never mentioned it?"

Lee smiled, reached across the table and patted Lewis' hand. "I'm glad you finally cleared it up," he said.

Yes, he carried feuds a long way.

The brothers' feud with the ticket brokers went back into high gear when the brokers petitioned the state to raise their legal "markup" from seventy-five cents to $1 per ticket, and the Shuberts objected loudly. Prices, they declared, are already too high, brokers don't contribute a damned thing to a show, why should prices go higher, with the difference going to the noncontributors?

On March 1, 1951, Jake wrote an indignant letter to Governor

Dewey. He thought that prices were already high enough, and that cheating practices that fleeced the public were a well-known fact. He threw up his hands in helplessness, proclaiming it impossible to keep tickets away from scalpers. He pointed out that ninety-three brokers were working the city of New York, which could support only thirty theaters.

In Jake's customary fashion, he used one nonpaying (to the Shuberts) activity to throw a rock at another Shubert target, the unions. Because of the unions, Jake claimed, the theater owner had no say about who sat in his box office or what happened to the tickets. His final bright thought was to get rid of brokers *and* unions. He was exceedingly happy with the idea.

Lee and Jake next sued the New York *Daily News*, the *Herald Tribune*, the *New York Times*, the Hearst Corporation, the New York *Journal American*, Hearst Consolidated Enterprises, and the New York *Post*—all of them at once. They claimed that the listed publishers had denied them advertising space.

The papers replied that they made theatrical advertising space available only to producers who have 51 percent of a production. "We do not make similar contracts with owners and operators of theaters, who are considered to be in the real estate business."

Jake was livid. Who said he was not a producer? The original Shubert suit had stated that they sought no damages, only their legal costs. Now Jake wanted damages too, but he was talked out of it.

They lost the suit.

Television made its first real impact in these same early fifties. Both Shubert brothers were dedicated watchers; Lee as a member of the board of two major film companies, MGM and United Artists, knew how this new medium had crippled Hollywood and its gate receipts. And he knew, too, that whatever TV was doing to Hollywood, it was also doing to Broadway.

Studios were cutting back radically in Los Angeles; the "stars" were seeing their contracts ended, canceled, bought up. There were wholesale layoffs. The established hierarchy no longer had a guaranteed tomorrow; great names were fired. As the studios cut back they even fired relatives! Whole empires were in transition. The interim regimes would learn to live with the new monster, TV.

Lee looked back on his own experience, and he made predictions: some were frighteningly accurate, and others were wide of the mark.

He did more than merely look at TV; he was seventy-eight years old and, lo and behold, there was a new way to make money out of entertainment. He started work on a TV series to be called "Shubert Alley." What else?

He called in a TV producer and suggested the series. In the course of it, he reminisced.

I remember when the first motion pictures happened. They used to show them in stores. My old friend, Marcus Loew, he showed them different; he had a flea circus kind of arcade, and he used to use the motion picture to get the people in so they spend the pennies in the arcade. [He shook his head, and scratched his ear.] In the store—they always were close to an undertaker's because an undertaker had chairs to rent—people sometimes used to get nervous and try to see where the people on the screen went. You know—when they went *off* the screen. Where did they hide in the walls? [He smiled reflectively.] Everybody thought it was a fad. People will get tired, we used to say. My God, *I* thought it was a passing fancy.

Some passing. We people in the theater said, "It will go away," and while we waited for it to go away, our bread and butter went away instead. We had to fight, and if we were going to survive, we had to do new things in the legitimate, and we did. We thought we were safe, and along came the talkies, and a brand-new struggle. Movies got bigger than ever, stealing whole pieces of our audience, and while they got bigger, we shrank.

[He turned to the TV producer and waved his letter opener.] You wouldn't believe this, but there used to be more than fifteen hundred theaters playing plays every day all across this country, and more in Canada. Now, if we're lucky, it's a hundred. So, that's what the movies did to us, and now it's television. What the movies did to us, television is doing to the movies, *and* to us.

I remember when you couldn't say "hell" on stage, unless you wanted to get padlocked. Well, let me tell you, pretty soon "hell" was in the movies, and we started talking about, you should forgive me, lesbians. To get an audience.

Well, young man, pretty soon, "hell" will be on television, movies will get excited with lesbians, and what are we going to have left to do, except maybe musicals?

Maybe I will be lucky and won't have to see what *we* are going to have to do to get an audience, when they learn to say "hell" on television. [Suddenly, he sat upright and began to chuckle.] Oh, my God, can you imagine what the legitimate is going to have to do for an audience when television starts with the lesbians?

[He was still laughing at himself, when he sobered.] It will be the worst time that the legitimate has ever experienced. When people can see things for nothing, in their own homes, why should they pay to see the same things? I feel sorry for the movies, but sorrier for us in the theater. The terrible thing that happens is that only the biggest successes will be successful. Nothing that is in the middle—nothing that needs encouragement, that needs help —for the beginner, for the actor, for the writer, for the one who needs the help—none of this will have a chance to make it.

For years, the movies, radio, everybody—they have lived on the legitimate. Broadway begins something—it takes the risks, it makes the experiment, and then, the movies move in, take on the idea, and they milk it like a rich cow. Now, I sit at night, and on the television, I see plays *we* started, and this is what they do— our plays. What are they going to do for themselves? I mean except for what we have already done.

[He waved at the gray walls of the small office.] I want to do a show about the theater—the legitimate theater. I have spent my whole life in it with my brothers, and, young man, I swear to you there are a million wonderful plays that people would love to see right in these walls. Wonderful, wonderful plays and stories about things that happened in our theaters, in our lives, with our actors and other people.

He had the zeal of an evangelist, and the energy of a youngster, and he was seventy-eight. He entered into an agreement to develop the TV series, and he agreed to make himself available for research, anecdotes, things he remembered.

Once cold, blustery October day, when the wind was gusting off the Hudson and marching the rain down 44th Street, he was in his office with the producer and Norman Lessing, a leading playwright and TV writer, who was to do a script. Lee was doing an imitation of Joe Jefferson, and he had sung "Lee's song" trying to remember an old tune, when suddenly he said, "Well, enough talk; it's time for lunch."

The producer protested. "We're working well; let's send out for lunch. Anyway, who wants to go out on a day like this?"

Lee stared at him. "I am a little older than you, young man, and if *I* can go out, *you* can go out."

The valet helped him on with his coat, and Lee's eyes were dancing impishly. He obviously had a trick up his sleeve. It was good to see him in this mood; earlier, when talking about Jefferson, he had mentioned his brother, Sam, and his eyes had filled with tears, and his voice had broken.

The three men descended in the elevator of the Shubert Theater, and made their way under the marquee that projects a few feet above the Alley, heading toward 45th Street. From the marquee of the Shubert, they moved under the marquee of the Plymouth Theater (Alley-side), then around in front of the Plymouth, and still untouched by a drop of rain, proceeded to the shelter of the Booth's marquee.

Now Lee watched the traffic, and then he darted swiftly across the street to the Imperial Theater (under the marquee, to be sure). He reached into his pocket, took out a key, opened the door to the Imperial, admitted the other two, and carefully locked the door. He led the way down the long lobby, through the theater, backstage, and out the stage door. He turned sharply, and entered Dinty Moore's. No one was damp.

His eyes were now mischievous as a child's, he was obviously very pleased with himself, and he ushered his guests to a table. When they were seated, the producer said to him, "Mr. Lee, now I know why you have so many theaters. You just don't like walking in the rain."

Everyone laughed, and then Lee said, "You know, my dear young man, when I and my *older* brother Sam (and here his eyes filled with tears again) first came to New York, we had a kind of a dream. We dreamed that one day, we would walk from New York to San Francisco, under our own roofs." He paused. "We came pretty damned close."

The only thing wrong with the scene was that Sam was *not* his older brother. Lee was the senior Shubert.

The preparation of the "Shubert Alley" series necessitated lengthy, late-night meetings, and endless checking of contracts on properties which the Shuberts claimed to own. This meant making the trek across 44th Street to "Jake's side," where the library and the records were stored.

J.J., ubiquitous and irascible, would peer around a door, discover the "alien"—the TV producer—and then he would nod his head vigorously on his pudgy neck and exclaim, "Ahah! Ahah! You came from the son of a bitch across the street! You think I don't know what's going on?"

He would glare suspiciously, and then add, "You tell the son of a bitch my brother that I am also planning television!" He actually was.

Nothing came of either idea. The rights were enormously complicated, and there were other headaches in the Shubert enterprises. It was always hard to pin anything down.

Someone had formed a "Show of the Month Club," and had made a deal with the producer of *Top Banana*, for some $43,000 worth of tickets. The Shuberts refused to honor the order, and "Show of the Month" sued—and lost.

Instantly, they filed a—guess what kind?—antitrust suit for $3,-000,000 against the Messrs. They lost that one too.

Despite their attorneys' protests, the Shuberts leased the Gayety Theater in Washington, rechristened it the Sam S. Shubert Memorial Theater, placed it under the guidance of Milton Shubert and Lawrence Shubert Lawrence, Sr., and started trying to make it the Number One Showcase in the nation's capital. The only competition was the National Theater, non-Shubert.

A group of independent producers within the New York League charged the Shuberts were intimidating producers into playing the Sam Shubert instead of the National, utilizing New York booking as the wedge. The Shuberts ignored it.

It was 1953, and for Thanksgiving Lee let the press know that he and his wife had been robbed in their Ritz Tower apartment. Some $59,000 worth of gems was missing. The Shuberts left for a ten-day vacation in Florida.

Lee returned and saw *The Starcross Story* go into production. It was a co-production with John Wilson, starring Eva Le Gallienne, Mary Astor, and Tony Ross, and introducing Christopher Plummer.

For five months now, Lee had been troubled with headaches, double-vision and bouts of vertigo. It all added up to one diagnosis: he had suffered a slight stroke. Lee refused to admit it. Occasionally, his lip would droop on the right side, and he would push it up with his finger, his vanity disturbed, his mind rejecting this sudden treason of his body. His eightieth birthday was approaching, and parts were wearing out.

On the morning of December 21, 1953, Lee Shubert awoke and could not get out of bed. First, it was sheer disbelief, and then it was unreasoning panic. He struggled to move, to beat back whatever it was that was imprisoning him, and he could not.

He was taken to Mount Sinai Hospital, and placed on the critical list. The doctors diagnosed a second stroke, and were grave in their prognosis.

John Shubert was notified and went to see his father.

"Uncle Lee is in the hospital," he told him.

Jake started. His eyes widened, and he asked quickly, "What happened?"

John gave him the doctor's report. "I think it would be nice if you went to see him," he told his father.

Jake shook his head violently. "No!" he said sharply, "I don't want to see him."

"Dad, I think you have to."

"I will not go!"

"He's your own flesh and blood, Dad. He's all that's left and—"

Jake cut him off. "I am not going, damn it," he said harshly. Then, he reached out to his son. "Don't you see, if he sees me there, then he'll know something is really wrong."

John nodded, and returned to the hospital.

There was little hope for Lee Shubert's survival that day and night, and then miraculously, indomitably, amazing the doctors, he rallied. The sturdy little body fought back, the black eyes challenged the enemy, and in an unbelievable two days, he was so much improved that he was to leave the hospital on the 23rd of December.

At 7:30 P.M. of the 23rd, his body was wracked by a series of what the doctors called "explosions." For an hour and a half, the gallant body fought back, recovered, only to shudder and shake with the next explosion. After the last one, Lee Shubert was unconscious.

For thirty hours, he stayed alive, defying the shattered blood vessels in his brain. He literally refused to die for more than a day, and then, finally, mercifully, at 5:24 P.M. on December 25, 1953, Lee Shubert was dead. The energy, the greed, the power—all were stilled.

Chapter Twenty

Marcella, Milton, Lawrence, Sr., Sylvia Golde (a niece), and John had maintained an almost ceaseless vigil. Jake had been summoned during the last comatose hours. He became semihysterical, weeping uncontrollably, almost duplicating the performance of his own father when Sam had died. When Lee was dead, he left the hospital, red-eyed and half-wild.

It is impossible to know what raced through his mind that night. The California trip, late in 1951, in re *Three Wishes*, had been aborted by his own illness. He had been rushed back to New York, entered the hospital, and made frantic efforts to put order into his life. He had married Muriel Knowles, who had been his faithful companion, confidante, friend for more than thirty years. (It was a Shubert marriage, complete with marital contract, and relinquishing of claims.) He had made a new will. He had reached out to John, trying to bring him closer. He was obsessed with a fear of death, and haunted by his own premonitions—"God help [the empire] if either of us dies"—and he was frightened. That's how he entered the hospital, where, anticlimactically, they took out his prostate. He was seventy-four, and recovery was slow.

But on this night, when his brother was lying dead, all his hopes, his fears, his doubts, his guilts—all of them must have gone racing through his brain. For twenty long years, he, J. J. Shubert, had been relegated to a secondary position. Did he still hate the man who had kept him there? Even after he was dead? Or was it an ambivalence of hate and love and the recognition of a finality? And had he secretly wanted this day to come, and now that it was here, was there elemental reaction?

And why did he cry? For the future? Or for the past? We are told that men do not weep for the dead but for the problems of the living. Then for whom did J. J. Shubert weep that night when his eyes grew red-rimmed and his sturdy body shook with sobs?

He must have known that now all the problems, the choices, the decisions, the responsibilities of empire were his. What would he do? ("God help it if either of us dies!")

He did not attend his brother's funeral—the state funeral they gave Lee Shubert. Fifteen hundred people, a cross-section of show business, came to Temple Emanu-El on Fifth Avenue, the synagogue for New

York's richest Jews and the synagogue Lee did not belong to. The honorary pallbearers were drawn from the elite of New York's Jewish and non-Jewish theatrical world, and some of them had actually known Lee in life. The presiding clergyman had not. But Jake did not attend. It was said he was "too disturbed."

They laid Lee Shubert to rest in the family mausoleum in Salem Fields Cemetery. Jake was there, speaking to no one.

In the close-knit confines of the Shubert family, and in the secretive cabals of the Shubert office, everyone awaited the reading of the will. Who had been bequeathed power? Who would it be? A personally held empire needs an heir, and Lee had no heir.

We are told Jake spent the day of Lee's funeral looking over papers in the office. He was assuming control. In the peculiar working arrangement that was the Shubert business pattern, each had held equal power; it was so stipulated in papers. But always, Jake had deferred to Lee. Why? Now he was in charge, and his first decisions were terrifying and almost irrational.

In the sentimentality and emotion that followed the shock of Lee's death, there seemed to be time for conciliation and truce. A family council was called. Willie Klein and Milton Weir attended, along with Larry, Sr., Milton, Sylvia, J. J., and John. For a short moment, it appeared possible that a dual regime would be instituted, with John and Milton steering things, and Jake, the chairman of the board, officiating. The Shuberts, still a family enterprise, would move ahead.

Any hope for this kind of solution was killed with the reading of Lee's will. He had reached back from the grave and insured the perpetuation of the feud. In the cold type of the legal document, Lee branded Jake "the other Shubert" once again. He stripped him of his newly won size and position, he denigrated him publicly, he left Jake no alternative but hatred. In addition, unwittingly, Lee had sowed the seeds of a dirty, avaricious, family-linen-washed-in-public squabble. It was a malicious will.

He had drawn the will in January of 1949, shortly after Marcella's divorce. It made all the usual provisions for charities and bequests, and it contained a number of key provisions. Most important was this clause.

It read: "I make no provision in this will for my brother, Jacob J. Shubert, for the reason that he has ample means of his own and requires no financial assistance from me. My love and respect for him, and my utmost faith in his honesty and integrity are evidenced by the fact that

380

I am naming him Executor and Trustee of my estate, content in the knowledge that he will do all within his power to conserve and administer my estate for the benefit of my beneficiaries. . . ."

It was the key clause. He had written the will shortly after the divorce. He changed it three times, always leaving the trustee clause intact. In October of 1952, he changed his will again, and this time drastically.

He ended the "brother" clause with the first sentence. Jake was no longer a trustee, no longer an executor. What happened in the short fifteen months to impel Lee to this decision cannot be ascertained. It might have been Jake's operation; it might have been the antitrust case. It might have been a sudden awareness of age and mortality. Whatever it was, it was destructive.

With the reading of the will, it was war. Of all the people Jake hated, his prime hatred was for his nephew Milton. He thought him untalented, incompetent, a fool. He had lost his temper each time Lee had placed Milton in a position of responsibility or importance. The implication that Milton would take Lee's place was intolerable.

Jake had taken to spending half his office time in Lee's office. He would sit in the round room, behind the small desk, poring over the papers, reading contracts which he did not know about, or understand, trying to grasp what had been done by his brother, in both their names. To this office, one day, came Milton Shubert and Milton Weir.

The trouble had already started. There was a strongbox in Lee's apartment, which Milton Shubert admitted having taken. He refused to turn it over to Jake. There were keys to the corporate vault, beside Lee's office—Milton held on to them. (Jake had already opened the vault. He did not need the keys.)

There was an angry meeting. There were loud voices, and the people in the outer offices stood looking at each other. It seemed as if they would come to blows—nephew and uncle. Milton Shubert and Milton Weir left, and Jake ordered the locks changed on his nephew's office. Milton Shubert was no longer part of the family company. He was fired.

What part the *Variety* story played in this is not easily ascertained. *Variety* had front-paged a story that Milton would take over for Lee and carry on. Jake read it, and the walls shook with his anger. To John he said, "Tell that son of a bitch to get out! You get that bastard out of there or, so help me God, I'll kill him."

John's role in this time of transition was impossible. On "Jake's side," only John knew the men who had worked for Lee—effectively or badly. He intervened with his father: he was persuasive and gentle, interposing when he could, yielding when he could not. He tried to temper his father's rages, tried to control the inevitable decimation of "Lee's side." Sometimes he succeeded; more often he failed.

He failed with Milton Weir. There was a long background for Jake's vendetta. Most of it stemmed from a minor piece of business—the lease on the Longacre Theater, which had been rented as a TV studio and which returned to the Shuberts. Ray Whittaker had proposed that they reassume the lease earlier than the end of the contract with the Mutual Broadcasting System. They could refurbish the house and get it ready for rental for the oncoming season. Milton Weir agreed. Jake disagreed, and vociferously. The proposal was sent to Lee, in London, and he approved. The deal was closed on Whittaker's terms, and Jake never forgave Milton Weir or Whittaker. Weir had to go; Whittaker, Jake would take care of later.

He demanded that Willie Klein and Weir sever their partnership, that Adolf Lund, already in the firm, replace Weir, and that Weir resign. It was only a beginning. He fired right and left, almost all on "Lee's side." He trusted no one, except John, and he told people, "My son is too soft for his own good." He pored over documents, suspicious of everything, certain he was being cheated, certain his rule was menaced, and he relied on no judgments except his own. And J.J. Shubert's judgments were being made by a seventy-five-year-old brain, and J.J. Shubert was tired, faulty, vacillating, and obsessed. It was the time of the terror on 44th Street.

It was also the time for greed and hatred, the time for the drawing of lines in a monetary war, the time when those, the heirs—characterized by Jake as the ones that "didn't make it, they never earned it, now they want to take it"—would hire lawyers and demand that Lee's will be interpreted in only one way, theirs. They wanted money, and position, and power. They would not get it from Jake Shubert.

There were two other interesting clauses in the will: Clauses XXI (g) and (h), and these Lee had not abridged or changed.

The first (g) read "that to the extent permitted by law, [my Executors and Trustees] shall be guided in the disposition of and administration of my said estate by the wishes of my brother, Jacob J. Shubert. . . . to the end that so long as my said brother shall live there shall be no forced liquidation or partition of the properties jointly owned by us. . . ."

Everything they owned was owned jointly—everything.

Clause (h) ran, "It is my express intent and desire that the final determination as to the sale and disposition of any business asset in which business my brother Jacob J. Shubert may be interested, during the lifetime of my said brother, shall be made by my said brother, and if there shall be any disagreement among my Executors and Trustees, then to the extent permitted by law the decision of my brother shall be final and shall prevail."

The retention of these two statements makes all the more puzzling the exclusion of Jake as executor and trustee. The clauses seemed explicit, and Jake behaved accordingly.

The legatees, Milton, Sylvia Wolfe Golde and, for a time, Larry, Sr., ignored Lee's words. They demanded accountings, they demanded liquidation, or failing liquidation, buy-out on their own terms. Milton demanded an employment contract, and they negotiated and negotiated. It was seamy, ugly, embittering. And Jake stayed firm. "I will see him in hell first!" he told John.

Five days after Lee's death, the federal district court ruled that the Shuberts were like baseball—they could not be held to antitrust laws, according to the Holmes precedent. In the Shubert office, there was a momentary sense of triumph, and then the letdown when the government announced it was taking the case to the Supreme Court.

The last show ever to bear the logo "The Messrs. Shubert Present" opened on January 13, 1954. *The Starcross Story* closed on January 14. It played one performance—a pitiful epitaph to a career that had brought nearly six hundred Broadway productions to New York in the name of the Shuberts. There would never be another.

Jake was negotiating with the various unions and bringing John into the meetings. "Someday, it will be yours," he would say. At one such meeting, John made a suggestion. Jake wheeled on him. "What the hell do you know about it?" he barked. "Keep your mouth shut!" He turned back to the union representatives. "*I* make the decisions," he informed them. "No one else."

No one else did. He issued instructions that in the vast Shubert chain of enterprises no bills would be paid until he had personally approved them. A two-dollar bill for deodorant cakes for flush bowls went unpaid until he had initialed it.

There was a state of catalepsy in the office. Meanwhile, the Lee Shubert heirs were making demands. Jake offered to buy them out. They refused the $7,500,000 he offered; Milton demanded $30,000,000. He felt the estate half of the Shubert empire was worth that.

At the same time, the estate was appraised for tax purposes by the I.R.S. at roughly $50,000,000. Milton protested, claiming the evaluation too high.

Jake grew more and more withdrawn. John was trying to function, trying almost desperately to "change the Shubert image." He was not succeeding. Jake began issuing an endless stream of memos from his office—to Whittaker, to John, to everyone he could think of. They betray his uncertainty, his lack of grasp of the real problems, his general sense of panic.

There were the multiple bills for twenty theaters in New York alone. There were more than three hundred nontheatrical Shubert tenants. Jake insisted on scrutinizing every item. He became an incredible bottleneck, paralyzing the functioning of the office. He was totally incapable of delegating authority without instantly, jealously, snatching it back.

He issued a paranoiac order. Not only were his key executives to report to him each day with full reports, but the assistants to the executives were to make personal reports, daily, in writing or by presenting themselves to him. Everything, repeat, everything must be told to him! It became almost impossible to get the work done. And he bombarded everyone with memos, notes, orders, picayune and pettifogging inconsequentials. Many of them made no sense. A sour and twisted man who had never been able to be articulate, to communicate, he insisted on communicating with everyone about everything.

In turn, he issued his barrages of instructions. On March 4, 1954, he advised that he felt that elevator services ought to be curtailed. When exchange of communications pointed out that they *had* to supply certain services, Jake ruminated, and on March 22 informed one and all that everything that Lee Shubert had said, written, or otherwise communicated was to be ignored. Jake didn't think Lee knew what he was doing. He said so.

After a short skirmish with Whittaker, where Jake flatly stated that he didn't want to hear anything about refrigerators in these various apartments where he had wanted to cut down the elevators, he turned his attention to John.

John had filled out the required (by Jake) form, requesting permission to paint one dressing room. After an endless exchange of thoughts, written and oral, Jake formally notified his son, in writing, that he could proceed with the job. There were seven thousand employees, a million per week in ticket receipts. And he was spending his time on a twenty-dollar paint job!

He was hardly finished with the paint job when new horizons opened. Henry Speckman, who collected rents and generally supervised real estate, made a normal request for a two-week vacation. Jake was outraged. He fired back a memo, informing Speckman and everyone else that he, Jake, did not believe in vacations and had no time for same. The idea of vacations *with pay* was totally repugnant. Jake had never heard of such an outlandish proposal and surmised that it was something cooked up by Lee and Whittaker. He refused to recognize the institution of vacations, with or without pay, and formally stated that the matter would be handled differently in the near future.

Of course, Speckman got his vacation with pay. But this endless messing with unimportant detail, the interminable flow of memos were totally crippling the work of the organization. John couldn't cut through; Whittaker was in left field; the ugly mess of the family wrangle was still going on; and Jake, in his office, would make no definite decisions. He became the stumbling block everyone tried to avoid.

He did not confine his efforts to the office. He had ousted Weir from the Shubert organization; now he demanded that Weir be dismissed as attorney for the league. Several unions took ads in the *Times*, protesting Jake's action. When the league did not accede to his request, Jake resigned from the league. It pretty effectively crippled the organization.

With Weir ousted from the Willie Klein partnership and replaced by Jake's nominee, Jake could now turn loose on Willie. In a series of letters, he intimated to Klein that Willie and Lee had connived to steal money from the company. He referred directly to Lee's divorce, insisted that it was a "personal" matter of Lee's and that Klein's doing what he did—acting as adviser to Marcella—had been deliberately designed to take money out of Jake's pocket.

Klein wrote back a placating letter and included a detailed expense account, showing exactly what monies he had received and how they had been paid.

Jake refused to pay any attention. Day after day, he sent long accusing letters to Klein. They were laced with phrases attacking Lee.

Finally, Klein weathered the storm.

Now Jake was ready to take on Equity. He wrote an angry letter, distributing copies to the press. He pointed out that he had produced plays for many years, sometimes as many as twenty-eight or thirty a year. Yet, in the last few years, he had produced none. Why? Equity and the other unions!

He was particularly resentful about benefit performances, which producers were asked to give for Equity. Equity had money in *its* treasury, and very often producers did not have money in theirs. Perhaps Equity ought to reconsider the arrangement, and try to do something for the producers. In Jake's opinion, this would be fair.

Equity pointed out that other producers, despite the losses Jake claimed, still were doing shows and showing them in Shubert theaters, in and out of New York, and presumably at a profit.

385

One columnist suggested that Jake seemed to want a benefit run for the Shuberts. Would anyone sponsor it?

John had been working overtime to keep the family mess out of the papers. Now it exploded again, and in print. Sylvia Wolfe Golde, the daughter of Jake's sister, Dora, sued for certain securities that were, she alleged, part of her mother's estate, and which Jake had seized.

When Mrs. Wolfe died, she owed the Shuberts some $200,000, and in the name of Lee Shubert, there were $200,000 worth of Mrs. Wolfe's blue-chip stocks in the Shubert vault. Sylvia wished to liquidate the debt, and take over the securities. Jake claimed the securities were part of the Lee Shubert estate, owned half by him, period.

The lines in the fight had been drawn. Milton was obdurate, greedy, and would settle for nothing reasonable. Larry, Sr., wanted to do it nicely and quietly. Sylvia was torn between them. Jake made no differentiation between them. "They are a lot of no-good parasites," he told a close associate. "They only want whatever they can get; I hope my brother is watching."

John wrote a bitter letter to a close friend and talked about the dirt and the death of rich relatives. He closed optimistically: the business was still generally running as if nothing had happened.

He was wrong. The business was continuing, but it had changed. The "banking" aspect was being cut back. They were almost totally a real-estate firm, but amazingly, the mystique still lived. They were the Shuberts. They did not produce, they hardly invested, all they did was manage their theaters and their bookings, but they were still universally feared.

In January of 1955, the Supreme Court ruled that the Shuberts were subject to antitrust laws. Justice Warren specifically noted that the Court had *not* decided whether or not the Shuberts had violated the Sherman Act. The Court's decision merely indicated that the Justice Department could proceed on a cause of action.

Jake refused to comment. He would not admit he had made a mistake in the Weir situation. Weir had successfully fought off the antitrust actions, and now they were back to haunt J. J. He sat in his office, seeing very few people, and brooding. He was growing more and more remote.

A former associate, visiting New York from California, dropped in to pay his respects. He had worked more closely with Lee than with Jake, but Jake knew him well enough to call into the outer office, "Come in, come in." No sooner had the caller entered than Jake's pudgy hand was pointing at him, and the harsh voice said, "And the son of a bitch was a thief besides! A thief!"

"Come on, Mr. J.J.," said the visitor, "Mr. Lee is dead, and what's the use of—"

"I got no time for that horse----," said Jake. "The son of a bitch was a thief, and I can prove it."

Herman Shumlin came to see him. He could feel the loneliness, the wistfulness of this complex man as he sat there on 44th Street, looking only inward.

"Why don't you do a play?" suggested Shumlin. "All those lovely shows you brought to the theater! Why don't you revive *Blossom Time* or do a new show?"

Jake would not look up. He stared down at the desk, his hands on the edge, as if poised to leap. He shook his head, still looking at the desk top. "Where would I get the people? Where?"

He was becoming more and more uncertain. No less irascible, but progressively less willing to make commitments. It was as if he were afraid of a mistake—a mistake that Lee might not have made. He was in competition with a dead man, and, therefore, if he did nothing, he could make no errors. He did nothing, and for Jake Shubert this was Hell.

He erupted by suing *Variety* for half a million dollars. They had run an article stating that the Shuberts were issuing new contracts under which the theater rental would be 50 percent of the gross, instead of the prevailing 30 percent; that the Shuberts were demanding that the ticket-printing costs be absorbed by the producer; *Variety* editorialized about "Shubert procedures."

Jake called it "false and defamatory . . . intended to and did injure his good name, fame, business and credit . . . exposed him to public contempt, ridicule, scorn, aversion, and disgrace." He didn't miss a trick.

The suit was not pursued.

He precipitated a second crisis when he barred Eliot Norton from the Boston theaters. The entire Shubert office staff and legal department tried to stop him, but he would not listen. Norton's reviews were bad. "No more free tickets. Let the son of a bitch buy his tickets! And I'll cut every ad out of his God-damned paper!" So it went.

With the antitrust case looming in the background, threatening the very existence of the Shubert empire, this was no time for Jake to demonstrate his power as czar by banning a critic. Logic and reason were unavailing. He stormed into Boston and issued the edict. Not content with the action against Norton, then drama critic for the Boston *Post*, Jake compounded his irrationality when he informed all producers coming into Boston that the Shuberts would not pay their proportion of the advertising fees in the *Post*. He more than intimated that if the

387

producer still insisted on advertising in the *Post*, he just might have a little difficulty getting a New York theater. His timing could not have been worse.

The *Post* called Thomas O'Neill, the representative from Boston, and the House of Representatives became interested (again) in Shubert affairs. The press picked up the story and wanted statements from Jake. He was unavailable. Someone had to speak for the Shuberts, and John was elected.

Dealing with the *Newsweek* reporter, John tried various approaches. He was urbane: "This is nothing. It's being blown up out of all proportion. It's only a matter of seven or eight bucks. He can get the seats, anyway. It's a tempest in a teapot."

He was "Shubert-consistent"—he had to be to save Jake's face: "You write a bad review and we'll fix you too!"

He was innocent: "I don't know a thing about it. I just work for my father."

Then he turned real Shubert, and not for Jake; this was all for John: "This is not an interview; you print one word of this, I'll sue you!"

Newsweek ran the story, including John's remarks. John was a true Shubert; he had threatened to sue. (He didn't.)

The "affair Norton" created a major problem for the Shubert legal eagles, and for John. What might conceivably happen if Jake were questioned on a witness stand? What intemperate sentences might be blurted out, in anger, or just because he was Jake? Willie Klein, for years, had tried to keep Jake out of courtrooms. Willie was a very old man by now, and his mind was not what it had been, but Willie was clear enough to back the consensus—Jake must never appear in the antitrust action.

This left one practical alternative: the Shuberts would sign a consent decree and "make a deal" with Uncle Sam. It was John's job to do the major chore of selling this to Jake. It was a wild scene.

Jake unknowingly paraphrased Churchill. He had not worked for sixty years to preside over the dissolution of the Shubert empire. He would fight the government to the finish. John pleaded, he cajoled, he tried logic, and he tried flattery. He called for reinforcements, and together with the "cabinet" of the Shuberts, they pleaded with Jake. Eventually they wore him down.

On February 18, 1956, with the Norton affair still in the news, Federal Judge I. T. Kauffman signed the consent decree, which bound the Shuberts to (1) sell off twelve theaters in six cities within two years, (2) give up the booking share of the business. It became more specific. They would sell the St. James in the two-year period, or lease it out, or lease the Imperial. They would sell the National in one year and two of the following within two years—Adelphi, Ambassador, Belasco, Elliott, Longacre, or the Ritz.

Within two years they would divest themselves, in Boston, of the Colonial or the Shubert, and the Wilbur. In Chicago, they would sell either the Blackstone or Great Northern and either the Erlanger or the Shubert. In Cincinnati, they would sell the Cox or the Shubert. In Detroit, the Shubert-Lafayette or the Cass. In Philadelphia the Locust or the Walnut, and the Shubert.

It was fairly obvious that the government was determined to break the Shubert monopoly on key out-of-town tryout cities. The Shuberts noted penitently that they had already sold their houses in Toledo and Pittsburgh.

Jake and the "cabinet" worked on a release, and, despite everything the legal minds could do, parts of the statement were pure Jake, and maybe he was entitled to his statement.

> I will live up to the decree, although I have my doubts as to whether some of its provisions will not hurt rather than benefit the legitimate theater. The decree requires us to sell a number of theaters which were assembled over half a century. Whether these theaters in other hands will continue to be operated as legitimate houses only time will tell.
>
> As the last survivor of the three Shubert brothers who practically alone developed the present theatrical districts in the larger cities of the United States, I can point out what my brothers and I contributed to the development of the legitimate theater in America.
>
> If we have been financially successful, the legitimate theater and the public will someday benefit from the fruits of our labor through the means of the Sam S. Shubert Foundation.

He made no comment beyond the published statement. It leaves room for conjecture. Did he think of his brother that night? And what were his thoughts? Would it have happened had Lee been the survivor? Would Lee have fought? After all, J.J. was the indomitable one, and he yielded without a struggle. What would Lee have done? Did Jake think these things that night? Or did he feel tired and beaten and old? He was seventy-eight. ("God help it if either of us or both of us die!")

At first, the blow seemed crushing. There were cold instructions that UBO must operate on an "impartial basis" and was not to have a financial interest in a theater or a show. And the Shuberts must forgo certain pressures, penalties, discriminatory practices that might give them unfair control over tickets, finances, or booking.

Certain Shubert stooges wrote angry letters. The legitimate theater would be crushed. Others wrote other letters—it will help the theater. Cold analysis—and it was made too in the Shubert office—was that they had been weakened but not undermined. They were not as badly hurt as they had been during Lee's receivership, and they had recovered from that. They would weather this.

Two months later, the House Judiciary Committee revived the Boston mess, and Jake fled to Europe. He had had it. In Washington, John McManus, editor in chief of the Boston *Post* testified that "there is no question that J.J. Shubert has tried to intrude upon freedom of the press in Boston." He went on to say that Michael J. Cavanaugh, a top Shubert employee in Boston, had made "definite attempts to control the writing of Eliot Norton." He had served "oral ultimatums and threats." He added that Cavanaugh had said he was there on orders from J.J. Shubert.

In New York, Johnny declined to comment.

A month later Jake told the House subcommittee that the advertising had been cut, but not because of Norton's reviews. There were "business reasons," he assured the committee. Why had they ceased giving "free tickets" to Norton? Norton was negative in his reviews, said Jake, and he didn't have to *invite* a man to be negative. If he wanted to be negative, let him pay. A month after that, the committee solemnly ruled that "the Shuberts had brought pressure on a critic," but technically "there was no violation."

Through all the mess, the matter of Lee's estate was creating its own problems. Milton Shubert and Sylvia Golde filed suit for an accounting of Lee's estate. The defendants were Jake, Willie Klein, as executor, and Larry, Sr., who wanted to get the matter settled and wasn't going to sue Uncle Jake. Ed Weisl, a New York attorney and political figure, was named referee to hear the accounting.

They began the liquidation of parts of the empire. They sold the National Theater for $900,000. In Boston, they had already leased the Colonial, and now, quickly, they dropped their lease on the Wilbur. They leased the Plymouth to the same man who had already taken on the Majestic, and its name was changed to the Gary. The Opera House was sold to the Allen Construction Company. They sold the Colonial and its office building for more than a million, netting $400,000 over what they had paid for it in 1952. They leased out the Copley.

They took an ad in *Variety* offering the United Booking Office for sale. There weren't any takers. And in the midst of it, a Philadelphia theater owner sued them for $2,000,000—the charge, violation of anti-trust laws.

They filed one suit of their own. They wanted a rebate of more than $143,000 on taxes paid in 1943, and the lower court had turned them down. They had gone to the Supreme Court with the case. It was a typical Shubert litigation.

The taxes involved were the excess profits taxes. Under the Internal Revenue rulings, the taxpayer was allowed to deduct a certain percentage of his invested capital from his gross income.

When the Shuberts, through Select, bought back the theaters in 1933, they had paid $400,000—on the books. In filing their 1943 return, they had used the $400,000 figure as the invested capital. They should have used, they contended, the figure of $4,000,000, the basis on which the Shuberts valued the purchase.

So, they said, please give us back $143,000. The Supreme Court agreed with the lower courts—Jake didn't get it.

They sold the St. James to a St. Paul group, headed by a top executive in Minnesota Mining, and sold the Shubert in Philadelphia to the same combine a short time later. The total was almost $2,500,000.

They faced a strike threat from their old friends at the Press Agents and Managers Union, and the musicians were giving them trouble too.

They dissolved UBO.

By now, Jake was almost a hermit. He would see no one, except for a trusted few. There were all the signs of an approaching senility; his hair had turned snow-white, his hands shook, and the blue eyes seemed almost genial—they weren't, he was seeing things that weren't always there.

No one can say, but there must have been memories of those first two years after his brother Sam died. The mad two years when they had either acquired or made agreements with fifty-two theaters while producing two dozen plays. Now, it was a slow replay, like a dream sequence, the film distorting as it played backward, and the theaters were going out of his hands, one by one.

He took to going to his costume lofts, where he would shamble down the aisles, fingering the fading cloths, admiring their texture, their opulence. He would mumble to himself, "So lovely! Such fine material!" He would caress the silks, and what did he see? What did he really see?

There were moments of transparent lucidity, when his frustration and his bitterness would come out. "Who made the money?" he would ask. "Who made the money? Mr. Lee Shubert? With his lousy London plays and his lousy productions? Who did the shows that made all the

391

An Award for His Contributions to the Theater. A benign J. J. Shubert being honored by Mayor Robert Wagner, New York, 1959.

money he should be a playboy, always on vacations and parties? *I* had no parties! I made the money, he could waste it! Who kept the theaters running with beautiful shows?" He would sit silently, brooding, hating.

He would glue himself to the TV screen, and bury himself in other people's fantasies, and then go back to his own. One day, he went to the costume loft and made them take out the entire costume list for *Blossom Time.* "They are still beautiful," he told the wide-eyed dressers. "Take good care of them. I may want to use them soon." He walked out slowly. "Take very good care."

He went to Europe again, with Muriel, and from there he appealed to the court for a little more time, and a revision of the consent decree. Judge Kauffman did grant a six-month extension, but refused to consider any revisions. He came back and retired to his cave in the Sardi Building.

Slowly, almost imperceptibly, he was losing touch with reality and the world in which he lived. Jake Shubert had never been a stable man. He was volatile, excitable, undisciplined, given to his giant rages and his physical releases. The past and the present were all at once merging in his memory, and yesterday was like that day in 1909, and today was almost like yesterday.

He had lived beyond his usefulness. There was no reason for him to be, and still he survived. Sometimes, the gods that are take pity, and they let a man die. Other times, they show mercy by veiling his mind. This they did for Jake Shubert, in his eightieth year. It was just as well. There were things that he was better off not knowing.

Chapter Twenty-one

As Jake Shubert was reluctantly, unknowingly relaxing his grip on the affairs of his company, his son was taking over. More and more of the responsibilities of decision were coming to him, and slowly he was trying to shape the future of the Shuberts.

John did not like the business, although he did like the power and wealth it insured. He would produce one play—he was not a producer. He didn't do much "banking"; he did not trust his judgment of theater that well. But he could work at changing the Shubert image; he could be genial and warm and cooperative.

What might he have been with another heritage or another set of parents? He loved boats. He loved sailing them, and he loved building them. He had gifted hands—he could design things and make them of wood, and they were lovely. As a young man, he had built his own apartment above the garage in Mamaroneck. Paneling, partitions, everything.

He might have been an architect, he might have been a shipbuilder, he might have been a very happy carpenter, and a well-adjusted man. He was none of these things. Torn between his father and his mother, torn between his Jewishness and his Catholicism, he walked a thin line between despair and elation.

He was drinking very heavily. It is odd that none of the founding Shubert brothers drank; possibly their father's example served them as a warning. Jake had had a few binges as a young man, but he soon found more interesting avenues for his "kicks." Lee hardly touched liquor, and Sam did not drink. In the next generation, Larry, Sr., did very well with the amber fluid, and now John was using it—as a prop, as nepenthe, to get through the days.

He was a strange man, accessible, open, seemingly candid, yet hard to know. He had a host of friends, and he had no enemies. It was as if he had made a pact with himself to be different from all other Shuberts—he would be liked. And he was. But there is something suspicious about a man who has no enemies.

He was odd about money. Heir to the Shubert fortune, in charge of what was still the largest theatrical empire in the world, he was niggardly. He would walk several blocks to buy two-dollar shirts at a surplus store. Out with a party of friends, he would call for the check, and then carefully break it down: "You had two drinks, and you had three, so that comes to three dollars you owe me, with the tip."

At home in the New York apartment, or in the big house he and Eckie had bought in Connecticut, he was a good host—fun-loving, relaxed, and lavish with his liquor. His mother was still cool to Eckie, and John either ignored the coldness between the women or really didn't see it. The latter seems incredible.

He built a house for his mother next to his own, and was "a good son." He and Eckie spent a great deal of time with his father, and each time they did, Catherine would become jealous and vicious-tongued. To compensate, he spent a lot of time with her. In 1958 he took Catherine to Europe with him.

He had adjusted his life to living two lives—at the same time. There was a part of him that walked through the Shubert offices, renting theaters, closing his eyes to what was already becoming a Broadway wisecrack—the ticket situation—and running a reasonably orderly shop. A second part of him was in search—of himself, of happiness, of some kind of fulfillment. His marriage was growing rocky. The strains on it were considerable. There was little peace anywhere for John Shubert.

He went back to Europe in 1960, without Eckie or his mother. He had grown much closer to his second cousin, Lawrence Shubert Lawrence, Jr., who was working in the office with him, and with Jack Small, his general manager.

In April of 1962, Jack Small died, and his death affected John Shubert in many ways. He began to become concerned with his own health. He was still drinking and now, with almost a hypochondriac's compulsion, he was taking all sorts of medicines. He saw a doctor for a complete physical. He went to a second physician.

He was invariably courteous, pleasant, charming, and his sweet, shy smile would break across his face as he greeted you. He was receiving some of the perquisites of his position—more money, appointment to the board of the City Museum, director of the Young Dramatists' Committee, presenter of Shubert Foundation awards. He was taking an active role in the bargaining process and getting some attention in the press. All of this he looked on with slightly ironic wonder; he had not earned it. It was something that went with the title on his letterhead—not with John Shubert, personally.

This duality of his existence was becoming more and more evident. He was assuming a mysterious personality, which was puzzling and unpredictable. In the midst of a party in Connecticut, he would disappear upstairs, come down in his blue serge suit, and wordlessly take off for New York. It was assumed he had "business."

During the day, he would leave his office, and no one seemed to know where he went or what he was doing. He seemed to be enjoying a private joke, and it was the kind of joke that contained very little humor or pleasure.

He would be desperately troubled and then serenely relaxed. Sometimes almost in the same instant. It was as if he and life shared some terribly amusing understanding, which no one else could possibly appreciate, and in his invariable courtesy there was almost a boyish superiority. "I know something you don't know," he seemed to be saying. "I dare you to guess what it is!"

His marriage was becoming more and more difficult for Eckie, checkered with separations and reconciliations, and friends were aware of it.

In the fall of 1962, John hosted a party at Sardi's for some forty or fifty friends, to celebrate their twenty-fifth wedding anniversary. He presented Eckie with a magnificent diamond clip. He seemed to be working at making things work.

A short time later, John left for Florida to visit "a dear friend." He never reached his destination. On the train, sometime during the day, he had suffered a massive coronary occlusion and was found dead in his compartment. He was fifty-three.

The body was returned to New York, and the papers announced that a private service would be held at Campbell's. The following day, the private service was canceled. The first act in John Shubert's "private joke" was about to play.

In all the years since Lee's death, there had been just one Shubert production—John's. It starred Claudette Colbert, and it played just one performance, on January 28, 1961. The titles of John's last two productions were sardonic; *Johnny on a Spot* and *Jules, Jake and Uncle Joe*. But if he couldn't produce plays, he could "produce" his own funeral. And he left instructions to do just that. He gave the theater a production it had never seen before.

On November 21, a non-matinée day, eight stagehands covered the sets of *Camelot* with black velour drops. The stage of the Majestic Theater was brightly lighted. Holding center stage was a mahogany coffin, containing the remains of John Shubert. A blanket of scarlet American Beauty roses covered the coffin. Alongside the coffin stood a tall black leather chair. In it sat John's widow, Eckie. She did not say anything. She merely sat there—the widow. It was exactly what John had requested.

Roger Stevens, now the director of the National Foundation for the Arts, then an active theatrical producer, who knew John Shubert only casually, delivered the eulogy. John had so left instructions. John

396

drew a good audience. It was an eerie, unreal scene, and the hush of the audience was partly because of the nature of the ceremony—it *was* a funeral—and partly because of the weird setting, the surrealist scene on stage, the irony of the gesture.

Jake was not informed of John's death. There were two reasons. It was doubtful that he would have understood the import of the news —he was too far gone. Second, there was genuine fear that if he did understand it, it would kill him.

Why the odd funeral? What depths lay behind the amiable, courteous exterior of this so-well-adjusted man? Whom was he spoofing? Was he laughing at the theater, the Shuberts, the world? What kind of warped sense of humor would order this garish, tasteless, preposterous ending? He had other "jokes" prepared. They were even less funny.

Although it was nearly nine years since Lee Shubert had died, his estate was still not settled. The government was still claiming more taxes than the heirs were willing to pay; and the legatees were still in litigation with Jake, and with each other. With John's death, Milton Shubert sensed an opportunity to assume control of the business. He wanted to run the shop. It was not to be. Lawrence Shubert Lawrence, Jr., was taking the reins.

Broadway was filled with rumors that the Shuberts were going to sell to a syndicate headed by Howard Cullman, the Broadway angel. And then, in the midst of the New York newspaper strike, the second act of John Shubert's "comedy" began to unfold.

The "nicest Shubert"—the man who had so often vowed to "change the Shubert image," the man who had pleaded with his mother not to sue his father with "There's enough dirt on the Shubert name!"—gave the press the most sordid personal scandal in Shubert history.

It explained his sly "secret." In retrospect, it seems like an inevitable consequence of his life.

The first bombshell was mercifully muffled by the New York press blackout. Only the New York *Standard*, one of the temporary newspapers, had the story. Eckie filed John's will for probate, petitioning that she be appointed temporary executrix, and a second Mrs. John Shubert contested the appointment.

By the time the matter came to trial before Judge Samuel DiFalco, the New York County surrogate, the newspaper strike was ended, and the tabloids had a field day.

Not only were there two wives, there were two children born to the second! And there were two wills. In addition to the document that Eckie had entered, there was a strange second will, presumably dictated by John on the eve of a European business trip. It was challenged, as was a divorce John had secured in Mexico.

There was a two-day binge in the newspapers, as they gleefully recounted the story. The wills were examined by handwriting experts; Catherine sided against Eckie; there was testimony about huge sums of money, and wisely DiFalco adjourned the public hearing, stating that he hoped a settlement could be found.

And in the interim of the recess, Broadway buzzed. There was the item of the sum of cash John had given Eckie. Where had John gotten *that* much cash? Milton Shubert wanted to know if it was "estate money." The Broadway smart money whispered, "Ice." Who was the real Mrs. John Shubert? And which was *the* will? And which documents were false, and which were genuine?

They all could have been genuine. John Shubert was a very troubled and confused man.

The out-of-court settlement was reached, and the dirty laundry was put away, out of the public spotlight. It was a unique settlement for a court to approve.

Eckie was the only Mrs. John Shubert, and heir to his estate, and the only female entitled to call herself Mrs. Shubert. Both children *could* call themselves Shubert. They were John's legitimate children, said the court. They agreed to surrender all claims to their father's estate, and to the estate of his father, Jacob J. Shubert—John's share of which, it was estimated, would be $15,000,000 at Jake's death. Finally, John Shubert's will was admitted to probate in January of 1964.

The case died away in the newspapers, and Jake Shubert never knew. He did not know that John was dead, he did not know he had two grandchildren, he did not know that his "educated" son had left a scandal behind him. Jake lay there in his oblivion in the Sardi Building, idling away his hours in reverie.

The government, facing ten years of appraisal in Lee's estate, filed a claim for more than $15,000,000 worth of estate taxes to avoid the estate's invoking the statute of limitations. Jake never knew.

They celebrated the fiftieth anniversay of Shubert Alley, with Larry, Jr., presiding, and Jake did not know.

A little more than a year after John's death, and ten years and a day after Lee's, Jacob J. Shubert, aged eighty-five, died. He was buried in the family mausoleum in Salem Fields, alongside Lee and Sam.

The last Shubert had left the Alley. He had never changed his will. His executors were "my loving son, John, and Milton Weir."

It is strange. They came down from Syracuse, these three little men, and they carved out theatrical districts in a dozen cities—carved them in their own image. Sam, the gentle Shubert, died in a violent catastrophe; Lee, the urbane Shubert died in a series of violent strokes; and Jake, the violent Shubert, dwindled away. Did he hear melodies those last years? *Blossom Time? Student Prince?* Did he relive all those "beautiful shows"? Were those the gentle smiles?

The Shuberts are all gone. But the theaters stand, and thousands of actors who might never else have worked, hundreds of directors and playwrights, other hundreds of composers, a hundred producers owe them a thank you. Or a damn you. So, too, does anyone who ever attends a theater performance. Either a Thank You, or a Damn You.

The brothers Shubert would not have cared much—not as long as you *bought* the ticket.

The Rotisserie Scene. From one of J.J.'s beautiful shows. The girls on the right presumably, were done.

Epilogue

As this is being written in the dying days of 1967, Lee Shubert has been dead for nearly fourteen years. His estate is still not settled, and when it is, there will be three beneficiaries: the United States Treasury, the Sam S. Shubert Foundation, and Lee's niece, Sylvia Wolfe Golde.

His two other heirs, Milton Shubert and Lawrence Shubert Lawrence, Sr., are dead. So are Willie Klein and Willie's wife, Peggy.

Marcella Swanson Shubert lives with her sister, Beatrice, and Beatrice's husband. She suffered a stroke a few years ago, and was confined to a wheelchair.

Muriel Knowles Shubert, Jake's widow, no longer lives in the apartment over the Sardi Building. It has been converted to office space.

Catherine Dealy Shubert, mother of John, occupies her apartment on Fifth Avenue, and spends a good deal of her time in the house her son built for her in Byram, Connecticut. From it, she can see her daughter-in-law as she comes and goes.

Eckie has the New York apartment and the house that John used to call "the big barn." From her front door, she can see her mother-in-law, but the women do not speak.

The Shubert empire is still the largest legitimate-theater operation in the country. It is directed by Lawrence Shubert Lawrence, Jr., from the offices in the Sardi Building. The Foundation is based at the same address, and makes periodic awards in the theater.

There are intermittent rumors that the Shuberts will return to production, but they have not produced a play since John's last attempt. They lease theaters and office space, and manage their real estate.

There are old employees who say that late at night the ghosts walk. Is it Lee checking the returns? Jake dreaming a dream of that outstanding production? Do they smile smugly, knowing that they are still the dominant force in the New York theater? Do they frown at the idea of "consultants"? (Whom would the Messrs. have consulted?) What would they think of Pinter and Ionesco and Albee? Would they have compared them with Pirandello and Shaw? A thousand questions—like the thousands of "stories in the walls" Lee saw, one day, as he planned a TV series.

There would have been some reassuring familiars. There has been another ticket scandal, involving another cousin.

All the rest, Lee 'n' J would have sneered at. Today, it runs like a business, not like an empire.

It is patently impossible to state what Lee and Sam and Jake are thinking as they look down (or is it up?) at what they built and left. Do they approve? And how would they do it all over again, given that second chance? And would they bother?

Shubert-Produced Musicals and Plays
in New York City

Productions	Theater	Date	Producer
Brixton Burglary	Herald Square	May 20, 1901	Sam S.
Chinese Honeymoon	Casino	June 2, 1902	Sam S.
Emerald Isle	Herald Square	Sept. 1, 1902	Sam S.
Night of the Party	Princess	Oct. 6, 1902	Messrs.
Heidelberg	Princess	Dec. 15, 1902	Sam & Lee
There and Back	Princess	Apr. 20, 1903	Messrs.
Runaways	Casino	May 11, 1903	Sam S.
Winsome Winnie	Casino	Dec. 1, 1903	Sam S.
Girl from Dixie	Madison Square	Dec. 14, 1903	Sam S.
Taming of the Shrew	Liberty	Feb. 6, 1905	Sam S.
The School for Scandal	Liberty	Feb. 13, 1905	Sam S.
Wang	Lyric	Apr. 18, 1904	Sam S.
Taps	Lyric	Sept. 17, 1904	Sam S.
Lady Teazle	Casino	Dec. 24, 1904	Messrs.
Fantana	Lyric	Jan. 16, 1905	Sam S.
Happyland	Lyric	Oct. 2, 1905	Messrs.
Earl and the Girl	Casino	Nov. 4, 1905	Messrs.
Babes and the Baron	Lyric	Dec. 25, 1905	Messrs.
Mexicana	Lyric	Jan. 29, 1906	Messrs.
Social Whirl	Casino	Apr. 9, 1906	Messrs.
Tourists	Majestic	Aug. 25, 1906	Messrs.
My Lady's Maid	Casino	Sept. 20, 1906	Messrs.
Love Letter	Lyric	Oct. 9, 1906	Messrs.
Shulamite	Lyric	Oct. 29, 1906	Messrs.
Love Route	Lincoln Square	Oct. 30, 1906	Messrs.
Blue Moon	Casino	Nov. 3, 1906	Messrs.
Pioneer Days	Hippodrome	Nov. 28, 1906	Messrs.
Belle of London Town	Lincoln	Jan. 28, 1907	Messrs.
Widower's Houses	Herald Square	Mar. 7, 1907	Messrs.
Ermete Novelli Repertory	Lyric	Mar. 18, 1907	Messrs.
Orchid	Herald Square	Apr. 8, 1907	Messrs.
The Other House	Majestic	Aug. 30, 1907	Messrs.
Anna Karenina	Herald Square	Sept. 2, 1907	Messrs.
Girl Behind the Counter	Herald Square	Oct. 1, 1907	Messrs.
Gay White Way	Casino	Oct. 7, 1907	Messrs.

Productions	Theater	Date	Producer
Girl of Holland	Lyric	Nov. 18, 1907	Messrs.
Auto Race	Hippodrome	Nov. 25, 1907	Messrs.
Lancers	Daly	Dec. 3, 1907	Messrs.
Lady Gay's Garden Party	Hippodrome	Feb. 17, 1908	Messrs.
Nearly a Hero	Casino	Feb. 24, 1908	Messrs.
Village Lawyer	Garden	Mar. 2, 1908	Messrs.
Girls	Daly	Mar. 23, 1908	Messrs.
Wolf	Bijou	Apr. 18, 1908	Messrs.
Mimic World	Casino	July 9, 1908	Messrs.
Sporting Days	Hippodrome	Sept. 5, 1908	Messrs.
Glorious Betsy	Lyric	Sept. 7, 1908	Messrs.
Mlle. Mischief	Lyric	Sept. 28, 1908	Messrs.
Marcelle	Casino	Oct. 1, 1908	Messrs.
Pied Piper	Majestic	Dec. 3, 1908	Messrs.
Mr. Hamlet of Broadway	Casino	Dec. 23, 1908	Messrs.
Vampire	Hackett	Jan. 18, 1909	Messrs.
Havana	Casino	Feb. 11, 1909	Messrs.
Goddess of Reason	Daly	Feb. 15, 1909	Messrs.
Return of Eve	Herald Square	Mar. 17, 1909	Messrs.
Going Some	Belasco	Apr. 12, 1909	Messrs.
Great John Ganton	Lyric	May 3, 1909	Messrs.
Ringmaster	Maxine Elliott	Aug. 9, 1909	Messrs.
Revellers	Maxine Elliott	Sept. 7, 1909	Messrs.
Girl and the Wizard	Casino	Sept. 27, 1909	Messrs.
Passing of the 3rd Floor Back	Maxine Elliott	Oct. 4, 1909	Messrs.
Belle of Brittany	Daly	Nov. 8, 1909	Messrs.
Old Dutch	Herald Square	Nov. 22, 1909	Messrs.
Lottery Man	Bijou	Dec. 5, 1909	Messrs.
The City	Lyric	Dec. 21, 1909	Messrs.
Don	New	Dec. 30, 1909	Messrs.
Affinity	Comedy	Jan. 3, 1910	Messrs.
King of Cadonia	Daly	Jan. 10, 1910	Messrs.
Twelfth Night	New	Jan. 26, 1910	Messrs.
A Man's World	Comedy	Feb. 9, 1910	Messrs.
Witch	New	Feb. 14, 1910	Messrs.
Son of the People	New	Feb. 28, 1910	Messrs.
Brand	New	Mar. 14, 1910	Messrs.

Productions	Theater	Date	Producer
Whirlwind	Daly	Mar. 23, 1910	Messrs.
Winter's Tale	New	Mar. 28, 1910	Messrs.
Beethoven	New	Apr. 11, 1910	Messrs.
Three Daughters of Monsieur Dupont	Comedy	Apr. 13, 1910	Messrs.
Lulu's Husbands	Maxine Elliott	Apr. 14, 1910	Messrs.
Little Eyolf	Nazimova	Apr. 18, 1910	Messrs.
The Mikado	Casino	May 30, 1910	Messrs.
Up and Down Broadway	Casino	July 18, 1910	Messrs.
International Cup, The Ballet of Niagara and The Earthquake	Hippodrome	Sept. 3, 1910	Messrs.
He Came from Milwaukee	Casino	Sept. 21, 1910	Messrs.
Bluebird	New	Oct. 1, 1910	Messrs.
Madame Troubadour	Lyric	Oct. 10, 1910	Messrs.
The Family	Comedy	Oct. 11, 1910	Messrs.
Mr. Preedy and the Countess	Nazimova	Nov. 7, 1910	Messrs.
Merry Wives of Windsor	New	Nov. 7, 1910	Messrs.
Thunderbolt	New	Nov. 12, 1910	Messrs.
Girl and the Kaiser	Herald Square	Nov. 22, 1910	Messrs.
Mary Magdalene	New	Dec. 5, 1910	Messrs.
Old Heidelberg	New	Dec. 19, 1910	Messrs.
Drifting	Nazimova	Dec. 21, 1910	Messrs.
Vanity Fair	New	Jan. 7, 1911	Messrs.
Balkan Princess	Herald Square	Feb. 9, 1911	Messrs.
Nobody's Daughter	New	Jan. 13, 1911	Messrs.
Arrow Maker	New	Feb. 27, 1911	Messrs.
As a Man Thinks	Nazimova	Mar. 13, 1911	Messrs.
Winter Garden	Winter Garden	Mar. 20, 1911	Messrs.
La Belle Paree	?	? 1911	Messrs.
H.M.S. Pinafore	Casino	May 29, 1911	Messrs.
Around the World	Hippodrome	Sept. 2, 1911	Messrs.
The Kiss Waltz	Casino	Sept. 18, 1911	Messrs.
Revues of Revues	Winter Garden	Sept. 27, 1911	Messrs.
Next	Daly	Sept. 28, 1911	Messrs.
Bunty Pulls the Strings	Comedy	Oct. 10, 1911	Messrs.
Duchess	Lyric	Oct. 16, 1911	Messrs.

Productions	Theater	Date	Producer
The Thunderbolt	Lyric	Nov. 16, 1911	Messrs.
Vera Violetta	Winter Garden	Nov. 20, 1911	Messrs.
Wedding Trip	Broadway	Dec. 25, 1911	Messrs.
Whirl of Society	Winter Garden	Mar. 5, 1911	Messrs.
Two Little Brides	Casino	Apr. 23, 1912	Messrs.
Patience	Lyric	May 6, 1912	Messrs.
Pirates of Penzance	Casino	June 3, 1912	Messrs.
H.M.S. Pinafore	Casino	June 27, 1912	Messrs.
Mikado	Casino	June 29, 1912	Messrs.
Passing Show of 1912	Winter Garden	July 22, 1912	Messrs.
Master of the House	39th Street	Aug. 20, 1912	Messrs.
Under Many Flags	Hippodrome	Aug. 31, 1912	Messrs.
Fanny's First Play	Comedy	Sept. 16, 1912	Messrs.
The Red Petticoat	Daly	Nov. 13, 1912	Messrs.
Broadway to Paris	Winter Garden	Nov. 20, 1912	Messrs.
All for the Ladies	Lyric	Dec. 30, 1912	Messrs.
Man with Three Wives	Weber and Fields	Jan. 23, 1913	Messrs.
The Honeymoon Express	Winter Garden	Feb. 6, 1913	Messrs.
The Five Frankforters	39th Street	Mar. 3, 1913	Messrs.
The Beggar Student	Casino	Mar. 22, 1913	Messrs.
The Geisha	44th Street	Mar. 27, 1913	Messrs.
The Mikado	Casino	Apr. 21, 1913	Messrs.
Gentlemen from Number 19	Comedy	May 1, 1913	Messrs.
H.M.S. Pinafore	Casino	May 5, 1913	Messrs.
Iolanthe	Casino	May 12, 1913	Messrs.
Passing Show of 1913	Winter Garden	July 24, 1913	Messrs.
The Lure	Maxine Elliott	Aug. 14, 1913	Messrs.
America	Hippodrome	Jan. 6, 1914	Messrs.
Lieber Augustin	Casino	Aug. 30, 1913	Messrs.
Forbes-Robertson Repertory	Shubert	Sept. 3, 1913 Dec. 29, 1913	Messrs.
At Bay	39th Street		Messrs.
Oh, I Say!	Casino	Oct. 7, 1913	Messrs.
Miss Phoenix	Harris	Oct. 30, 1913	Messrs.
The Pleasure Seekers	Winter Garden	Nov. 3, 1913	Messrs.
Ourselves	Lyric	Nov. 3, 1913	Messrs.
Girl on the Film	44th Street	Nov. 12, 1913	Messrs.
A Thousand Years Ago	Shubert	Dec. 29, 1913	Messrs.

Productions	Theater	Date	Producer
Whirl of the World	Winter Garden	Jan. 10, 1914	Messrs.
Midnight Girl	44th Street	Feb. 23, 1914	Messrs.
Marrying Money	Princess	Mar. 18, 1914	Messrs.
Panthea	Booth	Mar. 23, 1914	Messrs.
Belle of Bond Street	Shubert	Mar. 30, 1914	Messrs.
H.M.S. Pinafore	Hippodrome	Apr. 19, 1914	Messrs.
Madame Moselle	Shubert	May 23, 1914	Messrs.
Passing Show of 1914	Winter Garden	June 10, 1914	Messrs.
Dancing Duchess	Casino	Aug. 19, 1914	Messrs.
Wars of the World	Hippodrome	Sept. 5, 1914	Messrs.
A Modern Girl	Comedy	Sept. 12, 1914	Messrs.
What Is Love?	Maxine Elliott	Sept. 19, 1914	Messrs.
Consequences	Comedy	Oct. 1, 1914	Messrs.
Dancing Around	Winter Garden	Oct. 10, 1914	Messrs.
The Battle Cry	Lyric	Oct. 31, 1914	Messrs.
Mary Goes First	Comedy	Nov. 2, 1914	Messrs.
At the Barn	Comedy	Nov. 30, 1914	Messrs.
Tonight's the Night	Shubert	Dec. 25, 1914	Messrs.
A Mix-up	39th Street	Dec. 28, 1914	Messrs.
Taking Chances	39th Street	Mar. 17, 1915	Messrs.
Trilby	Shubert	Apr. 3, 1915	Messrs.
The Bubble	Booth	Apr. 5, 1915	Messrs.
Three of Hearts	39th Street	June 3, 1915	Messrs.
Hands Up	44th Street	July 22, 1915	Messrs.
The Last Laugh	39th Street	July 29, 1915	Messrs.
Blue Paradise	Casino	Aug. 5, 1915	Messrs.
Road to Happiness	Shubert	Aug. 30, 1915	Lee
The Bargain	Comedy	Oct. 6, 1915	Messrs.
Ruggles of Red Gap	Fulton	Dec. 25, 1915	Messrs.
Just a Woman	48th Street	Jan. 17, 1916	Messrs.
Payday	Cort	Feb. 26, 1916	Messrs.
The Co-respondent	Booth	Apr. 10, 1916	Messrs.
A Lady's Name	Maxine Elliott	May 15, 1916	Messrs.
Somebody's Luggage	48th Street	Aug. 28, 1916	Messrs.
The Girl from Brazil	44th Street	Aug. 30, 1916	Messrs.
Fixing Sister	Maxine Elliott	Oct. 4, 1916	Lee
Such Is Life	Princess	Nov. 25, 1916	Messrs.
Follow Me	Casino	Nov. 29, 1916	Messrs.
Her Soldier Boy	Astor	Dec. 6, 1916	Messrs.
Love O' Mike	Shubert	Jan. 15, 1917	Lee

Productions	Theater	Date	Producer
Stranger Than Fiction	Garrick	Mar. 5, 1917	Lee
The Knife	Bijou	Apr. 12, 1917	Messrs.
Peter Ibbetson	Republic	Apr. 17, 1917	Messrs.
The Highwayman	44th Street	May 2, 1917	Messrs.
My Lady's Glove	Lyric	June 18, 1917	Messrs.
The Inner Man	Lyric	Aug. 13, 1917	Messrs.
Maytime	Shubert	Aug. 16, 1917	Messrs.
Eyes of Youth	Maxine Elliott	Aug. 22, 1917	Messrs.
The Pawn	Fulton	Sept. 8, 1917	Messrs.
The Barton Mystery	Comedy	Oct. 13, 1917	Messrs.
The Torches	Bijou	Oct. 24, 1917	Messrs.
The Star Gazer	Plymouth	Nov. 26, 1917	Messrs.
Over the Top	44th Street	Nov. 28, 1917	Messrs.
Good Morning, Rosa-mond	48th Street	Dec. 10, 1917	Messrs.
The Heritage	Playhouse	Jan. 14, 1918	Messrs.
Girl o' Mine	Bijou	Jan. 28, 1918	Messrs.
Sinbad	Winter Garden	Feb. 14, 1918	Messrs.
A Cure of Curables	39th Street	Feb. 25, 1918	Lee
The Squab Farm	Bijou	Mar. 13, 1918	Messrs.
A Pair of Petticoats	44th Street	Mar. 18, 1918	Messrs.
Fancy Free	Astor	Apr. 11, 1918	Messrs.
The Passing Show of 1918	Winter Garden	July 25, 1918	Messrs.
The Blue Pearl	Longacre	Aug. 8, 1918	Messrs.
Freedom	Century	Oct. 19, 1918	Lee
Little Simplicity	Astor	Nov. 4, 1918	Messrs.
The Long Dash	39th Street	Nov. 5, 1918	Messrs.
A Place in the Sun	Comedy	Nov. 28, 1918	Messrs.
A Little Journey	Little	Dec. 26, 1918	Messrs.
Melting of Molly	Broadhurst	Dec. 30, 1918	Messrs.
The Climax	Comedy	Jan. 16, 1919	Messrs.
Good Morning, Judge	Shubert	Feb. 6, 1919	Messrs.
Monte Cristo, Jr.	Winter Garden	Feb. 12, 1919	Messrs.
A Sleepless Night	Bijou	Feb. 18, 1919	Messrs.
39 East	Broadhurst	Mar. 31, 1919	Messrs.
Shubert Gaieties of 1919	44th Street	July 17, 1919	Messrs.
Oh, What a Girl	Shubert	July 28, 1919	Messrs.
Those Who Walk in Darkness	48th Street	Aug. 14, 1919	Messrs.

Productions	Theater	Date	Producer
The Dancer	Harris	Sept. 29, 1919	Messrs.
Sothern-Marlowe Repertory	Shubert	Oct. 6, 1919	Lee
Hello, Alexander	44th Street	Oct. 7, 1919	Messrs.
Passing Show of 1919	Winter Garden	Oct. 23, 1919	Messrs.
The Purple Mask	Booth	Jan. 6, 1920	Lee
He and She	Little	Feb. 12, 1920	Messrs.
Florodora	Century	Apr. 5, 1920	J.J.S.
Not So Long Ago	Booth	May 4, 1920	Messrs.
Fall and Rise of Susan Lenox	44th Street	June 9, 1920	Messrs.
Cinderella on Broadway	Winter Garden	June 24, 1920	Messrs.
The Midnight Rounders	Century Grove	July 12, 1920	Messrs.
The Century Revue	Century Grove	July 12, 1920	Messrs.
The Americans in France	Comedy	Aug. 3, 1920	Lee
Blue Bonnett	Princess	Aug. 28, 1920	Messrs.
The Guest of Honor	Broadhurst	Sept. 20, 1920	Lee
The Outrageous Mrs. Palmer	39th Street	Oct. 12, 1920	Messrs.
The Prince and the Pauper	Booth	Nov. 1, 1920	Messrs.
When We Are Young	Broadhurst	Nov. 22, 1920	Messrs.
Passing Show of 1921	Winter Garden	Dec. 29, 1920	Messrs.
In the Night Watch	Century	Jan. 29, 1921	Messrs.
The Midnight Rounders of 1921	Century	Feb. 5, 1921	Messrs.
The Rose Girl	Ambassador	Feb. 11, 1921	Lee
Romance	Playhouse	Feb. 28, 1921	Messrs.
Toto	Bijou	Mar. 21, 1921	Lee
Just Married	Comedy	Apr. 26, 1921	Messrs.
Phoebe of Quality Street	Shubert	May 9, 1921	Messrs.
The Last Waltz	Century	May 10, 1921	Messrs.
The Whirl of New York	Winter Garden	June 13, 1921	Messrs.
March Hares	Bijou	Aug. 11, 1921	Messrs.
The Mimic World	Century	Aug. 15, 1921	Messrs.
The Detour	Astor	Aug. 23, 1921	Messrs.
The Triumph of X	Comedy	Aug. 24, 1921	Lee
Greenwich Village Follies	Shubert	Aug. 31, 1921	Messrs.
The Silver Fox	Maxine Elliott	Sept. 5, 1921	Lee

411

Productions	Theater	Date	Producer
The Blue Lagoon	Astor	Sept. 14, 1921	Messrs.
Blossom Time	Ambassador	Sept. 29, 1921	Messrs.
Beware of Dogs	Broadhurst	Oct. 3, 1921	Lee
Main Street	National	Oct. 5, 1921	Messrs.
Bombo	Jolson	Oct. 6, 1921	Messrs.
Sothern-Marlowe Repertory	Century	Oct., 1921	Messrs.
The Mad Dog	Comedy	Nov. 8, 1921	Messrs.
The Chocolate Soldier	Century	Dec. 12, 1921	Messrs.
The Squaw Man	Astor	Dec. 26, 1921	Lee
Face Value	49th Street	Dec. 26, 1921	Lee
The Blushing Bride	Astor	Feb. 6, 1922	Messrs.
The Rose of Stamboul	Century	Mar. 7, 1922	Messrs.
The Hotel Mouse	Shubert	Mar. 13, 1922	Messrs.
The Goldfish	Maxine Elliott	Apr. 17, 1922	Messrs.
Make It Snappy	Winter Garden	Apr. 13, 1922	Messrs.
Red Pepper	Shubert	May 29, 1922	Messrs.
Whispering Wires	49th Street	Aug. 7, 1922	Messrs.
Fools Errant	Maxine Elliott	Aug. 21, 1922	Messrs.
Sally, Irene and Mary	Casino	Sept. 4, 1922	Messrs.
Greenwich Village Follies	Shubert	Sept. 12, 1922	Messrs.
Passing Show of 1922	Winter Garden	Sept. 20, 1922	Messrs.
Thin Ice	Comedy	Sept 30, 1922	Messrs.
The Lady in Ermine	Ambassador	Oct. 2, 1922	Messrs.
Revue Russe	Booth	Oct. 5, 1922	Messrs.
Springtime of Youth	Broadhurst	Oct. 26, 1922	Messrs.
The Egotist	39th Street	Dec. 25, 1922	Lee
Jitta's Atonement	Comedy	Jan. 17, 1923	Lee
Dancing Girl	Winter Garden	Jan. 24, 1923	Messrs.
Mary the Third	39th Street	Feb. 5, 1923	Lee
Dew Drop Inn	Astor	May 17, 1923	Messrs.
Passing Show of 1923	Winter Garden	June 14, 1923	Messrs.
Home Fires	39th Street	Aug. 20, 1923	Messrs.
Artists and Models	Shubert	Aug. 20, 1923	Messrs.
A Lesson in Love	39th Street	Sept. 24, 1923	Lee
Cymbeline	Jolson	Oct. 2, 1923	Lee
For All of Us	49th Street	Oct. 15, 1923	Lee
The Dancers	Broadhurst	Oct. 17, 1923	Messrs.
Topics of 1923	Broadhurst	Nov. 20, 1923	Messrs.

Productions	Theater	Date	Producer
Time	39th Street	Nov. 26, 1923	Lee
The Business Widow	Ritz Theatre	Dec. 20, 1923	Lee
The Shadow	39th Street	Dec. 18, 1923	Lee
The Blue Bird	Jolson	Dec. 23, 1923	Lee
Vogues of 1924	Shubert	Mar. 27, 1924	Messrs.
The Kreutzer Sonata	Frazee	May 14, 1924	Lee
Blossom Time (revival)	Jolson	May 19, 1924	Messrs.
Innocent Eyes	Winter Garden	May 20, 1924	Messrs.
The Dream Girl	Ambassador	Aug. 20, 1924	Messrs.
Havoc	Maxine Elliott	Sept. 1, 1924	Messrs.
Passing Show of 1924	Winter Garden	Sept. 3, 1924	Messrs.
The Farmer's Wife	Comedy	Oct. 9, 1924	Lee
Artists and Models	Astor	Oct. 15, 1924	Messrs.
Firmin Gemier	Jolson	Nov. 10, 1924	Lee
The Desert Flower	Longacre	Nov. 18, 1924	Messrs.
Parasites	39th Street	Nov. 19, 1924	Lee
The Student Prince	Jolson	Dec. 2, 1924	Messrs.
Big Boy	Winter Garden	Jan. 7, 1925	Messrs.
The Love Song	Century	Jan. 13, 1925	Messrs.
Episode	Bijou	Feb. 4, 1925	Lee
The Virgin of Bethulia	Ambassador	Feb. 23, 1925	Lee
Sky High	Shubert	Mar. 2, 1925	Milton
The Fall Guy	Eltinge	Mar. 10, 1925	Messrs.
The Mikado	44th Street	Apr. 11, 1925	Messrs.
Taps	Broadhurst	Apr. 14, 1925	Messrs.
Man or Devil	Broadhurst	May 21, 1925	Messrs.
Artists and Models	Winter Garden	June 24, 1925	Messrs.
June Days	Astor	Aug. 6, 1925	Messrs.
Gay Paree	Shubert	Aug. 18, 1925	Messrs.
Big Boy	44th Street	Aug. 24, 1925	Messrs.
Courting	49th Street	Sept. 12, 1925	Lee
Harvest	Belmont	Sept. 19, 1925	Messrs.
Hayfever	Maxine Elliott	Oct. 5, 1925	Messrs.
The Crooked Friday	Bijou	Oct. 8, 1925	Messrs.
The Man with a Load of Mischief	Ritz	Oct. 26, 1925	Lee
Princess Flavia	Century	Nov. 2, 1925	Messrs.
The Offense	Ritz	Nov. 16, 1925	Messrs.
A Lady's Virtue	Bijou	Nov. 23, 1925	Messrs.

Productions	Theater	Date	Producer
Mayflowers	Forrest	Nov. 24, 1925	Messrs.
Greenwich Village Follies	46th Street	Dec. 24, 1925	Messrs.
A Night in Paris	Casino	Jan. 5, 1926	Messrs.
The Right Age to Marry	49th Street	Feb. 15, 1926	Lee
Blossom Time (revival)	Jolson	Mar. 8, 1926	Messrs.
The Two Orphans	Cosmopolitan	Apr. 5, 1926	Messrs.
Pinafore	Century	Apr. 6, 1926	Messrs.
What Every Woman Knows	Bijou	Apr. 13, 1926	Lee
Great Temptations	Winter Garden	May 18, 1926	Messrs.
The Merry World	Imperial	June 8, 1926	Messrs.
Naughty Riquette	Cosmopolitan	Sept. 13, 1926	Messrs.
Countess Maritza	Shubert	Sept. 18 1926	Messrs.
The Judge's Husband	49th Street	Sept. 27, 1926	Lee
Katja	44th Street	Oct. 18, 1926	Messrs.
Pearl of Great Price	Century	Nov. 1, 1926	Messrs.
First Love	Booth	Nov. 8, 1926	Messrs.
Gay Paree	Winter Garden	Nov. 9, 1926	Messrs.
Maitresse de Roi	Cosmopolitan	Nov. 30, 1926	Messrs.
The Nightingale	Jolson	Jan. 3, 1927	Messrs.
The Heaven Tappers	Forrest	Mar. 8, 1927	Lee
Cherry Blossoms	44th Street	Mar. 28, 1927	Messrs.
The Tightwad	49th Street	Apr. 16, 1927	Messrs.
The Thief	Ritz	Apr. 22, 1927	Lee
The Circus Princess	Winter Garden	Apr. 25, 1927	Messrs.
Mixed Doubles	Bijou	Apr. 26, 1927	Messrs.
A Night in Spain	44th Street	May 3, 1927	Messrs.
Padlocks of 1927	Shubert's Rose	July 6, 1927	Messrs.
Such Is Life	Morosco	Aug. 31, 1927	Messrs.
My Maryland	Jolson	Sept. 12, 1927	Messrs.
Murray Hill	Bijou	Sept. 29, 1927	Messrs.
The Love Call	Majestic	Oct. 24, 1927	Messrs.
And So To Bed	Shubert	Nov. 9, 1927	Lee
Artists and Models	Winter Garden	Nov. 15, 1927	Messrs.
Sisters	Klaw Theatre	Dec. 24, 1927	Messrs.
Lovely Lady	Harris	Dec. 29, 1927	Messrs.
Oh, Kay!	Century	Jan. 2, 1928	Messrs.
The Madcap	Royale	Jan. 31, 1928	Messrs.

Productions	Theater	Date	Producer
The Silent House	Morosco	Feb. 7, 1928	Lee
Greenwich Village Follies	Winter Garden	Apr. 9, 1928	Messrs.
Countess Maritza	Century	Apr. 9, 1928	Messrs.
White Lilacs	Shubert	Sept. 10, 1928	Messrs.
Luckee Girl	Casino	Sept. 15, 1928	Messrs.
Angela	Ambassador	Dec. 3, 1928	Messrs.
Sign of the Leopard	National	Dec. 11, 1928	Messrs.
Kingdom of God	Barrymore	Dec. 20, 1928	Lee
The Red Robe	Shubert	Dec. 25, 1928	Messrs.
Boom Boom	Casino	Jan. 28, 1929	Messrs.
Pleasure Bound	Majestic	Feb. 18, 1929	Messrs.
Security	Maxine Elliott	Mar. 28, 1929	Lee
Music in May	Casino	Apr. 1, 1929	Messrs.
Bird in Hand	Booth	Apr. 4, 1929	Lee
The Love Duel	Barrymore	Apr. 15, 1929	Lee
A Night in Venice	Shubert	May 21, 1929	Messrs.
Broadway Nights	44th Street	July 15, 1929	Messrs.
Rope's End	Masque	Sept 16, 1929	Lee
Nigger Rich (The Big Shot)	Royale	Sept. 20, 1929	Lee
Sweethearts	Jolson	Sept. 21, 1929	Messrs.
Mlle. Modiste	Jolson	Oct. 7, 1929	Messrs.
Naughty Marietta	Jolson	Oct. 21, 1929	Messrs.
A Wonderful Night	Majestic	Oct. 31, 1929	Messrs.
The Fortune Teller	Jolson	Nov. 4, 1929	Messrs.
Thunder in the Air	49th Street	Nov. 11, 1929	Lee
Robin Hood	Jolson	Nov. 18, 1929	Messrs.
Young Sinners	Morosco	Nov. 28, 1929	Messrs.
The Merry Widow	Jolson	Dec. 2, 1929	Messrs.
Babes in Toyland	Jolson	Dec. 23, 1929	Messrs.
Death Takes a Holiday	Barrymore	Dec. 26, 1929	Lee
Prince of Pilsen	Jolson	Jan. 13, 1930	Messrs.
Chocolate Soldier	Jolson	Jan. 27, 1930	Messrs.
Topaze	Music Box	Feb. 12, 1930	Messrs.
The Count of Luxembourg	Jolson	Feb. 17, 1930	Lee
The Serenade	Jolson	Mar. 4, 1930	Messrs.
The Matriarch	Longacre	Mar. 18, 1930	Lee
Three Little Girls	Shubert	Apr. 14, 1930	Messrs.

Productions	Theater	Date	Producer
Artists and Models	Majestic	June 10, 1930	Messrs.
Up Pops the Devil	Masque	Sept. 1, 1930	Lee
Insult	49th Street	Sept. 15, 1930	Lee
Symphony in Two Flats	Shubert	Sept. 16, 1930	Messrs.
Nina Rosa	Majestic	Sept. 20, 1930	Messrs.
Nine Till Six	Ritz	Sept. 27, 1930	Lee
His Majesty's Car	Barrymore	Oct. 23, 1930	Messrs.
The Last Enemy	Shubert	Oct. 30, 1930	Messrs.
The Man in Possession	Booth	Nov. 1, 1930	Lee
Bird in Hand	49th Street	Nov. 10, 1930	Lee
Hello Paris	Shubert	Nov. 15, 1930	Messrs.
Scarlet Sister Mary	Barrymore	Nov. 25, 1930	Lee
Purity	Ritz	Dec. 25, 1930	Lee
The Truth Game	Barrymore	Dec. 27, 1930	Lee
Meet My Sister	Shubert	Dec. 30, 1930	Messrs.
As You Desire Me	Maxine Elliott	Jan. 28, 1931	Lee
The Student Prince	Majestic	Jan. 29, 1931	Messrs.
Death Takes a Holiday	Ambassador	June 2, 1931	Lee
Blossom Time	Ambassador	Mar. 4, 1931	Messrs.
The Wonder Bar	Bayes	Mar. 17, 1931	Messrs.
The Silent Witness	Morosco	Mar. 23, 1931	Lee
Peter Ibbetson	Shubert	Apr. 8, 1931	Lee
Melo	Barrymore	Apr. 16, 1931	Lee
A Modern Virgin	Booth	May 20, 1931	Messrs.
If I Were You	Ambassador	Sept. 23, 1931	Messrs.
The Good Companions	44th Street	Oct. 1, 1931	Lee
The Father	49th Street	Oct. 8, 1931	Lee
Everybody's Welcome	Shubert	Oct. 13, 1931	Messrs.
Melo	Maxine Elliott	Oct. 19, 1931	Lee
The Venetian	Masque	Oct. 31, 1931	Messrs.
Cynara	Morosco	Nov. 2, 1931	Lee
The School for Scandal	Barrymore	Nov. 10, 1931	Lee
Marriage for Three	Bijou	Nov. 11, 1931	Lee
Experience Unnecessary	Longacre	Dec. 30, 1931	Messrs.
A Little Racketeer	44th Street	Jan. 18, 1932	Messrs.
Marching By	Chanin's 46th	Mar. 3, 1932	Messrs.
Happy Landing	Chanin's 46th	Mar. 26, 1932	Messrs.
Americana	Shubert	Oct. 5, 1932	Lee
There's Always Juliet	Barrymore	Oct. 27, 1932	Messrs.
The Silent House	Ambassador	Nov. 8, 1932	Lee

Productions	Theater	Date	Producer
Autumn Crocus	Morosco	Nov. 19, 1932	Lee
Best Sellers	Morosco	May 3, 1933	Lee
Hold Your Horses	Winter Garden	Sept. 25, 1933	Messrs.
Her Man of Wax	Shubert	Oct. 11, 1933	Lee
Ten Minute Alibi	Barrymore	Oct. 17, 1933	Lee
No More Ladies	Booth	Jan. 23, 1934	Lee
Bitter Sweet	44th Street	May 7, 1934	Messrs.
The Only Girl	44th Street	May 21, 1934	Messrs.
Life Begins at 8:40	Winter Garden	Aug. 27, 1934	Messrs.
No More Ladies	Morosco	Sept. 3, 1934	Lee
First Episode	Ritz	Sept. 17, 1934	Messrs.
Spring Freshet	Plymouth	Oct. 4, 1934	Lee
Music Hath Charms	Majestic	Dec. 29, 1934	Messrs.
Living Dangerously	Morosco	Jan. 12, 1935	Messrs.
Laburnum Grove	Booth	Jan. 14, 1935	Lee
A Journey by Night	Shubert	Apr. 16, 1935	Messrs.
Something Gay	Morosco	Apr. 29, 1935	Messrs.
At Home Abroad	Winter Garden	Sept. 19, 1935	Messrs.
Mid-West	Booth	Jan. 7, 1936	Messrs.
Follies	Shubert	Jan. 30, 1936	Messrs.
The Golden Journey	Booth	Sept. 15, 1936	Messrs.
Reflected Glory	Morosco	Sept. 21, 1936	Lee
The Laughing Woman	Golden	Oct. 13, 1936	Messrs.
Green Waters	Masque	Nov. 4, 1936	Messrs.
The Show Is On	Winter Garden	Dec. 25, 1936	Messrs.
Frederika	Imperial	Feb. 4, 1937	Messrs.
The Show Is On	Winter Garden	Sept. 18, 1937	Messrs.
The Abbey Theatre Players	Ambassador	Oct. 2, 1937	Messrs.
Hooray for What	Winter Garden	Dec. 1, 1937	Messrs.
Love of Women	Golden	Dec. 13, 1937	Messrs.
Between the Devil	Imperial	Dec. 22, 1937	Messrs.
Three Waltzes	Majestic	Dec. 25, 1937	Messrs.
You Never Know	Winter Garden	Sept. 21, 1938	Messrs. & John
Blossom Time	46th Street	Dec. 26, 1938	Messrs.
Night of Love	Hudson	Jan. 7, 1941	Messrs.
Streets of Paris	Broadhurst	June 19, 1939	Messrs.
Straw Hat Revue		Sept. 30, 1939	Messrs.
Foreigners	Belasco	Dec. 5, 1939	Messrs.

Productions	Theater	Date	Producer
Billy Draws a Horse	Playhouse	Dec. 21, 1939	Lee
Keep Off the Grass	Broadhurst	May 23, 1940	Messrs.
Walk with Music	Barrymore	June 4, 1940	Messrs.
Sons of Fun	Winter Garden	Dec. 1, 1940	Messrs.
Johnny on a Spot	Plymouth	Jan. 8, 1942	John
H.M.S. Pinafore	St. James	Jan. 21, 1942	Messrs.
The Mikado	St. James	Feb. 3, 1942	Messrs.
The Green Table	St. James	Feb. 10, 1942	Messrs.
The Big City	St. James	Feb., 1942	Messrs.
A Ball in Old Vienna	St. James	Feb., 1942	Messrs.
Pirates of Penzance	St. James	Feb. 17, 1942	Messrs.
Prodigal Son	St. James	Feb., 1942	Messrs.
Iolanthe	St. James	Feb. 23, 1942	Messrs.
Trial by Jury	St. James	Feb. 28, 1942	Messrs.
Gondoliers	St. James	Mar. 3, 1942	Messrs.
Priorities of 1942	46th Street	Mar. 12, 1942	Messrs.
Nathan the Wise	Belasco	Apr. 3, 1942	Messrs.
Keep 'em Laughing	44th Street	Apr. 24, 1942	Messrs.
Top Notchers	44th Street	May 29, 1942	Messrs.
I Killed the Count	Cort	Aug. 31, 1942	Messrs.
New Priorities of 1942	46th Street	Sept. 15, 1942	Messrs.
Wine, Women and Song	Ambassador	Sept. 28, 1942	Lee
Count Me In	Barrymore	Oct. 8, 1942	Messrs.
Proof Through the Night	Morosco	Dec. 25, 1942	Lee
Ziegfeld Follies	Winter Garden	Apr. 1, 1943	Messrs.
The Student Prince	Broadway	June 8, 1943	Messrs.
Blossom Time	Ambassador	Sept. 4, 1943	Messrs.
Ten Little Indians	Broadhurst	June 27, 1944	Messrs.
Laffing Room Only	Winter Garden	Dec. 23, 1944	Messrs.
A Lady Says Yes	Broadhurst	Jan. 10, 1945	J. J. S.
Dark of the Moon	46th Street	Mar. 14, 1945	Messrs.
The Wind in Ninety	Booth	June 21, 1945	Messrs.
The Ryan Girl	Plymouth	Sept. 24, 1945	Messrs.
You Touched Me!	Booth	Sept. 25, 1945	Lee
Hidden Horizon	Plymouth	Sept. 19, 1946	Messrs.
Under the Counter	Shubert	Oct. 3, 1947	Messrs.
Power Without Glory	Booth	Jan. 13, 1948	Messrs.
My Romance	Shubert	Oct. 19, 1948	Messrs.
Yes, M'Lord	Booth	Oct. 4, 1949	Messrs.

Productions	Theater	Date	Producer
Day After Tomorrow	Booth	Oct. 26, 1950	Messrs.
Ti-coq	Broadhurst	Feb. 9, 1951	Messrs.
Conscience	Booth	May 15, 1952	Messrs.
The Starcross Story	Royale	Jan. 13, 1954	Messrs.

Total: 520 productions

Index

430

About the Author

JERRY STAGG, native New Yorker, Columbia graduate, has been connected with broadcasting since he was a boy. After writing unsuccessful youthful plays, he migrated to Hollywood and wrote successful screen plays—a career which led to his becoming a successful, prize-winning television producer. He is now preparing a film on the urban crisis for AT&T.